T0301667

ENTREPRENEURSHIP IN AFRICA

ENTREPRENEURSHIP IN AFRICA

A Historical Approach

Edited by Moses E. Ochonu

Indiana University Press

This book is a publication of

Indiana University Press
Office of Scholarly Publishing
Herman B Wells Library 350
1320 East 10th Street
Bloomington, Indiana 47405 USA

iupress.indiana.edu

Manufactured in the United States of America

Library of Congress Cataloging-in-Publication Data

Names: Ochonu, Moses E., editor.
Title: Entrepreneurship in Africa : a historical approach / edited by
    Moses E. Ochonu.
Description: Bloomington, Indiana : Indiana University Press,
    2018. | Includes bibliographical references and index.
Identifiers: LCCN 2017053534 (print) | LCCN 2017051094
    (ebook) | ISBN 9780253032621 (e-book) | ISBN 9780253032607
    (hbk : alk. paper) | ISBN 9780253034380 (pbk : alk. paper)
Subjects: LCSH: Entrepreneurship—Africa—History. | New business
    Enterprises—Africa—History.
Classification: LCC HD2346.A55 (print) | LCC HD2346.A55 E583
    2018 (ebook) | DDC 338.642096—dc23
LC record available at https://lccn.loc.gov/2017053534

1 2 3 4 5   23 22 21 20 19 18

Contents

Acknowledgments

In the course of putting this collection together, I incurred much debt with colleagues and friends in and outside the academy. This volume would have been impossible to produce without the support and cooperation of my fellow authors. They responded enthusiastically to a call for papers and followed this up with encouraging words, timely submission of their chapters, and prompt responses to inquiries.

The foundational conversations that planted the seed of this book in me began several years ago and with several people. As director of the Tony Elumelu Foundation (TEF), Dr. Wiebe Boer generously invited me to partake, along with other scholars, in a research project designed to map the contemporary African investment and transnational entrepreneurial landscape.

This project led to my participation in another important conversation: a scholars' retreat in Calabar, Nigeria, organized by the foundation's Africapitalism Institute. The retreat was designed to formulate the outlines of an African business ethic under the rubric of Africapitalism. There, in the company of other scholars, I reflected harder on the nature of entrepreneurship in Africa, its character, history, and peculiarities. Subsequent reflections produced a mental outline for this book. I am grateful to TEF and to Dr. Boer for opening these avenues that enabled me to imagine the contours of this volume.

My conversation with Professor Kenneth Amaeshi of the University of Edinburgh Business School, a renowned scholar of African business and entrepreneurial cultures, reaffirmed my epistemological convictions on the topic of this volume.

Dr. Lucky Onmonya, the registrar and CEO of Nigeria's Institute for Development Finance and Project Management, Abuja, is one of Africa's authoritative voices on matters of entrepreneurial empowerment. Over the years, our conversations on the broad theme of African entrepreneurial potentials have enriched my perspectives and given me new ways of thinking about the subject outside my strict academic and disciplinary training.

At different stages of this book project, Scott Jossart helped with a variety of duties ranging from editing, to formatting, to coordination. His input was instrumental in resolving several technical challenges that arose as the volume gradually materialized.

I thank the reviewers, who not only thoroughly read the manuscript but also provided us with specific, actionable comments that, as they will see, have helped strengthen several aspects of the book.

Finally, I thank my wife, Margaret, and our two daughters, Ene and Agbenu, who persevered and supported me as I labored to get this collection ready for publication.

ENTREPRENEURSHIP IN AFRICA

Introduction

Toward African Entrepreneurship and Business History

Moses E. Ochonu

AFRICA IS SUFFUSED in entrepreneurship talk. Local and international development and antipoverty programs privilege entrepreneurship and recommend it as a bulwark against economic adversity and as a foundation for economic recovery. The figure of the entrepreneur has emerged as an organizing idiom for articulating the economic hopes and aspirations of various African societies. Globally recognized African entrepreneurs such as Aliko Dangote, Strive Masiyiwa, Patrice Motsepe, and Tony Elumelu are collectively regarded as the vanguard of a new African economic and developmental order that depends on the continuing ingenuity of entrepreneurs. These leading African entrepreneurs may indeed occupy the cutting edge of a new African economic age animated by entrepreneurial energies, but it is important to recognize that Dangote and his cohort stand on the unheralded shoulders of generations of African entrepreneurs, a tapestry of business histories and experiences that go back to precolonial and colonial times.

While Forbes-listed African entrepreneurs continue to capture the continent's imagination, Africa's rich entrepreneurial tradition calls for reflections on the role of innovation and enterprise in African history, as well as for a recovery of the multiple stories of entrepreneurial endeavor that foreshadowed today's entrepreneurial practices on the continent. This volume is a modest attempt to begin this task of recovery. Implicit in this effort is a historicization of Africa's intensifying fetishization of entrepreneurship as a path to individual, group, and societal economic prosperity. The facts of this entrepreneurship history, this volume demonstrates, should temper the entrepreneurial hysteria that has gripped Africa, but they also should foreground and lend credibility to ongoing conversations about the existence and contemporary utility of a distinct African business culture.

We live in a neoliberal moment in which entrepreneurship and entrepreneurs are celebrated as economic agents, catalysts for poverty reduction and economic growth. Whether entrepreneurship deserves this outsize reputation in our vast economic ecosystem or is itself a function of fundamental structural economic reconfigurations is an enduring question, one debated but never resolved. What can historical modes of analysis and a backward gaze into the *longue durée* reveal about what entrepreneurs can and cannot do? How can we engage with this question of entrepreneurial instrumentality from the unique perspective of African history? The latter question is the central focus of this volume.

Long monopolized by economics and its allied disciplines, entrepreneurship has morphed into a transdisciplinary subject of inquiry, with several humanistic and social scientific fields scrambling to contribute to our understanding of the role of entrepreneurial innovation and entrepreneurs in economic development. Historians have been slow to bring their methodological and analytical protocols to bear on the subject, and Africanist historians have been slower still to grapple with a subject matter for which Africa has increasingly become a laboratory.

This volume corrects this paucity of historical reflections, and specifically Africanist historical reflections, on the subject of entrepreneurship. We do not merely seek to historicize discourses and practices of entrepreneurship in Africa, although the following chapters do so with illuminating rigor. Rather, the volume is conceptualized to expand the field of analysis on entrepreneurship by posing expansive, even elastic, questions and advancing examples rooted in familiar and unfamiliar African historical contexts. These contexts are both spatial and temporal, personal and structural.

The question animating this volume is a simple one, but one with many possible iterations: What can the social, economic, and political histories of Africa, as well as African historical encounters, tell us about entrepreneurship as both a generic and a culturally inflected endeavor? The chapters that follow answer this question conceptually and empirically. The question correctly assumes the existence of a dominant theory of entrepreneurship, one that has not reckoned with the peculiar manifestations of entrepreneurial and innovative business endeavors in African history.

Much of today's paradigmatic economic theories have their intellectual origins in Western thought, even if the empirical circumstances that instantiate these theories and the ideational genealogies of their insights are of non-Western origins. This is not a radical statement to posit, given the fact that Western political and economic ascent and domination have helped mainstream, some might say naturalize, the Eurocentric semiotics of supposedly universal economic concepts such as entrepreneurship. Yet neither classical economic theory, an ideological component of Western imperialist expansion in the nineteenth and early twentieth centuries that is posited as the foundation of modern capitalism, nor the prevailing neoliberal consensus uncritically valorizes entrepreneurship as an engine of economic development.[1]

The Schumpeter Effect

It was not until the early twentieth century that entrepreneurship formerly entered the lexicon of Western economic theory. Economist Joseph Alois Schumpeter introduced to the field of economics systematic thinking about the concept of entrepreneurship, coining the term "entrepreneurial spirit" and positing the initial conceptual apparatuses for understanding and debating the role of entrepreneurs in a capitalist economy.[2] The historical newness of the concept belies its epistemological and programmatic sway in our world.

Although in the nineteenth century Jean-Baptiste Say identified entrepreneurial dexterity as being critical to effectively "combining together factors of production,"[3] today Schumpeter is regarded as the father of entrepreneurial studies. Whereas the former explained the process by which economic value is created through the instrumental agency of the entrepreneur, the latter showed that the entrepreneur is not just someone who engineers or supervises the process of value creation but also someone who creatively transforms or reinvents a familiar process of creating value, disrupting the existing value production equilibrium and ensuring economic development. The disruptive creativity of the entrepreneur entered the realm of economic thinking and is today taken for granted when discussing how large-scale corporate entrepreneurs recalibrate production to precipitate a qualitative leap forward, to use a Marxian shorthand. For good or ill, entrepreneurship and economic development became entwined.

Schumpeter's major contribution lies in going beyond understanding the entrepreneur as one who had the skill to "combine the factors of production." Whereas nineteenth-century philosophers such as John Stuart Mill and Alfred Marshall saw the entrepreneur as an individual and his or her function as merely managing and superintending the factors of production,[4] Schumpeter saw the entrepreneur not just in personal terms but also in terms of corporate agency, of the aggregate transformative impact of multiple, simultaneous, or successive entrepreneurial initiatives. More crucially, unlike other theorists, Schumpeter saw the entrepreneur not as a manager but as a catalyst, an innovator.

Schumpeter theorized that the entrepreneur not only combined the factors of production but created what he called "new combinations" and was responsible for "the doing of new things or the doing of things that are already being done in a new way."[5] The entrepreneur, Schumpeter posited, was thus responsible for structural and qualitative advancements in a capitalist economy; he or she was responsible for making the economy dynamic. If a capitalist economy was not to be static or to stagnate under the weight of monopolies, novelty, newness, and innovation had to be recurrent features of such an economy, Schumpeter contended. Markets and industries had to be reconfigured through the disruptive and catalytic intrusion of innovation since "capitalism is by nature a form or method of economic change and . . . never can be stationary."[6]

The expansive nature of Schumpeter's postulation on entrepreneurship and economic development has produced something of a fetish around both entrepreneurship and Schumpeter's theorization on it. Partly because of the iconoclastic and radically novel quality of the theory,[7] its subsequent enunciations tended to uncritically take it as a premise of analysis or as a settled analytical framework for examining entrepreneurial activities and behaviors in a multiplicity of contexts. The result that pertains to our purpose here has been a reductive understanding of entrepreneurship in largely industrial and capitalist terms, precluding the term in its broadest semiotics from being productively applied to preindustrial economies in Africa and other non-Western domains or even postindustrial economies in which the overarching agency of a foundational industrial behemoth is passé, replaced by the value and power of knowledge-based abstract, human, and digital products.

Furthermore, although Schumpeter himself seems to have been attuned to the importance of context, both spatial and temporal, and it is true that "entrepreneurial behavior, in the Schumpeterian framework, made little sense without equal analytical attention to the historical [and spatial] context in which it operated,"[8] the diverse historical and cultural experiences and settings in which particular forms of entrepreneurship manifested and thrived have rarely made it into the entrepreneurship literature with the same epistemological vigor as supposedly universal theorizations on the subject. The Schumpeterian framework and others rooted in the Western industrial capitalist experience, moreover, fail to account for instances in which the so-called corporate entrepreneur is the state and not individuals. Cases such as the one compellingly demonstrated in this volume by Marta Musso's chapter on Algeria, as well as numerous other African examples, show that, in the wake of independence, states drove the entrepreneurial process as part of a broader postcolonial effort to maximize control of, and benefits from, natural resources and to substitute import by investing directly in industrial manufacturing. The existing analytical lexicon of entrepreneurship is inadequate for explaining this reality of state entrepreneurial agency, of the state dominating the postcolonial business space and insisting on being the primary disruptive catalytic agent of economic development.

For these reasons, as well as our own commitment to supplying distinctly African historical perspectives on enterprise, business, value, wealth creation, prosperity, and innovation, the chapters in this volume both utilize and depart from the Schumpeterian frame of analysis. Not only were Schumpeter's theoretical observations set in a Western economic milieu and grounded in a decidedly Western capitalist reality, their empirical premises and assumptions fail to consider the socioeconomic realities, experiences, and productive endeavors of African and other non-Western peoples. The focus on large firms epitomizes this Eurocentric blind spot, and the advancement of industrial processes as embodiments and repositories of catalytic entrepreneurship is oblivious to the vast African field of agricultural, artisanal, healing, mining, and hunting entrepreneurship.

Conceptualizing African Entrepreneurship

As is discussed shortly, the definitional scope of the term "entrepreneurship" as conceived by Schumpeter and subsequent Western and neoliberal economic thinkers lack the flexibility to accommodate nonindustrial and noncapitalist experiences. Precolonial and colonial Africa was home to a variety of incipient and transitional capitalisms. The Western entrepreneurship conception is foregrounded by a Western capitalist ethos that is both narrow and unrepresentative of the plethora of capitalisms and gradations of capitalist behaviors discernible in African history. This is compounded further by the existence of several noncapitalist socioeconomic organizations and systems of production in which profits, personal gain, and value creation for their own utilitarian and exchange merit were not the norm. If the Schumpeterian model is adopted uncritically, it raises the question of whether, for instance, entrepreneurs could emerge and thrive in a communal economic setting, a question to which I will return shortly.

To frame a study of African entrepreneurial culture in a strictly Schumpeterian epistemology is thus to deny the historical and contemporary existence of seemingly contradictory but compellingly logical economic and commercial systems in which entrepreneurship thrived without the capitalist superstructures of the type considered by Schumpeter and other Western thinkers to be germane to innovation and entrepreneurial behavior. It is also to flatten a layered set of economic realities in which capitalist structures and relations are uneven, inconsistent, and mediated by multiple social, cultural, and political regimes. To speak of entrepreneurship in the African context is to invoke a much wider register of analysis than the Schumpeterian framework allows, expansive as it is. Historically, African entrepreneurs were hardly the one-dimensional economic catalytic machines that Schumpeter and his latter-day neoliberal disciples celebrate. They were much more than that depiction of mechanical agents of economic change. They were embedded in multiple networks and realms of economic, cultural, and political action, and they embraced a greater range of roles than terms such as "economic catalyst" or "agents of development" approximate. This volume challenges this conceptually liminal approach.

The problem is one of both a lack of interdisciplinarity in the study of entrepreneurship and the familiar marginalization of non-Western experiences in economic thought and policy. On the disciplinary side of the ledger, historical modes of analysis and inquiry have played only a marginal role in helping scholars understand the nature and role of entrepreneurship in society. Even in Western scholarship, this marginality of historical methods has been pronounced and consistent, marked largely by economists' insistence on owning and defining the contours of the field. The economists who dominate the field pay little attention to the kinds of questions that historians are trained and equipped to pose, such as how entrepreneurial cultures are constituted and how they evolve and change over time; how human agency is instrumental to this change; and how this change affects society outside the realm of economics.[9]

In the United States, the supposed capitalist bastion of the world, the only attempt to understand entrepreneurship through the lens of history was a short-lived, long-defunct 1941 initiative, the Committee for Research in Entrepreneurial History, and the creation of a research hub, the Research Center in Entrepreneurial History, which was funded by the Rockefeller Foundation.[10] The prevailing status quo in entrepreneurial studies, which is devoid of historical perspectives and is framed only in the esoteric theoretical and analytical lingo of economics, is traceable to these failed early experiments in the interdisciplinary study of entrepreneurship cultures. This analytical insularity continues to haunt studies of entrepreneurship cultures not only of the West but also of the non-Western world, including Africa. This volume is a modest contribution to efforts to historicize the study of entrepreneurship.

The second aspect of the problem concerns the marginalization and de-valuation of African economic histories and experiences and their resulting displacement from the canons and epistemologies of economic thought. Without belaboring the point, one should state from the outset that this is not an argument for rejecting theories and conceptual tools that originate outside Africa or outside Africanist scholarship, or for shunning scholarship that is empirically or theoretically located in the experiences of non-Africans. Rather, the point here is to identify, name, and recognize the limitations of theories that do not reckon with African modes of doing and seeing, and that are inadequate for analyzing the lived lives and actions of Africans for that reason.

As currently conceptually constituted, entrepreneurship is largely understood in starkly economistic terms, with a recent, marginal attention to insights from the subfield of social entrepreneurship. The advent of social scientific studies on social entrepreneurship, which is dominated by anthropologists, is a welcome scholarly development.[11] The social entrepreneur is an archetype close to the historical figure of the African businessperson or innovative value creator—a socioeconomic shapeshifter and versatile operative for whom professional and vocational boundaries are unwanted distractions from an elastic value-adding enterprise. This anthropologically sensitive conception has allowed African economic actors, historical and contemporary, to enter the discourse of entrepreneurial ferment and agency in ways that prior conceptions never permitted. Our work builds on this emerging corrective approach.

For generations anthropologists have been challenging economistic perspectives on entrepreneurship from the margins, but they seem to have broken through only in the 1990s, when a slew of studies appeared proposing or demonstrating the wisdom of applying anthropological concepts and methods, as well as the discipline's sensitivity to culture and context, to the study of entrepreneurship. One of the most influential of these studies is Alex Stewart's 1991 article in the journal *Entrepreneurship Theory and Practice*.[12] The essay argues for privileging the "anthropological focus on society and culture" in expanding the theoretical space of entrepreneurship.[13] Stewart contends that entrepreneurial studies would be enriched if non-Western cultural concepts and practices, long explored by anthropologists, were integrated into discussions of entrepreneurial activities. These realities, which Africanists would recognize as integral aspects of African economies, include informal economic networks; informalized markets; wealth in people and the intangibility of assets; unconventional storage of wealth; non-market definitions of resource access, rights, and utilization; and opportunity structures defined in both cultural and economic terms.

The popularity of the analytical grid of social entrepreneurship as a way of delineating alternative or parallel entrepreneurial paths has been habituated to the anthropological expansion of the discursive space of entrepreneurial culture. Yet the term "social entrepreneur" has its own baggage, its own blind spots that render it problematic for describing the people and activities discussed in the chapters of this book. At present, scholarly discussions on social entrepreneurship seem heavily skewed toward a focus on contemporary entrepreneurial actors, such as not-for-profit foundations that make seed money grants, microcredit institutions and pioneers, not-for-profit technology inventors and ventures, and other entrepreneurs motivated not by personal gain but by societal benefit.[14] This perspective inevitably privileges not only contemporary actors but also entrepreneurial actors in societies where technological invention and other kinds of technologically creative processes are well established, ignoring the many African settings where these processes are just emerging.

By ignoring historical social entrepreneurs, the impression is created that entrepreneurial practices that are not motivated solely by profit are a contemporary phenomenon or that they are anomalous manifestations, and insights from the experiences of many traditional societies in precolonial and colonial Africa that suggest otherwise remain untapped. One of the most cited articles on social entrepreneurship distinguishes between entrepreneurs and social entrepreneurs largely on the basis of the profit motive,[15] yet this distinction between "business entrepreneurs" and "social entrepreneurs" does not apply to many groups of precolonial and colonial African entrepreneurs who routinely transgressed and blurred this line. Several authors in this volume, notably Uyilawa Usuanlele, Martin S. Shanghuyia, and Mike Odugbo Odey, vigorously challenge this distinction by stressing that creative problem solving for both personal and communal benefit was a recurring dynamic of African entrepreneurship cultures. Usuanlele even posits a productively novel analytical trajectory that recognizes the entrepreneurial ingenuity of Benin warlords, spiritual consultants, priests, and religious purveyors. The professionalization of Africa's multiple social vocations entailed the adoption of business management principles that we associate with today's so-called business entrepreneurs. This fungible and flexible African entrepreneurial terrain is captured in several chapters of this volume.

Gloria Chuku's chapter drives this point hard with examples of Muslim Hausa, Yoruba, and Igbo female entrepreneurs of the colonial period who innovatively reconstituted the social and cultural realms of their milieus and made them function in the service of both business and personal prestige. For Hausa women, Islamic seclusion became a platform for entrepreneurial pursuits that leveraged the social and spatial cachet of privacy and gendered space in ways that defy current analytical categories of entrepreneurship. The example of Nwanyiemelie Nwonaku (the Triumphant Woman) in colonial eastern Nigeria poignantly demonstrates the symbiotic relationship between the social and the mercantile, the tangible and the intangible. Nwonaku used her wealth from trading to become a female husband to many women, a gesture that, in addition to offering traditional social benefits otherwise defined in masculine terms, was a form of business investment in itself. Nwonaku proceeded to rhetorically and physically deploy the human capital of her wives as collateral to gain access to both credit and patronage in a racist colonial trading system. Wives acquired with wealth gained from trading and leveraged for more trading advantages also provided a form of social service to the community, helping to solve the societal problem of devalued single womanhood. Female husbandry and trading strategies were interlinked, blurring the line between business and social obligations.

The concept of social entrepreneurship, purportedly a counterpoint to the conflation of entrepreneurship and the profit motive, also reifies a particular conception of the African entrepreneur as an exotic figure rooted exclusively in and animated by social impulses, and allergic to economic rationalities marked most recognizably by profit making, value creation, and innovative, self-interested problem solving. This is a restrictive frame of analysis. It concedes the normative space of entrepreneurship to capitalist, presumably Western, entrepreneurs operating on the logic of the market and its transactional accompaniments. It also participates in and perpetuates the notion that entrepreneurial activity—pure entrepreneurial activity—can only occur in a market-based economy governed and regulated by market incentives, an understanding that excludes African entrepreneurs who operate under conditions and logics that transcend market transactions, even if those transactions are part of a capacious, all-encompassing repertoire.

Thus, in this volume, although we find the concept of the social entrepreneur an improvement on parallel concepts located in strictly neoclassical and neoliberal bromides, we consider it a burdensome and restrictive improvement, one that does not encompass the range of mobility and flexibility that African entrepreneurs, historical or contemporary, engage in. The term "social entrepreneurship" presupposes a location in one transactional economy, in one discernible set of economic and cultural geographies designated as "social." It therefore occludes the very identity of the historical African entrepreneur that we are insisting on and that is operationalized in the following chapters: the flexible, malleable businessperson, artisan, or professional who combined characteristics and behaviors consistent with classic entrepreneurial routines with an eclectic repertoire of other engagements that may not be recognizable to scholars of the Western entrepreneurial experience.

Africa in the Shadow of Neoliberal Entrepreneurship Paradigms

The current incarnation of the Schumpeterian understanding of entrepreneurship, one with consequential implications for debates on Africa's economic development, is neoliberalism. The conceptual impact of Africa's long encounter with neoliberalism on discourses of African entrepreneurship is profound. The nexus of neoliberalism and entrepreneurship is not farfetched. The neoliberal economic regime imposed on African economies by the Bretton Woods institutions in the 1980s and 1990s dictated an economic paradigm shift for African countries, one that redefined the relationships, obligations, and responsibilities between states and their citizens. One of the most remarkable outcomes of this shift has been the "increasing dominance of the figure of the entrepreneur."[16] A corollary development has been the substitution of entrepreneurial self-help for redistributive and reconstructive structural economic reforms.

This lionization of the entrepreneur is a symptom of a deeper rhetorical, philosophical, and policy gesture in the direction of producing citizen-entrepreneurs who practice and pursue thrift and profits, creatively take charge of their own welfare, innovatively add value to the economy, and thus release the state from expensive financial obligations.[17] Neoliberal attempts to engineer into existence the ideal entrepreneurial citizen and to engender subjectivities that are self-reliant and removed from the nodes of state obligation were authorized by a new fetish of personal economic responsibility. This economic philosophy, hegemonic and ubiquitous, has inflected and even distorted familiar modes of understanding African enterprise and African business culture.

First, by seeking to make every postcolonial African an entrepreneur and by creating entrepreneurial imaginaries to anchor new paradigms of economic recovery, neoliberal economic interventions misread the African past as one in which Africans were pampered by the state and thus ceased to create value through entrepreneurial activity. In truth, there was never such a cessation of entrepreneurial ingenuity in African communities. Second, such interventions were cast against a foundational ignorance of the fact that value creation in most African societies was an organic social endeavor and not the intensely individualized enterprise intelligible to neoclassical and neoliberal economic frames. The political economy of neoliberal dominance has entrenched the entrepreneurial figure venerated by International Monetary Fund and World Bank policy documents as the discursive referent in studies of African entrepreneurial activity that are not rooted in African histories and cultures. The epistemological outcome has been profound, a transformation of the very vocabulary we use to designate some Africans as entrepreneurs and to withhold that nomenclature from other Africans.

The chapters in this volume are invested in restoring the conceptual and descriptive flexibility that predated Africa's neoliberal encounter and that allowed scholars to speak of merchants, enterprising warriors, craftsmen, artisans, ambitious farmers, praise singers, political organizers, musicians, priests, healers, miners, and other creative problem solvers and value creators as entrepreneurs. The chapters by Kwasi Konadu, Gloria Emeagwali, Michael Gennaro, and myself explore the lives and activities of African entrepreneurial mavericks who, acting in groups or as individuals, combined problem solving with value creation and social service—innovative economic actors who combined multiple elements and skills within and outside themselves to carve out niches in the economic and social spheres.

Toward a Business History of Africa

Entrepreneurship in Africa recovers and reconstructs Africa's rich histories of individual and group entrepreneurial activities and investments. It documents and casts new light on indigenous forms of enterprise and entrepreneurial leadership in African history. The chapters are animated by empirical case studies from all regions of Africa. Together, they demonstrate the infinite epistemological possibilities and insights that arise from studying the pasts of African business ventures and cultures on their own merits—in other words, a distinct field of African business history with its own analytical tools.

The volume is also a major intervention in the broad field of African economic history and seeks to rethink the field beyond familiar structural studies of African economies and Africa's economic entanglements. Unlike most works on African economic history, which focus on broad deterministic forces, structures, and nodes of production and exchange, as well as on political economy, broadly defined, this volume inaugurates the subfield of African business and entrepreneurial history in which the value-creating enterprise of Africans is considered alongside the wider economic and political environment in which these Africans operated. Our conceptualization of African business history places individual and group economic agency and initiative on the same instrumental arc as structural economic forces.

Several chapters illuminate conventional entrepreneurial activities in fields such as trading, mining, healing, agricultural production, goods distribution, manufacturing, craftsmanship, and other creative endeavors. However, we also understand entrepreneurship to include a range of unconventional value-creating activities that require organization, leadership, skill, and talent. Some of these activities were better coordinated than others, and in some cases they involved the mobilization of group interest and identity, thus highlighting the interface between individual creativity and communal enterprise, a fairly distinct feature of African entrepreneurial history.

Lynn Schler's and Ralph Callebert's chapters extend the unorthodox entrepreneurial field of Africa into the proletarian domain, further illustrating both the depth and diversity of African entrepreneurial experiences. Both chapters demonstrate that in colonial Nigeria and apartheid South Africa, workers moonlighted as entrepreneurs, engaging in arbitrage on the side even as they continued to work as seamen and dockworkers. Here entrepreneurship was a part-time activity, but it was no less constitutive of the worker-entrepreneurs' economic lives than were the dynamics of the workplace or the interactions between capital and labor. This new field of African business history, with its elastic analytical repertoire, is capable of exploring these complex economic lives in ways that traditional African economic history, with its neat dichotomies between proletariats and merchants, is incapable of doing.

Traditional debates in the field of African economic history have rarely acknowledged, let alone theorized, the entrepreneurial ingenuity of Africans in a sustained way. This erasure is particularly common in the field of African colonial economic history. Neodevelopmentalist interpretations of African colonial economic history such as A. G. Hopkins's *An Economic History of West Africa* celebrate the installment of an "open economy" through the instrumentality of colonial transport infrastructure, describing the process as providing a vent for Africa's surpluses.[18] Hopkins stresses the role of colonial infrastructure, especially transportation infrastructure, in opening up the world commodities market to African producers.[19] This theory clearly exaggerates the extent to which African producers willingly embraced the world market. It also focuses inordinately on an infrastructure-as-incentive argument while ignoring the role of coercion in compelling African producers to participate in colonially mediated structures of the world economy.[20]

The dependency/underdevelopment interpretation of the colonial economy sees a radically different process in which African agricultural producers, artisans, and other creators of value were tricked by colonial incentives and forced by coercive colonial measures into a volatile world market that impoverished them and distorted the evolution of their economies.[21] Studies in this radical tradition include Colin Bundy's *Rise and Fall of the South African Peasantry*, E. S. Atieno-Odhiambo's short article "The Rise and Decline of the Kenyan Peasant," Robert Shenton's *The Development of Capitalism in Northern Nigeria*, Jean Suret-Canale's *French Colonialism in Tropical Africa*, and Robin Palmer's *Land and Racial Discrimination in Rhodesia*. These studies lament how colonial policies on land, labor, taxation, and agriculture, as well as fiscal policies, led to a steep decline in the fortunes of African producers, stunting Africans' economic creativity.[22]

This interpretation, too, wears polemical blinders. Dependency theorists associate African peasants, artisans, and merchants with passivity, inertia, and helpless surrender,[23] a negation of the innovative, entrepreneurial, and creative instincts of African colonial subjects. One of our tasks in this volume is to write African entrepreneurs (back) into the colonial economic history of Africa and to do so by rejecting the subordination of African economic initiative to colonial catalysts or restrictions, an epistemic devaluation inherent in both the neoclassical and dependency readings of African colonial economic history.

Entrepreneurial Subalterns

The debate between the radical and neoclassical interpretations of colonial African history hardly allowed a space for Africans to be anything other than exploited or empowered colonial subjects. Africans' entrepreneurial accomplishments therefore went largely unrecognized and, where recognized, became fodder for radical-nationalist historiographical arguments that theorized Africans who innovatively maneuvered to create fortunes as handmaidens of and collaborators in colonial exploitation. Even as the narrow debate between the radical and neoclassical interpretations of African colonial economic history unfolded, other scholars explored a long tapestry of African wealth creation that extended from the precolonial to the colonial periods.

Ann Philips argues that African peasants, especially in the colonial economies of West Africa, surpassed the modest accumulation capacity that the "romantic anti-capitalism" of British policy in the interwar years expected of them. William Gervase Clarence-Smith makes a similar argument about how West African producers confounded the permutations of colonial economic planners by strategically and creatively positioning themselves to obtain maximum gains from the colonial system.[24] Whether these actors were peasants, craftspeople, merchants, artisans, wives who managed the family's portfolio of production and exchange, or even workers, these were entrepreneurial behaviors that have rarely been called by their proper name in the historiography.

Charles van Onselen's ethnological biography of Kas Maine, a South African sharecropper, was widely celebrated as an innovatively fine-grained and empathetic portrayal of African creativity and ingenuity in the face of daunting sociopolitical and economic circumstances and in the orbit of colonial domination.[25] However, Maine, the subject of the groundbreaking study, represents a peculiarly African entrepreneurial strain of creative survival, problem solving, and wealth accumulation under strict colonial and neocolonial conditions. Stories of unlikely African entrepreneurial success in the strictures of colonization have not been told in the vocabulary of entrepreneurship but should be. Chambi Chachage's chapter in this volume is thus an important revisionist approach that takes the mercantile successes of East Africa's South Asian merchants not as simply defying colonial expectations but as the culmination of remarkable entrepreneurial tenacity and effort.

The colonial economic space was a constricted one to be sure, but it was not a prison with no room for maneuvering and creativity. Indeed, as Chuku's, Isidore Lobnibe's, and Emeagwali's chapters in this volume demonstrate, the restrictive colonial economic space was an arena of remarkable entrepreneurial flourish not just for African men disproportionately empowered by Victorian colonial mores but also for a diverse group of women who broke free of colonial gender norms and the strictures of the colonial economy to build, increase, and sustain fortunes as traders, artisanal businesspeople, lenders, and investors. The colonial economic space was enriched by the entrepreneurial energies of a diverse group of African colonial actors. Chachage's aforementioned chapter on a distinctly East African South Asian community of businesspeople and middle-class professionals documents a history that was the unintended outcome of British migrant labor policies in East Africa, but Chachage's analysis situates the entrepreneurs' business success in multiple noncolonial registers. Finding an economic niche and expanding it, members of Tanzania's South Asian business class exploited the institutions of colonial mobility and rudimentary colonial infrastructures to build vast arbitrage, retail, and merchandizing businesses across East Africa.

Beyond Labor Aristocracy and Subsistence

Another debate within African economic history in which the chapters of this volume intervene concerns the nature of wage labor and whether paid disciplined work empowered Africans to pursue value-creating enterprises or robbed them of the freedom to do so. For the colonial period, the debate turns on the activism and revolutionary temperament of African workers, an issue summed up in the question of whether African colonial workers constituted a proletariat in the Marxian sense of the word or took on a more fluid identity. To varying degrees, stabilized African colonial laborers made demands and picketed their workplaces.

Some created informal unions. Some unions, such as those in South Africa and in the colliery of Enugu, Nigeria, became so powerful that the mines' management had to recognize and seek dialogue with them.[26] Even so, some scholars wrote off African colonial workers as possessing little or no capacity for creative action beyond the narrow aspirations of the workplace. The entrepreneurial initiatives of African workers have been unrecognized in the fog of this argument.

Frantz Fanon was the first to broach the so-called labor aristocracy debate when he argued that African colonial workers, urban and aristocratic in their ambitions, were not to be trusted with the revolutionary task of anticolonial mobilization.[27] Their temperament, Fanon contends, oriented them toward nonrevolutionary goals. This thesis touched off a long-running debate among labor historians of Africa, with critics of the labor aristocracy thesis finding abundant display of revolutionary behavior on the part of urban colonial African workers, the so-called labor aristocrats.[28] Later generations of critics that included authors such as Frederick Cooper went so far as to credit African colonial workers with broaching decolonization by pairing the "labor question" with larger questions of colonial oppression.[29]

Both sides of the labor aristocracy debate sidestep the nuances and complexities of labor organizing that required the skill and temperament of an entrepreneur, as well as the many sociological and historical factors that compelled some African workers to mobilize in support of the interests of the urban poor and some to not do so. There is also the question of historical contingency. As Jane Parpart argues, the behavior of workers on the Zambian Copperbelt defies the neat dichotomy of revolutionary versus nonrevolutionary workers that some scholars embraced in the wake of the debate.[30] To account for the diversity of proletarian responses and behaviors, one could speculate that some workers were more enterprising than others. This spirit of enterprise was not restricted to the pursuit of workplace benefits or political goals. Some of this creative energy was channeled to profit-making investments outside and within the workplace.

More crucially, and for our purpose here, it is worth noting that, despite their best efforts, colonial authorities did not succeed in turning African workers into proletarians in the pristine sense of workers whose identity was defined solely by the workplace. African workers were defined by much more than their working lives, as they maintained organic connections to the world outside work and to cultural and symbolic obligations that sometimes diluted their proletarian consciousness. The colonial project of proletarianization, as Fredrick Cooper, Bill Freund, and other labor historians of Africa have demonstrated, was as incomplete as it was contradictory.[31] African workers were immensely creative and enterprising actors whose impulses and socioeconomic aspirations transcended the workplace. They were entrepreneurs in our capacious definition of the term and also in its narrow, technical sense.

Callebert's and Schler's chapters in this volume present compelling iterations of the argument that African workers were and are much more than proletarians, and that, in fact, proletarian engagements, even in the strictures of the colonial economic space, provided pathways into entrepreneurial endeavors. The two chapters' analysis of the extracurricular entrepreneurial activities of two sets of colonial workers clearly demonstrates the intersection of wage labor and retail trade. The chapters show how African workers refused to let their working lives stand in the way of their entrepreneurial investments in their communities. Both authors contend that the workers profiled in the chapters routinely parlayed the resources and connections of the workplace into entrepreneurial engagements outside it, and vice versa.

The literature on precolonial African entrepreneurial activities is more robustly incorporative of the entrepreneurial accomplishments of Africans. The Swahili trading system in eastern and southeastern Africa and its oceanic tentacles are fairly well studied, and the role of African groups in building and sustaining it is well documented.[32] However, even here the African entrepreneurial agency in the Swahili system is often diluted by an excessive emphasis on the instrumentality of external forces in the commercial system. Within the same eastern and Central African precolonial commercial sphere, the mercantile exploits of the Nyamwezi of modern Tanzania, though well documented in the literature,[33] remain subsumed under factors that occlude the essential entrepreneurial independence and initiatives of the Nyamwezi people. The paradigm of the Nyamwezi as hired or indentured porters in the ivory and gold trades has overshadowed the entrepreneurial spirit and the rational business calculus that underpinned their long, monopolizing dominance of the interior transportation relay of the precolonial East African trading system.

The ways in which African entrepreneurial dexterity birthed and expanded the trans-Saharan trade between West and North Africa are adequately recognized in the literature.[34] However, much of this literature is dominated by research on external trade impetus or external stimuli, which tends to undermine the entrepreneurial contributions of African actors in these trading systems. The tension between highlighting the structural economic and commercial environment in which African entrepreneurs operated and telling the story of their quotidian and strategic business decisions and investments remains unresolved in much of the literature. Where attempts are made to resolve it, the balance is often upended in favor of external impetus. My own chapter on the Wangara trading network in precolonial West Africa analyzes this vast trading, production, extractive, and industrial system not as an appendage of a global trading system but as an internal West African entrepreneurial process that, far from being sustained by external stimuli, was undermined by it—by the advent of aggressive colonial merchant trading and quasi-imperial maneuvers.

For the precolonial period, another epistemological obstacle stands in the way of a full recognition of the role of enterprise, innovation, and private initiative in the economic evolution of African societies: the overwrought and influential theory of African socialism and of Africa's precolonial communal ethos. Julius Nyerere's seminal text *Ujamaa: Essays on Socialism* gave epistemic visibility to an incorrect notion of precolonial Africa as a site of subsistent communalism, an undifferentiated societal continuum supposedly unspoiled by the twin capitalist evils of the profit motive and private wealth accumulation.[35] Nor was precolonial Africa the haven of unbridled free-market capitalist transactions that scholars such as George B. N. Ayittey assume it to be.[36] Evidence adduced in multiple chapters of this volume indicates that a communitarian ethos underpinned and mediated the entrepreneurial pursuits of precolonial Africans. This suggests the coexistence of protocapitalist aspirations and communalist cultural constraints, not a displacement of the former by the latter. Moreover, Africa was hardly the communal or socialist paradise bereft of private initiative and enterprise that Nyerere makes it out to be. Even the most communally organized precolonial societies and economies had enterprising members who improved their lives through entrepreneurial initiatives, indicating that neither communalism nor subsistence, two hyperbolized and overgeneralized features of precolonial Africa, was incompatible with private property or the pursuit of individual wealth for self-improvement.

Most African societies had a malleable mix of communalism and systems of wealth accumulation, status acquisition, property ownership, and entrepreneurial innovation. Some societies were more oriented toward communal modes of socioeconomic organization and production than others, but even societies in which notions of wealth, status, and enterprise were well developed had an overlay of communal ethos that mediated the politics of wealth acquisition and the pursuit of profits. Decentralized societies and those that strategically developed communal modes of life did not forbid individual enterprise or innovation. This variegated reality is the basis for a foundational claim of this volume: that entrepreneurship was not incompatible with the social ethos of precolonial and colonial African economies and societies, and that it could be argued that entrepreneurship, broadly defined, was in fact integral to the evolution of precolonial societies, which are sometimes erroneously portrayed as idyllic sites of unfettered egalitarianism and subsistence, and as incubators of a cultural aversion to profit-motivated innovation.

In the colonial period, the emphasis on structural and policy factors and on the all-conquering behemoth of colonial exploitation has tended to undermine the entrepreneurial struggles and triumphs of Africans. The dominant historiographical lens for viewing the colonial economy in Africa was skewed because historians of the African colonial economy ascribed too much deterministic consequence to colonial structures, policies, intentions, goals, infrastructures, and visions. The power of nationalist historiography in the postcolonial period stunted any scholarly desire to recognize the limitations of these structures, the African enterprises that flourished in the shadow and vortex of colonial schemes, and the niches of innovation and intelligent profit making that Africans, as individuals and groups, carved out for themselves. The challenge for writing a history of African subaltern entrepreneurs has been how to circumvent this historiographical backdrop, how to write entrepreneurial African colonial subjects into this colonial economic story of omnipotent European exploiters and economic schemers and purportedly helpless African victims of, or marginalized participants in, these schemes.

Only recently has the organizational, associational, and leadership agency of African entrepreneurs broken through the wall of emphasis on colonial structural factors. Works on female entrepreneurs in the Lome-Cotonou-Lagos-Accra regional textile trade in colonial West Africa decidedly broke with the historiographical primacy of colonial policy determinants to highlight how an ethnic network of female traders and merchants with origins in the Mina ethnic group in Togo and their "Brazilian" coastal cousins in other parts of West Africa alternately sidestepped and utilized the structures of colonialism and drew on kinship and associational capital to build loci of female wealth that have been immortalized by the legend of Nana-Benz, and by the continuing entrepreneurship dominance of "merchant clans" that these enterprising women built.[37]

If the tension between the structural and the human, between structural constraints on African economic initiative and the tenacious economic agency of African peoples, has been the defining conceptual question in African economic history, a keen, deliberate attention to enterprise and entrepreneurial creativity as an engine of African history can move us closer to answering it. As a historical actor and agent, the African entrepreneur embodies the structural realities that shaped her economic age. On the other hand, her entrepreneurial activities, while in productive and disruptive tension with these structural conditions, transcend them and reveal a cultural and individual streak of value creation and organized problem solving. A history of African entrepreneurship is thus a window into how individual and group entrepreneurial agency interacted with and complicated the structural factors that are often deemed to be of overwhelming consequence. The historical African entrepreneur is a human clue to understanding this historiographical tension between structure and agency in African economic history.

The chapters of this volume build on emerging works in the genre of new African economic histories that depart from the consistent primacy of structural factors to emphasize the importance and insights of individual and group enterprise, and of the organizational, leadership, and innovative creativity that sustained such enterprise. We demonstrate here that the business of creating value and of creatively juggling the factors of production, investment, labor, and organization to produce profits for personal and group economic enhancement was neither impossible nor alien to Africans in their many internal and external economic entanglements in the precolonial, colonial, and postcolonial periods. Imagining Africans as historical entrepreneurial actors and African history as animated by multiple and infinitely diverse entrepreneurial activities ought to be a simple, timely exercise in restoring to Africans the instinct of value creation, creative problem solving, and innovative use of opportunity to fill a production, distribution, or service void. This restorative history is analogous to similar efforts to recover African initiative and agency from colonial and Eurocentric claims in the realms of politics and culture.

Contributions to African Entrepreneurship Studies

Ours is the first scholarly volume devoted solely to African entrepreneurial histories. It thus provides a historical backdrop to the emerging literature on the role of African entrepreneurs in African societies. It is also part of a group of pioneer publications in the area of African business and entrepreneurial studies. There are a few books already in print on the general subject of entrepreneurship in Africa. One is a publication titled *Africans Investing in Africa: Understanding Business and Trade, Sector by Sector.*[38] Another is *Entrepreneurship in Africa: A Study of Successes* by David Fisk.[39] The volume *Africa's Greatest Entrepreneurs* is another recent title in this general subject area.[40] As the titles of these works suggest, they are concerned with entrepreneurs and entrepreneurship culture in contemporary Africa. They also have little or no academic rigor, as they were written to provide an instrumental snapshot for a general audience seeking an introduction to, or an overview of, entrepreneurial endeavors on the continent.

Their narrow focus notwithstanding, these works served as inspirational references for our intervention. Our approach, however, differs markedly from those of these publications in two significant ways. First, our volume takes entrepreneurship as a vibrant subfield of African precolonial and colonial economic history, even while recognizing the historiographical arc that connects that history to contemporary entrepreneurial cultures on the continent. While the scattered body of writings on entrepreneurship on the continent tends to adopt an approach that privileges contemporary economic sectors and industries, a narrow conceptualization that does not capture the diversity of African entrepreneurial experiences, *Entrepreneurship in Africa* resists the restrictions of sectorial specializations and compartmentalization that have origins in more recent economic events. Second, our volume privileges the microhistories of entrepreneurship that are shown to connect to broad, consequential structural factors. Indeed, in addition to being informed by important historiographical preoccupations, several chapters (those by Usuanlele, Callebert, Schler, Lobnibe, and Chuku) are detailed microhistories of particular entrepreneurial families, groups, and individuals, stories unconstrained by the analytical straightjacket of sectors and rigid classifications.

Our volume takes a decidedly scholarly approach because of the marginality of African entrepreneurs and their stories to conceptual and theoretical formulations on the topic. We have subjected the topic to rigorous academic analysis while implicitly and explicitly highlighting policy-relevant insights and interventions. Our approach is in some sense an aggregation, one might say, of the various burgeoning approaches outlined above, as we began with the basic, all-encompassing question of why entrepreneurship is an important subject in and for Africa. That question cannot be answered without drawing on the histories of entrepreneurship on the continent.

In many ways, the sectorial surveys and inspirational biographical stories told in the books referenced previously have partly answered that foundational question and made our job a little easier. In that sense we owe a debt to these preceding studies, just as we hope that this volume will spawn, inspire, and establish a model for similar scholarly projects in the future. This is a legitimate aspiration, given the scholarly and general appetite for historical texts on African business leadership and entrepreneurial initiatives, and given the current epistemological nonexistence of the field of African business history.

The foregoing analysis demonstrates one thing: that African entrepreneurs and entrepreneurial initiatives have not been examined on their own terms in African economic history. This volume therefore plugs a yawning gap in the African economic history literature by focusing explicitly on indigenous African enterprise, business leadership, and entrepreneurship. Even as Africa's much-hyped entrepreneurial moment gathers speed, inspiring further scholarly and nonscholarly studies of individual and group enterprise on the continent, there is already a concern that, in stressing the historicity and prevalence of enterprise in African societies, the abiding structural environment that both constrains and necessitates enterprise could recede from the analysis. It is a legitimate concern that the authors in the volume rigorously address.

Each chapter situates itself in fascinating individual stories of entrepreneurial resilience, but these narratives are indexed at every juncture by an acute acknowledgment of the impersonal, external, and structural fundamentals that underpin the business initiatives under discussion. Furthermore, the chapters in this volume display a sustained awareness of the illuminating power of the biographical. It is by exploring the biographies of Africa's historical and contemporary entrepreneurial actors that the self-conscious deliberateness of their craft is revealed and fully understood. By paying equal attention to the histories of private enterprise and the professional biographies of individual Africans who engineered or pioneered business endeavors, our volume explores the human and lived dimensions of African economic and business history.

Although this is ancillary to our objective, several chapters in this volume break new methodological, conceptual, and theoretical ground, thereby supplying guideposts and theoretical formulations for the historical study of Africa's business cultures. The chapters in this volume make the epistemological case for African business history as a viable subfield of African economic history. The volume posits and explains the need for, and the modalities with which to approach, histories of African entrepreneurship endeavors. We have established a few foundational outlines for Africanist entrepreneurship epistemology. In particular, the chapters by Emeagwali, Odey, Gennaro, and Chuku take on this task frontally and effectively.

To the extent that a distinct tradition of African entrepreneurship exists, our goal in this volume is to retrieve, enunciate, and conceptualize it as a guide for future historical studies of African entrepreneurship, business, and innovation cultures. As entrepreneurship becomes increasingly important for scholarly and policy engagements with Africa's current economic predicaments and aspirations, it is important that historians formulate the conceptual apparatus for participating in the conversation and for advancing the historical backdrop for current discussions on Africa's entrepreneurial possibilities.

This volume demonstrates the tapestry of innovation, ideas, political economies, and commerce connecting the African entrepreneurial hubs of today with those of the past. The chapters document and establish clear patterns of African business creativity and entrepreneurship stretching back many centuries and generations, and they project these models of indigenous enterprise and home-grown commercial creativity as a historical backdrop for contemporary scholarly and policy debates on entrepreneurship on the continent.

In their own ways, the following chapters demonstrate the versatile repertoires of African entrepreneurs. African entrepreneurs differed from their purportedly archetypal Western counterparts in that, in instances such as those illustrated by Odey, Chuku, Chachage, Konadu, and me in this volume, the African entrepreneur shunned narrow, restrictive specialization and instead wore several entrepreneurial hats. For African entrepreneurs simultaneously participating in the processes of value creation and in precarious household economies, excessive specialization was disadvantageous, hence the embrace of entrepreneurial versatility as a strategy for inoculating economic risk takers against the natural and human vagaries that threatened African livelihoods from precolonial times to the postcolonial period.

Pushing the line of this contention even further, Usuanlele's chapter argues that entrepreneurial aspirations caused some Benins to migrate away from the Benin homeland. He further argues that these migrants cultivated a diverse repertoire that came to include warlordism, a form of political and military enterprise connected to securing and protecting lucrative trade. Without evaluating the morality of their craft, one can follow Usuanlele to conceptualize historical and contemporary African warlords, specialist warriors, and mercantile war makers as entrepreneurs in the business of power, violence, and control. However, a successful specialist warrior also dabbled in trade; devised efficient, self-interested strategies for dispensing loot; and often charged fees for protecting traders. He was a versatile entrepreneur, a composite of the flexible African mercantile actor. As the chapters in this volume contend, versatility was not the absence of specialization in the African historical context, nor did it emanate from a lack of awareness of niche building and comparative advantage. Rather, it was a strategy to exact maximum reward from entrepreneurial effort while minimizing risk. Versatility was a risk-management endeavor, an important insight that several authors in this volume advance.

The Architecture of the Book

The chapters in the volume are organized according to theme and without regard to chronology. For thematic coherence and compactness, the book is divided into five parts. Part 1 contains two chapters united by their keen attention to two phenomena: the centrality of networks to commercial and artisanal entrepreneurship, and the conceptual implications of studying these networks for the nascent field of African business history.

Part 2 focuses on the entrepreneurial initiatives and accomplishments of female traders, producers, and commercial innovators. The three chapters in this part explore how women in colonial and postcolonial Ghana and Nigeria negotiated multiple socioeconomic and political regimes to build, store, and leverage wealth for the purpose of improving their societies and enhancing their own status.

Part 3 contains two chapters that analyze, in different spatial and temporal contexts, the intersection of political decision making, politically charged events, and nationalism on the one hand, and entrepreneurship on the other. One is set in twentieth-century Algeria, the other in nineteenth- and early twentieth-century northeast Yorubaland in modern Nigeria. In both chapters, the state or, properly speaking, allegiance to the state and a sense of nationalist loyalty drove critical investments and commercial engagements that were imagined and calculated to bolster the state and enhance its prestige.

Part 4 features chapters that profile unlikely entrepreneurs or those whose entrepreneurial investments complemented their other economic identities. The chapters by Schler and Callebert examine two groups of workers in South Africa and Nigeria who established business ventures that pivoted on their working lives while enriching their proletarian identities. The chapter by Gennaro analyzes the business investments of boxing promoters in colonial Nigeria, shining a light on a previously neglected colonial business sector and the Africans who ran it. The third chapter in this section, by Konadu, examines the multifaceted entrepreneurial initiatives of Nana Kofi Donkɔ, a Ghanaian healer who painstakingly maintained logbooks, accounts, ledgers, and other records that give us a glimpse into his business repertoire.

Part 5 focuses on the theme of colonization as a context for African entrepreneurial flourishing. Two chapters, one by Odey and the other by Shanguhyia, consider how Africans exploited the narrow economic interstices of colonialism to establish small footholds in certain retail, production, and artisanal sectors of the economy. Their perspectives from the Turkana region of northwestern Kenya and the Igede area of central Nigeria complement each other and offer coterminous insights into rural microbusiness in the colonial economy.

MOSES E. OCHONU is the Cornelius Vanderbilt Chair in African History at Vanderbilt University. He is author of *Africa in Fragments: Essays on Nigeria, Africa, and Global Africanity*; *Colonialism by Proxy: Hausa Imperial Agents and Middle Belt Consciousness in Nigeria* (IUP), which was named finalist for the Herskovits Prize; and *Colonial Meltdown: Northern Nigeria in the Great Depression*.

Notes

1. Neither Adam Smith nor David Ricardo saw entrepreneurship as instrumental to economic development or even the creation and sustenance of capitalist prosperity.
2. Joseph A. Schumpeter, *The Theory of Economic Development: An Enquiry into Profits, Capital, Credit, Interest, and the Business Cycle* (Cambridge, MA: Harvard University Press, [1912] 1934), 2.
3. See Geoffrey G. Jones and Dan Wadhwani, "Schumpeter's Plea: Rediscovery History and Relevance in the Study of Entrepreneurship," *Harvard Business School Working Papers Series*, July 5, 2006, http://hbswk.hbs.edu/item/schumpeters-plea-rediscovering-history-and-relevance-in-the-study-of-entrepreneurship; J. B. Say, *A Treatise on Political Economy or the Production, Distribution, and Consumption of Wealth*, trans. C. R. Prinsep (London: Longman, Hurst, Rees, Orme, and Brown, 1821).
4. See John Stuart Mill, *Principles of Political Economy with Some of Their Applications to Social Philosophy* (London: Longmans, Green, 1848). Mill defines an entrepreneur as one who possesses the "labour and skill required for superintendence," p. 246.

5. Joseph A. Schumpeter, "The Creative Response in Economic History," *Journal of Economic History* 7 (1947): 149–59.

6. Joseph A. Schumpeter, *Capitalism, Socialism and Democracy* (New York: Harper and Row, 1942), 82.

7. Schumpeter broke with the conventional economic thinking of his time by arguing that large firms displayed entrepreneurial behavior and were thus catalysts of economic development. Other Western economists of the early twentieth century argued that big conglomerates, what we call big business in today's language, were detrimental to economic development because they were static monopolies that depressed wages and exploited workers and consumers alike.

8. Jones and Wadhwani, "Schumpeter's Plea," 5.

9. Naomi R. Lamoreaux, "Beyond the Old and the New: Economic History of the United States," Yale University Economics Department Working Paper, 2015, 27–28, http://economics yale.edu/sites/default/files/files/Faculty/Lamoreaux/beyond-old-2015.pdf.

10. Ibid., 7.

11. See Ann Pierre, Yvonne von Frederichs, and Joakim Wincent, "A Review of Social Entrepreneurship Research," *International Studies in Entrepreneurship* 29 (2013): 43–69.

12. Alex Stewart, "A Prospectus on the Anthropology of Entrepreneurship," *Entrepreneurship Theory and Practice* 16, no. 2 (1991): 71–91.

13. Ibid., abstract.

14. Roger L. Martin and Sally Osberg, "Social Entrepreneurship: The Case for Definition," *Stanford Social Innovation Review*, Spring 2007, 29–39.

15. Ibid., 34–35.

16. Thomas Martila, *The Culture of Enterprise in Neoliberalism* (London: Routledge, 2012). The quoted phrase is from the book's blurb.

17. See Yohei Miyauchi, "Imagined Entrepreneurs in Neoliberal South Africa: Informality and Spatial Justice in Post-apartheid Cities," *Mila*, special issue, 2014, 68–75.

18. A. G. Hopkins, *An Economic History of West Africa* (London: Longman, 1973).

19. Ibid.

20. A somewhat moderated version of this argument can be found in J. Forbes Munro, *Britain in Tropical Africa, 1880–1960: Economic Relationships and Impact* (London: Macmillan, 1984).

21. The literature on underdevelopment theory and world-system analysis is vast and varied, but a common denominator is that works promoting this paradigm tend to privilege structural, transnational, and exogenous factors over local individual and group economic agency. See Samir Amin, *Accumulation on a World Scale: A Critique of the Theory of Development*, trans. Brian Pearce (New York: Monthly Press, 1974); Immanuel Wallerstein, *The Capitalist World-Economy* (Cambridge: Cambridge University Press, 1979); and Samir Amin, *Unequal Development: An Essay on the Social Formations of Peripheral Capitalism* (New York: Monthly Review Press, 1977).

22. Colin Bundy, *The Rise and Fall of the South African Peasantry* (London: Heinemann, 1979); E. S. Atieno-Odhiambo, "The Rise and Decline of the Kenyan Peasant—1888–1922," *East Africa Journal* 9, no. 5 (1972): 11–15; Robert Shenton, *The Development of Capitalism in Northern Nigeria* (Toronto: University of Toronto Press, 1986); Jean Suret-Canale, *French Colonialism in Tropical Africa 1900–1945* (Ann Arbor: University of Michigan Press, 1971); Robin Palmer, *Land and Racial Discrimination in Rhodesia* (London: Heinemann, 1974).

23. See Frederick Cooper, "Africa and the World Economy," in *Confronting Historical Paradigms: Peasants, Labor, and the Capitalist World System in Africa and Latin America*, ed.

Frederick Cooper et al., 84–201 (Madison: University of Wisconsin Press, 1993); and Sara Berry, *No Condition Is Permanent: The Social Dynamic of Agrarian Change in Sub-Saharan Africa* (Madison: University of Wisconsin Press, 1993). Differentiation, maneuvering, and straddling were features of the African peasantry during colonialism, although the essentially racial character of the colonial bureaucracy erected limitations that restricted the extent to which African entrepreneurs could aspire to certain echelons of the colonial economy.

24. See Ann Philips, *The Enigma of Colonialism: British Policy in West Africa* (London: James Curry; Bloomington: Indiana University Press, 1989); William Gervase Clarence-Smith, "The Organization of 'Consent' in British West Africa, 1830s to 1960s," in *Contesting Colonial Hegemony: State and Society in Africa and India*, ed. Dagmar Engels and Shula Marks, 55–78 (London: British Academic Press, 1994).

25. Charles van Onselen, *The Seed Is Mine: The Life of Kas Maine, a South African Sharecropper, 1894–1985* (New York: Hill and Wang, 1996).

26. Keletso Atkins, *The Moon Is Dead! Give Us Our Money! The Cultural Origins of an African Work Ethic, Natal, South Africa, 1843–1900* (Portsmouth, NH: Heinemann, 1993); Caroline Brown, *"We Are All Slaves": African Miners, Culture, and Resistance at the Enugu Government Colliery, Nigeria* (Portsmouth, NH: Heinemann, 2002); Edward Roux, *Time Longer than Rope: A History of the Black Man's Struggle for Freedom in South Africa*, 2nd ed. (Madison: University of Wisconsin Press, 1967).

27. Frantz Fanon, *The Wretched of the Earth* (New York: Grove, 1967).

28. See Richard Jeffries, *Class, Power, and Ideology in Ghana: The Railwaymen of Sekondi* (Cambridge: Cambridge University Press, 1978); Bill Freund, *Capital and Labor in the Nigerian Tin Mines* (New York: Humanities Press, 1981).

29. This is the central thesis of Frederick Cooper's *Decolonization and African Society: The Labor Question in French and British Africa* (Cambridge: Cambridge University Press).

30. See Jane Parpart, "The 'Labor Aristocracy' Debate: The Copperbelt Case, 1924–1967," *African Economic History* 13 (1984): 171–91; G. Arrighi and J. Saul, *Essays on the Political Economy of Africa* (New York: Monthly Review Press, 1973).

31. See Cooper, *Decolonization and African Society*; Frederick Cooper, *On the African Waterfront: Urban Disorder and the Transformation of Work in Colonial Mombasa* (New Haven, CT: Yale University Press, 1987); Frederick Cooper, *From Slaves to Squatters: Plantation Labor and Agriculture in Zanzibar and Coastal Kenya, 1890–1925* (New Haven, CT: Yale University Press, 1981); and Bill Freund, *The African Worker* (Cambridge: Cambridge University Press, 1988).

32. For an insightful exploration of the Swahili trade system, see Abdul Sheriff, *Slaves, Spices, and Ivory in Zanzibar* (Athens: Ohio University Press, 1987).

33. A. D. Roberts, "Nyamwezi Trade," in *Precolonial African Trade: Essays on Trade in Central and Eastern Africa before 1900*, ed. Richard Gray, 39–74 (London: Oxford University Press, 1970). So prevalent is this denial of independent entrepreneurial agency to the Nyamwezi that the phrase "a nation of porters" is often uncritically applied to them in works that theorize them as part of a labor market system that developed in support of entrepreneurial traders with connections to external finance and logistics. See, for instance, Stephen Rockel, "'A Nation of Porters': The Nyamwezi and the Labor Market in Nineteenth-Century Tanzania," *Journal of African History* 41, no. 2 (2000): 173–95.

34. See Ghislaine Lydon, *On Trans-Saharan Trails: Islamic Law, Trade Networks, and Cross-cultural Exchange in Nineteenth-Century Western Africa* (Cambridge: Cambridge University Press, 2009).

35. Julius Nyerere, *Ujamaa: Essays on Socialism* (Dar es Salaam: Oxford University Press, 1968).
36. George B. N. Ayittey, *Indigenous African Institutions*, 2nd ed. (Leiden: Brill, Nijhoff, 2006).
37. See John R. Heilbrunn, "Commerce, Politics, and Business Associations in Benin and Togo," *Comparative Politics* 29, no. 4 (July 1997): 473–92.
38. See Terrence McNamee, Michael Pearson, and Wiebe Boer, eds., *Africans Investing in Africa: Understanding Business and Trade, Sector by Sector* (New York: Palgrave, 2015).
39. David Fisk, *Entrepreneurship in Africa: A Study of Successes* (Santa Barbara, CA: Praeger, 2002).
40. Moky Makura, *Africa's Greatest Entrepreneurs* (London: Penguin Global, 2009).

Bibliography

Amin, Samir. 1974. *Accumulation on a World Scale: A Critique of the Theory of Development.* Translated by Brian Pearce. New York: Monthly Press.
———. 1977. *Unequal Development: An Essay on the Social Formations of Peripheral Capitalism.* New York: Monthly Review Press.
Arrighi, G., and J. Saul. 1973. *Essays on the Political Economy of Africa.* New York: Monthly Review Press.
Atieno-Odhiambo, E. S. 1972. "The Rise and Decline of the Kenyan Peasant—1888–1922." *East Africa Journal* 9 (5): 11–15.
Atkins, Keletso. 1993. *The Moon Is Dead! Give Us Our Money! The Cultural Origins of an African Work Ethic, Natal, South Africa, 1843–1900.* Portsmouth, NH: Heinemann.
Ayittey, George B. N. 2006. *Indigenous African Institutions.* 2nd ed. Leiden: Brill, Nijhoff.
Berry, Sara. 1993. *No Condition Is Permanent: The Social Dynamic of Agrarian Change in Sub-Saharan Africa.* Madison: University of Wisconsin Press.
Brown, Caroline. 2002. *"We Are All Slaves": African Miners, Culture, and Resistance at the Enugu Government Colliery, Nigeria.* Portsmouth, NH: Heinemann.
Bundy, Colin. 1979. *The Rise and Fall of the South African Peasantry.* London: Heinemann.
Clarence-Smith, William Gervase. 1994. "The Organization of 'Consent' in British West Africa, 1830s to 1960s." In *Contesting Colonial Hegemony: State and Society in Africa and India,* edited by Dagmar Engels and Shula Marks, 55–78. London: British Academic Press.
Cooper, Frederick. 1981. *From Slaves to Squatters: Plantation Labor and Agriculture in Zanzibar and Coastal Kenya, 1890–1925.* New Haven, CT: Yale University Press.
———. 1987. *On the African Waterfront: Urban Disorder and the Transformation of Work in Colonial Mombasa.* New Haven, CT: Yale University Press.
———. 1993. "Africa and the World Economy." In *Confronting Historical Paradigms: Peasants, Labor, and the Capitalist World System in Africa and Latin America,* edited by Frederick Cooper, Allen F. Isaacman, Florencia E. Mallon, William Roseberry, and Steve J. Stern, 84–201. Madison: University of Wisconsin.
———. 1996. *Decolonization and African Society: The Labor Question in French and British Africa.* Cambridge: Cambridge University Press.
Fanon, Frantz. 1967. *The Wretched of the Earth.* New York: Grove.

Fisk, David. 2002. *Entrepreneurship in Africa: A Study of Successes*. Santa Barbara, CA: Praeger.

Freund, Bill. 1981. *Capital and Labor in the Nigerian Tin Mines*. New York: Humanities Press.

———. 1988. *The African Worker*. Cambridge: Cambridge University Press.

Heilbrunn, John R. 1997. "Commerce, Politics, and Business Associations in Benin and Togo." *Comparative Politics* 29 (4): 473–92.

Hopkins, A. G. 1973. *An Economic History of West Africa*. London: Longman.

Jeffries, Richard. 1978. *Class, Power, and Ideology in Ghana: The Railwaymen of Sekondi*. Cambridge: Cambridge University Press.

Jones, Geoffrey G., and Dan Wadhwani. 2006. "Schumpeter's Plea: Rediscovery History and Relevance in the Study of Entrepreneurship." *Harvard Business School Working Papers Series*, July 5. http://hbswk.hbs.edu/item/schumpeters-plea-rediscovering-history-and -relevance-in-the-study-of-entrepreneurship.

Lamoreaux, Naomi R. 2015. "Beyond the Old and the New: Economic History of the United States." Yale University Economics Department Working Paper. http://economics.yale.edu/sites /default/files/files/Faculty/Lamoreaux/beyond-old-2015.pdf.

Lydon, Ghislaine. 2009. *On Trans-Saharan Trails: Islamic Law, Trade Networks, and Cross-cultural Exchange in Nineteenth-Century Western Africa*. Cambridge: Cambridge University Press.

Makura, Moky. 2009. *Africa's Greatest Entrepreneurs*. London: Penguin Global.

Martila, Thomas. 2012. *The Culture of Enterprise in Neoliberalism*. London: Routledge.

Martin, Roger L., and Sally Osberg. 2007. "Social Entrepreneurship: The Case for Definition." *Stanford Social Innovation Review*, Spring, 29–39.

McNamee, Terrence, Michael Pearson, and Wiebe Boer, eds. 2015. *Africans Investing in Africa: Understanding Business and Trade, Sector by Sector*. New York: Palgrave.

Mill, John Stuart. 1848. *Principles of Political Economy with Some of Their Applications to Social Philosophy*. London: Longmans, Green.

Miyauchi, Yohei. 2014. "Imagined Entrepreneurs in Neoliberal South Africa: Informality and Spatial Justice in Post-apartheid Cities." *Mila*, special issue, 68–75.

Munro, J. Forbes. 1984. *Britain in Tropical Africa, 1880–1960: Economic Relationships and Impact*. London: Macmillan.

Nyerere, Julius. 1968. *Ujamaa: Essays on Socialism*. Dar es Salaam: Oxford University Press.

Palmer, Robin. 1974. *Land and Racial Discrimination in Rhodesia*. London: Heinemann.

Parpart, Jane. 1984. "The 'Labor Aristocracy' Debate: The Copperbelt Case, 1924–1967." *African Economic History* 13:171–91.

Philips, Ann. 1989. *The Enigma of Colonialism: British Policy in West Africa*. London: James Curry; Bloomington: Indiana University Press.

Pierre, Ann, Yvonne von Frederichs, and Joakim Wincent. 2013. "A Review of Social Entrepreneurship Research." *International Studies in Entrepreneurship* 29:43–69.

Roberts, A. D. 1970. "Nyamwezi Trade." In *Precolonial African Trade: Essays on Trade in Central and Eastern Africa before 1900*, edited by Richard Gray, 39–74. London: Oxford University Press.

Rockel, Stephen. 2000. "'A Nation of Porters': The Nyamwezi and the Labor Market in Nineteenth-Century Tanzania." *Journal of African History* 41 (2): 173–95.

Roux, Edward. 1967. *Time Longer than Rope: A History of the Black Man's Struggle for Freedom in South Africa*. 2nd edition. Madison: University of Wisconsin Press.

Say, J. B. 1821. *A Treatise on Political Economy or the Production, Distribution, and Consumption of Wealth*, translated by C. R. Prinsep. London: Longman, Hurst, Rees, Orme, and Brown.

Schumpeter, Joseph A. (1912) 1934. *The Theory of Economic Development: An Enquiry into Profits, Capital, Credit, Interest, and the Business Cycle.* Cambridge, MA: Harvard University Press.

———. 1942. *Capitalism, Socialism and Democracy.* New York: Harper and Row.

———. 1947. "The Creative Response in Economic History." *Journal of Economic History* 7:149–59.

Shenton, Robert. 1986. *The Development of Capitalism in Colonial Northern Nigeria.* Toronto: University of Toronto Press.

Sheriff, Abdul. 1987. *Slaves, Spices, and Ivory in Zanzibar.* Athens: Ohio University Press.

Stewart, Alex. 1991. "A Prospectus on the Anthropology of Entrepreneurship." *Entrepreneurship Theory and Practice* 16 (2): 71–91.

Suret-Canale, Jean. 1971. *French Colonialism in Tropical Africa 1900–1945.* Ann Arbor: University of Michigan Press.

Van Onselen, Charles. 1996. *The Seed Is Mine: The Life of Kas Maine, a South African Sharecropper, 1894–1985.* New York: Hill and Wang.

Wallerstein, Immanuel. 1979. *The Capitalist World-Economy.* Cambridge: Cambridge University Press.

1 Globalization and the Making of East Africa's Asian Entrepreneurship Networks

Chambi Chachage

> Asians have for the most part been solely concerned with their own economic salvation.
> —Dharam P. Ghai

THE WINDS OF change blowing across Africa in 1960 were swift.[1] Within a space of five years, the East African countries of Tanganyika, Uganda, Kenya, and Zanzibar won their independence—in 1961, 1962, 1963, and 1963/1964 respectively.[2] Filled with anticipation and apprehension, members of the Asian community in the region participated in this transition in varying ways. What lay ahead for them was as uncertain as it had been for their predecessors a century or two ago when they left Southeast Asia. As both agents and victims of global capitalism, they had become, predominantly and stereotypically, a business community. Africa's precolonial and colonial settings, though constraining in certain ways, had enabled a number of them to emerge as notable entrepreneurs. With the postcolonial era springing up in the context of African nationalism and the cold war between the predominantly capitalist West and primarily communist/socialist East, it was tempting to project the ideological trajectory that the newly independent nations would take since capitalism, as one economic historian has noted, was associated with colonialism.[3] Business, it seemed, would not be as usual.

This chapter traces the emergence and consolidation of East African Asian entrepreneurship networks. It argues that the marginalization of pioneering Asian entrepreneurs in the first global economy paved the way for the integration of their successors in the second global economy. Even though the transition from the former to the latter constrained them, the chapter further argues that they continued to form and maintain close bonds that enabled their business community to prosper. It is this entrepreneurship networking, and not an innate entrepreneurial spirit, that explains the reproduction of East African Asian entrepreneurs and their relative business success. "Historians," as Abdul Sheriff notes in the case of Zanzibar, "have hitherto tried to explain the rise of this section to the commercial hegemony in terms of race, ascribing business acumen to the Indians as if it were an inherent racial characteristic."[4] One of the leading East African businessmen, Ali A. Mufuruki, also shares such sentiments in regard to the Ismailis in Tanzania: "Their business acumen, experience and strong community network has enabled them to maintain a stronghold on many sectors of the economy."[5] Popular discourses also echo this stereotypical ascription, as this claim indicates: "It is an admitted fact that most of the Indian Ismailis came in Africa with industry in their blood, business in their brains and immense calibre to labour in their muscles, but with empty pockets."[6] Thus, it is important for this chapter to look at the concrete historical conjunctures that led to their rise.

Globalizing Asian Merchant Princes

Asians have been coming to East Africa since antiquity.[7] Through trade in the Indian Ocean and Mediterranean Sea, respectively, they were part and parcel of the first two series of waves—one starting from China in the eleventh century and the other from the Middle East and southern Europe—that Samir Amin refers to as contributing to the long history of capitalism.[8] However, it was after the third wave, which began in Atlantic Europe at the turn of the sixteenth century, that their presence in the region became relatively more pronounced and permanent. This last wave, as Amin notes, took the form of mercantilism for three centuries (1500–1800) after the conquest of the Americas and, later, various parts of Asia, Australia, and Africa.[9]

In the case of East Africa and South Asia, this wave buoyed the Portuguese interference in the Indian Ocean trade in the aftermath of Vasco da Gama's circumnavigation of the continent of Africa en route to India in 1498. Instead of opening up this free-trade zone to western Europe as allegedly envisaged, the Portuguese monopolized it and contributed to its decline. Reflecting on the "Chinese retreat and the 'Vasco da Gama epoch'" that occurred almost simultaneously, Sheriff laments, "Before the coming of the Europeans into the Indian Ocean in the sixteenth century it was indeed 'genuinely a *mare liberum* where no state tried to control maritime matters,' a sea open to all where the processes of sociocultural integration were not hampered by monopolistic seaborne empires."[10] It was replaced by armed trading.

"By 1596," notes Dana Seidenberg, "England and the Netherlands were challenging the Portuguese monopoly of the Indian coast, the English arriving in Surat in 1607, shortly after establishing trading centres at Bombay, Madras and Calcutta."[11] Even though India, like China, had contributed ingredients of capitalism to the three successive waves of the sociotechnological innovation that paved the way for capitalist modernity, it could not curb the great divergence that was emerging between western Europe and the rest of the world.[12] The factors that led to the industrial and political revolutions in Britain and France, such as accumulation and innovation, diffused more rapidly within western Europe relative to other corners of the world, which widened the gap in technological capacity, military strength, economic power, and other relative advancements that enabled the West to colonize.[13] Thus, "India, although well acquainted with artillery since the mid-fifteenth century, was no match for the Netherlands, England, and later France" by the seventeenth century.[14]

These growing European powers began utilizing the large-scale emigration of East Asians, through both force and free will, as a source of labor. This coincided with the emergence of imperial chartered companies. After the Imperial Dutch East Indian Company claimed the Mascarene island of Mauritius as an entrepôt, traders began importing slaves as early as 1641.[15] These slaves were tasked with cutting and carrying ebony trees, then highly valued raw materials in Europe. After the French took over in 1721 and established sugarcane plantations, the demand for slave labor increased, particularly in 1735 when sugar production became the main industry.[16] Meanwhile, the British East Indian Company and French East Indian Company were competing for dominance of the trade between Europe and Asia. Sheriff sums up the outcomes of this imperial contest and its implications for Oman, India, and East Africa:

> Although commercial and diplomatic contacts had earlier been established between Oman and those European powers that were competing for hegemony in the Indian Ocean, it was the spillover of Anglo-French rivalry into Asia that began to undermine the political independence of Oman. Struggle over the trade of the East involved concessions from oriental potentates. The chartered East India companies, both British and French, were therefore backed by the political power of the European mercantile nations. Rivalry between them was particularly virulent during the second half of the eighteenth century, partly because of the disintegration of the Mughal Empire which exposed the naked struggle for political control in India and the Indian Ocean. For Britain, which had emerged as the dominant power in India, the defence of its empire and its arteries became a constant preoccupation.[17]

Thus, it is this crystallization of capitalism as a globalizing yet marginalizing economic system that led to what is regarded as the first global economy (1840–1929).[18] It is important to note that 1840 was the year that Sultan Seyyid Said of Oman moved his capital from Muscat to Zanzibar. This move is of particular importance to a study on the globalizing dialectics of capitalism because it indirectly integrated and marginalized Asians in the first global economy. As Lois Lobo notes, many of them came to East Africa through Zanzibar around this time because the sultan and his sultanate actively encouraged them to live and work on the isle. "In fact," she stresses, "the position of Custom Master was always given to an Asian by the Sultan."[19] The "wise Sultan," affirms Manubhai Madhvani, "eager to speed up and encourage business transactions, invited the Indians [or Asians] to bring their families over, promising to honour and protect their religious beliefs and traditional values."[20]

As the Asian population in Zanzibar continued to grow steadily, notes Seidenberg—following Philip Curtin and Joel Kotkin—it formed a "capitalist diaspora" that constituted "a cohesive commercial network of uprooted merchants based on group solidarity and identity, seeking social progress" and locating its "identity in a common past."[21] It is the successful members of this business network, among others, who principally financed the caravan trade between the East African coast of Tanzania and its hinterland. These "merchant princes," documents Gijsbert Oonk, included "local South Asian kings of trade and commerce such as Tharia Topan (1823–1891), Sewa Haji (1851–1897), Allidina Visram (1851–1916) and Nasser [Virji] (1865–1942)."[22] Such Asian financiers, notes John Iliffe, "gave goods on credit to Arab or Swahili who undertook to repay two or three times the original sum in ivory on their return."[23]

The name that looms large is that of Topan. According to Blanche D'Souza, the self-taught trader left India at the age of twelve to join established relatives; however, he first worked from dawn to dusk for an agent of the firm of Jairam Sewji, known as Ladha Damji, before rising to own numerous enterprises.[24] Drawing from the biography that Topan's son wrote, Frederick Cooper notes how he managed to travel back to India to make agreements with Ismaili firms to purchase cloves from Zanzibar.[25] As Alia Paroo points out, he was also instrumental in laying the foundation for the migration of fellow Ismailis from India and developing their trade network on the East African coast.[26] Being a pioneering patron, Topan provided them with jobs, social services, and leadership.[27] Iliffe hails him as the most powerful capitalist of Zanzibar.[28] Topan later shifted his firm's headquarters to Bombay[29] and, as the following account highlights, boldly attempted to fully engage in the first global economy:

> From Bombay Tharia was to enter the lucrative China trade in the 1860s. Attempts were also made to develop trade with Europe by at least three merchants who either owned or chartered vessels for the trade. Tharia Topan, who owned three large vessels, had MT\$266,000[30] invested in his "London business" alone. He seems to have been discouraged from entering the American market directly, much to the relief of American merchants at Zanzibar. His London business, however, proved not so profitable for he clamed to have lost MT\$100,000 in 1867, and he contemplated withdrawing from it temporarily.[31]

During the same decade, Topan financed Tippu Tip, a prominent trader who is still remembered as far as the Congo for his central role in the slave trade. He also financed Rumaliza, another infamous slave trader.[32] Ironically, in 1875 the British knighted Topan to honor his role in ending the slave trade.[33] A new era was dawning.

However, these finances were circulating in—and thus their financiers were connected to—the first global economy, particularly through the Oman link to the British. Zanzibar had become its linking base on the East African coast as early as the 1740s, when the Busaidi dynasty seized control of Oman, "built their mercantile strength, [and] became satellites of British power in India."[34] This occurred after many of the Omani merchants had reverted to peaceful trade in the mid-1730s following a stint of armed trading and raiding of the Portuguese and their allies.[35] The centrality the British accorded Zanzibar cannot be overstated. When the French slave trade threatened to bypass it, they reoccupied Kilwa in the mid-1780s in order to make them trade through Zanzibar.[36] Kilwa, a town on the coast of Tanzania, was a slave-trading center. It had lost its earlier commercial glory as a Swahili city-state during the era of *mare liberum* due to the Portuguese conquest in 1505 that cut it off from the trade with the gold-rich Sofala and rendered it a worthless "establishment which they could ill afford to maintain in view of their limited resources of capital and manpower."[37] It had been reviving since the 1770s, not least because of "slave exports, first to the Persian Gulf and then to the Mascarene Islands, French plantation colonies developed after 1735."[38] Thus, what made Zanzibar prosper is the connection it had as a gateway with Kilwa and other towns on the East African coast and in the hinterland. Its prosperity even "attracted Asian merchants from Mozambique, where custom duties were crippling the ivory trade."[39]

A Knight with the Rockefellers of Uganda

In his memoir *A Knight in Africa: Journey from Bukene*, Jayantilal Keshavji Chande retraces the steps he took and the connections that made him one of the most famous entrepreneurs in East Africa.[40] He was born in the Kenyan coastal city of Mombasa on May 7, 1928, to parents who lived in then Tanganyika, and he married an Asian in Uganda, a testament to the vast East African Asian network. The story, however, begins in western India with his grandfather, who "was remarkable for the ineptitude [of] his speculative stock marketing trading."[41] Most weekdays, Chande recollects, his grandfather "would end up buying high and selling low."[42] When he contracted rabies and died in 1922, his family was left with a small farm whose value could not be realized due to local customs and a trading business on the verge of bankruptcy. Someone had to take drastic measures, with far-reaching implications: "It was then that my father, Keshavji, came to a momentous decision. Aged just twenty-two, he resolved to clear the family debts once and for all, not at home in India, but by taking a boat bound for Africa, leaving behind his widowed mother, his three brothers and two sisters, and an eighteen-year-old wife [Kanku Chande] and one young daughter of his own."[43] This happened in the twilight of the first global economy. It was waning not least because of the rise of communism after the Russian Revolution of 1917 and what the international historian Erez Manela refers to as the Wilsonian Moment that promised self-determination and internationalized anticolonial nationalism in the context of the 1919 peace conference in Paris.[44] World War I (1914–1918) had left the key players in this global economy ravaged; the Great Depression, which would put the last nail in the coffin by ushering in a period of disintegration (1930–1979), was less than a decade away.

Sir Andy Chande, as he has popularly been known after becoming a knight of the British Empire, narrates how his brave father made his way to and started a business in Africa:

> Like all those who have journeyed to Bukene, Keshavji arrived there by a roundabout route. His first stop on leaving his home village of Ged Bagasara in what is now Gujarat state was the port of Bombay. There he caught the SS *Karagola*, of the British India Steamship Company, bound for Mombasa. There, through the business connections of his father-in-law, Nanjibhai Damodar Ruparelia, who was commercially active up and down the Swahili coast from his base in Mombasa, Keshavji found work with an old established Indian merchant company, where under the watchful eye of the firm's owner, Haji Abdulrahman Issa, he worked for very little.[45]

The employer offered Keshavji partnership in the company after he impressed him with his diligence. Surprisingly, he declined. Chande attributes this to his unwillingness to tie his future to the company financially, but this does not mean he did not utilize existing networks to realize his dreams of owning his own business. Thus, after spending the year 1924 in India to treat his eyes, Keshavji went back to East Africa to join the firm of his cousin, Juthalal Velji Chande, who had sailed to Dar es Salaam on a dhow with his brothers in the late nineteenth century. However, he opted for Bukene in western Tanzania because the British colonial state had opened a railway line between Mwanza and Tabora that provided training opportunities.[46]

The railway station in Bukene attracted other Asian merchants. It was within this Asian merchant circle in East Africa that Chande learned his trade. In almost a literal sense, he was born and bred in the shop that his father opened. Reminiscing on his acquisition of the entrepreneurial aptitude that characterizes business geniuses, he states,

> My first childhood memory is of that shop—more precisely, of the machine that stood to one side of the counter, a small device for hulling maize. If I am certain of anything, it is that my lifelong passion, obsession almost, for find-

ing out how things and people can be made to work more efficiently and effectively stems from the many childhood hours I spent on those premises. Every small detail, down to the lid of a tin or the side of a jerrycan, has lodged itself in my memory, preserved forever in sharp focus, distinct, still exerting that primitive fascination even now.[47]

Business practice, not genetics, makes perfect. The tinges of nostalgia that can easily exaggerate things notwithstanding, such reminiscences underscore how the home environment can instill the entrepreneurship skills necessary to succeed. As I observed in a brief encounter with Chande in Mumbai on January 11, 2011, and later at the US embassy in Dar es Salaam, even at the age of eighty-three his mind was sharp in remembering, organizing, and connecting things and people. Apart from upbringing, it is business networking, family and otherwise, that enables many Asians to succeed in business and other related professions. The account that follows is illustrative:

> My sister's wedding [in 1938 to a Hindu from Misungwi in Mwanza, where he had a shop not unlike Chande's father's, though on a smaller scale] occurred at a time of rapid expansion in my father's business. In 1935 my cousin Juthalal Velji Chande sold his business to my father. It was my father's first such acquisition, and the springboard for accelerated future growth. Within a year Keshavji had invited his younger brothers, Ratansi and Amratlal, who were still living in India, to join him. Soon he had established a company by the name of Keshavji Jethabhai and Brothers, and was operating out of both Bukene and Tabora.[48]

The accelerated future growth included "a hard won agency for sugar (out of Uganda)," the "establishment in 1937 of a rice and flour milling business," and "processing facilities for oils and soaps."[49] His father's "acquisition of agencies for the products of Vacuum Oil company of South Africa Ltd., forerunners of ESSO, and also of Motor Mart and Exchange Limited, Tanganyika franchise-holders of General Motors," he further notes, "opened the door for the nascent truck market in Western Tanganyika."[50] The cars marketed were Chevrolet and Bedford trucks; most likely to minimize risks and losses, his father "operated this side of the business on a consignment basis, remitting money to Motor Mart only when trucks were sold."[51]

In his economic survey of the Asian community in East Africa in the 1960s, Dharam P. Ghai attributes their economic success to "their possession of certain qualities essential to economic development."[52] Clearly invoking Max Weber's *Spirit of Capitalism*,[53] he further asserts that the "early Asian settlers were imbued with quasi-Protestant ethics; they were remarkable for their strong commercial sense, capacity to work long hours, low propensity to consume, and passion for accumulation [of] riches."[54] Chande's account of his father seems to give credence to this explanation. Elsewhere Chande elaborates: "My father . . . purchased locally grown produce such as paddy and maize, sold consumable items and occasionally financed the growers. He operated on a small profit margin. Very often the sale of a gunnysack or empty four-gallon tin was his profit since the contents were sold at cost price. . . . In the 1950s and 1960s he became a prosperous man in the milling business but only after many years . . . of hard work and savings."[55]

However, Martha Honey provides a cautionary note on the basis of her then-ongoing seminal doctoral study on Asians: "There is a popular myth, internalized by many East African Asians, that Indians have innate commercial ability. In fact, Asians have concentrated heavily in commerce not only because it proved lucrative but also because other fields were not open to them. In other parts of the world overseas Indian communities have had different occupational patterns."[56] Such was the pervasiveness of the stereotype that Kleist Sykes, a contemporary of Chande's father and prominent African trader and political organizer, believed "the Asian way" of doing business "was the best for improving himself, and if all other Africans could follow the same pattern, life would be better for them too."[57] Sykes's attempt to copy them by establishing several shops, as his granddaughter Daisy Sykes Buruku further notes, hit a snag when the distant relatives he had asked for help while he continued to work as a civil servant ruined them due to untrustworthiness. He then resigned from the civil service and opened a large retail shop in Dar es Salaam. As the only prominent African competing with Asians in the lime business, he decided to cooperate with them by joining their retail traders' association. Nationalist African traders criticized him for this move. "Along with opposition," Buruku notes, "Kleist himself found it difficult to accept Asian ways and decided to form his African Retail Traders Association."[58] This highlights how an East African Asian business network closely guarded its competitive advantage, not least because this was one among the very few areas that was open to them. Chachage S. L. Chachage, following L. H. Gann and P. Duignan, traces it to the late precolonial era: "When the German chartered trading company—Deutsch-Ostafrikanische Gesellschaft (DOAG) or the German East African Company—took over the administration of Tanganyika in 1885, it 'could not compete with Arab or with Indian financiers who knew the country, relied on extensive networks of kinsmen, were willing to take high risks.'"[59]

As a minority group, for the Asians, embracing entrepreneurship was a matter of family and community survival. It is within this context that the myth and stereotype of inborn Asian entrepreneurship was produced and propagated. However, entrepreneurs are made, not born. Socialization, apprenticeship, and networking within community circles play a major role in breeding successful entrepreneurs. Chande is illustrative in this regard:

By 1952, my control of the export side of the business had seen me appointed, by my father and uncles, as Manager of Chande Brothers Limited. Most of the production side of the business was still concentrated within the separate entity of Chande Industries Limited, whose fifteen-acre plot on the Pugu Road was now being quickly developed. We had acquired the land, the headquarters of what was to be the National Milling Corp., on a ninety-nine year lease from Sheikh Ali Bin Said, who in turn had bought the site in the 1920s for next to nothing from the Custodian of Enemy (i.e., German) Property, and we had already built a number of mills and oil extraction plants. My side of the business, Chande Brothers Limited, had meanwhile not only become the largest exporter of coffee from Tanganyika, but had risen to second in the ranks of beeswax exporters, and into the top ten in the lucrative oil seed/oil cake market, against some serious multinational UK-based competition in the shape of Unilever, Gibson and Co., and the Steel Brothers.[60]

The sharp-minded Chande could not allow any opportunity to slip by to pick up cues from his father-in-law, Muljibhai Prabhudas Madhvani, as this message to his brother-in-law reveals:

I recall one incident in particular. Over dinner, at around 10pm (he always ate late, and always with his sons around him), he learnt that one of his staff, who was responsible for procurement of cans and tins for packing oils, had not been treated well by an English employee of the manufacturer, who operated out of Thika in Kenya. He was also earlier informed of the difficulty his firm was experiencing over price and delivery from this supplier. On learning this, he promptly got in touch with his confirming house in England and asked them to send a quotation for a factory to manufacture cans and tins, so he could make his own. When the Kenyan company came to know about this, its Managing Director tried to make amends, but Muljibhai stuck to his guns and in the process achieved vertical integration of his operations, which paid dividends.[61]

Marrying into the family that has been nicknamed "the Rockefellers of Uganda"[62] was just as much a lesson in business as it was a story of love.[63] A late dinner such as this, most likely due to lengthy working hours in the business, was not simply a family matter; it was also a business matter. Entrepreneurial networks were strengthened, business ideas developed, and best management practices exchanged. The younger Madhvani also documents this lesson on human resource management that his brother-in-law picked up from the elder Madhvani: "Jayantilal [Chande] remembers three instances of misappropriation or theft by Madhvani employees ('in each case he advised against imposing disciplinary measures'). He points out that 'Although Muljibhai did not often convey appreciation for services or for good work in words, he demonstrated his gratitude by actions.' For example, he named the avenue to the estate Ross Avenue, after our prized Australian engineer."[64] Marriage has played a significant role in forging business networks since ancient times, especially among communities that have run family businesses. Chande's marriage to his "wonderful Jayli," as he fondly called Jayalaxmi, is thus not exceptional. However, it underscores the role of business networking in enabling connected Asians to succeed in East Africa. Chande captures this well when he notes that it was hardly surprising that in both families the issue of their children getting married was raised and agreed on, given the families' background:

> For more than thirty years, my father had known the Madhvani family, who lived near Jinja, in Uganda. The Madhvanis were business people, and on a grand scale, too, being one of the most prosperous families in Uganda, if not the whole of Eastern Africa. Like my father, Muljibhai Madhvani was prominent in the Lohana community, even more so in fact, and on his many visits to Tanganyika Muljibhai would often stay with my father at the house in Tabora. Over time, the shared interest in business grew into a genuine friendship, a relationship of warmth and trust that was to last all their lives, and my father was appointed agent for the Madhvani sugar interests in Tanganyika. In time I, too, got to know the Madhvani businessmen, and struck up a friendship with Muljibhai's eldest son, Jayant. Like me, he served as a member of LEGCO [Legislative Council], in Uganda. Not surprisingly given the family's undoubted flair, some would say genius, for commerce, the Madhvani family crest is a gilded cogwheel. But between the Madhvanis and the Chandes the talk was increasingly as much about kinship as about business.[65]

As the celebrated year of 1960 and Africa's independence blew the winds of change across the coast of East Africa, these businessmen and statesmen must have contemplated the future of their business in postindependence eastern Africa. Like their fellows who published a symposium in the 1960s to analyze the "problems and prospects" of the Asian community in East Africa "at a crucial stage of its history,"[66] they must have been filled with anticipation and apprehension. Even though it was "becoming increasingly clear that the place of the Asians in the [then] new emerging societies . . . [constituted] the dominant problem in the field of race relations,"[67] to them there must have been another problem: that of the place and prospect of their private capital.

A Tale of Two Global Economies

The East African nations gained independence when a simultaneous, if not dialectical, process of the disintegration (1930–1979) of the first global economy (1840–1929) and the beginning (1950–1979) of the second global economy (1979–) was unfolding. It is thus not surprising that the political and intellectual debates that occurred in the 1960s and 1970s were preoccupied with the question of capial. All countries recognized the need for capital investment for socioeconomic development. However, there was no consensus among politicians and intellectuals on what form the new states should take to ensure both progress and equality. Two regional models were emerging: capitalism in Kenya and socialism in Tanzania. Reflecting on these debates in his Anstey Memorial Lectures at the University of Kent at Canterbury, one historian noted,

> In Africa the question is not merely theoretical. It is a matter of practical action. Should young Africans work with or against political movements whose purpose is to create national capitalism? Is national capitalism feasible? Is it desirable? Or is President [Julius] Nyerere [of Tanzania] right to argue that an autonomous national capitalism is impossible in Africa and that socialism is therefore "the rational choice"? During the last twenty years most young Africans would have had little hesitation: they would have agreed with Nyerere. Perhaps they still would, but I am not sure that they would still be quite so confident.[68]

It is within this context that the Madhvani family established Kioo Limited in 1963, a company that Chande came to later co-own. Despite Nyerere's socialist rhetoric as early as 1962, when he published *Ujamaa—The Basis of African Socialism*,[69] Tanzania encouraged private capital at least up to 1966.[70] Investors that were attracted in this period included Amental from France, Associated Portland Cement from Britain, Cementia Holdings from Switzerland, ENI from Italy, and Philips from the Netherlands, among others. Since the most readily available investors in the region were Asians who survived the transition from the first global economy, it was during this period that their capital, local and foreign, increased in being reinvested:

> Madhvani Brothers, based in Uganda set up Mtibwa sugar refinery (1965), Kioo Glass (1966)[71] and the Madhvani sugar refinery (1964). The Tanzania based milling operations of the Chande family, tied by marriage to the Madhvani Group, were extended. Karimjee Jivanjee, the largest Tanzania based Asian group, with large sisal estates, set up the biggest rope and twine factory. Industrial Promotion Services (IPS) started several projects including the £1.5 million Kilimanjaro Textiles, joint with German capital. IPS was set up by Asian Ismaili capital at the instigation of the Aga Khan who believed that if Ismaili capital did not move into industrial venture they would eventually lose their commercial interest to Africans. Local Asians also invested in Kibo Match (1965), and the Ugandan Sikh Saw Mills expanded rapidly. The Kenya based Chandaria Group begun Aluminium Africa Ltd, an aluminium rolling mill, in Dar es Salaam to serve the whole of East Africa (1964), as well as Paper Products Ltd. and Mabati Ltd. (galvanizing roofing).[72]

During this period, one expatriate who had worked in the Ministry of Planning in the 1970s observed, "There was a fairly impressive average annual rate of private capital formation of 15 percent."[73] In the case of Chande/Madhvani industries in the country, Honey stresses, the "bulk of the capital was, however, from Uganda, not Tanzania."[74]

What transpired after President Nyerere issued the Arusha Declaration on Socialism and Self-Reliance in 1967 remains contested as far as private capital is concerned.[75] Among other things, this party manifesto aimed to concentrate the commanding heights of the economy in the hands of the state and thus, in effect, make it socialist. Although it indeed became a central planning state, at no point did it delink Tanzania from international capital in and during the prelude to the second global economy (1950–1979). It only partially enabled the other side of that transition in the global economy—disintegration—when it nationalized a number of private firms and banks.

On February 11, 1967, the parliament passed an act that fully nationalized eight foreign business firms and partially nationalized seven subsidiaries through the state's control of the majority of shares.[76] A day earlier it had passed an act that fully nationalized nine companies involved in agricultural products.[77] Chande Industries Limited was in the latter list. Thus, these nationalizations mainly "affected Asians and Europeans and foreign capital in general."[78] Suleman Sumra's argument that this had a minimal effect on the investments of the Asian community is partly correct,[79] yet, for Chande, February 10, 1967, was the day that a country he "loved and was native of" had "seemingly forsaken him."[80] Madhvani's Kioo Limited, however, was spared.

Another wave of nationalization began on April 22, 1971, when the parliament passed an act that empowered the president to nationalize certain buildings.[81] This was a big blow to the Asian community, Timothy Ranja stresses, because they owned nearly all of the commercial and residential buildings in the centers of most towns in Tanzania.[82] Oonk's list of Karimjee Jivanjee family buildings that were nationalized runs to three spreadsheets yet is not exhaustive, making him settle for an estimate of over thirty-five houses in Dar es Salaam and probably more than fifteen in other places.[83] Reminiscing on these times, a then top government official and member of the Asian community, Al Noor Kassum, captures the mixed feelings among his fellows:

> When I first heard of the Arusha Declaration, it was through distorted reports from other people and the media. What I heard and read confused me. It was only when I obtained a copy of the Declaration and read it for myself that I realized that for the most part there was nothing new in it. . . . The only new aspect was the use of the term "nationalization," and that was a logical extension of TANU's [Tanganyika African National Union's] creed. I was not sure what the future would bring to Tanzanians but I was willing to give the party [TANU] the benefit of the doubt. . . . I was also glad that my family would not be affected, since we owned no industries. . . . In April 1971, when I was back in Tanzania, the government nationalized all private buildings from which the

owners were earning rent in excess of a certain amount. Our family owned many commercial properties in Dar es Salaam, including a very well known bar and restaurant, the Cosy Café, office and residential buildings, and cinemas. There was a hasty family gathering to discuss the government action. My brothers and I expected our father to be furious about losing the properties he had acquired through hard work over more than half a century. However, he surprised us. "I am happy the buildings have been nationalized—I will no longer have to pay income tax since I won't be earning rent," he said with a broad smile.[84]

For Chande's in-laws in Uganda, the situation had not yet reached the outrageous stage of the 1972 expulsion of the Asian community. In fact, nationalization had ironically provided an opportunity, as Mahmood Mamdani reveals:

So far as the 1970 nationalizations were concerned, the established sections of Indian capital had ample reason to cheer. The sector through which they primarily accumulated capital, export-import, earlier decreed as totally nationalized was now to be merely supervised by the state appointed Export-Import Corporation. The director and chairman of the Corporation, appointed by the president was none other than the most important Indian capitalist in Uganda—Jayant Madhvani! Its other five directors, according to the Minister of Commerce and Industry, were all "persons of fully proven business experience." In fact, an executive committee of the commercial bourgeoisie now sat and presided over the export-import trade! Predictably, it decided to let existing export import firms continue provided they gave the Corporation 10% commission on all transactions![85]

It is not surprising that by 1970 the Madhvani business group was contributing, through taxes and excise duties, about 10 percent of Uganda's income in terms of gross domestic product and had more than twenty thousand employees.[86] Their family also accounted for nearly 10 percent of the country's exports. When the Ugandan dictator Idi Amin's military coup toppled President Milton Obote's government in 1971 and expelled the Asian community in 1972, the Madhvani assets were valued at US$100 million.[87] Even though they regarded Kenya as one of the more probusiness and promising countries that conducted their operations in the mid-1970s, the Madhvanis' attempts to expand their Towel Manufactures Limited in Mombasa was not successful because it was never able to recover its overhead.[88] They ultimately sold it to another Asian family in Kenya. Ironically, Manubhai Madhvani's business continued to succeed in the mid-1970s in a country that he viewed as having a business climate that "remained hostile to private investment." "Nevertheless," he reminisces on Nyerere's Tanzania, "operations in my glass plant in Dar es Salaam (Kioo Ltd.) and the soap factory in Arusha (EMCO Industries Ltd.) continued to do moderately well, surviving the concerted effort for a fully government-controlled economy."[89] He recalls that

Chande and James Simpson, whom Seidenberg refers to as an economic adviser,[90] greatly assisted him in all three operations—glass, soap, and textiles—that remained in East Africa after the Madhvanis' fateful expulsion from Uganda.[91] As Carol E. Barker and David V. Wield's comprehensive list shows, Mtibwa Sugar Estates, then a Tanzanian subsidiary of EMCO Limited, became jointly owned by the state, with the Madhvanis holding 45 percent.[92] However, they maintained 100 percent holdings in Kioo Limited.[93]

J. V. S. Jones, building from Barker et al., provides details on its performance in the 1970s. By the middle of the decade, it was producing thirty tons of products per day. Whereas Barker et al. found that the company was producing 68 percent of its capacity instead of the usual capacity of 75 percent to 80 percent in 1976, Jones determined that the waste rate was much higher, implying poor performance. He cites Tanzania Breweries Limited's complaints about losing about 4 percent of its production due to breakages.[94] Having switched to Kioo bottles in 1974 from imported ones from Kenya, Tanganyika Bottling Company Limited also complained, citing a figure of 218 kilograms of breakages on the day Jones and his team visited.[95] Thus, "from the point of view of Kioo's customers," he observes, "it would seem that all is not well with the production process at the plant, and that some investment should be made in order to locate the source of the problems. . . . According to one view, the monopoly position of Kioo Ltd. produces little incentive to deal with the problem since profitability is guaranteed."[96] Nevertheless, "Kioo Ltd., along with Madhvani's other glass works, has a consultancy arrangement with Rockwell Glass, a British-based firm, who run training schemes for workers in all three East African factories. However, it is not known if they are involved in [an] attempt to solve the above problems."[97] The account that follows also highlights other challenges of the 1970s:

At Kioo Ltd., the workers were demanding equal disciplinary treatment because as they put it, "*Mwongozo* says we are equal."[98] Further research into this dispute revealed further salient silent facts. Why, for example, should the management, comprising of only twenty people, have about ten saloon cars for transport and use after work while the majority of the workers have only one omnibus for transport to work? And yet after work they have to find their own means home. Why, it was argued by the Chairman of the workers' committee, should the manual labourer toil for twelve years without substantial increment in salary while a clerk in the manager's office gets three promotions and therefore three increments within twelve months after his probation? Why should a simple worker, the so-called subordinate staff, incapable of purchasing *Uhuru* [the party newspaper] not be given a free newspaper [while a senior staff is entitled to a free newspaper even after he has purchased his own copy[99]]? Such were the inequalities that the workers at Kioo Ltd. had in mind when they demanded "equal disciplinary" treatment for all. To them discipline didn't mean the provisions of the disciplinary code and its sanctions or penalty but it meant the mode of distribution of rights—the discipline of material distribution amongst them and their superiors.[100]

These were the heydays of Ujamaa's nationalization. By the mid-1980s, when Nyerere retired from the presidency, Tanzania was already on its way to "Liberalize, Privatize and Marketize (LIMP)." Most of the over four hundred public corporations that were developed from scratch or through nationalization in the 1960s and 1970s were being sold or entered into joint ventures with the private sector. As was the case in the Arusha Declaration, it remains contested what happened to capital and capitalists after what is known as the Zanzibar Declaration of 1991 effectively nullified the former.

By the turn of the twenty-first century, when Tanzania was assessing the performance of companies and the impact of privatization, Kioo Limited was the only manufacturer of glass containers in the country. It was also the main supplier of bottles for liquor and soft drinks. After an investment of US$25 million aimed at upgrading its plant, the company acquired the capacity to produce fifty-two thousand tons of products per year. Moreover, it was generating over US$5 million per year in foreign exchange from its exports to twelve countries in Africa. These included South Africa after the end of apartheid (1994) opened it to the African subglobal economy. Ironically, it also included Kenya, which was typically the exporter of industrial products to Tanzania.

At its helm was Chande, although he had delegated day-to-day management to relatively young Asian entrepreneurs. The anecdote that follows captures this trajectory:

> The glass bottle maker was producing sub-standard products with a high breakage rate. Tanzania Breweries decided to explore sourcing from this company, but first it had to raise the bottle quality. The brewery guaranteed that it would buy all the bottles produced if they were of better quality and sent a South African engineer to assist in a major production system upgrade. Tanzania Breweries signed a contract ensuring that all bottle made would be bought, so the glass company was assured that it would get a return on its investment. Kioo Limited is now the primary glass manufacturer in Africa and supplies 100 per cent of Tanzania Breweries bottles, as well as producing for Coca Cola and Pepsi in Tanzania.[101]

The story of entry into the second global economy is not simply rosy. Torn between two regionalizing blocs—the Southern African Development Community (SADC) and the East African Community—Tanzania pulled out of the Common Market for Eastern and Southern Africa (COMESA) in 2004. The effects were as follows:

> Kioo Limited . . . reported losing orders of Coca Cola bottles of US $1.5 million to Zimbabwe and US $0.5 million to Malawi due to the substantial duty that

the buyers would pay. This company was created to meet the demand of the SADC and COMESA markets. However, since Tanzania withdrew from COMESA, the company has experienced difficulties exporting to COMESA countries as a result of which it now remains with excess capacity. The SADC market has not been able to replace the lost COMESA market largely due to the economic influence of South Africa on the SADC market.[102]

The journeys from India to East Africa that had brought tides of fortune in the midst of waves of misfortune for the Madhvanis and the Chandes continue. Since capitalism is still grappling with the effects of a recent financial crisis, one can hardly determine what shape the second global economy will take. Whichever way it goes, one thing is certain: East Africa's Asian entrepreneurship networks have a wealth of experience and resources derived from their engagements with the vagaries of global capitalism.

Conclusion

This chapter has shown how East Africa's Asian entrepreneurs have generally fared in the course of the long history of global capitalism. Before the rise of the first global economy, they were part and parcel of the Indian Ocean trade. Although the great divergence between the West and their country of origin, India, among other non-Western countries, led to slavery and colonialism, as a community the East African Asians forged entrepreneurship networks that produced some of the most illustrious entrepreneurs in the Indian Ocean World. Some, such as Tharia Topan, tried to break into the exclusive first global economy with relative success. Thus, even though both the East Asian subcontinent and East Africa were dialectically integrated by way of marginalization in the first global economy, some of their members managed to survive this exclusivity and seize the small window of opportunity provided by its disintegration to create business networks that enabled their descendants to participate more fully in the second global economy. The Madhvani and Chande families are classic cases of this creation of East African entrepreneurship networks.

However, no community is totally homogenous and unified. East Africa's Asian entrepreneurship networks have had their share of business conflicts, from the battle within the Indian Merchant Chamber of Dar es Salaam in the 1950s over "a bill threatening the interests of small millers that led the representative of Chande Brothers to walk out"[103] to the "bitter row in the Madhvani family over £60 million"[104] in the 1980s. Nevertheless, they continue to epitomize business success under duress.

CHAMBI CHACHAGE is a PhD candidate in African studies with a primary focus in history at Harvard University. He is coeditor of *Africa's Liberation: The Legacy of Nyerere*.

Notes

1. Derived from the then British prime minister Harold Macmillan's speech to members of Parliament in the then apartheid South Africa; see "1960: Macmillan Speaks of 'Wind of Change' in Africa," BBC, accessed December 20, 2012, http://news.bbc.co.uk/onthisday/hi/dates/stories/february/3/newsid_2714000/2714525.stm.

2. Zanzibar's contentious independence from Britain in 1963 under the sultan culminated in a controversial revolution in 1964, the same year it united with Tanganyika to form Tanzania.

3. Tiyambe Zeleza, "The Development of African Capitalism," *Africa Development* 17, no. 1 (1992): 129.

4. Abdul Sheriff, *Slaves, Spices and Ivory in Tanzania: An Integration of an East African Commercial Empire into the World Economy, 1770–1873* (Athens: Ohio University Press, 1987), 105.

5. Ali A. Mufuruki, "Embracing Change Is Key to Success in Today's Multi-cultural World," keynote address at the launch of the Ismaili Professionals Network, Dar es Salaam, June 19, 2013, http://www.infotech.co.tz/docs/Ismaili%20Professionals%20-%20Ali%20Mufuruki.pdf.

6. Mumtaz Ali Sadik Ali, *101 Ismaili Heroes* (Karachi: Islamic Book Publisher, 2007), 1:416.

7. See Dana A. Seidenberg, *Mercantile Adventurers: The World of East African Asians, 1750–1985* (New Delhi: New Age International, 1996), 2.

8. Samir Amin, "The Trajectory of Historical Capitalism and Marxism's Tricontinental Vocation," *Monthly Review* 62, no. 9 (2011): 1.

9. Ibid.

10. Abdul Sheriff, *Dhow Cultures of the Indian Ocean: Cosmopolitanism, Commerce and Islam* (London: Hurst, 2010), 25.

11. Seidenberg, *Mercantile Adventurers*, 7.

12. The term "great divergence" and its meaning are attributed to Kenneth Pomeranz, *The Great Divergence: China, Europe, and the Making of the Modern World Economy* (Princeton, NJ: Princeton University Press, 2000).

13. See Daron Acemoglu, Simon Johnson, and James A. Robinson, "The Rise of Europe: Atlantic Trade, Institutional Change and Economic Growth," *American Economic Review* 95, no. 3 (2005): 546–79.

14. Seidenberg, *Mercantile Adventurers*, 7.

15. Ibid., 8.

16. Ibid.

17. Sheriff, *Slaves, Spices and Ivory*, 21.

18. The globalization framework is primarily based on Professor Geoffrey Jones's lecture series, titled "Entrepreneurship and Global Capitalism," at Harvard Business School (HBS) in spring 2012, which I had the privilege to attend; regular personal communication with him in 2013; and a critical synthesis of his writings, especially Geoffrey Jones, "Entrepreneurs, Firms and Global Wealth since 1850," HBS Working Paper 13-076, March 12, 2013.

19. Lois Lobo, *They Came to Africa: 200 Years of the Asian Presence in Tanzania* (Dar es Salaam: Sustainable Village, 2000), 17.

20. Manubhai Madhvani, *Tide of Fortune: A Family Tale*, with Giles Foden (Noida, India: Random House India, 2009), 13.

21. Seidenberg, *Mercantile Adventurers*, 19.

22. Gijsbert Oonk, *The Karimjee Jivanjee Family: Merchant Princes of East Africa 1800–2000* (Amsterdam: Pallas, 2009), 13.

23. John Iliffe, *A Modern History of Tanganyika* (Cambridge: Cambridge University Press, 1979), 46.

24. Blanche R. D'Souza, *Harnessing the Trade Winds: The Story of the Centuries Old Indian Trade with East Africa Using the Monsoon Winds* (Nairobi: Zand Graphics, 2008), 129.

25. Frederick Cooper, *Plantation Slavery on the East Coast of Africa* (New Haven, CT: Yale University Press, 1977), 140.

26. Alia Paroo, "Aga Khan III and the British Empire: The Ismailis in Tanganyika, 1920–1957" (PhD diss., York University, 2012), 38.

27. Gijsbert Oonk, "South Asians in East Africa (1880–1920) with a Particular Focus on Zanzibar: Toward a Historical Explanation of Economic Success of a Middlemen Minority," *Journal of African and Asian Studies* 5, no. 1 (2006): 57–89.

28. Iliffe, *Modern History of Tanganyika*, 46.

29. Renamed Mumbai.

30. According to Sheriff, *Slaves, Spices and Ivory in Tanzania*, xix, the Maria Theresa dollar (MT$) was a coin used on the East African coast until the 1860s, when the US dollar began to replace it; during the first half of the nineteenth century, one MT dollar was equivalent to between 2.10 and 2.23 rupees, whereas one pound was equal to MT$4.75.

31. Sheriff, *Slaves, Spices and Ivory in Tanzania*, 107.

32. Iliffe, *Modern History of Tanganyika*, 46, 48, 211.

33. D'Souza, *Harnessing the Trade Winds*, 130.

34. Iliffe, *Modern History of Tanganyika*, 41.

35. Sheriff, *Slaves, Spices and Ivory in Tanzania*, 20–21.

36. Iliffe, *Modern History of Tanganyika*, 41.

37. Edward A. Alpers, "The Coast and the Development of the Caravan Trade," in *A History of Tanzania*, ed. Isaria N. Kimambo and Arnold J. Temu (Nairobi: East African Publishing House, 1969), 41.

38. Iliffe, *Modern History of Tanganyika*, 4.

39. Ibid., 41.

40. Jayantilal Keshavji Chande, *A Knight in Africa: Journey from Bukene* (Ontario: Penumbra, 2005).

41. Ibid., 13.

42. Ibid.

43. Ibid.

44. Erez Manela, *The Wilsonian Moment: Self-Determination and the International Origins of Anticolonial Nationalism* (Oxford: Oxford University Press, 2007), 7–9.

45. Chande, *Knight in Africa*, 17–18.

46. Ibid., 18.

47. Ibid., 19.

48. Ibid., 22.

49. Ibid., 22–23.

50. Ibid., 23.

51. Ibid.

52. Dharam P. Ghai, "An Economic Survey," in *Portrait of a Minority: Asians in East Africa*, ed. Dharam P. Ghai (Nairobi: Oxford University Press), 103.

53. Max Weber, *The Protestant Ethic and the Spirit of Capitalism*, trans. Talcott Parson (New York: Charles Scribner's Sons, [1904] 1930).

54. Ghai, "Economic Survey," 103.

55. Chande cited in Lobo, *They Came to Africa*, 19 cf. Chande, *Knight in Africa*, 17.

56. Martha Honey, "Asian Industrial Activities in Tanganyika," *Tanzanian Society* 75 (1974): 57.

57. Daisy Sykes Buruku, "The Townsman: Kleist Sykes," in *Modern Tanzanians: A Volume of Biographies*, ed. John Iliffe (Dar es Salaam: Historical Association of Tanzania, 1973), 109.

58. Ibid.

59. Chachage S. L. Chachage, "Socialist Ideology and the Reality of Tanzania" (PhD diss., University of Glasgow, 1986), 25.

60. Chande, *Knight in Africa*, 52.

61. Chande quoted in Madhvani, *Tide of Fortune*, 72–73.

62. Ibid., 7.

63. Chande, *Knight in Africa*, 58.

64. Madhvani, *Tide of Fortune*, 73.

65. Chande, *Knight in Africa*, 59.

66. Dharam P. Ghai, introduction to Ghai, *Portrait of a Minority*, ix.

67. Ibid.

68. John Iliffe, *The Emergence of African Capitalism* (London: Macmillan, 1983), 2.

69. In Julius K. Nyerere, *Freedom and Unity* (Dar es Salaam: Oxford University Press, 1966), 162–171.

70. Jeanette Hartmann, "The Rise and Rise of Private Capital," in *Capitalism, Socialism and the Development Crisis in Tanzania*, ed. N. O'Neill and K. Mustafa (Aldershot, UK: Avebury, 1990).

71. This is the year it began operations.

72. Carol E. Barker et al., *African Industrialisation: Technology and Change in Tanzania* (Aldershot, UK: Gower, 1986), 52.

73. Idrian N. Resnick, *The Long Transition: Building Socialism in Tanzania* (New York: Monthly Review Press, 1981), 60.

74. Honey, "Asian Industrial Activities in Tanganyika," 68.

75. In Julius K. Nyerere, *Freedom and Socialism* (Dar es Salaam: Oxford University Press, 1968), 231–50.

76. State Trading Corporation Short (Establishment and Vesting of Interests) Act (Act No. 2, 1967).

77. The National Agricultural Products Board (Vesting of Interests) Act (Act No. 3, 1967).

78. Chachage, "Socialist Ideology," 412.

79. In Timothy Ranja, "Success under Duress: A Comparison of the Indigenous African and East African Asian Entrepreneurs" (Economic and Social Research Foundation [ESRF] Working Paper 7, 2003), 1.

80. Chande, *Knight in Africa*, 13.

81. Acquisition of Buildings Act (Act No. 13, 1971).

82. Ranja, "Success under Duress," 4.

83. Oonk, *Karimjee Jivanjee Family*, 105, 162–67.

84. Al Noor Kassum, *Africa's Winds of Change: Memoirs of an International Tanzanian* (London: I. B. Tauris, 2007), 69.

85. Mahmood Mamdani, "Class Struggles in Uganda," *Review of African Political Economy* 4 (1975): 51.

86. Ranja, "Success under Duress," 11.

87. See the official website of the Muljibhai Madhvani Foundation, last accessed December 20, 2012, http://www.madhvanifoundation.com; and Neelima Mahajan-Bansal, "Experiences

of the Indian Diaspora in Africa," *Forbes Magazine India*, August 26, 2009, http://forbesindia
.com/article/magazine-extra/experiences-of-the-indian-diaspora-in-africa/3762/1.
88. Madhvani, *Tide of Fortune*, 198.
89. Ibid., 197.
90. Seidenberg, *Mercantile Adventurers*, 201.
91. Madhvani, *Tide of Fortune*, 198.
92. Carol E. Barker and David V. Wield, "Notes on International Firms in Tanzania," *Utafiti*
2, no. 3 (1978): 332.
93. Ibid., 327.
94. J. V. S. Jones, *Resources and Industry in Tanzania: Use, Misuse and Abuse* (Dar es Salaam:
Tanzania Publishing House, 1983), 77.
95. Ibid., 78.
96. Ibid.
97. Ibid., 105.
98. *Mwongozo* is a Swahili word meaning "guidelines." It was a name given to a party manifesto issued during the Ujamaa era of the single-party state to give voice to the workers and a
guide to the leaders.
99. Paschal Mihyo, "The Struggle for Workers' Control in Tanzania," *Review of African Political Economy* 2, no. 4 (1975): 64.
100. Paschal Mihyo, *Industrial Conflict and Change in Tanzania* (Dar es Salaam: Tanzania
Publishing House, 1983), 112–13.
101. Tamara Bekefi, *Tanzania: Lessons in Building Linkages for Competitive and Responsible
Entrepreneurship* (Cambridge, MA: United Nations Industrial Development Organization and
Kennedy School of Government, Harvard University, 2006), 26.
102. Zambia Business Forum, *Zambia Business Forum Study on Zambia's Dual Membership
of COMESA and SADC* (Lusaka, Zambia: Executive Financial Services, 2008), 51.
103. Iliffe, *Modern History of Tanganyika*, 450.
104. Madhvani, *Tide of Fortune*, 211.

Bibliography

Acemoglu, D., S. Johnson, and J. A. Robinson. 2005. "The Rise of Europe: Atlantic Trade,
    Institutional Change and Economic Growth." *American Economic Review* 95 (3): 546–79.
Ali, M. A. S. 2007. *101 Ismaili Heroes*. Vol. 1. Karachi: Islamic Book Publisher.
Alpers, E. A. 1969. "The Coast and the Development of the Caravan Trade." In *A History of Tanzania*,
    edited by I. N. Kimambo and A. J. Temu, 35–56. Nairobi: East African Publishing House.
Amin, S. 2011. "The Trajectory of Historical Capitalism and Marxism's Tricontinental Vocation."
    Monthly Review 62 (9): 1–18.
Barker, C. E., M. R. Bhagavan, P. V. Mitschke-Collande, and D. V. Wield. 1986. *African Industriali-
    sation: Technology and Change in Tanzania*. Aldershot, UK: Gower.
Barker, C. E., and D. V. Wield. 1978. "Notes on International Firms in Tanzania." *Utafiti* 2 (3): 316–41.
BBC. 2012. "1960: Macmillan Speaks of 'Wind of Change' in Africa." Accessed December 20.
    http://news.bbc.co.uk/onthisday/hi/dates/stories/february/3/newsid_2714000/2714525.stm.
Bekefi, T. 2006. *Tanzania: Lessons in Building Linkages for Competitive and Responsible Entrepre-
    neurship*. Cambridge, MA: United Nations Industrial Development Organization and
    Kennedy School of Government, Harvard University.

Buruku, D. S. 1973. "The Townsman: Kleist Sykes." In *Modern Tanzanians: A Volume of Biographies*, edited by J. Iliffe, 95–114. Dar es Salaam: Historical Association of Tanzania.

Chachage, C. S. L. 1986. "Socialist Ideology and the Reality of Tanzania." PhD diss., University of Glasgow.

Chande, J. K. 2005. *A Knight in Africa: Journey from Bukene*. Ontario: Penumbra.

Cooper, F. 1977. *Plantation Slavery on the East Coast of Africa*. New Haven, CT: Yale University Press.

D'Souza, B. R. 2008. *Harnessing the Trade Winds: The Story of the Centuries Old Indian Trade with East Africa Using the Monsoon Winds*. Nairobi: Zand Graphics.

Ghai, D. P. 1965. "An Economic Survey." In *Portrait of a Minority: Asians in East Africa*, edited by D. P. Ghai, 91–111. Nairobi: Oxford University Press.

———. 1965. Introdution to *Portrait of a Minority: Asians in East Africa*, edited by D. P. Ghai, ix–x. Nairobi: Oxford University Press.

Hartmann, J. 1990. "The Rise and Rise of Private Capital." In *Capitalism, Socialism and the Development Crisis in Tanzania*, edited by N. O'Neill and K. Mustafa, 233–54. Aldershot, UK: Avebury.

Honey, M. 1974. "Asian Industrial Activities in Tanganyika." *Tanzanian Society* 75:55–69.

Iliffe, J. 1979. *A Modern History of Tanganyika*. Cambridge: Cambridge University Press.

———. 1983. *The Emergence of African Capitalism*. London: Macmillan.

Jones, G. 2013. "Entrepreneurs, Firms and Global Wealth since 1850." Harvard Business School (HBS) Working Paper 13-076. March 12.

Jones, J. V. S. 1983. *Resources and Industry in Tanzania: Use, Misuse and Abuse*. Dar es Salaam: Tanzania Publishing House.

Kassum, A. N. 2007. *Africa's Winds of Change: Memoirs of an International Tanzanian*. London: I. B. Tauris.

Lobo, L. 2000. *They Came to Africa: 200 Years of the Asian Presence in Tanzania*. Dar es Salaam: Sustainable Village.

Madhvani, M. 2009. *Tide of Fortune: A Family Tale*. With G. Foden. Noida, India: Random House India.

Mahajan-Bansal, N. "Experiences of the Indian Diaspora in Africa." *Forbes Magazine India*, August 26, 2009. http://forbesindia.com/article/magazine-extra/experiences-of-the-indian-diaspora-in-africa/3762/1.

Mamdani, M. 1975. "Class Struggles in Uganda." *Review of African Political Economy* 4:26–61.

Manela, E. 2007. *The Wilsonian Moment: Self-Determination and the International Origins of Anticolonial Nationalism*. Oxford: Oxford University Press.

Mihyo, P. 1975. "The Struggle for Workers' Control in Tanzania." *Review of African Political Economy* 2 (4): 62–84.

———. 1983. *Industrial Conflict and Change in Tanzania*. Dar es Salaam: Tanzania Publishing House.

Mufuruki, A. A. 2013. "Embracing Change Is Key to Success in Today's Multi-cultural World." Keynote address at the launch of the Ismaili Professionals Network, Dar es Salaam, June 19. http://www.infotech.co.tz/docs/Ismaili%20Professionals%20-%20Ali%20Mufuruki.pdf.

Nyerere, J. K. 1966. *Freedom and Unity*. Dar es Salaam: Oxford University Press.

———. 1968. *Freedom and Socialism*. Dar es Salaam: Oxford University Press.

Oonk, G. 2006. "South Asians in East Africa (1880–1920) with a Particular Focus on Zanzibar: Toward a Historical Explanation of Economic Success of a Middlemen Minority." *Journal of African and Asian Studies* 5 (1): 57–89.

———. 2009. *The Karimjee Jivanjee Family: Merchant Princes of East Africa, 1800–2000.* Amsterdam: Pallas.

Paroo, A. 2012. "Aga Khan III and the British Empire: The Ismailis in Tanganyika, 1920–1957." PhD diss., York University.

Pomeranz, K. 2000. *The Great Divergence: China, Europe, and the Making of the Modern World Economy.* Princeton, NJ: Princeton University Press.

Ranja, T. 2003. "Success under Duress: A Comparison of the Indigenous African and East African Asian Entrepreneurs." Economic and Social Research Foundation (ESRF) Working Paper 7.

Resnick, I. N. 1981. *The Long Transition: Building Socialism in Tanzania.* New York: Monthly Review Press.

Seidenberg, D. A. 1996. *Mercantile Adventurers: The World of East African Asians, 1750–1985.* New Delhi: New Age International.

Sheriff, A. 1987. *Slaves, Spices and Ivory in Tanzania: An Integration of an East African Commercial Empire into the World Economy, 1770–1873.* Athens: Ohio University Press.

———. 2010. *Dhow Cultures of the Indian Ocean: Cosmopolitanism, Commerce and Islam.* London: Hurst.

Weber, M. (1904) 1930. *The Protestant Ethic and the Spirit of Capitalism.* Translated by Talcott Parson. New York: Charles Scribner's Sons.

Zambia Business Forum. 2008. *Zambia Business Forum Study on Zambia's Dual Membership of COMESA and SADC.* Lusaka, Zambia: Executive Financial Services.

Zeleza, T. 1992. "The Development of African Capitalism." *Africa Development* 17 (1): 129–36.

2 The Wangara Factor in West African Business History

Moses E. Ochonu

THIS CHAPTER FOCUSES on the extensive business and trading empire that Mande-speaking merchants, trade brokers, and financiers built and ran across West Africa between the fourteenth and nineteenth centuries.[1] The Wangara feature prominently in the economic and mercantile history of West Africa because they pioneered intraregional long-distance trading and investments. They faced and overcame obstacles to trade and investments in diverse cultural and political settings. They also failed to effectively respond to a new commercial dynamic introduced by the European commercial and colonial incursion. This chapter analyzes the story of the Wangara's mercantile successes and failures. I posit this expansive story as a foundational empirical crutch for understanding West African precolonial business, and the Wangara as a central factor in any research on West African business history.

For roughly five hundred years, these pioneers of regional intra-African investment with ancestral origins in the old Mali and Songhai empires mastered a uniquely African brand of product distribution, arbitrage, financing, manufacturing, credit, mining, currency swaps, bartering, and long-distance trading. Referred to in different sources as Wangara, Juula, Mandinka, Malinke, Mande, Mandingo, and Djula, the Wangara merchants built a vast regional economic network extending from the Sahel in the north to the Akan forest in the south, and from the Senegambia and the Mano River frontier in the west to modern Benin Republic and northern and western Nigeria in the east.

The West African commercial empire that the Wangara built connected territories in modern-day Mali, Senegal, Gambia, Guinea, Guinea Bissau, the Ivory Coast, Burkina Faso, Ghana, Benin, and Nigeria.[2] This trading and brokerage system involved many goods, including gold, kola nuts, cloth, salt, natron, and leather products. It also entailed a vast investment portfolio that spanned arbitrage, cottage manufacturing, credit, banking services, and mining. The Wangara were versatile entrepreneurs. They invested in economic endeavors that connected to or had the capacity to enhance their long-distance trading or gave them access to new, marketable products. The Wangara commercial network was an expansive, interconnected system of entrepreneurship hubs. It was held together by a trust system that evolved over centuries. The network's continuity was secured by two other factors: the Wangara's cultivation of strategic political alliances, and their skill in expanding the pool of participants and beneficiaries in a growing circuit of trade and prosperity.

In reading the commercial imaginaries of the Wangara, it is important to situate them within a larger matrix of transregional economic transactions and exchanges. Reading the Wangara in this way permits and culminates in an argument for their centrality to networks of production and exchange that hugged West Africa's borders and shrunk the temporal, spatial, and economic distance between a diverse array of West Africans from the early modern period to the nineteenth century. The Wangara are thus a preeminent factor in conceptualizations of West Africa's economic history, whether such conceptualizations emphasize political economy, merchandizing, craftsmanship, itinerant trading, or the integration of extractive and agricultural sectors with trade. I argue that scholars of West African business history and political economy should posit the Wangara not merely as precursors to the commercial economies of the colonial period but also as entrepreneurial actors who perfected a versatile repertoire of investment, commerce, production, and craftsmanship. They invented a distinctly African variety of commercial diversification and operational scaling that prefigures and complicates discussions of more-recent iterations of similar business techniques.

Wangara Mercantile Beginnings

The Wangara people were not a single, coherent ethnolinguistic unit. Instead, Wangara was a broad ethnic identity that included speakers of the Mande languages (mainly Malinke and Bambara), as well as speakers of the Azer dialect, a Soninke-derived "commercial lingua franca in Western Sudan."[3] Medieval sources attest to the Wangara's early mercantile preoccupations, which would later come to define and distinguish them. Beginning with early Arab travelers' accounts from the twelfth century through the mid-fourteenth century,[4] descriptions of the Wangara associated them with the supply of gold from the medieval gold mines of Bure and Bambuk in the kingdom of Mali to areas both north and south of the Sahelian base of the kingdom.

Gold was both a store and a standard of value. The value of other products was measured against the relatively stable value of gold. The Wangara's control of gold gave them leverage to dominate the trade in another valuable product: salt. Gold was the ultimate capital in medieval West African economies, and salt complemented its value. In that sense, the Wangara enjoyed the advantages conferred by membership in a geopolitical entity possessing resource wealth. Gold was exchanged for salt mined at the edge of the Sahara and salt brought by Arab,

Berber, and Jewish traders.[5] The Wangara then sold the salt, which was valued as both a seasoning ingredient and a form of currency in several parts of West Africa. The Wangara mobilized camel caravans that transported the salt from the Saharan mines to Timbuktu, a major Wangara distribution hub in which a large portion of the logistics for the Wangara's wholesale operations was based. Here Wangara bulk purchasers acquired blocks of salt to be caravanned to other West African commercial centers, where the product would then be retailed across vast hinterlands. The Wangara's salt distribution zone included a vast area in the kingdom of Mali, Mossi country in present-day Burkina Faso, the Guinea basin, and the Senegambia region (see map 2.1).

The Wangara positioned themselves as the first link in the trade chain that transported West African gold to North Africa and distributed salt from Sahel and North African salt-producing areas to many parts of West Africa. They were the commercial vanguard of a new regional economy, a regional trade "globalization." The new trans–West African trade relay began with them. This status conferred exclusive advantages on the Wangara, giving them the ability to shape the trajectory and structure of the network they were building. This early Wangara trade network was a de facto monopoly. They reaped the rewards of this monopolistic market, which helped them to consolidate their investments and seek new markets and commercial territories. The Wangara also established themselves as trade brokers between different points and actors in the emerging western African trade system. With this early, dominant involvement in commerce, the term "Wangara" quickly became synonymous with "trader" or "long-distance trader" and vice versa in much of West Africa. The process of mastering this trans–West African trade took time, but the spread of Wangara commercial influence from medieval Mali to other parts of West Africa was inevitable, given the importance of gold and salt to the economies of several states in West Africa.

Beginning probably in the late twelfth century, the Wangara began to expand their trading network to the Senegambia and Guinea areas, and southwest to modern-day Ghana, the Ivory Coast, and eventually modern-day Nigeria. Some of the Wangara hired porters who carried the salt on their heads; others relied on the familiar camel caravan system. After about twenty days of travel, they would arrive either in the forest states of modern-day Ghana or in Senegambia.[6] As they made their way south, they would sell some of the salt to defray expenses and buy trade goods from communities on the trade routes. Over the next three centuries, the Wangara perfected this trading system and not only opened up a set of recognized trade routes connecting the Sahara to multiple West African hinterlands (see map 2.2) but also established permanent trading centers in the regions of West Africa with which they conducted trade.

The following discussion of the Wangara's commercial activities across West Africa makes clear the complexity and reach of this trading and investment

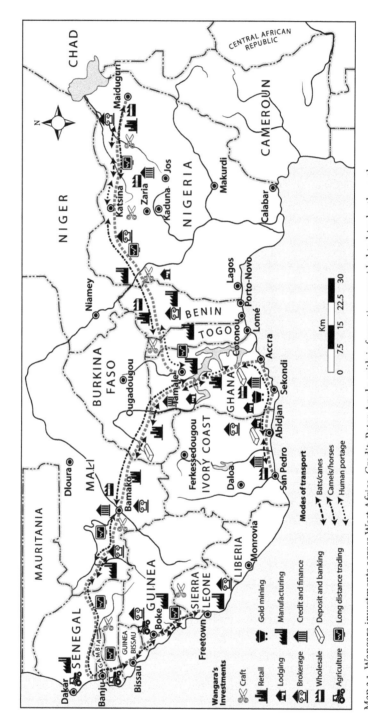

Map 2.1. Wangara investments across West Africa. Credit: Peter Anule, with information provided to him by the author.

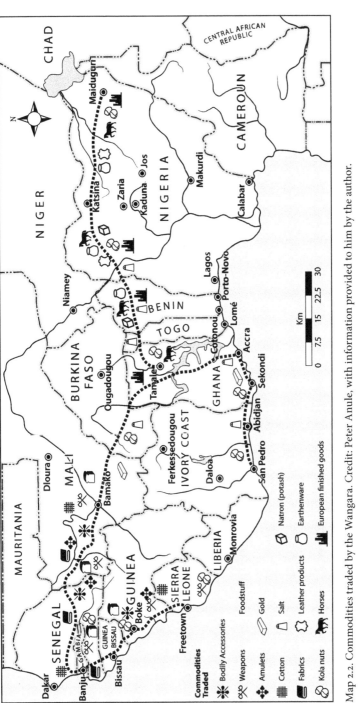

Map 2.2. Commodities traded by the Wangara. Credit: Peter Anule, with information provided to him by the author.

empire. The chapter begins with an overview of the Wangara's commercial activities in various parts of West Africa. This overview is accompanied by a multifactorial analysis of the strategies, strengths, successes, and challenges of the Wangara merchants in various West African trading and manufacturing nodes. I next answer the questions of when, why, and how this commercial empire collapsed. The chapter concludes by highlighting and analyzing the enduring insights of both the expansion and decline of the Wangara's vast trading network.

The Wangara in the Senegambia

To the west of the Wangara's Malian heartland lay the vast territory comprising the modern states of Senegal, Gambia, Guinea, and Guinea Bissau. The Wangara were very active here, given the contiguity of this region to Mali, and they set up social, political, and economic infrastructures to support their lucrative commercial activities. Many Wangara migrated to this region, helping to found small city-states and to consolidate kingdoms such as Kaabu.[7] Some of the Wangara migrants were warriors and clerics who became astute political leaders in their own right. Many others continued as itinerant traders, carrying goods back and forth between east (Mali) and west.

In the Senegambia region, the effect of this commercial and political influence of the "Wangara Diaspora," as Paul Lovejoy calls the Wangara commercial communities that emerged across West Africa,[8] was that, over time, Wangara warriors and clerics, some of them part-time merchants, provided a politically conducive religious and commercial environment for sedentary and itinerant Wangara traders to conduct their commercial activities without interference or security concerns. Even more valuable were the kinship networks that resulted, producing ever-expanding circuits of confidence that facilitated business transactions and credit.

Furthermore, some of the Wangara traders who settled permanently in the Senegambia region took up artisan pursuits, becoming cobblers and blacksmiths and manufacturing and supplying footwear, accessories, talismans, and weapons to Wangara and non-Wangara warriors, political leaders, priests, and long-distance traders. This group of Wangara artisans became valuable auxiliaries in the expanding trading system.[9] The trade system in turn sustained the Wangara artisans by keeping them employed. This diversification of the Wangara's commercial empire in the Senegambia region increased their forward and backward linkages, as well as their ability to move from one node of the supply and manufacturing chain to another. A small number of the Wangara may have also invested in agriculture, the products of which catered to the commercial, priestly, and political classes and supplied long-distance traders with specially preserved foods.[10] By catering to the commercial and spiritual demands of many communities in this region, the Wangara drew several non-Wangara peoples into the emerging Wangara economy.

The exchange of information regarding trade and commercial opportunity within the Wangara network was crucial to the ability of traders to spot demand, markets, and niches and to move to satisfy them with goods and services.[11] Information came through political contacts and insiders, and through participation in the politics of host communities. The Wangara were adept at this. The *Tarikh Bijini*, a Wangara text, tells the story of a wealthy Wangara merchant who exemplifies the versatile mercantile disposition of the Wangara. It states that he was a skillful caravan trader and a master commercial dealmaker, but also a gifted political mediator who routinely intervened in political matters along his trade routes in order to settle disputes that could affect trading. He was skillful at currying political favor that would be beneficial to trade.[12] This legendary Wangara merchant is a composite of the Wangara merchant class, his story an allegory for the ideal Wangara mercantile sensibility.

The Wangara traders established several rest stations (*ribats*) along their trade routes. The ribats later morphed into vibrant commercial centers "to which visitors flocked from all sides," and which served as links to other commercial and mining centers in Mali, Fouta Djallon, and as far as Casamance in modern-day southern Senegal.[13] One of the most prominent of these Wangara trade outposts in the Senegambia was Bijini, which evolved into an active commercial center whose legend lived on in popular lore long after its decline.

In the late sixteenth century and throughout the seventeenth century, the Wangara's trading activities spread even farther to the north of the Gambia River and probably all the way to the Lower Guinea coast. This was probably due to increased Wangara out-migration as a result of the decline and eventual collapse of the Songhai Empire. Contemporaneous Portuguese accounts from the Lower Guinea basin state that during this period the Wangara began to broker trade in European-manufactured goods between the Portuguese and Africans, and to sell gold to the Portuguese in exchange for manufactured goods.[14] These Wangara traders were said to trade seasonally with caravans, "conducting their business under the protection of fortified villages (*tata*) of the local *Sooninkee* chiefs."[15]

The influence of the Mande-speaking merchants was so great that the Mande language became a commercial lingua franca in this region, enabling commercial communication and connections between a network of local markets and trading stations through which the Wangara traders conducted their operations.[16] The Wangara created commercial hubs such as Badoora, Biafada, and Balanta, using these towns as platforms for long-distance trade in textiles, ivory, kola nuts, hides and skins, and salt, a commercial relay system that eventually reached as far as Sierra Leone.[17] The Wangara traders from Gambia and Sierra Leone met at

Badoora to exchange kola nuts, cotton, and fabrics, which each group then distributed throughout its commercial territorial sphere.

Portuguese traders seeking trade with local African communities in this region often went through the Wangara because the latter were revered and trusted as merchants, political mediators, and spiritual counselors. By combining a mastery of the private entrepreneurial sphere with an ability to work the political system through lobbying, the Wangara eliminated the familiar frictions that resulted from interactions between the realm of politics and the realm of commerce. Realizing the crucial interconnections between politics and business, the Wangara traders stationed political lobbyists "who served as ambassadors in many nations, and do this to make commerce."[18] In the process they built what one could call an early example of an African private-public partnership in the interest of commercial prosperity. The Wangara trade consuls supervised trade, smoothed over political challenges to trade, and helped resolve commercial disputes.

By pleasing political leaders and strategically inserting themselves into the political process, the Wangara not only secured their trade but also gave a stake to political leaders in the host communities of a growing West African trade diaspora. This ability to make private enterprise a compelling public interest and to reward political actors who bought into this vision ensured the Wangara's dominance in the growing Atlantic commerce between Africans and Europeans in this period. The Portuguese came to the Senegambia and the Upper Guinea coast in the fifteenth century to tap into the gold trade but found this trade already controlled by the Wangara. In the sixteenth century the Wangara continued to dominate and displace the aggressive European traders in this part of West Africa.[19] Their trading activities reached a peak in the mid-seventeenth century and then began to decline. This was probably due to the fact that as the political turmoil associated with the monarchical infighting and decline of Songhai engulfed much of the Middle Niger region—the trading base of the Wangara—they began to develop "new outlets for their trade in the far Western regions where the authority of the Malian king was still relatively intact."[20]

A final strategy of commercial penetration deployed by the Wangara in the Senegambia region was the building of a Mande merchant brand. As the Mande commercial empire flourished and expanded from the Sahel to the Gambia River and to the Atlantic, connecting Sahelian and hinterland West African peoples to the markets of North Africa and to European Atlantic products, Mande became a brand that ambitious commercial investors who were not ethnic Mande came to embrace in an honorary capacity in order to tap into the economic, social, and political capital of the Mande-speaking traders. In this process, a pan–West African merchant brand emerged, attracting many and further extending the frontiers of the Wangara commercial monopolies and trading networks. In a multiethnic region, the Wangara trading network created "a common [commercial] identity which transcended mere parochial interests" and gave everyone—host or settler, sedentary or nomadic—a stake in the commercial prosperity of the region.[21]

The Wangara in the Akan Zone

Another important trajectory of the Wangara's commercial expansion was southward toward the Akan forest, the vast forested territory encompassing modern Ghana and the southern Ivory Coast. From their Middle Niger base in Mali, the Wangara traders began trading south as early as the beginning of the fifteenth century. Transporting salt from the desert mines to Timbuktu, the Wangara merchants then transferred the cargo to boats that transported it to the inland city of Djene.[22] Djene served as a hub in the trade between Mali and the Akan forest states. From Djene the salt was broken into smaller tradable units that could be carried by camels and porters for the two- to three-week journey, spanning five hundred miles, to the vast Akan goldfields.[23] There the Wangara traded their salt for gold over a vast territory corresponding to modern Ghana and that stretched all the way to the coastal region encompassing the famous European trading port of Elmina.[24] After exhausting their stock of Saharan salt through bartering, the traders commenced the return journey to Djene, and then to Timbuktu, where Akan gold was sold to Arab and Berber trans-Saharan merchants. The Wangara traders then used the proceeds to buy salt, with which they would purchase their next supply of Akan gold.

The Wangara traders' expansion to and investment in the alluvial gold-mining production of the Akan region represented another strand in their fast-growing trading and investment repertoire. This expansion once again showcased the Wangara's ability to identify niches and needs between and within different regions of medieval West Africa, and to move to meet them. It was no accident that the extension of the Wangara's trading network to the Akan region occurred in tandem with "the development of new centers of gold production."[25] Wangara capital investments, credit, and the thriving Wangara gold trade with North Africa transformed Akan gold mining.

The Wangara's investment in the Akan goldfields expanded in the following centuries as more Mande-speaking traders moved south to partake in this lucrative trading system.[26] By building a vast distribution network that tied together the major West African centers of gold and salt production and by creating a virtual monopoly over this trade, the Wangara "became . . . the first link in a vast distributive network that extended northward from the goldfields to the greater entrepôts of the Western Sudan and Sahel."[27] Being the first link in this network gave the Wangara the leverage to put their imprimatur on the subsequent expansions of this Akan-Sahel trade.

The Wangara traders were not content with buying and selling gold across this vast long-distance route; they wanted to ensure an uninterrupted supply and production of gold in the Akan goldfields. This led them to establish, as they did in the Senegambia region, several trade settlements on the northern frontiers of the Akan area where Wangara kinsmen settled; these included Bitu, Baha, and Banbarranaa.[28] These settlements morphed fairly quickly into self-contained commercial hubs, with their own distinctly Wangara political and cultural traditions in the northwestern sectors of the vast Akan country.[29] The Wangara trading diaspora spread throughout the Akan hinterland as far as the modern-day Ivory Coast, with many of the hinterland Wangara communities identifying a foundational Juula trading metropolis called Bighu as the nucleus of their initial settlement among the Akan-speaking peoples.[30] Ivor Wilks argues that Bighu is Bitu, and that the ruins of the long-abandoned town "in present-day Ghana is well known locally."[31] This specific point may be disputed, but Wangara trade settlements in Akan country were precursors to today's many Mande-speaking communities in northern Ghana.

The Wangara trading settlements solved certain important interrelated challenges and enabled the Wangara to establish a commercial foothold and to eventually dominate the key trades in Akan country. First, being situated in the local Akan milieu, the Wangara settlers provided the itinerant Wangara gold and salt merchants with lodging and logistical services during their trading trips. Second, the settled Wangara provided brokerage and mediation services to both Akan gold producers and Wangara gold and salt traders. Their linguistic and cultural existence in both the Akan and Mande diasporic commercial worlds placed them in a unique position to play this role. Third, the settled Wangara provided security for the itinerant traders and their goods, helping with the safe depositing of gold and other valuables for a commission. In that sense, they provided deposit and safeguarding services analogous to modern banking services. Fourth, when the Wangara identified the European coastal demand for gold, they used Wangara trade towns as platforms to extend their trade empire to the Cape Coast, increasingly serving as middlemen in the trade between several Akan communities and European merchants on the coast.

The Wangara traders showed a remarkable capacity for nimbleness and adaptability, using their trade towns across West Africa, name recognition, control of credit, reputation for honesty, and political goodwill to move creatively within and between sites in their vast commercial networks as each occasion demanded. When one sector of the network became challenged, the Wangara simply moved to a different sector. Such was the case in the mid-sixteenth century when conflict in Akan coastal states reduced access to the coast and disrupted the Wangara's hinterland-coast operations. Many Wangara traders diverted their gold from Elmina and other southern coasts to the Gambia River and its extensive network of Wangara trading centers. In this way the Wangara traders ensured that the demand for Akan gold was met and that the Akan demand for salt and European-manufactured products was satiated. The advantages of scale and breadth proved decisive in staving off potentially devastating disruptions to trade.

There is yet another dimension to the Wangara's commercial penetration of the Akan region. Although Wilks attributes it to the backing of the king (or *mansa*) of Mali, there is little evidence that the Wangara traded as agents of the kings of Mali or that they were "concessionaires of the Malian government."[32] Nonetheless, the Wangara enjoyed the benefits of a political reputation that flowed from three symbiotic sources: the success of the Wangara's own brand; the myths of Malian political sophistication and strength; and the political, economic, and cultural reputation of the Wangara trading towns. This is probably what Wilks hints at, and the traders may well have invoked the widespread myths of Malian monarchical traditions to curry mercantile favors with political actors in polities with which they hoped to trade. Mercantile prestige tends to beget political prestige, and vice versa—whether the secondary reputation is deserved or not. This seems to have been the situation with the Wangara traders and trading communities of the Akan hinterlands. Their commercial reputation opened political doors as they expanded their trading network; open political doors in turn smoothed the path to more trade privileges and concessions, further giving the Wangara more political capital to parlay into commercial expansion.

A final factor that gave the Wangara traders preeminence in the trade of the Akan zone was the kola nut, a stimulant grown almost exclusively in the Akan forest[33] that enjoyed and still enjoys widespread demand for recreational and ritual use across West Africa and the Maghrebian lands north of the Sahara. This trans–West African and trans-Saharan market for kola nut and the Wangara's tentacles and settlements in regions that produced it gave the Wangara an opportunity to expand and consolidate their dominance over long-distance trade in West Africa. Ever alert to emerging demands and new trading opportunities, Wangara traders were quick to spot the vast kola nut export potential in the Akan forest and to correlate this to demand for the product across West Africa. Given the fact that "long-distance traders were usually in the best position to respond to new opportunities,"[34] the Wangara were in a unique position to develop a new trade in kola nuts. They leveraged their existing gold and salt trade infrastructures to add kola nut export to their trading portfolio. The ensuing trade in kola nuts gave the Wangara another opportunity to establish more trading outposts and settlements along new trade routes that they established to cater to the new kola nut economy. This Wangara-controlled kola nut trade opened up new trading routes, and with them new Wangara settlements and trading diasporas in the present-day Benin Republic, Niger, and Nigeria.

Wangara Traders in the Greater Borgu Axis

Trading under the corporate identity of the Wangara, Mande-speaking merchants began to trade kola nuts obtained from the Akan forest region to Hausaland (in modern-day Niger and Nigeria) probably as early as the middle of the fourteenth century or the early fifteenth century.[35] Much of this early trade followed clerics who came to Hausaland from Mali and the Senegambia region through Agadez, Air, and other towns in the present-day Niger Republic. Some of the Wangara who pioneered this trade were clerics, but one of the factors of Muslim clerical life, *al-harth* or travel, is virtually synonymous with trade or itinerant trading,[36] underscoring the entwinement of trade and clerical life among the Wangara. Although the clerical component of this Wangara commercial expansion to the east was very pronounced, commerce was at its center.

One of the most popular routes in this new trade was a fairly simple one, given the territorial contiguities that facilitated the journey. The Ghonja-Nikki-Borgu-Hausaland route became a natural trajectory for Wangara merchants. This direct kola nut trade between the Akan forest region and Hausaland exploded in the eighteenth century when there was "an upsurge in the demand for kola nuts in Hausaland, thus motivating the Wangara to obtain the commodity in large quantities from Gonja."[37] The eighteenth century marked the emergence of the Akan super-state, Asante, which, after uniting the dispersed Akan-speaking peoples, sought to expand and consolidate the frontiers of the state by increasing the production and export of gold and kola nuts. This new, state-backed economic imperative breathed new life into the kola nut trade and enabled the Wangara to expand, formalize, and secure their dominance over the trade through the partnership of the Wangara private trading initiative and the Asante public revenue imperative. In the eighteenth century the convergence of these two initiatives boosted the kola nut trade of the Wangara.[38] Once introduced to Hausaland and other Islamic polities such as Bornu, kola nuts became the recreational stimulant of choice for many Muslims because, as Lovejoy argues, kola nut was one of few stimulants not prohibited by the Islamic theological consensuses of the period.[39] The connection of this vast demand with the source of supply in the Akan region was another instance of the Wangara's adroitness in identifying arbitrage opportunities and moving in to create new trading activities. The Wangara were keenly aware of and operationalized the concept of emerging markets centuries before it became a buzzword in international trade and investment circuits.

Traveling in convoys that carried kola nuts, gold, and manufactured wares obtained from the coastal parts of the forest region of the Middle Volta, the Wangara traders usually set off from Ghonja, an Akan principality. The caravans then crossed territories in modern Togo, some of which were part of the greater Akan zone, into Nikki and other Borgu towns in modern Benin Republic. They then crossed into Yorubaland, Nupe, and Baatonu or Bariba land, as well as Bussa, the last two of which were part of the Borgu confederacy.[40] Many Wangara traders ended their journey in Baatonu land, selling their wares to Hausa or Wangara retailers who then took the goods to Hausaland, only a few days' journey away. Others made the trip into Hausaland themselves because they were interested in purchasing leather and other products there for trade.

As the Wangara's travel on this route increased in frequency and volume, they began to establish trading stations, ribats or makeshift markets, and refreshment centers along the different nodes of the route. Because these journeys lasted anywhere from five to seven months depending on the final destination and the particular route taken,[41] the Wangara traders sold some of their wares at these points in present-day Togo, Benin, and Yorubaland before arriving at the thoroughfare of Borgu. Engaging in the old arbitrage practice of buying low and selling high along the way minimized the cost of the long caravan journey, reduced loss of perishable products, and maximized profit and turnover. The Wangara thus connected a vast territory from the Akan region to the northernmost parts of Hausaland, creating an integrated regional market that facilitated access to a wide variety of goods that would not have been available to these communities without the agency of Mande-speaking traders. The repeat or return journey followed the same trajectory, though some Wangara traders instead returned to their Malian homelands or traded through Niger or Senegambia.

The Borgu states' location at the midpoint of the caravan route placed them at an advantage in this kola nut trade between Asante and Hausaland. With the influx of Wangara economic settlers and itinerant traders, the Borgu economy witnessed rapid growth and a transformation from an economy in which land was the currency and standard of value to a money-based economy in which barter exchange, weights, gold standards, and other systems of value and valuation came to dominate economic transactions.[42] Over the course of the eighteenth century, the range of goods flowing into and through Borgu to Hausaland on Wangara trade caravans increased to include horses, natron, salt, earthenware, and European-manufactured products such as jugs, brass, cotton cloth, processed wool products, and copper dishes.[43] Multiproduct arbitrage gave the Wangara a greater share of markets and an opportunity to spread their trading capital around, thereby minimizing losses due to fluctuations in prices and demand. The Wangara also opened up more subsidiary routes from kola-nut-producing areas in Asanteland to Hausaland. These routes included the Salaga-Dahomey-Oyo-Kandi-Illo-Sokoto route and the Ghonja-Djougou-Nikki-Bussa-Kano route. Once the traders arrived in Dahomey (modern-day Benin), they had even more options for getting their wares to the markets of Hausaland, such as the Nikki-Bussa-Zaria-Kano route or the Nikki-Yauri-Sokoto-Kebbi route. From Borgu, some Wangara traders preferred a river route, crossing the Niger River in

Kontagora territory, from where Kebbi, Sokoto, and other parts of Hausaland were easily accessible over land.[44]

Along with trading came Wangara migration to the Borgu states. As in other parts of West Africa, many became merchant-clerics, providing clerical services and engaging in Islamic proselytizing and trade. Others settled in Borgu, trading iron ore and shea butter to Hausaland and Nupe and bringing back leather products, mats, glass beads, and clothes.[45] Sedentary Borgu Wangara communities provided accommodations for visiting Wangara traders who ended their journey in Borgu or stayed there for days or weeks before proceeding to Hausaland or Nupe. The Wangara who settled in Borgu were the mediators in the commercial interactions between itinerant Wangara traders and local Borgu producers. The settled Wangara arranged safekeeping for valuables, negotiated safe passage for caravans with political authorities, arranged the political courtesies and gift giving that were instrumental in ensuring a political environment favorable to the traveling Wangara traders, and negotiated favorable trade tolls for the visiting traders. For performing these roles, members of the Borgu Wangara community were paid a commission in goods or were extended favorable trading terms as retailers and distributors.

The settled Wangara bought many of the itinerant traders' wares in wholesale transactions and retailed them for profit. In some cases this was a marketing partnership in which a commission was paid to the Wangara retailer. Other times the itinerant traders advanced credit to the settled Wangara retailer, who then repaid the sum when the goods were sold, often during the itinerant traders' return journey from Hausaland. In this way the benefits and profits of the Wangara's long-distance kola nut and gold trade from the Akan forest to Hausaland helped build a secondary commercial zone in the Borgu states. This in turn spawned a set of tertiary commercial transactions in the Borgu-Nupe-Gbagyi hinterland as Wangara and Hausa retailers carried the goods farther afield in a relay system of trade that connected distant and culturally diverse zones in a vast area corresponding to modern central Nigeria.

Finally, on the strength of their trading and clerical services of praying, advising, and making amulets for local aristocracies, as well as their role as cultural and trade brokers, the settled Wangara ingratiated themselves with the ruling houses of the Borgu states. This earned them a reputation as wealthy aristocrats, kingly advisers, and a privileged backbone of a Borgu economy that increasingly depended on its fortuitous location on a lucrative long-distance trade route.

Wangara Commerce in Hausaland

The expansion of the Wangara commercial empire into Hausaland began in the late fourteenth and early fifteenth centuries, as merchants from the rapidly growing Songhai Empire fanned out eastward. Through their involvement and investments in commerce, artisanal production, and professionalized vocations, they helped to transform the economies of Hausaland over the next several centuries.[46] Many Wangara merchants who operated in the Borgu sector merely used the area as an intermediate point or springboard in their quest for the big markets of Hausaland. Such was the importance of the Borgu-Hausaland connection in the expansion of the Wangara commercial influence in central Sudan that many Wangara merchants continued to travel to Hausaland from Mali and Borgu, even after the collapse of Songhai in the late sixteenth century. Lovejoy argues that one important legacy of the Wangara settlements in Borgu is that they were the "foundation of Wangara settlements in Hausa cities," which were extensions of preexisting "Songhay-oriented commercial diaspora[s]."[47]

The Wangara's southward and eastward expansion led to the emergence of Wangara merchant communities in Kano, Gobir, Kebbi, Katsina, and Air (in the present-day Niger Republic). However, the Wangara also utilized several novel trade routes that led directly from Mali to Hausaland. The route through Azelik and later through Agadez (both in present-day Niger) led straight to Katsina and then Kano. The *Kano Chronicle,* an undated precolonial account of the Hausa people of Kano, their interactions with their neighbors, and their kings, records a large migration of Wangara merchants and Islamic scholars from Mali into Kano through Air and Katsina in the late fifteenth century. In the fifteenth and sixteenth centuries the Azelik trading corridor brought Wangara traders to Gobir and Borno from the Songhai Empire. They came bearing gold, salt, and other products of the Sahel. They may also have introduced the use of cowries as legal tender and a unit of standardized value with convertibility tied to gold.[48] In the late fifteenth century Agadez appears to have taken over Azelik's position as the major trade artery connecting Songhai to Hausaland. Agadez gradually came to house a significant population of Wangara merchants who coordinated trade between the Sahel and Hausaland. In addition, the city served as a major hub in the traffic of goods and finance between Kebbi, Katsina, and parts of Kano on one hand and Songhai on the other. Located between Songhai and the two major Hausa commercial centers of Kano and Katsina, Kebbi gradually came to host a significant population of occupationally diverse Wangara immigrants. Kebbi's large Wangara settlements gave Mande- and Soninke-speaking merchants a base from which to trade to Katsina and Kano.[49] In Kano and Katsina the Wangara settled in designated Songhai merchant quarters,[50] establishing merchant guilds and mosques that aided them in carrying out trading and clerical duties that were often entwined. Like Wangara merchant communities elsewhere, the settled traders in Kano brokered trade between their traveling kinsmen and Hausa product buyers. They also provided landlord services for visiting Wangara traders.[51]

Residing in urban centers as they did in Borgu, Wangara migrants in Hausaland invested their capital in the butchering arts and established themselves in legal consultancy, Islamic mysticism, the booming religious book trade, and

Islamic scholarship. By embracing such a wide variety of professions, the Wangara ensured that the auxiliary services that long-distance trading required were readily available within their diasporic community. Investment in these professions was thus closely linked with the imperative of efficient trading.

In diversifying their commercial endeavors, Wangara traders expanded their stake in the dominant industries and crafts of sixteenth- and seventeenth-century Hausaland. Wangara merchants also invested in Hausaland's famous leather industry. The manufacture of leather bags, pouches, shoes, straps, amulet holders, cushions, fans, and other valued leather products was made possible partly by Wangara initiatives and investments.[52] The Wangara merchants invested in the processing of rawhide, which they then exported, along with finished leather goods, across the Sahara to North Africa, especially Morocco. Mediterranean and European purchasers would later identify these Hausaland-originated leather products as Moroccan leather. This name brand functioned to conceal, at least to consumers in far-flung Mediterranean lands, the fact that the manufacturing and distribution center of the referenced leatherwork was in Hausaland and that its human catalysts were migrant and settled Wangara traders, financiers, craftspeople, and leather workers. Such was the geographical and commercial breadth of the Wangara entrepreneurial network.

The Wangara merchants became central economic actors in Hausaland when they invested in textile production, historically the most viable sector of the economy. Gobir, a state with a large population of Wangara settlers, and Kano both hosted the dyeing arts. There the making of turkudi, a shiny, thin fabric used for ceremonial turbans by aristocrats, royals, and clerics across West Africa, was an established craft.[53] The Wangara merchants saw potential for growth and invested heavily in this industry. The Kano, Katsina, and Kebbi cloth industries were fully integrated, from the ginning of cotton, to the weaving of cloth on looms, to dyeing and beating, to tailoring and embroidery and complex gown design. With financing from Wangara merchants, production was optimized and the export of Hausa luxury and consumer cloth to other parts of West Africa and across the Sahara to North Africa increased, boosted by the existing trade tentacles and reputation of the Wangara.

Wangara merchants took further steps to secure their growing trading empire in Hausaland. They initiated marriage alliances between themselves and the indigenous aristocracies of Hausaland. They also built a moral economy through Islam. These innovations, although seemingly social in nature, "solidified common [economic] interests between the government and the commercial sector . . . and led to the assimilation of [Wangara] immigrants as a privileged class."[54] In the period between the fifteenth and nineteenth centuries, the economy of Hausaland experienced remarkable growth. This was also the period in which Wangara merchants invested heavily in multiple sectors of the economy and built a credit and monetary system that facilitated exchange across a vast network of trade routes and commercial centers throughout Hausaland. Lovejoy summarizes the transformative impact of the Wangara merchants thus: "The founding of settlements, the extension of a common monetary system, the introduction of new products, and the participation in early craft production suggest one conclusion: the Wangara founded the Muslim commercial diaspora in . . . Hausa[land] . . . and contributed significantly to the development of the Central Sudan economy."[55] By the late nineteenth century, the Wangara merchants' influence was waning in Hausaland, as was also the case in Borgu, Senegambia, and the Akan area. Given the profound impact it had on many economies across West Africa, the decline and demise of the Wangara's pan–West African trading empire deserves to be understood in the context of multiple factors that interrupted what seemed like the early signs of a private-sector and trade-driven regional economic integration.

Decline of the Wangara Trading Network

By the eighteenth and nineteenth centuries, some of the Wangara's commercial dominance had begun to wane because states, kingdoms, and empires were trying to directly conduct trade with an increasingly ubiquitous group of European traders. States such as Asante and the Sokoto Caliphate when it emerged in the first decade of the nineteenth century began to imagine their commercial destinies outside the Wangara system and increasingly sought to cultivate their own direct trade ties to Europeans on the coast. The European merchants resented the dominant brokering position of the Wangara and welcomed the commercial self-assertion of the West African polities. As these states recruited and empowered their own commercial groups—in the case of Asante and the caliphate, Akan and Hausa traders—the Wangara's dominance over long-distance coastal and hinterland trade began to decline.

European merchants, especially those not as well financed, preferred to bypass middlemen like the Wangara and deal directly with the producers of peanuts, palm produce, cocoa, cotton, and other goods they desired, and to sell their goods directly to consumers. Producers were located in hinterlands controlled by states that were now using these resources and the increased demand for them during the Industrial Revolution as leverage to exact profits and strategic goods from European merchants. Commercial agreements and contracts between European merchants and powerful West African states became common in the nineteenth century, further marginalizing the Wangara. These commercial treaties began to take on the character of quasi-colonial accords in which European companies such as the Royal Niger Company and the French companies operating in the lower Niger area increasingly acted on behalf of the British and French governments, respectively.[56]

With the advent of informal imperial arrangements in the mid- to late nineteenth century, European states, invoking treaties and territorial claims as part of the scramble for Africa, began to use military might and their state-backed monopoly trading companies to decimate African trading networks, commercial groups, middlemen, and trade brokers. As the alliance of European commercial and political interests moved more aggressively to capture and monopolize African trade within increasingly defined and protected territories, the commercial empire of the Wangara was squeezed and began to disintegrate. Moreover, the increased emphasis on and policing of territorial sovereignties struck a blow at one of the foundational bases of the Wangara trading system: easy movement across West Africa. The ability to move freely by simply observing some traditional protocols required of strangers and visitors in a new land was central to the commercial success of the Wangara. Territorial barriers defined first as European commercial spheres and later as colonial possessions limited free movement over long distances across West Africa. This, along with several emerging colonial realities, broke up the Wangara trading network.

The process of decline in the Wangara trading system and its correlation to colonial events unfolded differently in the various parts of West Africa. In the Akan sector, the expansion of Asante in the nineteenth century, as well as the rivalry between it and the Fante states, had three consequences for the Wangara's involvement in trade in the forest region of modern Ghana. First, these realities gave the Asante an impetus to discard the commercial mediation of Wangara and Hausa traders and to directly control trade with Europeans on the coast through their own indigenous agents. Second, these circumstances made it possible for Britain to intervene and gradually assert imperial control in the region. Imperial control meant the erosion of sovereignty and the usurpation of previously existing regulations over trade. Quasi-colonial maneuvers resulted in the increased dominance of British merchants over the trade on the Gold Coast at the expense of African traders and brokers like the Wangara. Finally, a series of wars between Asante and Fante and between the Asante and the British between 1867 and 1901 rendered the region—hinterland and coast—insecure for trade and for itinerant Wangara merchants.

In the Senegambia area and in the Sahel region covering modern Mali and Niger, French imperial maneuvers in the form of military, political, and commercial expansion began to take a toll on the activities of Wangara merchants and communities. Between 1822 and 1855 the French presence in the Upper Senegal expanded through the activities of the French monopolistic trading company, the Compagnie de Galam. With the backing of the French government, the company took over the trade in gum arabic,[57] which was previously controlled by the Wangara. In the 1870s, when French control in this region stabilized after the defeat of Al-Haj Umar Tal and the subsequent obliteration of other expressions of African resistance, a rudimentary French administration was established.[58] One casualty of the prolonged period of colonial "pacification" was Wangara trade, since insecurity made movement difficult. Once colonial administration was in place, one of the earliest priorities of the French colonial administration was revenue.

The quest for revenue led to the imposition of taxation, which had to be paid in colonial currency. Although Francois Manchuelle argues that the tax burden was light,[59] the introduction of taxation had profound implications for the Wangara trading network. First, French colonial taxation undermined the commercial provenance of bartering, which had been an essential part of Wangara trading. Second, it made local currencies such as cowries and salt lose their power as legal tender, again undermining the monetary system central to the Wangara network. Finally, taxation by the colonial government forced many Wangara—ethnic Soninke, Bambara, and Mande-speaking peoples—out of trading and into professions in which they could earn the colonial currency. With long-distance trading losing its appeal as a result of the new logistical, security, and monetary problems, some Wangara continued to trade, but only within specific locales. Others became migrant laborers, working for wages as *laptots*, Africans who fought on the side of France and then worked in the colonial system between the eighteenth and the mid twentieth century. Many *laptots* served in the French Navy as boat hands for French merchants, as porters, as agricultural hands in the growing colonial export crop industry, and in other new colonial enterprises in distant African lands.[60] This was a significant reversal of fortunes for the Wangara.

Meanwhile, the National African Company, formed in 1879 and headed by George Goldie, had militarily commandeered several territories bordering its lower Niger trading base.[61] By doing so, the British quasi-imperial trading company disrupted the Wangara river-borne trade in Nupe and Yauri. The company's enforcement of its trading monopoly also disrupted the secondary trade in manufactured goods, salt, and kola nuts that the Wangara's merchant community in Borgu had created. When the charter of the company was revoked in 1899 and its territorial and military assets taken over by the British government, it signaled a British intention to use the Niger-Benue confluence region as a base to subdue the Sokoto Caliphate encompassing all of Hausaland and Nupe.[62] The conquest of the caliphate, which began in 1900 and concluded with the defeat of the caliphate forces in Burmi in 1903, brought the vast trading network of the Wangara within and between different Hausa locales under the British and their Fulani aristocratic allies.

In Borgu the situation was a little dicey because the transition from informal empire to direct imperial control was a messier, more disruptive process than it was in other areas. French and British imperial interests collided in the vast confederacy of Borgu in modern north-central Nigeria and the northern Benin Republic. This led to confrontational military invasions and maneuvers that disrupted trade and agriculture and entrenched insecurity throughout the 1890s.[63] All the major Wangara trade hubs in Borguland, including Nikki, Parakou, Illo, Kande, and Bussa, were affected by this Anglo-French imperial military confrontation, which culminated in the famous race to Nikki and the subsequent military stalemate. Wangara long-distance trade into and between these nodes suffered in this climate of imperial rivalry.

When the dispute was eventually settled through the exchange of territories between the two European imperial states in June 1898, the settlement had a profoundly negative impact on the Wangara trading network. Borgu was divided between the British and the French, with Kande, Parakou, and Nikki going to the French and Bussa, Kiama, and Okuta going to the British. This destroyed the territorial contiguity and political uniformity and continuity that had been so central to Wangara trading operations. Furthermore, with formalized, policed borders dividing French Dahomey from the British protectorate of Northern Nigeria, and with the territories of German Togoland and French Dahomey standing between the Akan, Mossi, and Senegambia regions on one hand and the Borgu-Hausa axis on the other, Wangara long-distance trade all but ended.

Insights from the Rise and Fall of the Wangara Trading Network

The trading network built by the Wangara confronted and overcame many obstacles and proved adaptable to varying socioeconomic and political regimes. The Wangara leveraged the advantages of scale, their diverse portfolio of investments, and their nimble versatility to avoid or weather disruptions to trade. Their ability to spot market opportunities and emerging demands and to invest in mechanisms for satisfying them gave the Wangara control over the long-distance trade in several commodities. The Wangara saw West Africa as a vast, interconnected zone of trade and investments. Their investment in trade, the extraction industry, and artisanal manufacturing helped to commercially integrate the region and dissolve political, cultural, and economic barriers to trade. Understanding the ways in which the Wangara creatively solved the problems of long-distance trade and trans-African investing requires a distillation of insights from this rich commercial and entrepreneurial history. To underscore the Wangara factor in the business history of West Africa, key insights from their commercial operations need to be distilled and highlighted.

The Wangara were adept at identifying demand and supply nodes and moving to connect them. By doing so, they also built new commercial niches. In several of the commercial and investment theaters in which the Wangara operated, the ability to spot opportunities in production, distribution, and arbitrage was central to their success, although this also exposed them to new challenges that they had to surmount. The Wangara recognized the power of what is known in contemporary business lingo as brand building. They built their brand using multiple strategies. Trading in multiple political and cultural contexts, they gave a stake to non-Wangara traders in several polities, allowing the latter to buy into the Wangara franchise and parlay the commercial, social, cultural, and political capital associated with that name into primary or secondary trading activities. The Wangara thus established a brand that was permissive, panethnic, and pan–West African. They viewed local merchants as partners and potential distributors of their goods rather than as competitors. This attitude further enhanced the reputation of the Wangara trading network and made it attractive to more West African groups of traders.

Another insight that is discernible from the mercantile operations of the Wangara is that they recognized the important entwinements of the business and political realms and worked hard to dissolve antagonism between them and to bring them into a productive, cooperative relationship. In all the polities where the Wangara established trading communities and supply chains, they designated Wangara merchants and trade consuls to lobby the host political establishment. This lobbying infrastructure was instrumental in securing trade, getting a set of uniform trade rules enforced, and opening up new markets. The Wangara lobbyists used their powers of persuasion and the symbols of their commercial success to make political entities believe in their capacity to spread prosperity. When necessary, the Wangara did not hesitate to give varying stakes to political actors in a private-public commercial partnership. By pushing political policies that favored trade, enterprise, and free exchange, the Wangara ensured the security and continuity of their trading system.

The Wangara succeeded through a conscious diversification of their investment portfolios. They invested their capital and knowledge across the economic value chain—in manufacturing, wholesale, retail, distribution, consultancy, and support professions and crafts, as well as in cultivating political ties for the benefit of business. Diversification gave the Wangara more economic leverage. Their forward and backward linkages gave them a unique and dominant foothold in the West African long-distance trade sector. The much-discussed trade monopoly of the Wangara was thus de facto and not de jure, a product of the ability to spread investments across multiple points of a value chain and across different sectors. The Wangara reaped the commercial advantages of the economy of scale due to the breadth of their investments in polities connected to their network. The vastness of their investments also meant that the Wangara effectively connected interiors to coasts, rural areas to cities, and, more crucially, wholesale sectors to retail points. In other words, diversification facilitated integration.

A major obstacle to long-distance multistate commerce is variation in currency and credit and related policies. Although the Wangara adapted to the varieties of currency used for exchange in the many polities in which they operated and participated in bartering operations where necessary, they overcame the problem of currency proliferation by introducing the gold standard of value to commerce in many regions of West Africa. This form of standardization helped the Wangara to invest and trade in multiple cultural and geographical contexts without the problem of monetary differentiation undermining their commercial empire.

The Wangara also developed a system of credit that helped many West African groups to trade with or for the Wangara as retailers and partners in localized areas. Much of this credit system was based on a system of trust, which was cultivated over long periods of repeated transactions. A related innovation of the Wangara merchants was the development of the concept of trading transactions built on trust, which was anchored on adherence to both shared moral codes and, in some regions, forms of Islamic literacy. In the Wangara's trading empire and in their many commercial communities across West Africa, Islamic moral codes governed transactions. This, along with written contracts and honor-based business practices, helped build trust in two layers—one oral and relational, the other in binding, legal documents. In areas where the Wangara traded with and among non-Muslims, trust was also the basis of business and transactions. This trust developed from repeated transactions and familiarity. Here too the sanctity of the written contract, aided by the Wangara's status as purveyors of literacy, bookkeeping, and accounting, provided another layer of transactional integrity. By alternating between these two mechanisms of protection, the Wangara managed risks to their investments and built confidence in their trading partners while remaining flexible enough to conduct transactions across literate and nonliterate, and Muslim and non-Muslim, regions of West Africa.

One of the Wangara's accomplishments was their ability to compress time and distance by using multiple means of transportation to get goods from source to destination. The Wangara used porters, camel and donkey caravans, canoes on rivers, and horses to reduce the amount of time it took to transport goods between different regions. At times all these means were deployed during a single trip in alternating relays, with the traders switching from one mode of mobility to another in order to cut the time and distance of travel, minimize costs, and maximize profits and efficiency. The Wangara demonstrated a type of improvisational flexibility that made mobility easier in a time of treacherous instruments of mobility.

The insights of the Wangara commercial network are not inherent only in its success; its collapse also harbors valuable information. One of the important insights to be gleaned from the collapse of the network is that the Wangara could not adapt to changing tastes, changing consumption patterns, changing demands, and, of course, the restrictions and protectionist policies of colonial regimes. One example of this failure to adapt is the Wangara's inability to match the speed with which Europeans delivered products to the West African interior and bought African products from the same source. Although, as mentioned, one of the Wangara's earlier strengths was their ability to use multiple means of transportation, when European trading ships began to navigate West Africa's rivers to reach deep into the hinterlands, the Wangara had no answer and were marginalized as a result.

The Wangara simply could not compete with better-financed traders who could offer cheaper, more efficiently manufactured goods. The failure to adapt to changes brought on by external factors—changes over which an African business actor had no control—has been a recurring theme of business stagnation and failure in West African business history. When European merchants and their African allies began to challenge the trade monopoly of the Wangara with a flood of cheap European goods, they catalyzed a new dynamic. Overwhelmed, the Wangara could not adapt. As imperial control made the influx of foreign goods possible and as the Wangara lost political allies who could protect their trading rights, their commercial empire atrophied.

The Wangara also faced another problem: in the era of European commercial and imperial expansion in West Africa, they came up against the perception that foreign goods, manufactured or not, were superior to and thus better markers of status than the locally manufactured or locally sourced products that the Wangara traded. This problem was particularly acute in the period of so-called legitimate trade throughout the nineteenth century. This perception took the Wangara by surprise, and they could not counter it effectively.

Conclusion

Over five hundred years the Wangara built a formidable pan–West African trading empire with a diverse range of investments. This chapter has documented the successes of this commercial network and the strategies and circumstances that catalyzed this success. It also analyzed the challenges, decline, and eventual collapse of this influential commercial diaspora. Some of these challenges and failures opened the door to European competitors in the era of Atlantic commerce to build and consolidate their own trading and quasi-political empire, for which the Wangara were no match. The Wangara were slow to respond to the advent of the European factor in West African trade. They also failed to anticipate and respond to new mercantile dynamics.

One manifestation of this failure to stay actively innovative is that, despite investing in several sectors and trading in a diverse array of products, the Wangara traders and investors were incapable of meeting certain demands. For example, the Wangara neglected to invest in the technology and manufacture of firearms, despite soaring demand for them during the late eighteenth century and the nineteenth century. Despite the Wangara's well-deserved reputation for spotting emerging demands and markets and for being able to forecast changing patterns of need, they failed to identify this growing demand for, and increased valuation of, firearms. By the early nineteenth century, the firearms trade was the most lucrative commercial activity in many regions of West Africa, aside from the waning Atlantic slave trade. By failing to see that times were changing and by failing to adapt to these changing times and their mercantile implications, the Wangara missed out on a new lucrative trade.

This is one of several examples of how the Wangara's commitment to the trade patterns of earlier centuries prevented them from keeping up with the trends and demands of the nineteenth century, and how, without competitors for hundreds of years, they were unprepared for the commercial threats posed by European merchants and political actors. In spite of these failures, the legacies of the Wangara trading system remain relevant as historical markers and as points of reference in discussions and debates in the emerging field of African business history.

MOSES E. OCHONU is the Cornelius Vanderbilt Chair in African History at Vanderbilt University. He is author of *Africa in Fragments: Essays on Nigeria, Africa, and Global Africanity*; *Colonialism by Proxy: Hausa Imperial Agents and Middle Belt Consciousness in Nigeria* (IUP), which was named finalist for the Herskovits Prize; and *Colonial Meltdown: Northern Nigeria in the Great Depression*.

Notes

1. This title is inspired by Adamu Mahdi's *The Hausa Factor in West African History* (Oxford: Oxford University Press, 1979), which, much like the ethnocommercial thrust of this chapter, analyzes the pan–West African economic and social instrumentality of long-distance Hausa trading and migration.

2. Andreas W. Massing, "The Wangara, an Old Soninke Diaspora in West Africa?," *Cahiers d'etudes africaines* 158 (2000): 281–308.

3. Ghislaine Lydon, *On Trans-Saharan Trails: Islamic Law, Trade Networks, and Cross-cultural Exchange in Nineteenth-Century Western Africa* (Cambridge: Cambridge University Press, 2009), 64.

4. Ivor Wilks, "Wangara, Akan and Portuguese in the Fifteenth and Sixteenth Centuries: I. The Matter of Bitu," *Journal of African History* 23, no. 3 (1982): 333–49.

5. Lydon, *On Trans-Saharan Trails*.

6. E. W. Bovill, "The Silent Trade of Wangara," *Journal of the Royal African Society* 29, no. 113 (1929): 27–38.

7. Cornelia Giesing and Valentine Vydrine, eds. and trans., *Tarikh Mandinka de Bijini/La Memoire des Mandinka et des Sooninkee du Kaabu* (Leiden: Brill, 2007), 161–62. This work has been translated from French to English for this project by Carolyn Taratko.

8. Paul Lovejoy, "The Role of the Wangara in the Economic Transformation of the Central Sudan in the Fifteenth and Sixteenth Centuries," *Journal of African History* 19, no. 2 (1978): 173–93.
9. Giesing and Vydrine, *Tarikh Mandinka*, 173.
10. Ibid., 242.
11. Ibid., 174.
12. Ibid., 230.
13. Ibid.
14. A. A. de Almada, *Tratado Breve dos Rios de Guine do Cabo Verde*, ed. Antonio Brasio (Lisbon: Editorial LIAM, [1594] 1964), cited in Giesing and Vydrine, *Tarikh Mandinka*, 231.
15. Giesing and Vydrine, *Tarikh Mandinka*, 231.
16. Ibid., 232.
17. Ibid., 240.
18. Manuel Padre Alvares, *Etiopia Menor e descricao geografica da Serra Leoa* ([1616] 1916), typed manuscript at the Bibliothèque du Centre de Recherches Africaines, Université de Paris I, a copy of MS 141-C-1 at the Société de Géographie de Lisbonne, quoted in Giesing and Vydrine, *Tarikh Mandinka*, 249.
19. Giesing and Vydrine, *Tarikh Mandinka*, 245–46.
20. Ivor Wilks, "Wangara, Akan and Portuguese in the Fifteenth and Sixteenth Centuries: I. The Struggle for Trade," *Journal of African History* 23, no. 4 (1982): 467–72, 468.
21. Lovejoy, "Role of the Wangara," 173.
22. Wilks, "Wangara, Akan and Portuguese I," 340–42.
23. Ibid., 340.
24. Ibid., 337.
25. Ivor Wilks, "The Juula and the Expansion of Islam into the Forest," in *The History of Islam in Africa*, ed. Nehemiah Levitzion, 93–114 (Athens: Ohio University Press, 2000), 103.
26. Wilks, "Wangara, Akan and Portuguese I," 339–43.
27. Wilks, "Juula," 94.
28. John Blake, *Europeans in West Africa, 1540–1560: Documents to Illustrate the Nature and Scope of Portuguese Enterprise in West Africa* (London: Hakluyt Society, 1942), 1:65–68.
29. See Wilks, "Wangara, Akan and Portuguese I," 344. So profound was this Wangara commercial-demographic penetration of Akan country that many Muslim communities in this region of modern Ghana claim Wangara, Juula, and Mande origins.
30. Ibid.
31. Ibid., 345.
32. Wilks, "Wangara, Akan and Portuguese II," 468.
33. Wilks, "Wangara, Akan and Portuguese I," 343.
34. Lovejoy, "Role of the Wangara," 173.
35. Ibid., 174; Julius Adekunle, "Borgu and Economic Transformation 1700–1900: The Wangara Factor," *African Economic History* 22 (1994): 1–18.
36. Lovejoy, "Role of the Wangara," 174.
37. Adekunle, "Borgu and Economic Transformation," 8.
38. Ibid.
39. Paul Lovejoy, *Caravans of Kola: The Hausa Kola Trade, 1700–1900* (Zaria, Nigeria: Ahmadu Bello University Press, 1980), 1–6.
40. Adekunle, "Borgu and Economic Transformation," 1.
41. Ibid., 9.
42. Ibid., 8.

43. Ibid.
44. Ibid., 9.
45. Ibid., 13.
46. Lovejoy, "Role of the Wangara," 174.
47. Ibid., 176.
48. Ibid.,182. Lovejoy quotes extensively from the *Kano Chronicle* in his discussion of the role of Wangara in Kano.
49. Ibid., 182–83.
50. In Kano the Wangara merchants who specialized in trade with the Akan goldfields were housed in Agalawa quarters in the old city, a testament to their importance to the economy of the state. See Lovejoy, "Role of the Wangara," 184.
51. Ibid., 184.
52. Ibid.
53. P. J. Shea, "The Development of an Export-Oriented Cloth Industry in Kano Emirate in the Nineteenth Century" (PhD diss., University of Wisconsin, 1975). See also P. J. Shea, "Big Is Sometimes Best: The Sokoto Caliphate and Economic Advantages of Size in the Textile Industry," *African Economic History* 34 (2006): 5–21.
54. Lovejoy, "Role of the Wangara," 177.
55. Ibid., 185.
56. See J. E. Flint, *Sir George Goldie and the Making of Nigeria* (London: Oxford University Press, 1960), 9–33. Flint discusses the United Africa Company's frantic and aggressive acquisition of French competitors in the Niger trade.
57. Francois Manchuelle, *Willing Migrants: Soninke Labor Diasporas, 1848–1960* (Athens: Ohio University Press; London: James Curry, 1997), 43.
58. For a full account of the French imperial conquest of the Upper Niger and Senegambia regions, see Thomas Pakenham, *The Scramble for Africa: The White Man's Conquest of the Dark Continent from 1876–1912* (New York: Avon Books, 1991), ch. 10.
59. Manchuelle, *Willing Migrants*, 66–79.
60. Ibid., 74–84.
61. Pakenham, *Scramble for Africa*, 191–99.
62. Obaro Ikime, *The Fall of Nigeria: The British Conquest* (New York: Africana, 1977); R. A. Adeleye, *Power and Diplomacy in Nigeria, 1804–1906: The Sokoto Caliphate and Its Enemies* (New York: Humanities Press, 1971).
63. See S. C. Ukpabi, "The Anglo-French Rivalry in Borgu: A Study of Military Imperialism," *African Studies Review* 14, no. 3 (1971): 447–61; and Pakenham, *Scramble for Africa*, 512–14, 520–22.

Bibliography

Adamu, M. 1979. *The Hausa Factor in West African History*. Oxford: Oxford University Press.
Adekunle, J. 1994. "Borgu and Economic Transformation 1700–1900: The Wangara Factor." *African Economic History* 22:1–18.
Adeleye, R. A. 1971. *Power and Diplomacy in Nigeria, 1804–1906: The Sokoto Caliphate and Its Enemies*. New York: Humanities Press.
Alvares, M. P. (1616) 1916. *Etiopia Menor e descricao geografica da Serra Leoa*. Typed manuscript at the Bibliothèque du Centre de Recherches Africaines, Université de Paris I. Copy of MS 141-C-1 at the Société de Géographie de Lisbonne.

Blake, J. 1942. *Europeans in West Africa, 1540–1560: Documents to Illustrate the Nature and Scope of Portuguese Enterprise in West Africa.* Vol. 1. London: Hakluyt Society.

Bovill, E. W. 1929. "The Silent Trade of Wangara." *Journal of the Royal African Society* 29, no. 113: 27–38.

De Almada, A. A. (1594) 1964. *Tratado Breve dos Rios de Guine do Cabo Verde.* Edited by Antonio Brasio. Lisbon: Editorial LIAM.

Flint, J. E. 1960. *Sir George Goldie and the Making of Nigeria.* London: Oxford University Press.

Giesing, C., and V. Vydrine, eds. and trans. 2007. *Tarikh Mandinka de Bijini/La Memoire des Mandinka et des Sooninkee du Kaabu.* Leiden: Brill.

Ikime, O. 1977. *The Fall of Nigeria: The British Conquest.* New York: Africana.

Lovejoy, P. 1978. "The Role of the Wangara in the Economic Transformation of the Central Sudan in the Fifteenth and Sixteenth Centuries." *Journal of African History* 19, no. 2: 173–93.

———. 1980. *Caravans of Kola: The Hausa Kola Trade, 1700–1900.* Zaria, Nigeria: Ahmadu Bello University Press.

Lydon, G. 2009. *On Trans-Saharan Trails: Islamic Law, Trade Networks, and Cross-cultural Exchange in Nineteenth-Century Western Africa.* Cambridge: Cambridge University Press.

Manchuelle, F. 1997. *Willing Migrants: Soninke Labor Diasporas, 1848–1960.* Athens: Ohio University Press; London: James Curry.

Massing, A. W. 2000. "The Wangara, an Old Soninke Diaspora in West Africa?" *Cahiers d'etudes africaines* 158:281–308.

Pakenham, T. 1991. *The Scramble for Africa: The White Man's Conquest of the Dark Continent from 1876–1912.* New York: Avon Books.

Shea, P. J. 1975. "The Development of an Export-Oriented Cloth Industry in Kano Emirate in the Nineteenth Century." PhD diss., University of Wisconsin.

———. 2006. "Big Is Sometimes Best: The Sokoto Caliphate and Economic Advantages of Size in the Textile Industry." *African Economic History* 34:5–21.

Ukpabi, S. C. 1971. "The Anglo-French Rivalry in Borgu: A Study of Military Imperialism." *African Studies Review* 14, no. 3: 447–61.

Wilks, I. 1982. "Wangara, Akan and Portuguese in the Fifteenth and Sixteenth Centuries: I. The Matter of Bitu." *Journal of African History* 23, no. 3: 333–49.

———. 1982. "Wangara, Akan and Portuguese in the Fifteenth and Sixteenth Centuries: II. The Struggle for Trade." *Journal of African History* 23, no. 4: 467–72.

———. 2000. "The Juula and the Expansion of Islam into the Forest." In *The History of Islam in Africa,* edited by Nehemiah Levitzion, 93–114. Athens: Ohio University Press.

PART II

FEMALE ENTREPRENEURS AND GENDERED INNOVATION

3 Women Entrepreneurs, Gender, Traditions, and the Negotiation of Power Relations in Colonial Nigeria

Gloria Chuku

Women's involvement in the act of creating and the day-to-day management of their businesses has a long history in Africa because success as a merchant or a trader was one of the routes by which they achieved an elite status in different parts of the continent, including Nigeria. The history of women's domination of local and regional trade on the continent is therefore well established. Whereas some female traders traveled with their men and families as partners in enterprise, others engaged in independent commercial enterprises between the eighteenth and early twentieth centuries. Examples can be drawn from the Bete women of the Guinea forest who dominated all stages of kola production and marketing,[1] the Krio women of Sierra Leone,[2] the Wolof women of Senegal,[3] the Kikuyu and Kamba women of Kenya,[4] and the Nyamwezi caravan women of Tanzania.[5] In the nineteenth century the Yoruba caravans were predominantly female affairs; here women dominated trading activities using slaves and members of their households as porters.[6] The entrepreneurial ingenuity of market women in colonial and postcolonial Africa has also attracted scholarly attention.[7]

This chapter provides profiles of some southern Nigerian women of Igbo and Yoruba extraction who distinguished themselves as successful traders and influential business brokers in late nineteenth- and twentieth-century Nigeria; it also describes the entrepreneurial activities of Muslim Hausa women who, due to their seclusion, engaged in "hidden" productive ventures and thus demonstrated the intersections of gender, power, traditions, age, and entrepreneurship. Since gender conventions shaped how people achieved different kinds of power and prestige through varied activities, the chapter explores how these women continually renegotiated their relationships with men based on their distinct and complementary sources of power and status. In addition to its examination of gender conventions, the chapter discusses other cultural traditions that guided individual and group relationships and also influenced or determined how these women related to men and other social groups, how they moved through society, and how they created their own social identities within their communities and the wider Nigerian society and beyond. The chapter also examines the cultural and political dynamics within which they conducted their businesses, as well as the ways in which they struggled to maximize available opportunities and navigated challenging circumstances to become successful entrepreneurs.

Using multiple sources, the following questions are addressed: What motivated these women to enter into business? Was it a question of necessity for survival or the availability of opportunities, a quest for self-actualization and security, or a combination of factors? How did the strategies they employed and their ability to navigate patriarchal, social, and other inhibitions, as well as their differential social standing and claims to power, determine their degree of entrepreneurial accomplishments? How did these women negotiate spatial, cultural, social, ideological, and political differences and commonalities between them and men, and between them and other women, within indigenous and colonial contexts? How did they deal with the reciprocal processes of negotiation and domination as they acted to support or challenge the existing system of gender relations that affected their ability to successfully bargain for privileges and resources? How did they construct and contest gender asymmetries within the household and the larger interlinked arenas of the market, the community, and the colonial state of Nigeria? What lessons can we learn from their individual experiences?

Colonial Nigeria

Various parts of the territory that became independent Nigeria in 1960 were colonized by Great Britain at different points in time.[8] The British colonial domination of the coastal areas of modern Nigeria began with the consular rule (1849–1885), when consuls were appointed by the British government to oversee British commercial interests along the Bights of Benin and Biafra. In 1851 the British annexed Lagos, the last stronghold of the Portuguese and Spanish slave traders. In 1861 Lagos was proclaimed a Crown colony of Britain. On the eastern coast, the Oil Rivers Protectorate was established in 1885, later renamed the Niger Coast Protectorate in 1893, with the subjugation by George Goldie's National African Company (later, the Royal Niger Company [RNC]) of kingdoms, states, and communities within the area, including Bonny, Brass, Degema, Calabar, Benin, Opobo, Itshekiri, Warri, Lokoja, Aboh, and Onitsha. Consular and company rule ended here when the administration of the protectorate was transferred to the Colonial Office in 1899. In 1900 the territory was renamed the Protectorate of Southern Nigeria. Some parts of northern Nigeria were secured by the RNC through treaties and military campaigns between 1894 and 1899. In 1900 the British government declared the Protectorate of Northern Nigeria over the territories and placed Frederick Lugard in charge of it. By 1903 Lugard had succeeded in conquering the rest of the polities in the north, including Bornu and the Sokoto Caliphate. With successful military campaigns against Yoruba states, the western areas and Lagos became the Colony and Protectorate of Lagos in 1906, and later the Colony and Protectorate of Southern Nigeria, with the addition of the Protectorate of Southern Nigeria. In 1914 the two administrations of Northern and Southern Nigeria were amalgamated and the whole territory that later became Nigeria was called the Colony and Protectorate of Nigeria, with Lugard as the governor and Lagos the headquarters. Since then, Lagos has occupied a unique status in the history of Nigeria as a leading commercial and administrative capital in the nineteenth century, the most important city in twentieth-century black Africa, and Nigeria's federal capital and unrivaled industrial and business hub.

The British colonial system of indirect rule entailed the deposition and deportation of some powerful local rulers and the appointment of and collaboration with the more malleable ones. It had a transformative impact on the indigenous sociopolitical structures and institutions, and in most places it was a radical departure from the indigenous forms of government. In addition to the new political system and new laws and courts that were dominated by men, colonialism introduced a new monetary system—British coins and paper money—that facilitated growth in the internal market, taxation, land alienation and commercialization, new technologies, and improved transportation in the form of railways and roads suitable for motorized vehicles, bicycles, ports and ships, and other social amenities. Colonialism led to the expansion of Christianity and Islam; the creation of formal schools run by missionaries and the colonial government that increased literacy and multilingualism among Nigerians; increased urbanization and rural-urban migration; and an increased number of European trading firms with special privileges, including banking monopoly. It resulted in the integration of Nigeria into the global capitalist system as a producer of agricultural produce and minerals and as a consumer of European-manufactured goods, as well as the expansion of commerce and the indigenous capitalist class.

Colonial policies, institutions, and technological innovations had complex and differential impacts on Nigerians. In particular, they had far-reaching and ambivalent consequences for women and their sociopolitical roles and economic activities. While some of the innovations were restrictive and undermined women's political and economic independence, others offered them new opportunities to improve their status. The period of the two world wars and the global depression was characterized by increased hardships, alienation, exploitation, and racial discrimination and consequently escalated Nigerian resistance to colonial domination. Price-control measures and the restriction of the sale of foodstuffs or their confiscation by colonial officers and their agents dealt direct blows to the economic independence of Nigerian women and were therefore resisted by them.[9] Similarly, post–World War II marketing boards, which fixed a flat scale of produce prices and issued licenses to their agents, mainly large foreign firms with male local representatives in towns and markets, adversely affected women. The marketplace, which served different functions as a place to buy and sell, socialize, disseminate information, and carry out ritual performances, had been the domain of southern Nigerian women. However, with the construction of new markets and stalls, especially in the emerging cities and towns, and the appointment by the local government of male officials who served as market masters, women began to lose their control over the market. Although both foreign and indigenous male traders displaced many of them, some female traders acquired enough capital through their entrepreneurial skills to purchase or rent stalls.

Emphasis on cash crop production increased women's workload without commensurate rewards. For instance, among the Igbo and Yoruba, men owned palm fruit and its oil, while their wives played a dominant role in processing and marketing the produce. Gloria Chuku and Susan M. Martin have demonstrated how the rise in the production of palm oil and kernels, which belonged to women, took much of their time away from food production and other economic activities.[10] In the cocoa-producing areas of the Western Region, women put in 265 workdays, compared to men's 221 days, yet the cocoa belonged to men. Due to the large amount of time women allocated to cocoa production and the poor remuneration they received for it, in the 1940s Ijebu women abandoned the cocoa industry and served as porters for more-rewarding activities such as *gari* (cassava flour) production and the kola nut trade.[11] Except in the world war years from 1914 to the 1940s, when indigenous crafts and industries flourished, colonialism led to a decline in the indigenous industrial production associated with women, such as salt production, cloth weaving, pottery, soapmaking, basketry, and mat weaving. In addition to flooding Nigerian markets with European-manufactured substitutes and, later, locally manufactured goods that affected local consumption patterns, the increase in formal education and access to more-remunerative occupations also contributed to the decline in these indigenous industries. For instance, with time, Nigerians realized that enamelware, metal pots, and plastic objects were more durable than pottery and baskets.

However, *Pax Britannica* and the establishment of law and order enabled more women to take advantage of the established security and freedom of movement as they pursued their economic activities. Improvement in modes of transportation enabled women to travel widely and to convey their trade goods from far and near markets. Throughout the colonial period, trading remained the most important and remunerative economic activity for Nigerian women. Although most women remained petty traders, buying and selling foodstuffs and other goods with marginal profits, those who were more enterprising and well positioned took advantage of their financial base and familial ties and support, as well as credit lines advanced to them by foreign trading firms, to expand or launch their businesses in imported and indigenous textiles, kola nuts, palm produce, gari, coral beads and ivory ornaments, cooked food, and imported commodities.[12] The discussion that follows focuses on the entrepreneurial activities of Muslim Hausa women of northern Nigeria, Igbo women in the southeast, and Yoruba women in the west. These women continued to play important roles in the political economy of colonial Nigeria as farmers, food processors, traders, and skilled craftswomen. While delicately navigating acceptable cultural and religious codes of behavior and inhibitions, as well as familial responsibilities, and also taking into consideration their skills and education, their finances, and new techniques, these women successfully responded and adapted to the new opportunities and technologies unleashed by colonialism.

Muslim Hausa Female Entrepreneurs

Hausa women of colonial northern Nigeria were actively involved in both the commodity-based export colonial economy and the rural economy of food production. Their activities ranged from harvesting, pounding, threshing, winnowing, cleaning, and bagging export products to processing and storing foodstuffs and cooking and selling food. M. G. Smith notes that while all the 421 women he enumerates in his 1949–1950 study of Zaria had at least one income-generating activity, some engaged in four to five in addition to their responsibilities as wives and mothers.[13] In fact, as Emmy B. Simmons states, just as "it is socially unrespectable [for a Hausa woman] not to have an occupation . . . it is rare . . . to find a rural woman who has never set up production in some food-processing enterprise."[14] Polly Hill's studies of Batagarawa and Kano show that virtually all Hausa women worked. Their economic activities included embroidering, knitting and sewing, plaiting hair, spinning raw cotton into thread, farming, and trading. Some engaged in shelling beans for traders or grinding and pounding grain for pay. It has been noted that all Hausa women engaged in trade and that "the wives of rich men . . . [were] those most likely to flourish."[15] In Batagarawa "the wives of poorer farmers [were] as apt to participate in [house] trade as those of richer farmers."[16] However, the nature and degree of the economic activity of a Hausa woman depended on her community, household, class, age, and marital status. For instance, while poor rural women could engage in different kinds of agricultural activities, helping their husbands for a reward in cash or produce, royal women and wives of wealthy men, who were usually secluded, often engaged in entrepreneurial activities within the confines of their homes or compounds.

Ideologically and spatially, Muslim women were restricted through the practice of purdah (wife seclusion). However, whereas married women's mobility was restricted by purdah, children and older women, especially widows and divorcées, were not subjected to such religious and cultural injunctions. Thus, Muslim Hausa women were able to circumvent purdah and remain economically active by exercising control over the allocation of children's time and labor.[17] Through their children and older women of a certain status, Muslim women gained access to the market and engaged in what Hill refers to as "hidden trade" or "house-trade."[18] Hill notes that Batagarawa farmer-traders, known as *kwarami*, obtained their supplies from farmers and markets outside the town but entrusted most of the retailing of those goods to their secluded wives, who conducted their transactions at home through the agency of children. These secluded women were free to raise or lower the price they charged, and also to grant credit without their husbands' permission. Any profit made above the market or agreed price belonged to them. Only a small number of women sold produce (grains, groundnuts, and cowpeas) on behalf of their husbands for some commission.

Most Hausa women engaged in house trade on their own, using their own money to buy from either their husbands or relatives and other farmers and managing the sale. According to Hill, about two-thirds of Batagarawa women engaged in house trading on their own account.[19] More than 30 percent prepared cooked food for sale, the most popular being groundnut oil and its by-product *kulikuli*; millet and sorghum porridge (*fura*); various types of cakes made of grain, beans, or tiger-nut flour; roasted groundnuts; locust-bean cakes (*daddawa*); boiled cassava; rice porridge (*tuwo*); and guinea corn gruel (*koko*). Others engaged in retail trade in essential condiments and spices such as salt, natron, and pepper; in vegetables (such as dried baobab leaves); kola nuts; and sour milk supplied by Fulani pastoralists. It is important to note that the wives of Fulani pastoralists, whether settled or transhumant, were not secluded. They processed and sold milk and butter inside and outside the marketplace. Mary F. Smith notes that the mother of Baba of Karo produced millet balls, bean cakes, groundnut cakes, roasted salted groundnuts, and groundnut oil entirely for sale at her house or through children at a nearby marketplace.[20]

The demand for cooked and processed foodstuffs was high in Hausa society because of people's domestic consumption patterns, in which the typical family bought at least one meal or snack daily to supplement family-prepared meals. In fact, most men and children, who spent more time outside the home, ate one meal at home but otherwise relied on purchased cooked food or snacks. These eating patterns guaranteed a market for prepared foodstuffs. Thus, whether there was a nearby marketplace or not, a great part of food consumed by a household consisted of prepared foods bought from other houses. Even when wives prepared food for sale, they usually required their husbands to pay for any portion fed to their family.

The practicality of purdah varied according to the economic circumstances of the Hausa families. For example, Hajiya Asabe, who lived a life of seclusion in her husband's compound in Kano in the early 1900s, turned to a relatively autonomous life without supervision in order to engage in more income-generating activities when they relocated to the Kaduna suburb in the 1920s.[21] Kaduna was established in 1912 as a colonial military and administrative headquarters, as well as a railway and commercial town, a unique status that made it attractive. Asabe and her husband were among the earliest Kano Hausa to settle in Kaduna. To supplement her husband's income, Asabe turned to midwifery and ritual services and the selling of henna and kola. By diversifying her income-generating activities, Asabe became a wealthy woman. When her husband died, she inherited his compound and rented out some portions. She was able to sponsor her own pilgrimage to Mecca three times and her daughter's once. She sent her daughter to a primary school and arranged her marriage at the age of thirteen. As an independent, wealthy woman, Asabe negotiated a more advantageous second marriage for herself.

Colonialism brought increased migration and the concentration of large and mixed populations in urban centers. It created new job opportunities for men. Many Hausa women accompanied their husbands to the new centers of administration, employment, and markets. However, the Islamic practice of purdah, which was reinforced by colonial patriarchal ideology, did not extend similar job opportunities to Hausa women. Part of the problem was that Hausa women and girls had limited access to formal education and therefore could secure little employment outside their homes. They could not even engage directly in open-market trading due to religious injunctions. As a result, the important commercial activities of Hausa women were largely conducted within their local communities. There was a virtual absence of women, including those who were unmarried and nonsecluded, in older and large marketplaces such as the Kurmi market in Kano, Kaduna's Central Market, or the Katsina city market. Even in newly established markets in emerging towns such as those in *sabon gari* (strangers' quarter) areas where women had permanent stalls, they were mostly Nupe, Yoruba, and other Nigerian women. The stalls of unmarried and nonsecluded Hausa women were located within residential neighborhoods. Many of the women continued to participate in the food industry, processing, storing, cooking, and selling food. However, colonialism expanded these women's customer bases through the concentration of large populations in certain areas. For instance, Abner Cohen reports that Hausa housewives "engaged in business from behind their seclusion" in the Yoruba town of Ibadan, where one-third of them dominated retail trade in "kola, oranges, and plantain, while the remaining two-thirds [dominated] the cooking industry" of the Hausa quarters, supplying "thousands of bachelors [and] streams of strangers" and other Hausa households. "One of the most significant paradoxes," Cohen observes, was the acquisition of wealth by Hausa women who engaged in entrepreneurial activities under the "bondage of seclusion and wifehood, but [could not] do so when they [were] free as prostitutes."[22] Cohen's remarks may be questionable, but what is undeniable is that Hausa women in purdah transformed the household from an arena of unpaid labor to one of production and exchange.

Another benefit of colonialism for Muslim Hausa women was the improved means of transportation, especially for those who engaged in large-scale food processing and trade. Hausa women who processed food such as groundnut oil and cakes were able to transport them by train or lorry road to such southern cities as Lagos, Ibadan, and Enugu. They used the agency of their male or female relatives who were residing in these towns to transact their business. Some of the women relied on personal relationships they had established with Muslim and non-Muslim southern women foodstuff dealers who had visited the north and dealt with the Hausa women producers directly. Once trust and personal relationships were established between the buyers and producers or suppliers, it was no longer necessary to visit the north as frequently as in the beginning of such commercial relationships. Instead, orders of consignments were placed, goods delivered by rail or lorry, and money collected by a relative upon delivery. This group of Hausa women bulked foodstuffs from rural areas during harvest season when they were relatively cheap, stored them in their own granaries or those of their sons, and later processed or resold them when prices rose in local or urban areas. Many of these women were older, semisecluded, widowed, or unmarried and enjoyed a certain degree of spatial mobility.[23] In a period that coincided with the early colonial era, Baba of Karo informed Mary Smith that women owned granaries in order to maximize profit.[24]

Colonialism brought about the expansion of the business sector in northern Nigeria. This business expansion did open up income-generating avenues for women in seclusion. Some secluded women increased the assorted goods they sold by adding imported and locally manufactured products, such as soap, detergent, sugar, matches, cigarettes, biscuits, perfumes, cosmetics, and kerosene. Hill lists sixty-five different items sold by the secluded Hausa women she studied.[25] Other secluded and nonsecluded Hausa women diversified their income-generating activities by taking advantage of new technologies introduced during the colonial period, such as mechanical grinding mills, groundnut decorticators, oil presses, and sewing machines. These technologies increased production, usually required less labor, and saved time. For instance, some women were able to engage in small-scale soapmaking and the production of vegetable oil and plastic bags.[26] A few privileged ones were involved in international business transactions during Islamic pilgrimages to Mecca by cultivating and nurturing business connections made during such occasional trips. Jewelry, clothing materials, and religious and aesthetic objects and souvenirs were the most popular merchandise in this type of trade.

Hausa women's economic activities were carried out independently from their husbands. They raised their capital, controlled the marketing of their produce, and retained incomes generated from their economic activities. Hausa women raised the initial capital for their businesses through household allowances from husbands, their dowries, gifts from relatives and friends, and loans from rotational credit associations called *adashe* or *adashi*. Dowry items included articles of clothing, pieces of furniture, and household utensils—enamel, brass, and glass pots and bowls of different sizes; plates and cups; bedroom furniture; carved and decorated calabashes; and pieces of jewelry. These could be sold to raise the initial capital. In fact, they constituted capital, savings, and insurance or economic security, especially in times of need and in case of widowhood or divorce. They were also a measure of one's status. Since women controlled their income, they could advance loans to their husbands and recover them through any means within their power. For instance, M. G. Smith observes that any loans women made to their husbands were recoverable in court.[27] As Hill notes, "A wife's economic autonomy is often sufficient to insulate her from her husband's poverty—as shown by the examples of prominent house-traders whose husbands are notably poverty-stricken."[28]

Hausa women invested their surplus income in durable cloth, which could be resold; their own and their children's clothing; cosmetics; jewelry; household items, including cooking pots and plates, grindstones and mortars, enamel and brass bowls, glassware, modern appliances, cupboards, carpets, mattresses, pillows, and other "things of the room" (*kayandaki*); gifts for female relatives and friends; daughters' dowries (usually household furnishings, such as an assortment of cooking utensils, plates, dishes for decorative purposes, and loads of cloth); and contributions to sons' bridewealth. There were some who owned sheep, goats, and poultry as a form of investment. Hill reports that women owned two-thirds of the sheep and goats in the *gari* (town) she studied, where there were three hundred sheep and seven hundred goats.[29] A goat sold for three pounds in the mid-1960s, and a woman could own ten goats and sheep or more. As Simmons aptly notes, rather than sources of family food, these animals were considered to be stores of value and investment, a "good banking procedure" and cash savings bearing interest in the form of their offspring.[30]

In spite of the progress made as a result of colonialism and Hausa women's agency, these women faced enormous challenges and inhibitive barriers as female entrepreneurs in colonial northern Nigeria. One such challenge was the navigation of the delicate line between Islamic values and injunctions and Western innovations and modernity. Some Hausa women may have triumphed under purdah's spatial restrictions, but this practice did limit their level of social interaction and information gathering outside the home. Their restricted movement may explain the certain lack of dynamism in Hausa women's productive and distributive activities compared to those of their southern counterparts. For instance, where spatial mobility was restricted, as in the case of secluded Hausa women, new products and information on how to utilize them were slow to spread; women usually learned by observing other women within the confines of their homes.

Hausa women also faced limited financial resources. While some of the businesswomen in the south could establish certain lines of credit with large expatriate firms and later with banks, and travel overseas on the invitation of such firms, the secluded women in the north did not enjoy such opportunities and privileges. Moreover, their limited capital and trade goods, such as cooked food, were more likely to be diverted to family consumption and other needs in spite of their attempts to protect them and remain in business. These secluded women were more likely to be put out of business, even temporarily, by poor health conditions and the necessity of relying on children for their business than were southern businesswomen, who were surrounded by paid assistants and apprentices. In fact, whenever the children used by secluded women in their entrepreneurial activities were preoccupied with other responsibilities, such business ventures were threatened. For instance, Enid Schildkrout remarks that "more than any other single factor, the enrollment of children in primary school challenges the position of secluded West African Muslim women, or, perhaps, threatens the institution of purdah itself."[31] In addition to religious and cultural factors, the labor need that Hausa children, especially girls, fulfilled for secluded women may explain why they fell behind in formal educational enrollment and retention during this period and even beyond.[32] Hausa women's businesses were also threatened by stiff competition from large-scale expatriate firms and industrial plants that produced similar products, such as groundnut oil, milk, and soap, as well as by urban-centered firms of all scales and levels of technology that produced competitive products from largely imported raw materials.

Igbo Women and Entrepreneurship

The Igbo women of southeastern Nigeria have a long history of entrepreneurship dating back to the period before the European colonial conquest. While they controlled local trade in every Igbo village or community, some from certain culture zones, such as the Aboh, Aku, Aro, Oguta, Ossomari, and Onitsha, were active in long-distance commercial exchanges.[33] In many of these areas, a woman who did not know how to trade was regarded as a "senseless woman"; in fact, she was "not a woman at all."[34] In some places, men did not engage in trade until the twentieth century. For instance, it was not until the twentieth century that men from Oguta and Onitsha, who had previously regarded trade as a woman's affair, began to trade with foreign firms. Accounts of powerful Igbo women traders such as Ojobo and Okwuenu Ezeiwere of Aboh; Ikpeaku Ifeobu, Ruth Onumonu Uzoaru, and Madam Naomi of Oguta; Ezenwanyi Nnenne Mgbokwo of Arochukwu; and Omu Okwei of Ossomari, whose commercial activities extended beyond their immediate communities and spanned from the eighteenth to the early twentieth century, have been studied.[35] These women dealt mainly in slaves, palm produce, foodstuffs, and an assortment of imported goods.

While colonialism created conditions that forced the majority of Igbo women to remain in petty trade, it also unleashed new opportunities that some women exploited to evolve from petty traders into powerful merchants and middlewomen who traded directly with European merchants and expatriate firms. The involvement of these women in the export-import trade of the colonial Igbo economy required them to bulk palm oil and kernels and break bulky imported goods. They were able to successfully navigate the cultural, familial, and financial barriers and challenges amid stiff competition from Syrian, Lebanese, European, and African traders of Sierra Leonean and Brazilian descent in the major commercial centers of southeastern Nigeria, especially Onitsha and Port Harcourt. This group of women included Lucinda Okwunne, Iyaaji Nwadigwu, Nwanyiemelie Mgbogo Nwonaku, Izadi Ugboma, Eunice Abiana Nnoruka, Iyaaji Enwezor, Janet Ifeyinwa Romaine, Iyaji Akaya, and Madam Eleanor Ndalaku Brodie-Mends. These women deployed their business acumen, familial ties, and personal relationships to expand their commercial empires.

For instance, Nwanyiemelie Nwonaku, "the Triumphant Woman," was the daughter of Adiebo Eseagba of the Ofuluzo family of Umu Dei village and the wife of Ifeajunna Okwugbele of Umuasele village, both in Onitsha. She started as a petty trader in fish. Later she added palm produce, which she supplied to European traders and firms in exchange for cloth, tobacco, and matches. While she was still married to Okwugbele, Nwonaku became a female husband, marrying many wives of her own. She strategically negotiated personal companionships between her wives and European and Sierra Leonean traders and agents, a network of familial ties that provided her a competitive advantage in her business operations. As companions of important, foreign, male agents in Onitsha, Nwonaku's wives helped her cement her creditworthiness by serving as her business collateral and vital channels of information. Her two sisters served as her most reliable assistants in her trading and investment operations. By the time Nwonaku died in 1919, she had accumulated a great deal of wealth, some of which she invested in landed property, expensive cloth, and jewelry.[36]

Eleanor Ndalaku Brodie-Mends (1905–1974) was another prominent Igbo woman with a distinguished career as a merchant queen, a term referring to both her beauty and her commercial success. She was born in Onitsha of Igbo and Yoruba parentage. She later married Theophilus Dogan Brodie-Mends, an administrative officer in Nigeria who was from the then Gold Coast Colony and was honored by the British monarch in 1954 as a Member of the Order of the British Empire. They had one son, Zaccheus Eko, who became a medical doctor in the 1950s. Eleanor Brodie-Mends attended elementary school and also a training class in dressmaking and domestic science at the YWCA. She combined dressmaking with petty trading in provisions. Later she started trading in palm oil and kernels. In the 1920s she formed a trading group with two of her closest friends, Eunice Abiana Nnoruka and Janet Ifeyinwa Romaine. The name of their company was Eunice and Company. The three women became wholesale agents of John Holt in Onitsha, supplying the company with palm produce in exchange for imported goods, including tobacco and cloth. In the 1940s, Brodie-Mends and her two business partners entered into the transport sector by establishing the God Leads Man of War lorry business. Their lorries serviced major towns in Nigeria, connecting the eastern part with Lagos in the west and the Kano-Kaduna axis in the north. Brodie-Mends's business transactions took her to Lagos and Port Harcourt several times. She was a close associate of Mary Nzimiro, who dominated the Port Harcourt business circle and whose annual turnover with one of the large European trading firms ran to six figures.[37] In 1948 the two women traveled together on a business trip to England. By this time their children, Nzimiro's daughter Priscilla and Brodie-Mends's son Zaccheus, were pursuing their medical degrees in Britain. In 1953 *Venture*, the journal of John Holt and Company, described Eunice and Company as one of the largest trading partnerships in eastern Nigeria.[38]

Brodie-Mends was a leader and a spokeswoman for women traders in Onitsha. In 1956 she demonstrated her leadership skills when women in the Eastern Region protested against the introduction of a new tax system by the government led by the National Council of Nigeria and the Cameroons (NCNC). In a press release, Brodie-Mends, as the leader of the market women's association, threatened to withdraw the association's support from the NCNC for an independent candidate in the upcoming regional elections. On March 27, 1957, the Eastern House of Assembly made some concessions to appease the women through an amendment to the finance bill that increased the minimum taxable income for women and added children above sixteen years old to tax deductions.[39] Brodie-Mends remained a devotee of the NCNC.

In addition to these activities, Brodie-Mends invested in real estate. Her Venn Road residence was one of several properties she owned in various parts of Onitsha. She rented out some of her properties to local and foreign businesses and individuals, one of which was Messrs. Argeian and Melikian, an Armenian company.[40] She was also among the earliest Nigerian women in Onitsha to own a private car, and one of the first women to drive a car in that community. In the 1950s her private car was a luxurious Chevrolet. She also invested in membership in exclusive female clubs. For instance, Brodie-Mends and her two business partners belonged to the Jolly Rose Society, an association of the elite women of Onitsha. She was a philanthropist who contributed generously to the development of human capital through her scholarships and the expansion of Anglicanism in Onitsha. In recognition of her generosity, the All Saints Cathedral in Onitsha engraved her name on one of the church's individual plaques in 1952.

In the late 1950s Brodie-Mends left Onitsha for Lagos, where she continued her business activities. In 1965 the Lagos monarch invested her with the chieftaincy title of Iyalaje of Lagos. She built herself a residence near Ikorodu road and acquired other properties in the city, including a hospital for her son's medical practice. She died in Lagos on July 24, 1974. She was undoubtedly a merchant queen whose successful business career, leadership, and generosity earned her titles and public recognition. It is not surprising that she was the subject of the popular musical number "Elina nwa Mama" and was popularly called "Kpajie," a diminutive for "Kpajie Ego," in Onitsha, which meant one who had "garnered astounding wealth."

Another prominent Igbo woman entrepreneur was Eunice Abiana Nnoruka, born in the riverine town of Atani in 1902. Eunice was raised in Onitsha, where she attended the same primary schools as Brodie-Mends, her lifelong friend, and Nnamdi Azikiwe, the famous African nationalist who later became the first president of independent Nigeria. Like Brodie-Mends, Eunice trained in dressmaking and domestic science. In 1922 she married Stephen Chukwuka Nnoruka, a native of Otolo Nnewi. They had three children, of whom only one, Josephine, survived.

Eunice Nnoruka began trading as a child, picking and selling seasonal fruits early in the morning before school. When she had saved enough money, she began selling rice, buying a small bag and selling it in cups. Her industriousness was prompted by necessity, since she had to put herself through primary school and the YWCA training with minimum assistance from her family. After her training, Nnoruka began buying textile materials and making dresses. By the 1920s she had abandoned dressmaking in favor of buying and supplying palm produce to John Holt and Company in Onitsha, while building her reputation as a credible and hardworking businesswoman. It was during this period that she entered into partnership with Brodie-Mends and Romaine to form Eunice and Company. They dealt in assorted imports, including tobacco, but their main line was clothing materials. Impressed by the uncanny business acumen and entrepreneurial ingenuity of these three partners, Peter T. Bauer remarked: "I met in Onitsha three African ladies who have been in partnership as traders for twenty-five years. Two of them had been at school together and had attended Y.W.C.A. sewing classes. In their spare time they sewed, sold cloth, saved their earnings and with their savings bought palm kernels, which they sold to a European firm. Subsequently, they bought merchandise, mainly textiles, from the same firm, thus trading both in produce and in merchandise. Later, they withdrew from produce buying and began to deal exclusively in imported merchandise. Today their annual turnover exceeds £100,000."[41]

Bauer further commented on the dignified manner with which Brodie-Mends, Nnoruka, and Romaine conducted their business transactions with John Holt: "In Onitsha I witnessed a remarkable transaction in which the three partners of an African trading firm (all women) bought on credit over £9000 worth of tobacco from a European trading house; the informal elegance and dignity of the proceedings and the obvious mutual respect and confidence could not have been excelled in the most select trading circles of London and Amsterdam."[42]

In addition to serving as an agent of John Holt in Onitsha, Nnoruka also imported goods from overseas. She traveled to various parts of Nigeria on business ventures. She invested her surplus capital wisely, especially in real estate. While in her twenties, Nnoruka bought a piece of land and built the first of her many houses in Onitsha. In the 1940s she built a new residence on Moore Street in Onitsha, a Victorian-style fourteen-room mansion on spacious grounds. In 1949 she built a five-bedroom house in her ancestral home in Atani. It was one of the first private cement and pan-roof houses in that community. Nnoruka built several other houses in Onitsha. Indeed, one of her wedding presents to her daughter, Josephine, in 1953 was a two-story, lavishly furnished house located in Fegge District, Onitsha. The chairman and directors of John Holt and Company in Liverpool presented a "solid silver tea service" to Josephine as a wedding gift "in view of the Company's long connection with the firm of Eunice and Company."[43] In 1977 Nnoruka toured England on the invitation of John Holt and Company. She and her three travel companions were feted and accommodated by the company in the Atlantic Tower Hotel in Liverpool. Like other merchant princesses, Nnoruka sent her daughter to study in England in the 1950s. She trained her younger brothers, arranged and financed their marriages, and also helped raise their children. She was a pillar of support to her six grandchildren.

Nnoruka contributed greatly to the construction and establishment of All Saints' School (later Premier Primary School) in Onitsha. In 1952 her name was inscribed on a plaque in All Saints' Cathedral in Onitsha in recognition of her contributions to the church. One of the earliest members of the National Council of Women's Societies in Onitsha, Nnoruka was appointed a life member in 1980 in recognition of her dedicated service to the society over the past decades.[44] Nnoruka was also patron of the Onitsha Festival of Arts and leader of Otu-Umu-Otu, an association of persons born or bred in Otu (downtown) Onitsha. She bore the agnomen "Ogbatuluenyi" (one who bagged an elephant) in recognition of her stature and achievements. She died on March 19, 1990, as an accomplished businesswoman and a distinguished philanthropist.

Yoruba Women Traders and Entrepreneurs

Yoruba women traded in multiple ways and at various levels during the colonial period. Age, family condition, and capital were key determining factors. While some engaged in local trade within a given market or local area by selling farm produce, processed foodstuffs, or small manufactured goods, others hawked their wares on the streets or sold from their homes or rented shops. There were others who visited a cluster of rural markets to buy and sell goods, as well as those who operated as intermediaries, middle women, and wholesalers, going either to farms and small markets to accumulate farm produce and craft objects for city markets or to ports to export goods and distribute imported manufactured goods to middlemen and retailers. As examples, in 1926 in Epe, one Osenatu amassed forty bags of farina for sale at a higher price; Raliatu supplied eight bags of processed garri to her agent at Ejinrin market through a canoe man; and Musitura delivered corn flour to police barracks in 1927. Osenatu Taiwo of Ibadan was a successful government contractor, supplying bags of foodstuff to the prisons from 1914 to 1940.[45] By the 1930s Ijebu women had developed and controlled the lucrative gari business, processing and marketing the foodstuff. Similarly, in the 1930s at Dugbe market, Ibadan, women took over from men the control of the wholesale trade in yams. While some non-Ijesa yam traders were men, in Ijesa all the Ilesa traders were women, both wholesalers and retailers. A single Ilesa dealer could purchase up to eight hundred yam tubers at a time from Ijesa farmers and at village markets with cash or partial credit. Some of these Ilesa middlewomen had been in the business for over twenty years and had long-established personal relationships (*onibara*) and lines of credit from their suppliers, and these women extended lines of credit to their own customers in turn.[46]

While many of the women were described locally as petty traders, some of them accumulated hundreds of pounds through their trading activities. For instance, it was reported in 1933 that one Lagos-based elderly female petty trader had a savings of £600, plus jewelry valued at £309.[47] There were others who traded textiles, kola nuts, and other goods along the West African coast. Wholesaling of imported merchandise, including textiles, provisions, food, beverages, alcohols, cosmetics, soap, cigarettes, needles, metal and plasticwares, and baby toys, and bulking locally produced goods required significant amounts of capital and credit, as well as time, and were therefore limited to a few women.[48] For instance, in Egba and Ijebu regions, women traders accumulated food crops by buying from male farmers and then carried them to city markets for sale or sold to those with better means of transportation. This group of women traders usually gained considerable profit and economic power over male producers.

Yoruba women, who were heavily involved in the preparation and marketing of kola nuts, bought raw nuts from their husbands and the other men who owned the trees and then fermented, processed, and stored them to dry before selling to visiting Hausa traders or carrying them to northern cities, where they made more profit. Women also organized kola nut traders' associations, such as the one founded by Madam Emily Patience Fayemi of Ado-Ekiti in the 1940s, to facilitate the marketing of their kola nuts in Lagos, where they often sold to Ekiti women migrants.[49] Some of these successful kola nut traders also traded in other goods. Fo example, an Ibadan woman in the 1940s traveled to northern cities to sell kola nuts and also dealt in a wide range of textiles.[50] Some of the wealthiest women in Nigeria were cloth dealers, and Yoruba women played a prominent role in this trade. The cloth included various kinds of locally made fabrics and imported textiles such as velvets, silk, brocade, lace, and woolen and flannel wrappers.

Examples of Female Yoruba Entrepreneurs

Humuani (Humani) Alaga was born around 1907 and was the fourth child of Alfa Alaga, a Muslim cleric and trader, and Asmau Ladebo Alaga. Both parents later became prominent textile and bead dealers whose commercial activities took them to different parts of Yoruba territory, including Lagos, Ejigbo, Oshogbo, and Ogbomosho. Humuani started as an apprentice to her parents when she was very young. She and her two sisters accompanied their parents on several trading trips. Although the youngest, Humuani was virtually in control of her mother's trade by the age of fifteen, relaying accurate accounts of all daily transactions to her. In 1923, at the age of sixteen, Humuani began her own independent business, hawking textiles and other goods at the old Gbagi Market, the central market of Ibadan. At the age of eighteen, she married Sanusi Oshinusi, an Egba man.

Between 1928 and 1929 she established her own shop along Lebanon Street at a cost of one hundred pounds. She became the first woman textile trader to own a shop where the large European firms were located. In 1932 she became one of the registered customers of G. B. Ollivant, John Holt, and the United African Company (UAC) as these foreign firms established their branches in Ibadan and other inland Yoruba areas. In addition to buying and selling textiles, she advised European firms on the designs and textures for cloth in high demand by local populations in the West African region. By the mid-1930s she had become one of the most successful merchants in Ibadan, employing over ten assistants and a number of apprentices. Even though she perfected her good accounting skills, Alaga employed a bookkeeper and a secretary who helped her in interpreting business contracts and transactions. It was reported that in 1953 she had established enviable accounts with European trading companies and had over five hundred local customers to whom she advanced credit. She kept detailed accounts of her business dealings. In recognition of her business success, trustworthiness, and leadership skills, in 1934 Alaga was appointed the Iya Egbe Alaso (the leader of textile dealers) at the Gbagi Market. In this capacity she settled market-related disputes between traders and customers. She was also recognized as a community leader, especially among Muslims. As a result, cases relating to land, inheritance, and other family matters were brought to her, and she always strictly applied Islamic principles of dispute settlement to resolve them.[51]

A philanthropist who contributed in various ways to the development of Ibadan, Alaga helped many people financially, including paying for their education. She organized Quranic classes for Muslim children, as well as courses for girls interested in trading. She employed and provided accommodations for the teachers who taught those classes, collecting two shillings a month from each of the students to augment the teachers' salaries. She also taught some of the classes. Although a wealthy Muslim businesswoman with minimal education, Alaga recognized the importance of formal education. She attended adult training classes in Quranic and Western education. In 1958 she attempted to enroll one of her daughters, Musliat, in a mission grammar school, Saint Anne's School, but she was rejected by the school authority, who gave admission preference to Christian girls. Angered by this policy, Alaga called a special meeting of her Muslim women's association, the Isabatudeen Society, and mobilized the women, most of whom were illiterate traders, to raise funds to build their own secondary school for girls. Each of the women contributed nine pounds toward the school project. The Isabatudeen Girls' Grammar School in Ojoo, Ibadan, was completed in the early 1960s, and sixty-six girls, both Muslim and non-Muslim, began attending classes in January 1964. It was the first Muslim girls' secondary school in Ibadan.[52] Alaga and members of the Isabatudeen Society also built a maternity clinic in Mapo, Ibadan. She single-handedly arranged for the construction of a mosque in the Sango area of Ibadan. Alaga held landed properties in Nigeria and the United Kingdom.

She was also politically active. In 1930 she founded the Egbe Ifelodun, an association that focused on fashion and modernization of Ibadan, with other wealthy and influential women of the area. In 1938 she led the Women's Cotton Trade Union in a protest against Lebanese merchants who began retailing their merchandise at reduced prices, thereby undercutting the female dealers. The Ibadan Municipal Council investigated the matter and ordered the Lebanese traders to end the practice. In 1953 Alaga led a delegation from the Ibadan African Textile Association to Mapo Hall, the seat of the municipal government, to protest policies detrimental to textile traders, including plans to relocate Dugbe Market to a new site. She led market women, who marched barefooted and without their headgear, to Olubadan Yesufu Kobiowu's palace and gave him a three-day ultimatum to rescind the decision to relocate the market. They were successful. Alaga also led a group of female civil servants before the colonial governor in favor of equal pay for equal work. She asked why women were placed on a daily pay system while their male counterparts received monthly salaries. Mrs. Folayegbe Akintunde-Ighodalo, who later became the first woman permanent secretary in Nigeria, was among the female civil servants who met with the governor over the gender disparity in the civil service pay structure.[53] As the president of the Isabatudeen Society, Alaga helped to introduce its branches in major Yoruba towns, such as Ijebu-Ode and Abeokuta, which had over one hundred members in the late 1950s. She led the women in a protest against speculators who hiked the prices of goods, an action that earned her the description "a fearless fighter for Ibadan women traders" in 1953.[54]

Alaga was a cofounder of the National Council of Women's Societies in Ibadan in 1959, a member of the Ibadan Progressive Union, and a member of the women's wing of the Action Group, a major political party in western Nigeria. Her fund-raising and mobilization skills earned her an appointment on the Olubadan's Palace Committee. Her political activism also earned her many chieftaincy titles, including that of the Iyalaje of Ibadan. As the Iyalaje, Alaga oversaw the welfare and economic well-being of all traders in Ibadan, both women and men. She was described as "a Muminaat [Believer in Allah] who influenced women to play [an] active part in [community], state, national and international affairs."[55] In 1961 she received an award as a Member of the Order of the British Empire from the Queen of England. Alaga also held the title of Otun Iyalode of Ibadan. Humuani Alaga was no doubt a dutiful wife, a dedicated and respectful mother, an astute and successful entrepreneur, a devoted Muslim, a fearless activist, and a philanthropist.

Ayantoya of Okuku began producing palm oil in 1917 and in 1922 started preparing and selling kola nuts. As her business expanded, Ayantoya acquired palm groves and used hired labor to process palm fruits to maximize profit. She also entered into the meat market and imported alcoholic drinks. She employed women to assist her in managing her business empire as it expanded. She outlived two husbands; as a widow, her household expanded with children, grandchildren, and other dependents, whom she employed in her business and took care of, including seeing to their education. Realizing the importance of the railway, she built an iron-roofed house and a shop by the train station. She invested in horses and rode them. Karin Barber reports that the "newness of the trade in European imports [with no gender differential] gave Ayantoya an opening."[56] She also took advantage of her experience in local trade and the well-established trading networks within and around Okuku. Successful women were often demonized and branded as witches, and Ayantoya was one of those prosperous women rumored to have negative supernatural powers. As a result, her achievements were not celebrated in *oriki* (Yoruba Praise Poetry).[57] The fact that she outlived two husbands and remained an independent and wealthy widow with a large household filled with dependent people may have contributed to her demonization as a witch.

Comfort Oguntubi, born in 1910 in Ado-Ekiti, learned the arts of weaving and trading from her parents as a young girl. In the 1920s she became an itinerant trader between Ado-Ekiti and Ile-Ife. With capital accumulated over the years, in the mid-1930s she ventured into and specialized in imported textiles. By Nigeria's independence in 1960, Oguntubi had become the largest dealer in textiles in her town. She was the Iyaloja (titled market leader) of Ado-Ekiti, a title bestowed on her due to her entrepreneurial prowess and contribution to the development of the town and its market. She cofounded the Egbe Ifelodun with Alaga. She was always consulted on important issues concerning her town. Comfort Oguntubi was a major player in Ado-Ekiti politics, especially in the town's political crisis of the early 1940s.[58]

Chief Esther Bisoye Tejuoso (1916–1996) was the fourth child of Chief Josiah Ajayi Karunwi, a farmer, and Victoria Aina Karunwi (née Osoba), a trader. The Karunwi family was one of the royal families of Abeokuta. Bisoye's parents were devout Christians who believed in the value of girls' education. In the 1920s they enrolled her in local schools, including the Baptist Girls' School, Idi-Aba, and the Idi-Aba Teachers Training College. Even though Bisoye earned a teaching certificate, she never took up teaching as a career. In 1934 she married Joseph Somoye Tejuoso, who had taught her in elementary school. The couple moved to Lagos in 1937, where Somoye was employed by the Nigerian Railway. Bisoye started trading as an apprentice to her husband's relative in Lagos who dealt in imported textiles, including headgear, khaki, and shirting materials. She began trading on her own with modest capital, dealing in textiles and provisions. In 1940 Bisoye accompanied her husband when he was transferred to Zaria in northern Nigeria. In her first six years in Zaria, she devoted her time to being a housewife and mother, raising their five children. Two of the children survived to adulthood: a daughter, who later died as a student in Ireland, and a son, Adedapo Adewale, who later became a medical doctor and Osile of Oke Ona, one of the four traditional rulers of the Egba Federation.[59]

Free of childcare responsibilities, Bisoye went back to trading in the mid-1940s, dealing in local foodstuffs (tomatoes, onions, and groundnuts). She later added such imported merchandise as hardware, provisions, and cigarettes. She took advantage of her husband's employment by the railway to travel and transport her goods without cost from south to north, and she utilized his network of fellow workers to consolidate and expand her trade in imported goods and hardware. She later became an agent of the UAC, with a substantial credit line and many subagents who traded on her behalf and to whom she supplied hardware and enamelware on wholesale. In 1957 she returned to Lagos with her husband.

Her position as an agent of the UAC and her return to Lagos, the commercial hub of Nigeria, helped her to expand her business empire. The campaign for self-government and the Nigerianization of the civil service and the economy created new opportunities for Nigerians with capital, expertise, and vision. Similarly, the import substitution policy ushered in lucrative partnerships between European businessmen and Nigerians with proven records of business success and a strong financial base. With the split of the UAC in 1959, Tejuoso became a distributor for G. B. Ollivant and Vono Industry with a dealership in building materials, beds, mattresses, and cushions. Tejuoso benefited from the growing Nigerian middle-class and the presence of an expatriate community and foreign diplomats.[60]

In 1962, Tejuoso was approached by a Norwegian businessman for a joint business venture. After initially rejecting the proposal, she agreed and formed a joint venture—the Nigerian Polyurethane Company Limited—that included E. E. Eribo, a businessman from Benin. While the Norwegian became the managing director, Tejuoso served as the sales director and Eribo and her son Adedapo served as members of the board of directors. The company was located in Benin due to its proximity to rubber production sites. Production began in 1964 and included such products as mattresses, pillows, upholstery sheets, carpet underlay sponges, and foam chairs. They set up two showrooms in different parts of Lagos. In 1971 Tejuoso and her son bought out their Norwegian and Benin partners and renamed their company Teju Industries Limited, with Tejufoam as their trademark.

A loan from the Nigerian Industrial Development Bank helped mother and son to build a lucrative factory in Ilupeju, Lagos. Tejuoso personally supervised the factory workers and sales personnel. The company later maintained eighteen depots outside Lagos, strategically located in five zones of Nigeria with over two thousand employees. A woman of humble beginnings who utilized a combination of hard work, business acumen, and good public relations, Tejuoso became Nigeria's first woman industrialist and a multimillionaire. Before she was brutally assassinated at the age of eighty by a gang of four men in her residence in Surulere, Lagos, Tejuoso had diversified her commercial empire to include Tejufarms Limited, a poultry farm; Teju Investment and Property Company Limited; Avis Petroleum Company Limited, which manufactured petrochemicals; Regent Hotel, a two-star hotel in Lagos; and a partnership with Grizi Nigeria Limited for specialized furniture.[61]

Tejuoso acquired landed properties in Nigeria and abroad, including a seventeen-room mansion with tennis courts and a chapel in Surulere, Lagos. She also invested in the overseas education of her children and relatives. She mentored girls and young women in the areas of education and career choices. She deployed some of her wealth for self-adornment and the acquisition of titles that conveyed high status, such as the Lika Oloja Obinrin of Ago Oko and the Iyalaje of Egbaland in 1973. Tejuoso also invested her wealth in community development, church activities, and politics, donating generously to a number of projects. With her wealth, wisdom, independent mind, and selfless service to her community, and unencumbered by familial obligations as a respectable widow, Tejuoso was crowned the third Iyalode of Abeokuta in 1982, a title that had been vacant for fifty years, and the Iya Ijo of her church. The nationalist politics of decolonization and early years of independence helped shape Tejuoso's political outlook. While in Zaria, she actively supported the Action Group political party of Obafemi Awolowo, but upon her return to Lagos she put her time and resources into expanding her distributorship to foreign firms and manufacturing ventures. However, she was deeply involved in the chieftaincy politics of Abeokuta. She ran open houses in both Lagos and Abeokuta, extending her generosity and hospitality to her business associates and clients, women leaders, chiefs, relatives, friends, and other visitors. Tejuoso won regional and national recognition for her contributions to development.[62]

Abigasi Bolajoke Ladejobi of Oshogbo began her trading career as a petty trader. After her marriage in 1936, she started dealing in textile materials, crockery, and enamelware. In 1942 her husband was transferred to Zaria in northern Nigeria. Ladejobi moved her business to Zaria, where she continued dealing in cotton goods she obtained from two foreign trading companies. She returned to Oshogbo following the death of her husband in 1946. Ladejobi expanded her trade by adding the milling of corn and the baking of bread. The bread industry was relatively new to the Yoruba during this period, but Ladejobi was fearless in venturing into new areas of business. In order to consolidate her bakery industry and expand business in food supplies, Ladejobi applied for a loan of £1,000 from the Western Region's Production Development Board in 1952 in order to acquire three motorized corn mills and erect a building over them. The mills were needed to process and grind a large quantity of such foodstuffs as corn, guinea corn, yams, and pepper for consumers. Although Ladejobi received a loan to buy only one mill, she never gave up in her efforts to expand her food industry in Oshogbo. In 1955 when the government was planning to extend public utilities to the town, Ladejobi applied for a second loan of £3,000 to purchase an electric mill for an expanded modern bakery.[63]

Conclusion

This chapter has demonstrated how gender power relations in the home and outside it, as well as cultural traditions, religious values and injunctions, age, and class, affected the entrepreneurial activities of Nigerian women during the colonial period. Motivated by the necessity of survival, the availability of new opportunities, and a quest for self-actualization and security, Nigerian women engaged in the politics of negotiation and successfully navigated challenging circumstances in pursuit of their entrepreneurial activities. They faced familial responsibilities; cultural and religious inhibitions; limited access to capital and technology; stiff competition from European, Lebanese, Syrian, and African traders of Sierra Leonean and Brazilian descent, as well as local men; and the discriminatory practices of large trading firms and the exploitative colonial conditions in which they operated. In spite of spatial restrictions imposed on Muslim housewives, Hausa women in purdah were able to transform their homes from arenas of unpaid labor to ones of productive and distributive ventures. However, their southern counterparts, with relative freedom in spatial mobility, enjoyed the benefits of extensive social interactions and relationships, networks, and information dissemination as they built more dynamic commercial empires that extended beyond Nigeria and Africa.

Through their uncanny business acumen, entrepreneurial ingenuity, hard work, and resilience, the women discussed in this chapter carved a niche in the highly competitive colonial market and economy by becoming distinguished businesswomen. Whether literate or illiterate, Nigerian women entrepreneurs were alert and imaginative, with immense mental capacity for dealing with new commodities, making profits, managing their time effectively, and calculating the value of their goods and credit. They had effective sales techniques to woo customers and bargain over prices. What is remarkable is that the majority of these women were able to successfully combine their responsibilities as wives, mothers, and members of extended families, communities, and women's associations as they transformed their status from invisible subsistence producers and petty traders to prominent businesswomen and international merchant queens. Many of them became the breadwinners of their households and formidable agents of human capital and community development. Through strategic investment of their surplus capital, political activism, and philanthropy, they became visible and highly respected in their respective communities and beyond. Their successes helped them create new identities both in colonial Nigeria and internationally. There is no doubt that these women entrepreneurs were and will continue to serve as role models for girls and young women of their generation and generations to come.

GLORIA CHUKU is Professor and Chair of Africana Studies, Affiliate Professor of Gender and Women's Studies, and Affiliate Professor of the Language, Literacy and Culture PhD Program at the University of Maryland, Baltimore County. She is author of *Igbo Women and Economic Transformation in Southeastern Nigeria, 1900–1960*, as well as two edited volumes: *The Igbo Intellectual Tradition: Creative Conflict in African and African Diasporic Thought*, and *Ethnicities, Nationalities, and Cross-Cultural Representations in Africa and the Diaspora*.

Notes

1. Paul Lovejoy, *Caravans of Kola: The Hausa Kola Trade, 1700–1900* (Zaria, Nigeria: Ahmadu Bello University Press, 1980), 16.

2. E. Frances White, *Sierra Leone's Settler Women Traders: Women on the Afro-European Frontier* (Ann Arbor: University of Michigan Press, 1987).

3. George E. Brooks Jr., "The *Signares* of Saint-Louis and Goree: Women Entrepreneurs in Eighteenth-Century Senegal," in *Women in Africa: Studies in Social and Economic Change*, ed. Nancy J. Hafkin and Edna G. Bay, 19–44 (Stanford, CA: Stanford University Press, 1976).

4. Claire C. Robertson, "Gender and Trade Relations in Central Kenya in the Late Nineteenth Century," *International Journal of African Historical Studies* 30, no. 1 (1997): 23–47.

5. Stephen J. Rockel, "Enterprising Partners: Caravan Women in Nineteenth Century Tanzania," *Canadian Journal of African Studies* 34, no. 3 (2000): 748–78.

6. Toyin Falola, "The Yoruba Caravan System of the Nineteenth Century," *International Journal of African Historical Studies* 24, no. 1 (1991): 111–32; Niara Sudarkasa, *Where Women Work: A Study of Yoruba Women in the Marketplace and in the Home* (Ann Arbor: University of Michigan Press, 1973).

7. Gracia Clark, *African Market Women: Seven Life Stories from Ghana* (Bloomington: Indiana University Press, 2010); Gracia Clark, *Onions Are My Husband: Survival and Accumulation by West African Market Women* (Chicago: University of Chicago Press, 1994); Mary J. Osirim, *Enterprising Women in Urban Zimbabwe: Gender, Microbusiness, and Globalization* (Washington, DC: Woodrow Wilson Center Press, 2009); Bessie House-Midamba and Felix K. Ekechi, eds., *African Market Women and Economic Power: The Role of Women in African Economic Development* (Westport, CT: Greenwood, 1995); Barbara C. Lewis, "The Limitations of Group Action among Entrepreneurs: The Market Women of Abidjan, Ivory Coast," in Hafkin and Bay, *Women in Africa*, 135–56.

8. See A. I. Asiwaju, *Western Yorubaland under European Rule, 1889–1945* (London: Longman, 1976); A. E. Afigbo, *The Warrant Chiefs: Indirect Rule in Southeastern Nigeria, 1891–1929* (New York: Humanities Press, 1972); T. N. Tamuno, *The Evolution of the Nigerian State: The Southern Phase, 1898–1914* (New York: Humanities Press, 1972); R. A. Adeleye, *Power and Diplomacy in Northern Nigeria, 1804–1906* (New York: Humanities Press, 1971); and Robert Heussler, *The British in Northern Nigeria* (London: Oxford University Press, 1968).

9. Gloria Chuku, "'Crack Kernels, Crack Hitler': Export Production Drive and Igbo Women during the Second World War," in *Gendering the African Diaspora: Women, Culture, and Historical Change in the Caribbean and Nigerian Hinterland*, ed. Judith A. Byfield, LaRay Denzer, and Anthea Morrison, 219–44 (Bloomington: Indiana University Press, 2010); Judith A. Byfield, "Feeding the Troops: Abeokuta (Nigeria) and World War II," *African Economic History* 35 (2007): 77–87; Nina Emma Mba, *Nigerian Women Mobilized: Women's Political Activity in Southern Nigeria, 1900–1965* (Berkeley: University of California Press, 1982); Cheryl Johnson, "Madam Alimotu Pelewura and the Lagos Market Women," *Tarikh* 7, no. 1 (1981): 1–10; Cheryl Johnson, "Grass Roots Organizing: Women in Anticolonial Activity in Southwestern Nigeria," *African Studies Review* 25, nos. 2/3 (1982): 137–57; Wale Oyemakinde, "The Pullen Marketing Scheme: A Trial in Food Price Control in Nigeria, 1941–1947," *Journal of the Historical Society of Nigeria* 6, no. 4 (1973): 413–23.

10. Gloria Chuku, *Igbo Women and Economic Transformation in Southeastern Nigeria* (New York: Routledge, 2005); Susan M. Martin, *Palm Oil and Protest: An Economic History of the Ngwa Region, South-Eastern Nigeria, 1800–1980* (London: Cambridge University Press, 1988).

11. LaRay Denzer, "Yoruba Women: A Historiographical Study," *International Journal of African Historical Studies* 27, no. 1 (1994): 24.

12. Gloria Chuku, "Nzimiro, Mary," in *Dictionary of African Biography*, ed. Emmanuel K. Akyeampong and Henry Louis Gates Jr., 4:525–26 (Oxford: Oxford University Press, 2012); Gloria Chuku, "Okwei," in Akyeampong and Gates, *Dictionary of African Biography*,5:26–28; Chuku, *Igbo Women and Economic Transformation*; Gloria Chuku, "From Petty Traders to International Merchants: A Historical Account of the Role of Three Igbo Women of Nigeria in Trade and Commerce, 1886 to 1970," *African Economic History* 27 (1999): 1–22; Enid Schildkrout, "Dependence and Autonomy: The Economic Activities of Secluded Hausa Women in Kano, Nigeria," in *Women and Work in Africa*, ed. Edna G. Bay, 55–81 (Boulder, CO: Westview, 1982); Sudarkasa, *Where Women Work*; Felicia I. Ekejiuba, "Omu Okwei of Osomari," in *Nigerian Women in Historical Perspective*, ed. Bolanle Awe, 89–104 (Lagos, Nigeria: Sankore, 1992); Felicia I. Ekejiuba, "Omu Okwei, the Merchant Queen of Ossomari: A Biographical Sketch," *Journal of the Historical Society of Nigeria* 3, no. 4 (1967): 633–46.

13. M. G. Smith, *The Economy of Hausa Communities of Zaria*, Colonial Research Series No.16 (London: Her Majesty's Stationery Office, 1955).

14. Emmy B. Simmons, "The Small-Scale Rural Food-Processing Industry in Northern Nigeria," *Food Research Institute Studies* 14, no. 2 (1975): 155 and 158.

15. Polly Hill, *Population, Prosperity and Poverty: Rural Kano, 1900 and 1970* (London: Cambridge University Press, 1977), 173.

16. Polly Hill, *Rural Hausa: A Village and a Setting* (London: Cambridge University Press, 1972), 268.

17. Enid Schildkrout, "Hajiya Husaina: Notes on the Life History of a Hausa Woman," in *Life Histories of African Women*, ed. Patricia W. Romero, 78–98 (Amherst, NY: Humanity Books, 1988); Schildkrout, "Dependence and Autonomy"; Hill, *Rural Hausa*; Polly Hill, "Hidden Trade in Hausaland," *Man* 4, no. 3 (1969): 392–409.

18. Hill, "Hidden Trade in Hausaland."

19. Hill, *Rural Hausa*.

20. Mary F. Smith, *Baba of Karo: A Woman of the Muslim Hausa* (London: Faber and Faber, 1954), 54.

21. Catherine M. Coles, "Three Generations of Hausa Women in Kaduna, Nigeria, 1925–1985," in *Courtyards, Markets, City Streets: Urban Women in Africa*, ed. Kathleen Sheldon, 73–85 (Boulder, CO: Westview, 1996).

22. Abner Cohen, *Custom and Politics in Urban Africa: A Study of Hausa Migrants in Yoruba Towns* (Berkeley: University of California Press, 1969), 64–65.

23. Renee Pittin, "Documentation of Women's Work in Nigeria: Problems and Solutions," in *Sex Roles, Population and Development in West Africa*, ed. Christine Oppong, 25–44 (Portsmouth, NH: Heinemann, 1987).

24. M. F. Smith, *Baba of Karo*, 119.

25. Hill, "Hidden Trade in Hausaland," 400.

26. Yakubu Zakaria, "Entrepreneurs at Home: Secluded Muslim Women and Hidden Economic Activities in Northern Nigeria," *Nordic Journal of African Studies* 10, no. 1 (2001): 117–18.

27. M. G. Smith, *Economy of Hausa Communities of Zaria*, 115.

28. Hill, "Hidden Trade in Hausaland," 398.

29. Hill, *Rural Hausa*, 317–18.

30. Simmons, "Rural Food-Processing Industry," 158.

31. Schildkrout, "Dependence and Autonomy," 57.

32. Jean Boyd and Beverly Mack, *Educating Muslim Women: The West African Legacy of Nana Asma'u, 1793–1864* (Oxfordshire, UK: Interface, 2013); Jean Trevor, "Western Education and Muslim Fulani/Hausa Women in Sokoto, Northern Nigeria," in *Conflict and Harmony in Education in Tropical Africa*, ed. Godfrey Brown and Mervyn Hiskett, 247–70 (London: George Allen and Unwin, 1975); A. Babs Fafunwa, *History of Education in Nigeria* (London: George Allen and Unwin, 1974).

33. Gloria Chuku, "Nwagboka," in Akyeampong and Gates, *Dictionary of African Biography*, 4:509–11; Chuku, *Igbo Women and Economic Transformation*; Chuku, "Petty Traders to International Merchants."

34. Flora Nwapa, *Idu* (Ibadan, Nigeria: Heinemann Educational Books, 1970), 29.

35. Chuku, "Nwagboka"; Chuku, "Okwei"; Chuku, *Igbo Women and Economic Transformation*, ch. 6; Chuku, "Petty Traders to International Merchants"; Felix K. Ekechi, "Aspects of Palm Oil Trade at Oguta (Eastern Nigeria), 1900–1950," *African Economic History* 10 (1981): 41–58; Ekejiuba, "Omu Okwei, the Merchant Queen."

36. Patrick Mbajekwe, "'Landlords of Onitsha': Urban Land, Accumulation, and Debates over Custom in Colonial Eastern Nigeria, ca. 1880–1945," *International Journal of African Historical Studies* 39, no. 3 (2006): 413–39; Nkiru U. Nzegwu, *Family Matters: Feminist Concepts in African Philosophy of Culture* (Albany: State University of New York Press, 2006); Chuku, *Igbo Women and Economic Transformation*.

37. Chuku, "Nzimiro, Mary"; Chuku, *Igbo Women and Economic Transformation*; Chuku, "Petty Traders to International Merchants."

38. Correspondence with Reginald Chiedu Ofodile, writer/actor, London, UK, February 19, 2007.

39. Gloria Chuku, "Okala, Janet," in Akyeampong and Gates, *Dictionary of African Biography*, 5:12–14; Mba, *Nigerian Women Mobilized*, 102–3.

40. Mbajekwe, "'Landlords of Onitsha,'" 431.

41. Peter T. Bauer, *West African Trade: A Study of Competition, Oligopoly and Monopoly in a Changing Economy* (London: Cambridge University Press, 1954), 31.

42. Ibid., 3.

43. Correspondence with Reginald Chiedu Ofodile, writer/actor and grandson of Eunice Nnoruka, London, UK, February 19, 2007.

44. Correspondence with Reginald Chiedu Ofodile, 2007.

45. Marjorie K. McIntosh, *Yoruba Women, Work, and Social Change* (Bloomington: Indiana University Press, 2009), 153.

46. Lillian Trager, "Customers and Creditors: Variations in Economic Personalism in a Nigerian Marketing System," *Ethnology* 20 (1981): 133–46.

47. *Nigerian Daily Telegraph*, February 8, 1933, 1.

48. McIntosh, *Yoruba Women*; Susan J. Watts, "Rural Women as Food Processors and Traders: Eko Making in the Ilorin Area of Nigeria," *Journal of Developing Areas* 19 (1984): 71–82; Lillian Trager, "Market Women in the Urban Economy: The Role of Yoruba Intermediaries in a Medium-Sized City," *African Urban Notes* B, no. 2 (1975/1976): 1–9.

49. Olatunji Ojo, "More than Farmers' Wives: Yoruba Women and Cash Crop Production, c. 1920–1957," in *The Transformation of Nigeria*, ed. Adebayo Oyebade (Trenton, NJ: Africa World, 2002), 392.

50. McIntosh, *Yoruba Women*, 152.

51. Jadesola Oyewole, "Humuani's Life Is a Pride to Muslims," *Vanguard* (Nigeria), February 28, 2014; McIntosh, *Yoruba Women*; LaRay Denzer, "Alhaja Humuani Alaga (c. 1903–1993): A Tribute," *WORDOC Newsletter* (Ibadan, Nigeria) 1, no. 2 (November 1997): 8–10; LaRay

Denzer and Glenn Webb, eds., *Traders and Traders' Associations in Southwest Nigeria* (Ibadan, Nigeria: Ibadan University Press, 1990).

52. Oyewole, "Humuani's Life"; Peter B. Clarke, *West Africa and Islam: A Study of Religious Development from the 8th to the 20th Century* (London: Edward Arnold, 1982).

53. LaRay Denzer, *Folayegbe M. Akintunde-Ighodalo: A Public Life* (Ibadan, Nigeria: Sam Bookman, 2001).

54. McIntosh, *Yoruba Women*, 73, 164.

55. Oyewole, "Humuani's Life."

56. Karin Barber, *I Could Speak until Tomorrow: Oriki, Women, and the Past in a Yoruba Town* (Washington, DC: Smithsonian Institution Press, 1991), 234.

57. Karin Barber, "Going Too Far in Okuku: Some Ideas about Gender, Excess, and Political Power," in *Gender and Identity in Africa*, ed. Mechtchild Reh and G. Ludwar-Ene (Münster, Germany: Lit Verlag, 1995), 77–78.

58. Ojo, "More than Farmers' Wives," 400–401.

59. LaRay Denzer, "When Wealth Kills: The Assassinations of Three Yoruba Businesswomen, 1996," in *Nigeria's Struggle for Democracy and Good Governance*, ed. Adigun A. B. Agbaje, Larry Diamond, and Ebere Onwudiwe, 303–26 (Ibadan, Nigeria: Ibadan University Press, 2004); Omodele Karunwi, *A Woman Industrialist: A Biography of Chief (Mrs.) Bisoye Tejuoso, Yeye-Oba Oke-Ona Egba, 3rd Iyalode of Egbaland* (Lagos, Nigeria: Cow-Lad Enterprises, Nigeria Limited, 1991); Adedapo A. Tejuoso, *The Ultimate Honour* (Lagos, Nigeria: Nelson, 1989).

60. McIntosh, *Yoruba Women*; Denzer, "When Wealth Kills"; Karunwi, *Woman Industrialist*.

61. Karunwi, *Woman Industrialist*; Tejuoso, *Ultimate Honour*.

62. Denzer, "When Wealth Kills"; Karunwi, *Woman Industrialist*; Tejuoso, *Ultimate Honour*.

63. McIntosh, *Yoruba Women*, 163–64.

Bibliography

Adeleye, R. A. *Power and Diplomacy in Northern Nigeria, 1804–1906*. New York: Humanities Press, 1971.

Afigbo, A. E. *The Warrant Chiefs: Indirect Rule in Southeastern Nigeria, 1891–1929*. New York: Humanities Press, 1972.

Asiwaju, A. I. *Western Yorubaland under European Rule, 1889–1945*. London: Longman, 1976.

Barber, K. "Going Too Far in Okuku: Some Ideas about Gender, Excess, and Political Power." In *Gender and Identity in Africa*, edited by Mechtchild Reh and G. Ludwar-Ene, 71–83. Münster, Germany: Lit Verlag, 1995.

———. *I Could Speak until Tomorrow: Oriki, Women, and the Past in a Yoruba Town*. Washington, DC: Smithsonian Institution Press, 1991.

Barkow, J. H. "Hausa Women and Islam." *Canadian Journal of African Studies* 6, no. 2 (1972): 317–28.

Barnes, S. T. "Gender and the Politics of Support and Protection in Precolonial West Africa." In *Queens, Queen Mothers, Priestesses, and Power: Case Studies in African Gender*, edited by F. E. S. Kaplan, 1–18. New York: New York Academy of Sciences, 1997.

Bauer, P. T. *West African Trade: A Study of Competition, Oligopoly and Monopoly in a Changing Economy*. London: Cambridge University Press, 1954.

Biobaku, S. "Madam Tinubu." In *Eminent Nigerians of the Nineteenth Century*, edited by K. O. Dike, 33–41. Cambridge: Cambridge University Press, 1960.

Boyd, J., and B. Mack. *Educating Muslim Women: The West African Legacy of Nana Asma'u, 1793–1864*. Oxfordshire, UK: Interface, 2013.

Brooks, G. E., Jr. "The *Signares* of Saint-Louis and Goree: Women Entrepreneurs in Eighteenth-Century Senegal." In *Women in Africa: Studies in Social and Economic Change*, edited by Nancy J. Hafkin and Edna G. Bay, 19–44. Stanford, CA: Stanford University Press, 1976.

Byfield, J. A. "Feeding the Troops: Abeokuta (Nigeria) and World War II." *African Economic History* 35 (2007): 77–87.

Callaway, B. *Muslim Hausa Women in Nigeria: Tradition and Change*. Syracuse, NY: Syracuse University Press, 1987.

Chuku, Gloria. "'Crack Kernels, Crack Hitler': Export Production Drive and Igbo Women during the Second World War." In *Gendering the African Diaspora: Women, Culture, and Historical Change in the Caribbean and Nigerian Hinterland*, edited by J. A. Byfield, L. Denzer, and A. Morrison, 219–44. Bloomington: Indiana University Press, 2010.

——. "From Petty Traders to International Merchants: A Historical Account of the Role of Three Igbo Women of Nigeria in Trade and Commerce, 1886 to 1970." *African Economic History* 27 (1999): 1–22.

——. *Igbo Women and Economic Transformation in Southeastern Nigeria*. New York: Routledge, 2005.

——. "Igbo Women and Political Participation in Nigeria, 1800s–2005." *International Journal of African Historical Studies* 42, no. 1 (2009): 81–103.

——."Nwagboka." In *Dictionary of African Biography*, edited by E. K. Akyeampong and H. L. Gates Jr., 4:509–11. Oxford: Oxford University Press, 2012.

——. "Nzimiro, Mary." In *Dictionary of African Biography*, edited by E. K. Akyeampong and H. L. Gates Jr., 4:525–26. Oxford: Oxford University Press, 2012.

——. "Okala, Janet." In *Dictionary of African Biography*, edited by E. K. Akyeampong and H. L. Gates Jr., 5:12–14. Oxford: Oxford University Press, 2012.

——. "Okwei." In *Dictionary of African Biography*, edited by E. K. Akyeampong and H. L. Gates Jr., 5:26–28. Oxford: Oxford University Press, 2012.

Clark, G. *African Market Women: Seven Life Stories from Ghana*. Bloomington: Indiana University Press, 2010.

——. *Onions Are My Husband: Survival and Accumulation by West African Market Women*. Chicago: University of Chicago Press, 1994.

Clarke, P. B. *West Africa and Islam: A Study of Religious Development from the 8th to the 20th Century*. London: Edward Arnold, 1982.

Cohen, A. *Custom and Politics in Urban Africa: A Study of Hausa Migrants in Yoruba Towns*. Berkeley: University of California Press, 1969.

Coles, C. M. "Three Generations of Hausa Women in Kaduna, Nigeria, 1925–1985." In *Courtyards, Markets, City Streets: Urban Women in Africa*, edited by K. Sheldon, 73–102. Boulder, CO: Westview, 1996.

Coles, C., and B. Mack, eds. *Hausa Women in the Twentieth Century*. Madison: University of Wisconsin Press, 1991.

Denzer, L. "Alhaja Humuani Alaga (c. 1903–1993): A Tribute." *WORDOC Newsletter* (Ibadan, Nigeria) 1, no. 2 (November 1997): 8–10.

———. *Folayegbe M. Akintunde-Ighodalo: A Public Life.* Ibadan, Nigeria: Sam Bookman, 2001.

———. "When Wealth Kills: The Assassinations of Three Yoruba Businesswomen, 1996." In *Nigeria's Struggle for Democracy and Good Governance*, edited by A. A. B. Agbaje, L. Diamond, and E. Onwudiwe, 303–26. Ibadan, Nigeria: Ibadan University Press, 2004.

———. "Yoruba Women: A Historiographical Study." *International Journal of African Historical Studies* 27, no. 1 (1994): 1–39.

Denzer, L., and G. Webb, eds. *Traders and Traders' Associations in Southwest Nigeria.* Ibadan, Nigeria: Ibadan University Press, 1990.

Ekechi, F. K. "Aspects of Palm Oil Trade at Oguta (Eastern Nigeria), 1900–1950." *African Economic History* 10 (1981): 41–58.

Ekejiuba, F. I. "Omu Okwei of Osomari." In *Nigerian Women in Historical Perspective*, edited by B. Awe, 89–104. Lagos, Nigeria: Sankore, 1992.

———. "Omu Okwei, the Merchant Queen of Ossomari: A Biographical Sketch." *Journal of the Historical Society of Nigeria* 3, no. 4 (1967): 633–46.

Fafunwa, A. B. *History of Education in Nigeria.* London: George Allen and Unwin, 1974.

Falola, T. "The Yoruba Caravan System of the Nineteenth Century." *International Journal of African Historical Studies* 24, no. 1 (1991): 111–32.

Frobenius, L. *The Voice of Africa.* Vol. 1. London: Hutchinson, 1913.

Funeral Program of Chief Eleanor Brodie-Mends, 1974, obtained from family friend.

Funeral Program of Mrs. Eunice Abiana Nnoruka (née Osadebe), 1990, obtained from a family member.

Henderson, H. K. "Onitsha Women: The Traditional Context for Political Power." In *Queens, Queen Mothers, Priestesses, and Power: Case Studies in African Gender*, edited by F. E. S. Kaplan, 215–43. New York: New York Academy of Sciences, 1997.

Heussler, R. *The British in Northern Nigeria.* London: Oxford University Press, 1968.

Hill, P. "Hidden Trade in Hausaland." *Man* 4, no. 3 (1969): 392–409.

———. *Population, Prosperity and Poverty: Rural Kano, 1900 and 1970.* London: Cambridge University Press, 1977.

———. *Rural Hausa: A Village and a Setting.* London: Cambridge University Press, 1972.

Hodder, B. W., and U. I. Ukwu. *Markets in West Africa: Studies of Markets and Trade among the Yoruba and Ibo.* Ibadan, Nigeria: Ibadan University Press, 1969.

House-Midamba, B., and F. K. Ekechi, eds. *African Market Women and Economic Power: The Role of Women in African Economic Development.* Westport, CT: Greenwood, 1995.

Johnson, C. "Grass Roots Organizing: Women in Anticolonial Activity in Southwestern Nigeria." *African Studies Review* 25, nos. 2/3 (1982): 137–57.

———. "Madam Alimotu Pelewura and the Lagos Market Women." *Tarikh* 7, no. 1 (1981): 1–10.

Johnson, E. J. "Marketwomen and Capitalist Adaptation: A Case Study in Rural Benin, Nigeria." PhD diss., Michigan State University, 1973.

Karunwi, O. *A Woman Industrialist: A Biography of Chief (Mrs.) Bisoye Tejuoso, Yeye-Oba Oke-Ona Egba, 3rd Iyalode of Egbaland.* Lagos, Nigeria: Cow-Lad Enterprises, Nigeria Limited, 1991.

Lewis, B. C. "The Limitations of Group Action among Entrepreneurs: The Market Women of Abidjan, Ivory Coast." In *Women in Africa: Studies in Social and Economic Change*, edited by N. J. Hafkin and E. G. Bay, 135–56. Stanford, CA: Stanford University Press, 1976.

Lovejoy, P. E. *Caravans of Kola: The Hausa Kola Trade, 1700–1900.* Zaria, Nigeria: Ahmadu Bello University Press, 1980.
———. "Concubinage and the Status of Women Slaves in Early Colonial Northern Nigeria." *Journal of African History* 29, no. 2 (1988): 245–66.
Mack, B. "Hajiya Ma'daki: A Royal Hausa Woman." In *Life Histories of African Women*, edited by Patricia W. Romero, 47–77. Amherst, NY: Humanity Books, 1988.
Mann, K. "Women, Landed Property, and the Accumulation of Wealth in Early Colonial Lagos." *Signs* 16, no. 4 (1991): 682–706.
Martin, S. M. *Palm Oil and Protest: An Economic History of the Ngwa Region, South-Eastern Nigeria, 1800–1980.* London: Cambridge University Press, 1988.
Mba, N. E. *Nigerian Women Mobilized: Women's Political Activity in Southern Nigeria, 1900–1965.* Berkeley: University of California Press, 1982.
Mbajekwe, P. "'Landlords of Onitsha': Urban Land, Accumulation, and Debates over Custom in Colonial Eastern Nigeria, ca. 1880–1945." *International Journal of African Historical Studies* 39, no. 3 (2006): 413–39.
McIntosh, M. K. *Yoruba Women, Work, and Social Change.* Bloomington: Indiana University Press, 2009.
Nwapa, F. *Idu.* Ibadan, Nigeria: Heinemann Educational Books, 1970.
Nzegwu, N. U. *Family Matters: Feminist Concepts in African Philosophy of Culture.* Albany: State University of New York Press, 2006.
Ojo, O. "More than Farmers' Wives: Yoruba Women and Cash Crop Production, c. 1920–1957." In *The Transformation of Nigeria*, edited by Adebayo Oyebade, 383–404. Trenton, NJ: Africa World Press, 2002.
Osirim, M. J. *Enterprising Women in Urban Zimbabwe: Gender, Microbusiness, and Globalization.* Washington, DC: Woodrow Wilson Center Press, 2009.
Oyemakinde, W. "The Pullen Marketing Scheme: A Trial in Food Price Control in Nigeria, 1941–1947." *Journal of the Historical Society of Nigeria* 6, no. 4 (1973): 413–23.
Oyewole, J. "Humuani's Life Is a Pride to Muslims." *Vanguard* (Nigeria), February 28, 2014.
Pittin, R. "Documentation of Women's Work in Nigeria: Problems and Solutions." In *Sex Roles, Population and Development in West Africa*, edited by C. Oppong, 25–44. Portsmouth, NH: Heinemann, 1987.
Robertson, C. C. "Gender and Trade Relations in Central Kenya in the Late Nineteenth Century." *International Journal of African Historical Studies* 30, no. 1 (1997): 23–47.
Robson, E. "Sub-Saharan Africa: Hausa Societies." In *Encyclopedia of Women and Islamic Culture: Family, Law and Politics*, edited by Suad Joseph, 2:135–37. Leiden, Netherlands: Brill Academic, 2005.
Rockel, S. J. "Enterprising Partners: Caravan Women in Nineteenth Century Tanzania." *Canadian Journal of African Studies* 34, no. 3 (2000): 748–78.
Ronald, C. "Oedipus Rex and Regina: The Queen Mother in Africa." *Africa* 47, no. 1 (1977): 14–30.
Schildkrout, E. "Dependence and Autonomy: The Economic Activities of Secluded Hausa Women in Kano, Nigeria." In *Women and Work in Africa*, edited by Edna G. Bay, 55–81. Boulder, CO: Westview, 1982.
———. "Hajiya Husaina: Notes on the Life History of a Hausa Woman." In *Life Histories of African Women*, edited by Patricia W. Romero, 78–98. Amherst, NY: Humanity Books, 1988.
Simmons, E. B. "The Small-Scale Rural Food-Processing Industry in Northern Nigeria." *Food Research Institute Studies* 14, no. 2 (1975): 147–61.

Smith, M. F. *Baba of Karo: A Woman of the Muslim Hausa*. London: Faber and Faber, 1954.

Smith, M. G. *The Economy of Hausa Communities of Zaria*. Colonial Research Series No. 16. London: Her Majesty's Stationery Office, 1955.

Sudarkasa, N. *Where Women Work: A Study of Yoruba Women in the Marketplace and in the Home*. Ann Arbor: University of Michigan Press, 1973.

Tamuno, T. N. *The Evolution of the Nigerian State: The Southern Phase, 1898–1914*. New York: Humanities Press, 1972.

Tejuoso, A. A. *The Ultimate Honour*. Lagos, Nigeria: Nelson, 1989.

Trager, L. "Customers and Creditors: Variations in Economic Personalism in a Nigerian Marketing System." *Ethnology* 20, no. 2 (1981): 133–46.

———. "Market Women in the Urban Economy: The Role of Yoruba Intermediaries in a Medium-Sized City." *African Urban Notes* B, no. 2 (1975/1976): 1–9.

Trevor, J. "Western Education and Muslim Fulani/Hausa Women in Sokoto, Northern Nigeria." In *Conflict and Harmony in Education in Tropical Africa*, edited by Godfrey Brown and Mervyn Hiskett, 247–70. London: George Allen and Unwin, 1975.

VerEecke, C. "Muslim Women Traders of Northern Nigeria: Perspectives from the City of Yola." *Ethnology* 32, no. 3 (1993): 217–36.

Watts, S. J. "Rural Women as Food Processors and Traders: *Eko* Making in the Ilorin Area of Nigeria." *Journal of Developing Areas* 19 (1984): 71–82.

White, E. F. *Sierra Leone's Settler Women Traders: Women on the Afro-European Frontier*. Ann Arbor: University of Michigan Press, 1987.

Williams, P. "Impact of Islam on Women in Hausaland and Northern Nigeria." In *The Foundations of Nigeria: Essays in Honor of Toyin Falola*, edited by Adebayo Oyebade, 591–621. Trenton, NJ: Africa World, 2003.

Yemitan, O. *Madame Tinubu: Merchant and King-Maker*. Ibadan, Nigeria: Ibadan University Press, 1987.

Zakaria, Y. "Entrepreneurs at Home: Secluded Muslim Women and Hidden Economic Activities in Northern Nigeria." *Nordic Journal of African Studies* 10, no. 1 (2001): 107–23.

4 From Artisanal Brew to a Booming Industry

An Economic History of Pito Brewing among Northern Ghanaian Migrant Women in Southern Ghana

Isidore Lobnibe

SINCE PRECOLONIAL TIMES African peasants have produced a myriad of alcoholic beverages. These drinks are made from either grains or root trees, and they aid agricultural production or mark ritual and celebratory occasions.[1] With the consolidation of the cash economy during the colonial period, African rural women responded to nascent commercial opportunities by purchasing grains on their own to brew beer for sale in village markets and urban centers instead of having to rely on household elders to supply them with the materials.[2] The historical and sociological literature on drinking and alcohol production in Africa has shed considerable light on artisanal brewing and its ritual implications across time and space. In rural West Africa, for example, highly ritualized agricultural cycles have been shown to correspond with the making of beer by peasant households to pacify Earthshrines during the farming season or to celebrate and thank the ancestors after a good harvest.[3]

As rural people started to migrate to the cities and drinking became commercialized, scholars turned to analyzing the effects of the commercialization of alcohol on traditional life.[4] In southern and eastern Africa, earlier ethnographic accounts from the school that viewed alcohol as a disruptive social force emphasized intergenerational and gender conflicts that resulted from commoditized drink; the disrespect of elders by the young and moral degeneration were blamed on the rise of female-headed households and the evils of urban drinking.[5] A later body of work takes a more positive approach by highlighting the new income-generating opportunities created by the commercialization of women's brewing activities; this approach allows brewing to be seen more in terms of female economic empowerment and entrepreneurship.[6]

In present-day Ghana there is also a rich body of literature on the changing drinking patterns and modalities[7] and the ways in which locally produced brews and imported European-style beer or liquor interact in ritual or daily social life.[8] Among the Akan of southern Ghana, Emmanuel Akyeampong not only presents alcohol as a metaphor for social differentiation and hierarchies in pre-colonial Akan society but also shows that the flow of liquor was the center around which chiefly Akan protocol revolved.[9] According to him, although "young men (commoners) and women tapped and served chiefs and the elders liquor or palm wine, they were often excluded from drinking because of 'strict sumptuary laws.' "[10] Only in the colonial and postcolonial periods did ordinary people's increased access to alcoholic drink emerge, as a new culture that permitted social drinking interpreted and mediated the social experiences of new urban migrants and their entry in cosmopolitan settings.[11]

The Ghanaian historiography on alcohol production has erected a glass wall between the former southern colony, where earlier contact with imported European liquor occurred, and the Northern Territories of the British protectorates, where the colonial authorities prohibited the import and consumption of liquor during the interwar period.[12] There is a need to break this glass wall if we are to understand the dynamic interactions between regional indigenous drinks and the contemporary cultural dialogue they engender. For instance, the bifurcated approach to the social history of drinking in Ghana has created a gap in our understanding of the commercialization of sorghum beer, thereby glossing over the important contributions of the actors behind the spread of the staple savanna drink to major cities.

In Ghana the past few decades have indeed witnessed the proliferation of *pito* (sorghum beer) bars in major cities;[13] these bars are typically owned and operated by northern immigrant women, and they bear the name of the ethnicity of the brewer or that of the village or town from which the brewer hails—for example, Nandom Base, Kaleo Base, Konkomba Base, or Damongo Base—or they refer to a historical event. Although in Ghana people classify pito based on the ethnicity of the brewer,[14] the quality and taste of the drink, which varies from sweet to very sour, are not necessarily determined by the ethnicity of the brewer, as each brewer differs slightly in how long he or she boils the brew on the fireplace and in the wort extraction and fermentation techniques used.[15] Scientific analysis of the drink has detected the presence of lactic acid, sugars, amino acids, about 5 percent alcohol, and some vitamins and proteins.[16] The owners range from small-scale brewers who employ young girls to carry the drinks to customers, to the more established brewers who own large, established bars and taverns powered by electricity.

Brewing pito can be a laborious process. To prepare the malt, the grains are soaked in water and covered for six to seven days to allow the sprout to germinate and grow under careful observation.[17] The actual brewing entails grinding the malt and fetching large quantities of water and firewood. Next, a roughly ground flour is mixed with a large amount of water. This is boiled for about an hour and left overnight to settle in order for the liquid beer to be separated from the wort. On the second day the beer water is boiled for several hours into first-grade beer, ready for fermentation. The brew is then transferred to cooling jars before yeast is applied. When ready for consumption, pito has a golden-yellow to dark-brown color. Until recently, the drink was stored in earthenware pots and served fresh in calabashes.

Because of the profits derived from urban pito brewing, generations of northern Ghanaian women have taken to the commercial brewing of it as a means by which to supplement their incomes and contribute to the family upkeep.[18] For the single mother or widow struggling to raise or educate her children in the village, migrating to an urban area or city to take up brewing is an escape route from oppressive patriarchal homes. Evidence suggests that Dagara and Konkomba women from the Upper West and Northern Regions, respectively, have long dominated the urban commercial pito industry.[19] Their monopoly can partially be attributed to the fact that women from these ethnic groups are often exposed earlier in life to brewing for large farming groups and beer parties. As major producers of cereal crops,[20] the women of these ethnic groups are expected to brew beer to entertain the reciprocal labor exchange of farming groups during the rainy seasons, and also for ceremonial or ritual occasions during the dry season. The skills they acquire in the process make it easy for them to transition to the commercial production of the drink.

This chapter explores the expansion of the commercial brewing of pito from the rural savanna region of northern Ghana to major cities of southern Ghana, and the role that northern Ghanaian immigrant women from the economic margins of the city or urban periphery play in the thriving industry. I interrogate the place of these "subaltern entrepreneurs"[21]—Mary N. Kinyanjui's phrase—by examining the ways in which they operate and navigate the competition of imported liquor or industrial beer, as well as the dynamic interactions between those competing drinks and this indigenous brew. Drawing on fieldwork conducted in major Ghanaian cities, I describe and analyze the activities of pito brewers in order to show the strategies and social networks they develop to support their brewing activities. The career trajectories of four women are highlighted to underscore individual women's entrepreneurial prowess and contributions to the national economy. I argue that a closer look at women's urban brewing activities and their experiences presents a lens through which to view contemporary Ghanaian history, social transformation, women's social history, and entrepreneurship in Ghana as well as the broader West African region.

The chapter begins by examining the ways in which the brew evolved from a household drink of the rural savanna into a vibrant urban cottage industry. The political economic context within which the drink spread to southern Ghana is presented next, alongside the entrepreneurship literature, to situate the commercialization of the drink within the Ghanaian informal economy. The last sections take up an analysis of four individual women's brewing experiences in order to show how they contributed to unseating Eurocentric entrepreneurial models. These cases also show similarities, and even entanglements, with contemporary notions of entrepreneurship.

Pito: A West African Savanna Drink

Present-day northern Ghana forms part of the vast West African Sudanic belt lying between the Akan forest to the south and the great bend of the river Niger to the north. This area now consists of three administrative regions of Ghana: the Upper East, Upper West, and Northern Regions. During the trans-Saharan trade, this middle Volta basin was the gateway to the outside world, and it also served as a commercial crossroad between the resource-rich Akan forest region to the south and the Sahel.[22] Its strategic location in the open grasslands may have attracted Mole-Dagbani and the commercially minded Mande-speaking peoples to settle around the fifteenth and mid-sixteenth centuries, respectively. Armed with knowledge of centralized political organization, the newcomers easily imposed their political authority over the mainly subsistence agricultural producers and stateless original settlers.

In terms of social organization, the agrarian culture has been crucial in influencing the daily experiences and economic strategies of the region. Not only has land remained the main source of livelihood, but people also generally live in homesteads close enough to one another to ensure labor recruitment through reciprocal aid and the inheritance of land for social reproduction.[23] The earth priest, once the central figure of community and ritual life, has continued to enjoy some privileged relations within each community, assuming responsibility for all acts of sacrifice and sanction of daily life. In fact, the maintenance of a productive and healthy community called for the making of beer from the staple cereals of millet and sorghum to facilitate ritual conversations concerning the propitiation of the earth during the cultivation of the land and after the harvest period.

As with other parts of precolonial West Africa, grains featured prominently in many economic transactions in northern Ghana, and their widespread circulation served partly to meet the need for beer production.[24] It is quite possible that most West African urbanites came to associate pito, a term rooted in the pre-Islamic Hausa lexicon, with sorghum beer in the context of the early urbanization of the beer-producing areas that was fueled by the vibrant regional grain market. Before Islam came to Hausaland in the Central Sudan, the Hausa communities brewed and drank sorghum beer and may have coined the term "pito" to designate the fermented drink and "burukutu" for a version of the drink.[25] These words may have then traveled via the Hausa constabulary during the era of colonial pacification from northern and central Nigeria, its main areas of consumption in Nigeria.[26] Most of the soldiers recruited by the British into the initial Hausa constabulary were ex-slaves captured from the non-Muslim areas of northern Nigeria, where Hausa was spoken as a second language and where burukutu and pito would have been popular drinks. Since Hausa was a trade lingua franca even before the advent of Islam, these terminologies were spread farther by the soldiers to other non-Hausa parts of modern northern Nigeria and to similar cultures of sorghum beer brewing and beer drinking, such as in northern Ghana.

In the Voltaic region, early colonial reports on the Northern Territories of the Gold Coast point to widespread drinking of sorghum beer by the time the British annexed the area in 1901.[27] In the former Lawra District of northwest Ghana, the district commissioner Duncan Johnstone voiced his concerns about the competence of Danye of Brurutu, who had been earmarked to replace Kyiir, the first colonially installed chief of Nandom, upon his death in 1908. The commissioner was quoted as attributing Danye's incompetence to his weakness for the drink; he described Danye as a "useless old drunkard whose hand is always inside a pito (sorghum beer) pot" and pressured him to hand over power to "his nephew Boro who is a good man, strong and energetic."[28] Carola Lentz suggests that because pito was originally brewed in this area for household consumption or ritual celebrations, elderly women were the only ones who depended on household elders to supply them with the grains to brew beer.[29] The growing need for cash to buy consumer goods, cloth, detergent, and kitchen necessities motivated younger women to independently purchase the ingredients to brew beer.

It appears that in the immediate aftermath of World War II a thriving commercial brewing industry had begun to emerge, and it crystallized in the 1950s thanks to the consolidation of the cash economy, the migration of labor, and the resultant growth and expansion of local and regional grain markets.[30] My interviews with older informants from northern Ghana also suggest that, by the 1960s, commercial brewing of pito had indeed become a common feature in Gambaga (the first colonial administrative center), Tamale, Wa, Bawku, Bolga, and the district capitals. The expansion to commercial brewing was a response to the broader social processes engendered by the out-migration of rural residents to the towns and cities. The major driving force behind the commercialization of the drink beyond its production base in the north, however, was the female migrant brewers whose activities have largely remained veiled in the urban economic history of Ghana.

The Political Economy of the Spread of Brewing Pito: 1960s–Present

As was the case elsewhere on the continent, the Africanization of the civil service in the newly independent state of Ghana fueled rural-urban migration. Ghanaians were drawn from the colonial backwater regions, such as northern Ghana, to the southern part of the country in search of jobs. However, lacking the necessary educational skills and training with which to enter the nascent white-collar job market, nonliterate male migrants from the north of Ghana who arrived in the south mainly took up employment in the underground gold mines or served as laborers and security guards in government agencies.[31] As opportunities to earn a stable income improved, some of these migrants invited their wives to join them. Compared to the eastern and southern African regions where the movement of migrant women was strictly regulated (despite the fact that they comforted and entertained their male counterparts with beer),[32] West African women were freer to migrate to the cities, but they also suffered discrimination. Beverly Grier notes that the unfriendly nature of the colonial city ensured that the few women who followed their husbands did not find employment, and that "a single woman was easily branded as a prostitute and treated as such."[33] In northern Ghana the gender ideology of the patrilineal societies discouraged women from embarking on long-distance travels on their own. Not even daring women in search of jobs traveled alone to the southern cities before independence in 1957.

Female migration in search of employment started to change during the early postindependence years as the informal labor market expanded and opportunities opened up for a few of them to engage in petty trading.[34] Based on interviews I conducted with older retired migrant mine workers and service men from northern Ghana, the wives in this group were the first to experiment with brewing pito in the southern coastal cities, partly to earn an income and satisfy the tastes of their husbands, but also to escape boredom and homesickness. Largely through such modest efforts, drinking pito became popular in the police and military barracks, the coastal railway and mining towns, and immigrant neighborhoods such as Nima, Maamobi, Kwisimitim, Ashaiman, Labardi, Kwadaso Santaasi, and Playground, near Kejetia in Kumasi. In the subsequent decades, as discussed later, consumption of the drink and patronage of drinking establishments came to depend more on north–south migration trends and the vicissitudes of the national political economy.

In analyzing the social economy of pito drinking, it is also important to understand the dynamic interaction between African locally brewed beer and distilled or imported liquor. Several scholars have revealed how patronage of either drink was predicated largely on the postcolonial national political economies. In Tanzania, Deborah F. Bryceson found a link between the economic decline of the

.980s and changing drinking habits of the urbanites. She observes that "rural home or cottage-brewed supplies dominated European imported drinks for the most part of pre-colonial and colonial periods . . . until urbanization and national independence reversed the trend in the 1960s."[35] The reversal, she notes, was occasioned by the production of lager beer by the newly established postindependence state breweries. However, when the national economy declined and the wages of workers dropped, workers were compelled to turn away from the more expensive lager beer and returned to consuming locally produced beer.

A similar pattern has also been reported in Ghana, with direct implications for the present analysis.[36] In Accra some brewers claimed that many of their customers who originally drank bottled beer had turned to drinking either the locally distilled gin (*akpeteshie*) or pito because of unemployment. Their joblessness resulted from the mass retrenchment of government workers with the implementation of structural adjustment programs. The economic situation was exacerbated by a prolonged drought and the outbreak of bushfires during the mid-1980s that destroyed the southern forest region. The volume of distillation of staple brews of southern Ghana dropped as a result of the scarcity of palm trees and sugarcane.[37]

This scarcity of forest trees may have created a space for the pito industry to flourish in the south. However, the high cost of shipping grains from the north, a result of the poor quality of the roads, discouraged potential commercial pito brewers from taking up the trade in the south. Some veteran brewers reported that they tried substituting corn in brewing pito but found that many experienced customers disliked corn beer because it caused headaches and nausea. From the 1990s onward, an improving economy, coupled with a demographic boom of rural migration from the north to Brong Ahafo and the Afram plains, drove down the cost of grains, since many rural immigrants who settled in those areas began to farm sorghum. The combination of this with their consumption habits and the entrepreneurial prowess of individual brewers helped pave the way for pito brewing to flourish in the south and middle belt of Ghana.

While the constellation of these environmental and demographic factors created favorable conditions for commercial brewing and the consumption of pito to thrive in the south of Ghana, rapid urbanization and the effects of climate change were detrimental to brewing in the north. For one thing, brewers stated they often faced a shortage of firewood because of the disappearance of "village commons" from which village women traditionally gathered firewood for cooking and brewing. For another, women in northern Ghana generally do not control the felling of trees, and hence only a few family farms have access to firewood unless they can afford to buy logs. The financial burden associated with this added high energy cost and the amount of water needed to brew beer is exacerbated by the gradual shifting of the production base for sorghum away from the coarse

Guinea savanna to the forest fringes as desiccation of the savanna intensifies in the north. It has become very difficult for many commercial brewers to make profits or even recover production costs while maintaining the desired quality of beer for their customers.

Not surprisingly, widespread complaints regarding the deteriorating quality of pito abound as a result of the outward migration of brewers. While many customers blame it on the profit motive of some brewers, others attribute the problem to the previously mentioned challenges facing the industry. Some pito-drinking connoisseurs that I interviewed claimed that the finest pito is not found in northern Ghana these days, but rather in the southern transit cities of Sunyani, Wenchi, Techiman, Ejura, Atebubu, Kintampo, and Nkoransa. Here on the forest fringes, the prospects for the pito industry have improved, especially in the peri-urban areas of middle Ghana, due to easy access to firewood, water, and grain. Likewise, there is a growing consumer base made up of immigrants.

It is important to note that rural migration from northern Ghana to Brong Ahafo and other parts of southern Ghana dates as far back as the early colonial period in the late nineteenth and twentieth centuries.[38] During the latter decades of the twentieth century, the Gold Coast economy witnessed a sharp increase in labor demand; the area's need to fill mining and cocoa plantation jobs attracted migrant laborers from the northern territories and neighboring French colonies who exploited the gold mines, manned the cocoa farms, and participated in government works in the fast-growing southern economy.[39] However, from the 1980s onward, a phenomenal growth and expansion of new farm settlements resulted from widespread agricultural colonization from the north, the destruction caused by drought and bushfires in the 1980s, and the concomitant decline of the agricultural export economy in the forest region. The decline also affected the staple-food crop production in the forest fringes[40] and helped shift the production base of sorghum southward. There several land owners responded to the food crisis by welcoming northerners with generous terms to settle on their fallow lands in order to satisfy their basic food requirements. The result was that the migrants' easy access to farmlands, obtained either by paying affordable fees or sharecropping (*dominyenkye*), encouraged families to settle permanently.

As the next section shows, the expansion of pito drinking among the local population of the middle belt of Ghana has had significant implications for the improved economic conditions of many immigrant women. For rural migrant women, the positive local perception of the drink presents an entrepreneurial opportunity. This contrasts with the negative attitude that earlier generations of migrant pito brewers faced and continue to face in the larger southern cities, such as Accra, Takoradi, Cape Coast, and Kumasi. The political economy I have described provides the broader context for the female commercialization of brewing and the structural factors that helped shape their entry into the southern cities. However, the key to individual brewers' success lies in their entrepreneurial ingenuity and ability to adapt to the new urban settings. Before turning to the brewers' experiences to highlight this dynamic, a few observations are needed about the informal economy within which pito brewers operate, as well as some considerations of modern entrepreneurial requirements.

Brewing Pito: Subaltern Urbanism and the Informal Economy

Since Keith Hart's pioneering study of the urban subproletariat of Accra, economic informality has been at the center of both historical and sociological analysis in much of the developing world.[41] The African urban landscape in particular has witnessed an upsurge of studies on female grassroots economic activities, partly due to the recognition of their importance by both governments and NGOs. As Francesca Locatelli and Paul Nugent note, employment in this sector is seen as a means of subsistence for the majority of African urbanites because of recent and rapid urbanization, allowing ordinary women to demonstrate extraordinary ingenuity in capturing the city from the dominant business and economic elite.[42] Catherine Coquery-Vidrovitch argues that economic informality should not be viewed as a new reality in Africa, but rather as a phenomenon that came about as soon as Western capitalism took hold. She notes that some people, especially women, were prevented entry to the official urban labor market because they were not perceived as directly useful producers or auxiliaries serving the dependent order.[43]

Since women were often denied the natural right to become urban dwellers, their economic activities did not receive scholarly attention until the 1970s and 1980s.[44] Gracia Clark notes that the shift was due to the influx of rural women to the city in response to the prolonged economic stagnation of the 1970s and 1980s.[45] The deleterious effect of the economic crisis on the countryside and the subsequent implementation of the structural adjustments program further drew many rural women out of their productive and reproductive roles into the cities, where they engaged in petty trading in the informal sector. In Nairobi, Kenya, Kinyanjui observes what she terms "the rise of subaltern urbanism" or "solidarity entrepreneurialism" as a feature of the intensified claims on urban space.[46] In highlighting the activities of female garment sellers in the informal sector, she demonstrates how they faced obstacles and exclusion. Although women were perceived as encroachers in the urban space, they saw opportunities in the informal sector and were able to cross boundaries in the city to become important players in the economy. The trend provides useful insights with which to analyze pito brewers' experiences, as both encroachers in Ghanaian urban space and members of a marginalized group that forged its own mechanism of survival in extreme economic conditions.

The next section discusses the life stories of four individual women brewers and the strategies they used to adapt in the face of challenges in the urban economy. I also underscore how they defy Eurocentric models of entrepreneurship. The choice of these particular brewers was based on the different levels of success they achieved in their brewing enterprises across time and space. Whether finding spaces to brew and sell pito or welcoming first-time migrants and constituting solidarity networks in southern Ghana, these urban pito brewers, like their Kenyan counterparts, demonstrated considerable adaptability and enterprise in extending mutual support to one another. Analyzing their experiences from historical and life-course perspectives[47] allows us to place them in the context of their individual environments and those of their families, as well as in the larger context of history. As Tamara K. Hareven notes, a life-course perspective reveals the adaptation of individuals and their families to social and economic conditions, in this case the urban informal economy. Depending on the mutual support they receive, many are able to successfully respond to historical circumstances, such as migration, wars, and the decline or collapse of local economies, encountered in the course of their lives.[48]

Christina, Age Fifty-Eight, Accra

In 1971 Christina was a bubbly teenage girl who had just dropped out of middle school. Like many of her peers, she was recruited by her mother to help brew pito for sale in a town located on the Ghana–Burkina Faso international border. Christina related that although the 1970s were very difficult economic times, she cherished the memories from that decade because that is when she met her future husband. Hoping for a better life in the city, the new couple eloped to Accra, but, upon arrival, Christina discovered that she would be welcoming her first child despite having no source of income to support the family. She received some support from an extended family member, but it was her ability to develop a wider social network through her village women's association in Nima and Maamobi that allowed her to procure a few items to ease her settlement.

Nima and Maamobi are neighborhoods in Accra that have long been popular weekend destinations for most of the northern immigrant working class of the city. The Christians worship at the Saint Kisito Catholic church in Nima on Sundays, then usually go to Maamobi to socialize over calabashes of pito and dance to xylophone music or simply experience the dense social and leisure networks that they have developed through church, ethnic, or hometown associations. This was the social environment in which Christina first found herself helping to brew and serve pito in Accra. On weekdays she also carried pito to sell around the city. Unfortunately, she had to relocate to a different part of the city when her husband lost his job. At her new place, she contacted her village women's association, which extended her a much-needed line of credit. In order to start brewing her own pito for sale, she bought two enamel pots and a bag of red sorghum and established a wayside bar that not only thrived but also attracted so many customers that she had to invite two former pito colleagues to assist her.

In major cities of southern Ghana, the lack of space to brew pito meant that members of the early generation of brewers, such as Christina, were often compelled to brew (and continue to brew) in courtyards of either rented compound houses or bungalows assigned to government officials. Most brewers erected wooden structures without roofs, with long benches arranged to serve as drinking bars.[49] Those without such premises solicited uncompleted buildings from the property owners that they turned into taverns. From the taverns, brewers would rotate sending out their pito sellers to carry the drink in ten-liter bottles or rubber cans as they walked several miles across the city to reach more customers.

When I first met and interviewed Christina in 2006, she was operating a vibrant pito bar (*pata*). Her wooden facility, situated away from her family residence and neighborhood, had enough space to brew, house the salesgirls, and seat customers. In this bar she employed two girls from her home village; three former employees had already gone on to start their own pito-brewing enterprises in different parts of the city. Few brewers are able to afford the considerable resources needed to acquire a space and invest in the infrastructure. That Christina was able to build and operate such a facility underscores the transformation of her life's trajectory by her decision to become an urban brewer.

Madam Long, Age Sixty-Two, Kumasi

One of my other interlocutors was a brewer known to her customers as Madam Long who lived in Kumasi, Ghana's second-largest city. Madam Long launched her career during her second marriage; previously, she had farmed in a remote village in the Afram Plains for twenty years with her first husband. Following his death, she married Mr. Long, who was a laborer in Kumasi-Kwadaso-Agric. This suburb is known for attracting a large numbers of immigrants seeking employment as watchmen, cleaners, and agricultural field laborers. In 2002 Mr. Long earned a promotion to chief laborer in one of the institutes, which also allocated him a residential quarter. This house was well situated at the center of the housing complex of the laborers; it had a spacious courtyard that was well shaded by a large mango tree. It was at this location that Madam Long found a business opportunity. She started to brew pito for sale, and also bought grains from villages in the Afram Plains to sell to other brewers. In 2010 when I visited the couple, Madam Long explained that her pito enterprise had begun to pay off, allowing her to employ three girls to help with the business. Moreover, she and her husband had already built their own house, largely with the proceeds from her pito bar. That the couple was able to do this well before Mr. Long's retirement from the formal sector is a rare achievement among the laboring class.

Adjusting and Settling in the City

The brewing careers of both Christina and Madam Long highlight the entry of pito brewers into the city. Furthermore, they reveal the constraints and challenges associated with starting a commercial brewing enterprise in a major city of southern Ghana. Brewers such as Madam Long usually relied on young, first-time migrant female relatives to help carry the drink from their residences to customers. These pito carriers, as they are known, take advantage of the opportunity provided by more-established brewers in return for their support with initial accommodations and other basic needs. Despite the ever-shifting and difficult economic terrain of the informal sector, both of these women were able to adjust to their new urban environments, relying on initial support received from either their immediate relatives or other social networks to launch their commercial enterprises.

Over decades, the face of the commercial pito industry in the south has remained the roaming pito seller or carrier. In fact, she has come to signify the marginal status of the poor northern immigrant in the city and is recognizable to customers who consume the drink. This experience is well captured by Stella, a former pito carrier who related the harassments she and her colleagues suffered at the hands of unwelcoming customers in Kumasi during the 1970s and 1980s: "The Ashanti boys used to call us from a distance, shouting in Twi, '*Pito wura bra ha*' ["Pito seller, come here"] and once you got to them, they started teasing; those who wanted to make fun of us called the drink 'tea without bread.' Today I see that everybody drinks pito and the Ashantis sometimes buy drums of pito from us when they have funerals."[50] Stella's account of her experience selling pito points to the social exclusion and negative perception with which the roaming pito seller is associated in southern Ghana. At the same time, it also underscores the recent expansion of the customer base beyond poor urban immigrant drinkers. One of my southern informants, Nsieh-Gyabaah, noted this development and the fact that when he was growing up in the 1960s in Busunya in remote Brong Ahafo, nobody drank pito because it was not brewed in the area. These days, however, pito is a very popular drink not just in this area but throughout the region.[51] How did this happen?

Retreat to Peri-urban Ghana

In contrast to cities such as Accra, Kumasi, Obuasi, and Sekondi-Takoradi, where pito bars had begun to dot the slums and city margins, the consumption of the drink had not yet penetrated the rural and peri-urban centers of the middle belt of the country by the late 1960s. One reason was the vibrant tapping of palm wine and the distillation of local gin (akpeteshie).[52] Because rural migration from northern Ghana to the south was largely seasonal and undertaken by males, there was no large, sedentary immigrant population or brewers to sustain the industry. The migrants' lack of easy access to farmland on which to produce their own grains was another factor. By the 1980s it seemed that the problems associated with the latter obstacle had been minimized when the economic crisis compelled many landowners to relax restrictions on immigrants' access to farmland.

Stella's statement that today everybody drinks pito is clearly an exaggeration, but it serves to capture the extent to which rural southerners have now warmed up to pito drinking. In fact, my conversations with local Brong informants suggest that there is now a booming pito industry throughout the middle belt, and a number of the people I talked to said that they preferred pito to palm wine and akpeteshie. The fact that many of the major cities and peri-urban centers in Brong Ahafo had pito bars that attracted customers from multiple ethnic groups confirms Nsieh-Gyabaah's observation of the widespread embrace of the drink and its declining negative perception in the region.

Surveys of pito brewers in Brong Ahafo (see table 4.1) show that the majority of brewers were immigrant wives of civil servants from the Upper West Region. Others were single, separated, divorced, or widowed women, a group whose members, in patrilineal societies, have few attachments in rural areas beyond their nuclear families.[53] In two cases, I found that professional female brewers had recruited young girls from their extended families and home villages to help brew and serve the drinks. In addition to their normal tasks, these pito sellers are expected to attract male customers and encourage them to drink more.[54]

In the discussion that follows, my highlighting of the drinking activities of two pito bars serves to underline the entrepreneurial skills and strategies that brewers deploy to mobilize customers and ensure the survival of their businesses. My aim is to contrast the performance of bars located in large cities with that of bars in peri-urban towns with close proximity to farm settlements, but also to underline the strategies brewers employ in dealing with the high costs of brewing in the major cities, which include retreating to the peri-urban areas of Brong Ahafo. The proximity to the farming population means that these brewers face less competition from industrial beer and other distilled drinks, in addition to having easy access to the grain supply chain. The career trajectories of the following women are presented here as illustrative examples.

Cecilia, Age Forty, Wenchi

In 1998 Gmankurnaa pito bar was established in Wenchi by Cecilia, a very enterprising woman. In the port city of Takoradi, where her husband used to work, Cecilia had failed to establish a brewing business because of the obstacles discussed

Table 4.1 Survey of Pito Bars in Major Towns of Brong Ahafo

Name of Bar	Ethnicity of Brewer	Marital Status	Husband's Occupation	Region	City/Town	Ye Estab
New Foundland	Dagara	Single	NA	Upper West	Sunyani	19
KKB	Konkomba	Widow	NA	Northern	Sunyani	19
Zanzibar	Dagara	Single	NA	Upper West	Sunyani	19
New Market	Dagara	Married	Retired teacher	Upper West	Wenchi	19
Blackie Ma	Dagara	Married	Farmer	Upper West	Wenchi	20
Nandom Pito Bar	Dagara	Married	Driver	Upper West	Wenchi	19
Quality Pito Bar	Dagara	Married	NA	Upper West	Wenchi	20
Ernestina's Bar	Dagara	Married	Farmer	Upper West	Wenchi	19
Roman Church Pito	Dagara	Married	Cocoa farmer	Upper West	Techiman	20
Mary Pito Bar	Dagara	Widow	NA	Upper West	Techiman	20
Magazine Pito Bar	Dagara	Married	Teacher	Upper West	Techiman	20
Tiegber Pito Bar	Dagara	Married	Pensioner	Upper West	Techiman	Unk
Tigo Pole Pito Bar	Dagara	Married	Teacher	Upper West	Techiman	Unk
Aggie Pito Bar	Dagara	Widow	NA	Upper West	Chiira	19
Nandom Pito Bar	Dagara	Married	Farmer	Upper West	Chiira	19
Nyami na ye Pito Bar	Dagara	Married	Retired educationist	Upper West	Chiira	19
Tandee Pito Bar	Wala	Married	Farmer	Upper West	Chiira	20
Sampiaga pito bar	Nakana	Married	Educationist	Upper East	Chiira	Unk

ɔle 4.1 *(continued)*

me of Bar	Ethnicity of Brewer	Marital Status	Husband's Occupation	Region	City/Town	Year Established
kooase Pito Bar	Dagara	Married	Educationist	Upper West	Bouku	2001
-50 Pito Bar	Dagara	Widow	NA	Upper West	Bouku	1998
ppy-Home Pito	Dagara	Widow	NA	Upper West	Bouku	1980
ho Is Free Pito Bar	Dagara	Married	Retired policeman	Upper West	Bouku	1983
meabra Pito	Dagara	Married	Watchman	Upper West	Bouku	1983
pa Pito	Konkomba	Single	NA	Northern	Sunyani	1980

previously. Now in Wenchi, Cecilia stated that she was very happy with her brewing activities; she said that she usually increased the quantity of beer on market days in order to meet the higher demand of customers who attended the weekly Wenchi market. At the time of my fieldwork, she employed five young girls to help with the brewing and selling of pito while she occupied herself with the acquisition of grains from the nearby villages.

On the several occasions that I visited Gmankurnaa, villagers from near Wenchi and faraway villages visited the bar as early as eight o'clock in the morning. During this time, most of the customers said they were there to taste (Lem) the drink and exchange early morning pleasantries with the female pito sellers.[55] Their presence also indicated the intention to reserve pito for a more relaxing drinking session later in the day, since the supply of beer frequently ran out by the close of the market. It was typically during this initial visit that nonregulars made their reservations for a specific quantity of drink. Regular customers, especially the lovers of the salesgirls, did not need to make such reservations because their orders, or "reserves," were already known and handled by the salesgirls.

By early evening, when the well-attended market was about to disperse, the pito bar was filled to capacity. Recorded xylophone, highlife, and hiplife music could be heard from the bar, as well as the chatter of laughter or voices talking. Such noises reflected the sense of happiness and convivial atmosphere that typically characterizes market-day drinking in this peri-urban town on the rural-urban interface. After several days of intensive farm work, market day presents an opportunity for the immigrant farming population to leave the remote villages in order to sell their farm produce, drink, and relax with friends in the urban areas.

In Gmankurnaa pito bar, pepper or light soup prepared from either pork or goat meat is one of the popular items on the menu, and the late-night drinkers who regularly organize beer parties with the salesgirls look forward to drinking beer over a meal of well-seasoned dog meat (a sought-after delicacy in urban pito bars in Ghana). Many patrons of Gmankurnaa said that light soup bars experience high demand because many villagers leave the house without eating breakfast. They maintained that it is not advisable to drink with an "empty stomach" (*puzagla*), and that the cooked meat complements and helps neutralize the effect of alcohol and diminishes inebriation among customers. Outside Gmankurnaa, Guinness was sold at a small kiosk, catering to customers who wanted to mix the pito with the bottled drink. The combination of the two is one innovative feature of urban drinking, and patrons said that the mixture improves the texture of the drink and makes it taste better. The convivial atmosphere in and around Gmankurnaa became more intense in the late evenings as people drank, flirted, and socialized with friends throughout the day. On market days, the inebriated traders from faraway villages do not have to worry about traveling back home late at night or securing accommodations, since a room is reserved for them.

The vibrant drinking activities of this pito bar demonstrate the mutually reinforcing link between the farming activities of migrants who have settled on the forest fringes and the now-flourishing pito industry in the middle belt of Ghana. Locations that link the urban and rural, peri-urban areas of middle Ghana have become sites for women's agency and entrepreneurship. As with Cecilia, the life course of Maame Konkomba, whose brewing career we next examine, demonstrates a pattern in which an increasing number of both rural and urban women looking for better life opportunities are forced into peri-urban settings by the pressures of urban life or rural depression.

Maame Konkomba, Age Seventy, Sunyani

Konkomba Base (KKB) was one of the pito bars that I visited regularly during fieldwork in Sunyani. The seventy-year-old brewer who owned the bar said she started brewing pito as a teenager in the 1960s in the northern regional capital of Tamale. With the help of her younger sister, she established two very popular bars, which they named after the Biafra civil war in Nigeria. Maame Konkomba explained the reason behind the names of the bars: "At that time there was war in Nigeria, and a Yoruba trader living in Ghana visited the bar. After tasting my pito, he compared the strength of the drink [alcoholic content] to the bitterness of the raging Biafra war. Because Biafra was all over the place at the time, we decided to give that name to our bars. The unique name attracted many people to our pito."

By the late 1970s and early 1980s, Maame Konkomba and her sister had begun to face stiff competition from other pito brewers. However, she noted that "business was still good" until the so-called Konkomba-Nanumba Guinea Fowl Civil War of 1994, when a faction warring against the Konkomba stormed the bars and razed the buildings to the ground. Maame Konkomba said she barely escaped the wrath of the attackers, and she relocated to Sunyani in middle Ghana with the help of the Ghana army. She brought her business experience with her to the Brong Ahafo regional capital. When I first interviewed her in 2006, she had virtually relinquished the daily routine of brewing to her daughter because of old age, continuing to supervise her only to ensure, in her words, "that the family tradition as well as the quality of pito would be maintained."[56]

Like Gmankurnaa, KKB had daily brews for sale and drew its customers from the multiethnic urban youth of the city. Most customers said that they were attracted to the good pito and lively social atmosphere that prevailed in the bar on Sundays. One other attraction was the fact that the son of Maame Konkomba also sold Guinness, which customers bought to mix with the pito. Maame Konkomba stated that through her brewing she was able to buy a KIA truck, which she used in support of her business, and was also able to finance her son's education to become a professional teacher.

Urban Brewing: Unsettling Eurocentric Entrepreneurial Models

Over the past few decades, the dual conceptualization of African economies into formal and informal has allowed scholars of African business and entrepreneurship to shine an ethnographic light on the economic activities of the informal sector.[57] The focus on the sector has sensitized scholars to the need to incorporate indigenous African business norms and practices, which hitherto were deemed inimical to the success of business and entrepreneurship, into their analysis.

In her review of the Ghanaian entrepreneurship landscape, Anita Spring defines entrepreneurship as one's "ability to establish new businesses that create employment, and provide services and products to increase the wealth of their local and national economies." For her, therefore, "entrepreneurship prowess includes the idea that through their own achievement, entrepreneurs can significantly increase their incomes and lifestyle—that is upward mobility or rags to riches."[58] Political economy–minded scholars who study the so-called microentrepreneurs in the informal sector have helped illuminate the experiences of operators within the unregulated urban economy. However, the tendency to analyze these economic activities through the lens of neoliberal economic models means that the economic activities of most urban poor are dismissed as entrepreneurial ventures.

Spring and John Kuada acknowledge the fine line between the formal and informal sectors but note that although entrepreneurs of the formal sector can move into the latter sector—especially in times of crisis, such as when businesses collapse—there is usually little chance for microentrepreneurs to move into the formal sector because they lack the educational, capital, and business network requirements.[59] What this means is that operators such as those who run pito bars may be classified as microentrepreneurs, but because they are at the bottom of the economic ladder and engage in subsistence activities in the informal sector, their economic activities are not considered as entrepreneurial enough

This Eurocentric perspective is reflected in the theoretical distinction often made between opportunity-based and necessity-based entrepreneurship.[60] Under the former category, entrepreneurs with growth-oriented goals have the propensity to engage in high-expectation entrepreneurial activities. Necessity-based entrepreneurs, on the other hand, are driven mainly by economic survival requirements. This means that most informal-sector workers who are self-employed and concerned with meeting their daily needs are not growth oriented.[61] Kinyanjui critiques the pessimistic view proffered by Eurocentric entrepreneurial models of economic informality, especially in terms of "what is wrong with it and what it does not do," arguing that the sector should not have to be assessed in terms of the government-regulated sector.[62] According to her, the preponderance of economic informality in Africa represents a transition from a post-Western capitalist mode to an African mode of production in terms of business norms. Hence, rather than viewing economic informality in terms of the formal sector, it needs to be treated in its own right and understood in the context of the creation of an indigenous African social economic order.[63]

To be sure, pito bar owners may lack the necessary education, social capital, and international networks to move into the formal sector, but should these requirements preclude them from establishing new businesses that create employment and provide services and products to increase the wealth of their local and national economies, which is the hallmark of entrepreneurship? An examination of this question makes the activities of the brewers appear to be equally viable entrepreneurial ventures.

This study has already noted the ways in which the decline of the rural economy affected brewing activities in northern Ghana and compelled potential brewers to migrate to the south. This shift represents an economic loss to the poorer savanna regions, as the once-thriving brewing cottage industry, around which the livelihoods of many rural women in the north depended, has suffered. By migrating to establish their own commerce in the south, pito brewers provide a vital economic link between the largely rural north and the urban south, generating entry-point jobs for most of the young girls arriving in the south for the first time. In doing so, brewers earn their own income and educate their children but also provide an opportunity for younger female migrants to make a living and learn an indigenous trade.

In fact, many of the migrant girls who gain the trust of the shop owner are occasionally given a chance to make their own brew using the owner's facilities, and they are allowed to keep the income without any commission. From such income, unmarried girls are able to buy the necessary household items and utensils to prepare for their future married life. Ernestina made this point when she noted that "some good madams provide us with clothing during our transition period into city life,"[64] explaining that, thanks to the generosity of her former madam, she was able to save enough money to buy a sewing machine, with which she was able to learn an additional trade. She believed that her sewing skills ensured a more regular income than work as a bargirl, while increasing her marriage prospects. Some girls who were working for other brewers were not as lucky as Ernestina, but they too said that they were happy with the accommodations and meals their jobs in the bars guaranteed them. Rather than becoming *kayayei* (head porters) in the larger cities, with all the vagaries associated with that position, they were lucky to live and work with familiar people in a much safer environment. When I asked pito brewers why they could not pay the girls better wages, many of them cited the stiff competition from industrial beer and akpeteshie sellers. Unlike other cottage industries whose owners had easy access to credit and could easily obtain loans from banks, they complained that they were not viewed as viable entrepreneurs. They were also convinced that the negative attitude toward the drink exhibited by their fellow immigrants who were members of the educated middle class was to blame.

Lentz suggests that in the 1980s and 1990s the consumption of factory-produced beer served as a marker of social status in northern Ghana.[65] According to her, although middle-class, educated, northern Ghanaians occasionally drank pito, they rarely did so among their colleagues, fearing a loss of prestige associated with the settings in which pito is normally consumed. The attitude of the immigrant middle class, many of whom grew up drinking pito but now avoid it, can be viewed in the context of current economic and social challenges, such as urbanization, ecological change, and class formation, that have given rise to changing drinking and consumption habits.

The transformation of Maame Konkomba's pito bar from Biafra to KKB seems to reflect the pattern by which many pito brewers from the north establish drinking bars in southern Ghana. However, a closer look at the unique circumstances under which she settled in Sunyani following the Konkomba-Nanumba civil war demonstrates women's knowledge of social history. In using the Yoruba trader's statement about the Biafra civil war to brand her business, Maame Konkomba not only demonstrated her shrewd business skills but simultaneously succeeded in inscribing the historical memory of the Yoruba traders' presence in Ghana in the 1960s and their discourses about the war that erupted in their country for ordinary Ghanaians. Her decision to change the name of the bar reflects her own traumatic experience with the Konkumba-Nanumba civil war and her attempts to silence her past experiences as a refugee in order to start anew. The naming of her popular bars thus provides a window into the ways in which ordinary northern Ghanaian women remember and memorialize important historical events. Furthermore, Maame Konkomba's technique of operating an entirely family-run business, rarely hiring outsiders, is one of the residual features of artisanal brewing that continues to be embraced by most brewers in peri-urban towns surrounded by farming settlements. Situated in the rural-urban interstices, such bars draw their customers from the farming population; the bars are characterized by more vitality and are likely to survive longer than those in major cities.

Conclusion

This chapter has outlined and analyzed the historical context within which the staple rural savanna drink pito evolved from a purely home-brewed beverage into a thriving urban cottage industry in the south of Ghana. It has historicized the political economy of the commercialization of the drink following the consolidation of the colonial cash economy and examined the role that migrant women played in the spread of the industry. In northern Ghana, rural women first responded to new business opportunities by brewing beer for sale instead of relying on household elders to supply them with grains. The patronage of migrant young men who spent money earned from wage labor on the drink allowed them to enhance their efforts. From the early postcolonial period, rural economic depression, increased migration involving women, and environmental changes helped accelerate the spread of the commercialization of women's brewing activities to southern Ghana.

In highlighting individual female brewers' experiences, this chapter has argued that although the expansion of commerce in beer was a response to the social processes engendered by the out-migration of rural folks to towns and cities, the major driving force behind the commercialization of the drink beyond its production base was the female migrant brewers who recognized and seized opportunities presented in major cities. Faced with economic marginalization and social exclusion in the southern cities, pito brewers overcame social harassment and economic obstacles and succeeded in popularizing the consumption of pito. The now-vibrant patronage of the drink in peri-urban centers of middle Ghana exemplifies the entrepreneurial activities and strategies that generations of brewers have used to generate incomes, not only for themselves but also for their auxiliaries, in the brewing industry. By analyzing the career trajectories of these subaltern entrepreneurs, the chapter also contributes to contemporary women's social history and ongoing social transformation.

ISIDORE LOBNIBE is Associate Professor of Anthropology at Western Oregon University, and Fellow of the WissenschaftKolleg zu Berlin / Institute For Advanced Study. His research interests center on social organization, the agrarian and household economy, and relations of gender in Ghana and Burkina Faso. His current research is about ongoing changes in funeral practices among northern Ghanaians.

Notes

1. Mahir Saul, "Beer, Sorghum and Women: Production for the Market in Rural Upper-Volta," *Africa: Journal of the International African Institute* 51, no. 3 (1981): 746–64; Elizabeth Colson and Thayer Scudder, *For Prayer and for Profit: The Ritual, Economic and Social Importance of Beer in Gwmenbe District, Zambia, 1950–52* (Stanford, CA: Stanford University Press, 1988); Emmanuel Akyeampong, *Drink, Power, and Cultural Change: A Social History of Alcohol in Ghana, c. 1800 to Recent Times* (Portsmouth, NH: Heinemann, 1996); Carola Lentz, "Alcohol Consumption between Community Ritual and Political Economy: Case Studies from Ecuador and Ghana," in *Changing Food Habits: Case Studies from Africa, South America and Europe*, ed. Carola Lentz, 155–79 (Amsterdam. The Netherlands: Harwood Academic, 1999); Deborah F. Bryceson, "Pleasure and Pain: The Ambiguity of Alcohol in Africa," in *Alcohol in Africa: Mixing Business, Pleasure and Politics*, ed. Deborah F. Bryceson, 267–91 (Portsmouth, NH: Heinemann, 2002).

2. Barbara L. Hagaman, "Beer and Matriliny: The Power of Women in a West African Society" (PhD diss., Northeastern University, 1977); Saul, "Beer, Sorghum and Women"; Lentz, "Alcohol Consumption."

3. Hagaman, "Beer and Matriliny"; Sabine Luning, "To Drink or Not to Drink? Beer Brewing, Rituals, and Religious Conversation in Maane, Burkina Faso," in Bryceson, *Alcohol in Africa*, 267–91.

4. Monica Wilson, *For Men and Elders: Changes in the Relations of Generations and of Men and Women among the Nyakusa and Ngonde* (London: International Institute of African Studies, 1977); Justin Willis, "For Women and Children: An Economic History of Brewing among the Nyakusa of Southwestern Tanzania," in Bryceson, *Alcohol in Africa*, 56–73; Lentz, "Alcohol Consumption."

5. Wilson, *For Men and Elders*; Colson and Scudder, *For Prayer and for Profit.*

6. Akyeampong, *Drink, Power, and Cultural Change*; Bryceson, "Changing Modalities of Alcohol Usage"; Lentz, "Alcohol Consumption"; Willis, "For Women and Children."

7. Bryceson, 2002, defines "modalities" as the norms, attitudes, and values associated with patterns of drinking and intoxication.

8. Akyeampong, *Drink, Power, and Cultural Change*; Emmanuel Akyeampong, "Drinking with Friends: Popular Culture, the Working Poor and Youth Drinking in Independent Ghana," in Bryceson, *Alcohol in Africa*, 215–30.

9. Akyeampong, *Drink, Power, and Cultural Change*; Emmanuel Akyeampong, "Chiefs and Socio-political Change in the Gold Coast: Insights from Reports on Liquor Consumption, 1919–1934," in *Chieftaincy in Ghana: Culture, Governance and Development*, ed. Irene K. Odotei and Albert K. Awedoba, 309–23 (Accra, Ghana: Sub-Saharan, 2006).

10. Akyeampong, "Chiefs and Socio-political Change," 309–10.

11. Akyeampong, *Drink, Power, and Cultural Change*; Akyeampong, "Drinking with Friends," 220.

12. Akyeampong, "Chiefs and Socio-political Change," 309–10.

13. See Richard L. K. Glover, "Diversity within Yeast Involved in Spontaneous Fermentation of Pito" (PhD diss., Kwame Nkrumah University of Science and Technology, 2007).

14. Such categories include Dagati pito, Konkomba pito, Kassena pito, Kusasi pito, and Frafra pito.

15. Sigrun Helmfrid, "Thirsty Men and Thrifty Women: Gender, Power, and Agency in Rural Beer Trade in Burkina Faso," in *Beer in Africa: Drinking Spaces, States and Selves*, ed. Steven Von Woputte and Mattaia Fumenti, 196–285 (New Brunswick, NJ: Transaction, 2010).

16. Glover, "Diversity within Yeast."

17. See Saul, "Beer, Sorghum and Women."

18. Hagaman, "Beer and Matriliny."

19. See Lentz, "Alcohol Consumption."

20. Jack Goody, *Death, Property and the Ancestors: A Study of the Mortuary Customs of the LoDagaa of West Africa* (London: Tavistock, 1962); and David E. Tait, *The Konkomba of Northern Ghana* (London: Oxford University Press, 1961).

21. Mary N. Kinyanjui, "Women Informal Garment Traders in Taveta Road, Nairobi: From the Margins to the Center," *African Studies Review* 56, no. 3 (2013): 147–64.

22. Kwame Arhin, "Transit Markets in Asanti Hinterland in the Nineteenth Century," *Odu: Journal of Yoruba and Related Studies* 9 (1974): 5–22.

23. Goody, *Death, Property and the Ancestors*.

24. Francoise Heritier, "Des Cauris et des Hommes," in *L'eclavage en Afrique Precolonial*, ed. Claude Meillassoux, 477–508 (Paris: Maspero, 1975).

25. Personal Communication with Moses Ochonu.

26. Robert M. Netting, "Beer as a Locus of value among the West African Kofyar," *American Anthropologist* 66, no. 2 (1964): 375–84.

27. Lawra District Record Book, GNA, ADM 61/5/11; Carola Lentz and Veit Erlmann, "Working Class in Formation?: Economic Crisis and Strategies of Survival among Dagara Mine Workers in Ghana," *Cahiers d'études africaines* 29, no. 113 (1989): 69–111.

28. Carola Lentz, "Histories and Political Conflict: A Case Study of Chieftaincy in Nandom, Northwestern Ghana," *Paideuma* 39 (1993): 191.

29. Lentz, "Alcohol Consumption."

30. Hagaman, "Beer and Matriliny"; Saul, "Beer, Sorghum and Women"; Lentz, "Alcohol Consumption."

31. Roger Thomas, "Forced Labor in British West Africa: The Case of the Northern Territories of the Gold Coast, 1906–1927," *Journal of African History* 14, no. 1 (1973): 79–103; Raymond Dumett is the correct spelling *The Eldorado of West Africa: The Gold Mining Frontier, African Labor and Colonial Capitalism in the Gold Coast, 1898–1910* (Oxford: James Curry, 1998); Lentz and Erlmann, "Working Class in Formation?"

32. Kenneth Little, *Women in African Towns* (Cambridge: Cambridge University Press, 1973); Luise White, *The Comforts of Home: Prostitution in Colonial Nairobi* (Cambridge: Cambridge University Press, 1990).

33. Beverly Grier, "Pawns, Porters and Petty Traders in the Transition to Cash Crop Agriculture in Colonial Ghana," *Signs* 17, no. 2 (1992): 322.

34. Keith Hart, "Informal Economic Opportunities and Urban Unemployment in Ghana," *Journal of Modern African Studies* 11, no. 1 (1973): 61–89.

35. Bryceson, "Changing Modalities of Alcohol Usage," 36–38.

36. See Akyeampong, "Drinking with Friends," and Akyeampong, *Drink, Power, and Cultural Change.*

37. Akyeampong, *Drink, Power, and Cultural Change.*

38. Thomas, "Forced Labor in British West Africa."

39. Andrew Shepherd, "Agrarian Change in Northern Ghana: Public Investment, Capitalist Farming and Famine," in *Rural Development in Tropical Africa,* eds. J. Heyer, P. Roberts, and G. Williams, 169–92 (London: Palgrave Macmillan, 1981).

40. Sara Berry, *Chiefs Know Their Boundaries: Essays on Property, Power, and the Past in Asante, 1986–1996* (Portsmouth, NH: Heinemann, 2001); Isidore Lobnibe, "Going to Jong: A Burden of History and Current Options among Northern Ghanaian Migrant Farmers in Southern Ghana" (PhD diss., University of Illinois at Urbana-Champaign, 2007).

41. Hart, "Informal Economic Opportunities."

42. Francesca Locatelli and Paul Nugent, "Introduction: Competing Claims on Urban Spaces," in *African Cities: Competing Claims on African Cities,* ed. Francesca Locatelli and Paul Nugent, 1–13 (Leiden: Brill, 2009).

43. Catherine Coquery-Vidrovitch, "The Process of Urbanization in Africa: From the Origins to the Beginning of Independence," *African Studies Review* 34, no. 1 (1991): 59.

44. See Little, *Women in African Towns.*

45. Gracia Clark, *Onions Are My Husband: Survival and Accumulation by West African Market Women* (Chicago: University Chicago Press, 1994).

46. Kinyanjui, "Women Informal Garment Traders."

47. Tamara K. Hareven, "Aging and Generational Relations: A Historical and Life Course Perspective," *Annual Review of Sociology* 20 (1994): 437–61.

48. Ibid., 438.

49. Lentz, "Alcohol Consumption."

50. Stella (former pito seller), interview with the author, July 2006, Kumasi.

51. Nsiah-Gyabaah, January, 2005 Sunyani

52. Akyeampong, *Drink, Power, and Cultural Change.*

53. Josef Gugler, "Life in a Dual System Revisited: Urban-Rural Ties in Enugu, Nigeria, 1961–87," *World Development* 19, no. 5 (1991): 399–409.

54. Bryceson, "Changing Modalities of Alcohol Consumption," 38.

55. For a fascinating discussion of Lenga as a central concept in beer drinking among the Mossi and Bisa of neighboring Burkina Faso, see Saul, "Beer, Sorghum and Women."

56. Maame Konkomba (pito bar owner), interview with the author, Sunyani, July 2005. For a discussion of the mother-daughter dyad in beer brewing, see Luning, "To Drink or Not to Drink?"

57. Anita Spring, "African Women in the Entrepreneurial Landscape: Reconsidering the Formal and Informal Sector," *Journal of African Business* 10, no. 1 (2009): 11–30; John Kuada, "Gender, Social Networks, and Entrepreneurship in Ghana," *Journal of African Business* 10, no. 1 (2009): 85–103; Kinyanjui, "Women Informal Garment Traders"; Agnes Atia Apusigah, "Transcending Gendered Economics: Grassroots Women's Agency in the Informal Ghanaian Economy," *Ghana Studies* 9 (2006): 131–76.

58. Spring, "African Women," 14.

59. Kuada, "Gender."

60. See ibid.

61. Ibid., 88.

62. Kinyanjui, "Women Informal Garment Traders," 149.

63. Ibid., 150.
64. Interview with Stella, January 4, 2005, Wenchi.
65. Lentz, "Alcohol Consumption."

Bibliography

Akyeampong, E. 1996. *Drink, Power, and Cultural Change: A Social History of Alcohol in Ghana, c. 1800 to Recent Times.* Portsmouth, NH: Heinemann.
———. 2002. "Drinking with Friends: Popular Culture, the Working Poor and Youth Drinking in Independent Ghana." In *Alcohol in Africa: Mixing Business, Pleasure, and Politics*, edited by D. F. Bryceson, 215–309. Portsmouth, NH: Heinemann.
———. 2006. "Chiefs and Socio-political Change in the Gold Coast: Insights from Reports on Liquor Consumption, 1919–1934." In *Chieftaincy in Ghana: Culture, Governance and Development*, edited by Irene K. Odotei and Albert K. Awedoba, 309–23. Accra, Ghana: Sub-Saharan.
Apusigah, A. A. 2006. "Transcending Gendered Economics: Grassroots Women's Agency in the Informal Ghanaian Economy." *Ghana Studies* 9:131–76.
Arhin, K. 1974. "Transit Markets in Asanti Hinterland in the Nineteenth Century." *Odu: Journal of Yoruba and Related Studies* 9:5–22.
Berry, S. 2001. *Chiefs Know Their boundaries: Essays on Property, Power, and the Past in Asante, 1986–1996.* Portsmouth, NH: Heinemann.
Bryceson, D. F. 2002. "Changing Modalities of Alcohol Consumption." In *Alcohol in Africa: Mixing Business, Pleasure, and Politics*, edited by D. F. Bryceson, 23–52. Portsmouth, NH: Heinemann.
Clark, G. 1994. *Onions Are My Husband: Survival and Accumulation by West African Market Women.* Chicago: University Chicago Press.
Colson, E., and T. Scudder. 1988. *For Prayer and for Profit: The Ritual, Economic and Social Importance of Beer in Gwmenbe District, Zambia, 1950–52.* Stanford, CA: Stanford University Press.
Coquery-Vidrovitch, C. 1991. "The Process of Urbanization in Africa: From the Origins to the Beginning of Independence." *African Studies Review* 34, no. 1: 1–98.
Crips, J. 1984. *The Story of an African Working Class: Ghanaian Miners' Struggles, 1870–1980.* London: Zed.
Dumett, R. 1998. *The Eldorado of West Africa: The Gold Mining Frontier, African Labor and Colonial Capitalism in the Gold Coast, 1898–1910.* Oxford: James Curry.
Geschiere, P., and J. Gugler. 1998. "Introduction: The Urban-Rural Connection: Changing Issues of Belonging and Identification." *Africa: Journal of the International African Institute* 68, no. 3: 309–19.
Glover, R. L. K. 2007. "Diversity within Yeast Involved in Spontaneous Fermentation of Pito." PhD diss., Kwame Nkrumah University of Science and Technology.
Goldstein, D. 2003. *Laughter Out of Place: Race, Class, Violence, and Sexuality in Rio Shantytown.* Berkeley: University of California Press.
Goody, J. 1962. *Death, Property and the Ancestors: A Study of the Mortuary Customs of the LoDagaa of West Africa.* London: Tavistock.

Grier, B. 1992. "Pawns, Porters and Petty Traders in the Transition to Cash Crop Agriculture in Colonial Ghana." *Signs* 17, no. 2: 304–28.

Gugler, J. 1991. "Life in a Dual System Revisited: Urban-Rural Ties in Enugu, Nigeria, 1961–87." *World Development* 19, no. 5: 399–409.

Hagaman, B. L. 1977. "Beer and Matriliny: The Power of Women in a West African Society." PhD diss., Northeastern University.

Hareven, T. K. 1994. "Aging and Generational Relations: A Historical and Life Course Perspective." *Annual Review of Sociology* 20:437–61.

Hart, K. 1973. "Informal Economic Opportunities and Urban Unemployment in Ghana." *Journal of Modern African Studies* 11, no. 1: 61–89.

Helmfrid, S. 2010. "Thirsty Men and Thrifty Women: Gender, Power, and Agency in Rural Beer Trade in Burkina Faso." In *Beer in Africa: Drinking Spaces, States and Selves*, edited by Steven Von Woputte and Mattaia Fumenti, 196–285. New Brunswick, NJ: Transaction.

Heritier, F. 1975. "Des Cauris et des Hommes." In *L'eclavage en Afrique Precolonial*, edited by Claude Meillassoux, 477–508. Paris: Maspero.

Kinyanjui, M. N. 2013. "Women Informal Garment Traders in Taveta Road, Nairobi: From the Margins to the Center." *African Studies Review* 56, no. 3: 147–64.

Kuada, J. 2009. "Gender, Social Networks, and Entrepreneurship in Ghana." *Journal of African Business* 10, no. 1: 85–103.

Lentz, C. 1993. "Histories and Political Conflict: A Case Study of Chieftaincy in Nandom, Northwestern Ghana." *Paideuma* 39:177–215.

———. 1999. "Alcohol Consumption between Community Ritual and Political Economy: Case Studies from Ecuador and Ghana." In *Changing Food Habits: Case Studies from Africa, South America and Europe*, edited by Carola Lentz, 155–179. Mainz, Germany: Harwood Academic.

———. 1999. "Changing Food Habits: An Introduction." In *Changing Food Habits: Case Studies from Africa, South America and Europe*, edited by Carola Lentz, 1–25. Amterdam, The Netherlands: Harwood Academic.

Lentz, C., and V. Erlmann. 1989. "Working Class in Formation? Economic Crisis and Strategies of Survival among Dagara Mine Workers in Ghana." *Cahiers d'études africaines* 29, no. 113: 69–111.

Little, K. 1973. *Women in African Towns*. Cambridge: Cambridge University Press.

Lobnibe, I. 2007. "Going to Jong: A Burden of History and Current Options among Northern Ghanaian Migrant Farmers in Southern Ghana." PhD diss., University of Illinois at Urbana-Champaign.

Locatelli, F., and P. Nugent. 2009. "Introduction: Competing Claims on Urban Spaces." In *African Cities: Competing Claims on African Cities*, edited by F. Locatelli and P. Nugent, 1–13. Leiden: Brill.

Luning, S. 2002. "To Drink or Not to Drink? Beer Brewing, Rituals, and Religious Conversation in Maane, Burkina Faso." In *Alcohol in Africa: Mixing Business, Pleasure, and Politics*, edited by D. F. Bryceson, 267–91. Portsmouth, NH: Heinemann.

Netting, R. M. 1964. "Beer as a Locus of Value among the West African Kofyar." *American Anthropologist* 66, no. 2: 375–84.

Saul, M. 1981. "Beer, Sorghum and Women: Production for the Market in Rural Upper-Volta." *Africa: Journal of the International African Institute* 51, no. 3: 746–64.

Shepherd, A. 1981. "Agrarian Change in Northern Ghana: Public Investment, Capitalist Farming and Famine." In *Rural Development in Tropical Africa*, edited by J. Heyer, P. Roberts, and G. Williams, 169–92. London: Palgrave Macmillan.

Spring, A. 2009. "African Women in the Entrepreneurial Landscape: Reconsidering the Formal and Informal Sector." *Journal of African Business* 10, no. 1: 11–30.

Tait, D. E. 1961. *The Konkomba of Northern Ghana*. London: Oxford University Press.

Thomas, R. 1973. "Forced Labor in British West Africa: The Case of the Northern Territories of the Gold Coast, 1906–1927." *Journal of African History* 14, no. 1: 79–103.

White, L. 1990. *The Comforts of Home: Prostitution in Colonial Nairobi*. Cambridge: Cambridge University Press.

Willis, J. 2002. "For Women and Children: An Economic History of Brewing among the Nyakusa of Southwestern Tanzania." In *Alcohol in Africa: Mixing Business, Pleasure, and Politics*, edited by D. F. Bryceson, 56–73. Portsmouth, NH: Heinemann.

Wilson, M. 1977. *For Men and Elders: Changes in the Relations of Generations and of Men and Women among the Nyakusa and Ngonde*. London: International Institute of African Studies.

Von Wolputte, S., and M. Fumanti, eds. 2010. *Beer in Africa: Drinking Spaces, States and Selves*. New Brunswick, NJ: Transaction.

5 Interconnections between Female Entrepreneurship and Technological Innovation in the Nigerian Context

Gloria Emeagwali

BEFORE THE TWENTIETH century, the Nigerian region consisted of various city-states, kingdoms, and empires. These included the nineteenth-century Sokoto Caliphate in northern Nigeria and city-states such as Ijesha, Ekiti, Owo, Ijebu, and Egba in western Nigeria, where the empire of Ibadan also prevailed.[1] In the context of village democracies, political power in the Igbo-speaking region in eastern Nigeria was centralized in areas such as Nri but diffused elsewhere in the region.[2] The Nupe kingdoms were among the centralized political entities in the central Nigerian region. The 1900 British occupation of various city-states, kingdoms, and empires eventually triggered a vibrant anticolonial movement in resistance to high taxation, segregated residential areas, discriminatory workplaces, divide-and-rule politics, forced recruitment to fight European civil wars, and a host of human-rights violations. Interestingly enough, women were at the forefront of some of these anticolonial protests at various times, having lost some of the economic advantages they enjoyed in the precolonial era.[3]

This chapter focuses on the activities of women, with emphasis on female entrepreneurship and innovation before the twentieth century. I point out that Nigerian female entrepreneurs were at their peak in this period. The discussion reflects on the circumstances that facilitated and encouraged this trend and focuses on some of the diverse modes of innovation and inventiveness that emerged alongside entrepreneurial activities. First, however, I analyze in methodological terms some of the theoretical constructs related to innovation and entrepreneurship, concepts that inform this analysis.

Innovation and Entrepreneurship

The innovativeness of humankind has shaped the way we live and revolutionized many facets of our world.[4] Innovation is "the act of introducing something new, be it a method or a thing."[5] The variables associated with this activity include curiosity, inquisitiveness, and the willingness to change and modify earlier methods and procedures in favor of the new.[6] Innovative Africa is indeed an Africa in which ordinary people build on "what is already within Africa itself with Africans themselves as the central agent."[7] It is an Africa in which ordinary people are at the center of change and innovation in the creation of the building blocks of society and community over time and space. Innovators question, observe, experiment, and network.[8] Innovations can be potentially disruptive; as Michael Tushman and Philip Anderson point out, we can distinguish between "competence-destroying" and "competence-enhancing" innovative activities.[9] In their view, some innovations make a clear technological break, while others do not. They also note that there are conceptual distinctions between "product innovation" and "process innovation."[10] Innovations can involve new methods of production, marketing, and design.[11]

What is clear from ongoing discussions on innovation is that its relationship to entrepreneurship is intricate. Peter Drucker sees innovation as an "instrument" of entrepreneurship, facilitating and making possible "the new capacity to create wealth."[12] This is done through the creation of new needs, demands, and satisfactions, and through activities such as the standardization of products and the exploitation of new opportunities. Drucker focuses on the contemporary United States, but his insights seem to be applicable to earlier periods and our area of focus. According to a few recent successful entrepreneurs in various fields, entrepreneurs view things from a fresh perspective and have a positive approach. Driven by vision, passion, and mission, they are confident that they can move forward "from zero to one."[13] By implication, entrepreneurs are often self-employed actors, committed to changing existing realities through their endeavors, which can include micro- or mega enterprises.

What kinds of innovation did women entrepreneurs initiate? Were their innovations "product" and "process" innovations, and, if so, what effects did these have on entrepreneurial activity? How did they pass on their knowledge and experience? Niklas Zennstrom suggests that the relation between innovation and the entrepreneur is a "horse-and-cart relationship," with innovation being the cart.[14] How accurate is this analogy for our subject of focus? These are some of the issues that I will focus on.

Gendered Entrepreneurial Activities before the Twentieth Century

In pre-twentieth-century Nigeria, the processing of vegetable oils, the making of condiments and soap, the manufacturing of different types of pulverized grain, and the brewing of beer were done primarily by females, who often created surplus products beyond their household needs for sale in their microenterprises. Female entrepreneurs also made pots, processed salt, and created a wide range of textiles in the context of numerous innovations.[15] In their discussion of "the innovator's DNA," Jeff Dyer, Hal Gregersen, and Clayton Christensen remark that there are no "differentiating features" between entrepreneurs and small-business owners in terms of the variables that they famously identified—namely, questioning, observing, networking, and experimenting.[16] Dyer, Gregersen, and Christensen were referring to entrepreneurship in the contemporary US economy, with a focus on "lone-wolf" entrepreneurs, but their observations seem applicable here. There was clearly a convergence between entrepreneurship and small business in the Nigerian case, with a good measure of observation and experimentation in ceramics, salt processing, and textiles, sectors that are discussed later.

In his discussion of pottery in eastern Nigeria, Thurstan Shaw points to the impressive collections of indigenous receptacles found in Igbo-Ukwu in the ninth century,[17] which may have been produced by women. Females have been at the center of the ceramics industry in most areas of Nigeria, creating pots that were diverse in terms of design, shape, motifs, and usage. The function of the pot influenced the design, with differentiation between water pots; cooking pots; pots for storage of vegetable oil, grain, or medicaments; pots for religious purposes; and musical instrumentation. Pots reflected a high level of innovation and collaborative creativity.[18] Ceramics entailed identification of the appropriate clay, mixing, pounding, molding, and firing. Over time, female potters, who manufactured saucers, bowls, plates, pipes, and ritual utensils, made cumulative innovations in these techniques. We should note that in the Gbagyi-speaking area of Abuja and the environs, the Hausa-populated region of Kano, the Plateau region in the Middle Belt, and Ojaba in western Nigeria, female manufacturers and entrepreneurs were also central to pottery.[19] Female potters came from three main polities in the Birom region of the Middle Belt, while in Wukari, also in the Middle Belt, pottery was dominated by the Ba-zimi, a group of female potters-cum-entrepreneurs who made pots of various shapes and sizes and became well known for their technical innovation.[20] The Abuja potters were known to create pots that had high thermal shock resistance and did not crack when firing. Innovations included improved methods of clay selection and improved firing techniques. Using the red liquor from locust bean pods to baste pots improved their durability, an innovation arrived at through careful observation and experimentation. This was clearly a process innovation with competence-enhancing features.

Another sector that was exclusively under the control of Nigerian female manufacturers and entrepreneurs was salt processing. In this industry, eastern Nigerian women "developed specific technological innovations related to the filtration process and the use of condensers," creating "depth filters" whereby sand "was filtered through strategically located pots."[21] This method was used in areas such as Okposi and Uburu in eastern Nigeria, Gloria Chuku points out.[22] She also notes that the women of Abakaliki designed five types of pots of various sizes and functions for salt processing. Innovations took place in the design and range of pots used. I note similar innovations in Abuja pottery.[23]

Women were prominent in the various activities and techniques associated with the production of cloth; process innovations took place at the levels of spinning, weaving, and dyeing in terms of design and the utensils and techniques used.[24] Technological innovations took place in both process and product in the production of Akwete cloth in eastern Nigeria. Color dyes, motifs, loom design, and the width of the strips of cloth utilized underwent change. In an earlier discussion on textile technology in Nigeria in the nineteenth and early twentieth centuries, I pointed out that one of the major areas of innovation was the dyeing process and the range of colors that was made available to the consumer.[25] In her discussion of innovation in the Igbo area, Chuku points out that instead of sewing together two or three narrow strips, women eventually produced a wider panel of forty-five inches.[26]

Based on Chuku's illuminating discussion on Igbo textiles, table 5.1 lists several types of cloth and their significance, as well as the nature of the innovations made by the female entrepreneurs.

Unlike in the cases of pottery and salt processing, however, in the case of textiles, female exclusivity prevailed only in some regions. For example, according to Chuku, in Igbo society males were involved in weaving Ukara-Ekpe, a type of cloth used by the Ekpe Society, an exclusively male organization.[27]

Innovative Marketing Strategies

In the Nupe region in central Nigeria, females dominated all local and regional trade.[28] Eyewitness reports from the mid-nineteenth century attest to exclusive control of this sector by women who introduced innovative expertise in the areas of purchasing, the storage of commodities, banking, and investment. Initially these activities were centered in local communities in which male farmers sold their wives' farm produce for resale at a profit.[29] However, the first major innovations in investment occurred with the advancement of loans by female entrepreneurs to farmers and manufacturers.[30]

One of the most significant innovations of female entrepreneurs in the region was the creation of rotating savings and credit clubs, known as *roscas*. Membership in these mobile banking schemes was an asset for borrowers, and it enhanced the creditworthiness of participants. Entrepreneurs used these credit programs to provide start-up capital on a rotating basis. These banking systems emerged in various parts of the region under such names as *esusu* in the west and *dashi* in Nupeland. These systems are still highly popular in various parts of Nigeria and in the old and new African diaspora. They enable women to bypass

Table 5.1 Innovations of Female Entrepreneurs of Eastern Nigeria

Type of Cloth	Significance	Innovation
Akwa-ocha	Anioma	Inlays on a white background; product innovation
Ikaki	Represents wisdom of the leadership	Motifs; cross-regional influence from Ijebu-Ode (Yoruba region); repetitive motifs in three different models of Ikaki; use of vegetable color dyes; product innovation
Ikependioma	Religious	Religious motifs; product innovation
Iioji (George)	Ceremonial	Embroidered motif, influenced by South Asian Madras plaid; product innovation
Nnadede	In honor of a military hero of the 1860s	Motifs; use of vegetable color dyes; product innovation
Popo	Named after place of sale	Motifs; use of vegetable color dyes
Ukara-Ekpe	Woven by Abakaliki males	NA

Source of data: Chuku (2005).

bureaucratic paperwork and male-centric banking systems, engage in social networking, and provide psychological and social support for their peers.[31] Moneylending at high interest rates, flexible loan agreements contingent on profit or collateral, and loans generated from the household were among some of the other mechanisms used for obtaining capital in the nineteenth century.

Specialist female entrepreneurs, such as the *kodagbazhi* in the Nupe region, purchased produce in bulk from distant villages and conveyed it from the source. This was an innovation in marketing that expanded on the initial practice of wives buying their husbands' agricultural produce. The *shiyanzhi* were another group of women entrepreneurs who focused on retail trade rather than wholesale.[32] The major innovation of the *dilaliyah*, a third group of female entrepreneurs, was the introduction of a system called *soke* that was designed to undercut male competitors through commissions from wholesale purchase, according to Carolyn Ezeokeke.[33] In the Nupe region, we observe a spectrum of innovative techniques at the levels of marketing, banking, and investment (see table 5.2). The entrepreneurs responded to change and exploited available opportunities in an entrepreneurial spirit, in keeping with some of Drucker's expectations of entrepreneurship.[34]

Table 5.2 Female Entrepreneurs of Central Nigeria

Female Wholesalers (Kodagbazhi)	Female Brokers Working for Commissions (Dilaliyah)	Retailers (Shiyanzhi)
Created a trading monopoly	Created a system to compete with male brokers	Created a trading monopoly in retail

Source: Ezeokeke (2014).

Women dominated trade in eastern and western Nigeria as well. In the west, traders selling similar commodities organized into guilds with their own executive members. These indigenous organizations checked illegal trade, enforced organization rules and disciplined members, resisted price control, went on strike, and created links between entrepreneurs and political agencies.[35] Through innovations at the organizational level, the women were able to empower themselves and accumulate political clout. Over time, the marketplace itself became a political space because of changes made during various periods. Outstanding entrepreneurs such as Tinubu, a trader of Egba identity, and Efunseta Aniwura of Ibadan stood out in the mid-nineteenth century for building bridges to politics and linking entrepreneurs to the political arena.[36]

Overview of the Pre-twentieth-century Era

Nigeria before the twentieth century provides an example par excellence of group collaboration in the creation of goods and utilitarian objects. Innovation was collective, correlating with the views of S. Alexander Haslam, Immaculada Adarves-Yorno, and Tom Postmes on the social context of ingenuity.[37] We note "lone-wolf" inventors such as Madam Dada Nwakata in textiles in the mid-nineteenth century and Efunseta Aniwura of Ibadan in the west, yet the norms and values of the society as a whole prevailed throughout the discovery and implementation process. What Keith Sawyer refers to as "improvisational collaboration" took place from time to time.[38]

The Nigerian context generally presents a cumulative innovative process involving female entrepreneurs and part-time homemakers in the making of products and processes at the local and regional levels. In this case, creativity was the product not only of the thinking of individuals but also of behavioral and sociological circumstances. Female Nigerian innovators relied deeply on community approval and acceptance of their products and the processes associated with their innovations, even when such innovations were revolutionary and disruptive. They also helped shape the demand for their commodities. In some cases, they created customized cloth; in others, they helped create certain tastes and expectations for their products. Innovation was largely generated by groups of people who sought to make their production and consumption activities more enduring and efficient. A "shared social identity" reinforced by shared cultural norms and values facilitated this exercise.[39] What motivated these entrepreneurs and their innovations? They appear to have been largely motivated by the desire for economic independence, which they attained to a large extent before British occupation. In the regions discussed, the acquisition of prestigious titles and honors was a motivating factor for wealth accumulation. With such titles, women gained prestige in the society and competed with their peers. They invested in costly clothing that enhanced their prestige and served as capital if the need for collateral emerged. They lent money to their husbands when requested and competed with cowives in fulfilling their obligations. Men and women were expected to contribute to the upkeep of the family in specified areas, and they were equal to the task. Some entrepreneurs reinvested portions of their profits in their enterprises.

On the basis of my research, I conclude that the relationship between innovation and entrepreneurship is often not sequential but dialectic. The image of the horse and cart is seductive, but each innovation had an incremental impact on product and process and stimulated the emergence of a new bout of innovation in fits and starts. The imposition of alien rule by the British disrupted the process of organic growth, although it did not destroy such processes completely.

The Colonial Era

British occupation was motivated by the search for raw materials, captive markets, and outlets for surplus products. Competition with Germany and France instigated preemptive occupation and internecine rivalry among European contenders. During the colonial era, the development of indigenous technology was directly and indirectly inhibited for several reasons. First, a shift to cash-crop production destabilized internal agricultural development and the supply of raw materials for local manufacture. Most significantly, the Nigerian market was flooded with cheap, imported, mass-produced items that affected female-dominated sectors such as pottery, textiles, and salt processing. Some male-dominated sectors, such as metallurgy, were also affected, but it can be argued that women bore the brunt of the negative impact and responded accordingly with protests.[40]

Colonial rule enforced male supremacy. Women were excluded from legislative executive and judicial power, and the parallel female institutions of power were completely ignored by the new colonial chauvinists. In some cases, mindless Westernization processes, combined with Eurocentric missionary education and misinformation, weakened the passionate attachment to indigenous culture that motivated consumers and entrepreneurs.

With colonial rule, a new, male-centered philosophy regarding credit and extension services emerged. Males now swamped the sectors traditionally associated with female initiative.[41] Some of the economic roles and technical innovations that nurtured and accompanied successful female entrepreneurship were undermined by patriarchal administrators.

Postcolonial Nigeria

The process of female disempowerment inherited from the colonial period prevailed, to a large extent, in the postcolonial era.[42] Although women still held a strategic place in sectors such as fast-food vending and retail trade, the percentage of female entrepreneurs had declined. The introduction of International Monetary Fund (IMF)/World Bank structural adjustment programs in the postcolonial era, two decades after political independence, had significant implications for the economy as a whole. The liberalization of trade, privatization, currency devaluation, and the removal of subsidies for health and education proved to be largely toxic. The liberalization of trade meant the expansion of the old colonial strategy of dumping cheap products on captive markets, and it was a blow to infant businesses and industries that were unable to compete with the new dispensation.[43] Privatization was in the interest of conglomerates and foreign firms, many of which influenced IMF/World Bank policy making.[44] The removal of subsidies in health and education led to high school fees and student withdrawals. These fallouts of structural adjustment policies further burdened the household economy, the domain of women, and reduced access to maternal and children health services, a development that validates the argument that women invariably paid the price for IMF/World Bank programs.[45] These programs essentially feminized poverty. The structural adjustment programs were monetarist and led to intense deflation and a drastic reduction in purchasing power. Women were forced to bear the brunt of the negative impact on the household, and their responsibilities were expanded. Profits from business entities had to be channeled into the household budget to make up for the financial deficit brought about by these programs. Female entrepreneurs involved in wholesale and retail trade were actually blamed for the high cost of commodities.

The Better Life Programme for Rural Women, launched by Nigeria's first lady Maryam Babangida, highlighted small businesses, cooperatives, and cottage industries through high-profile trade fairs and exhibitions.[46] Local fabric manufacture and indigenous rice milling and food processing were among the targeted sectors. Although accused of deceit, contradictory goals, and diversionary rhetoric, the program had some benefits in that it granted female entrepreneurs some access to revolving loans. Its funding programs made no attempts to differentiate women by age, marital status, or class, and follow-up measures for startups were largely nonexistent. The IMF/World Bank conditionalities dealt a severe blow to many women. The Better Life Programme was a drop in a huge bucket of deficits, but it gave legitimacy to female entrepreneurial programs. This may be one of the program's most enduring contributions to an anticipated renaissance in female entrepreneurship and innovation.

The Way Forward

As I have discussed elsewhere, China's presence in Africa brought mixed blessings.[47] The condescending paternalism of the West has been somewhat subdued, and to a large extent a hypocritical, self-serving language of development and aid has been replaced by a narrative of dignity and mutual respect. More favorable terms of trade and interest rates on loans have emerged. However, locally produced consumer goods, including textiles, have been among the major casualties of China-Africa trade relations.[48] To date, the Nigerian textile industry in particular has witnessed a loss of millions of jobs to cheap Chinese imports. Female entrepreneurs engaged in the importation of Chinese-made clothing have done well, while those engaged in the manufacturing of indigenous clothing continue to struggle. At this juncture, the renaissance of female entrepreneurial capabilities with respect to manufacturing necessitates new modes of innovation and ingenuity.

New and creative developmental strategies are needed from policy makers in the context of globalization.[49] The pitfalls of export-led growth, as well as of overreliance on foreign consumer markets, are real, a point that is no doubt as valid for Nigeria as it is for China.[50] Capacity building and the utilization of indigenous human capital remain key variables in self-sustained growth. In today's volatile world, small and locally owned business enterprises may have advantages over mega industries and businesses that generate income for foreign corporations and elites and that may become "too big to fail."[51] In order for female entrepreneurs to recapture lost ground, an inward-looking agenda must be put in place, infused by the spirit of innovation and ingenuity manifested by the pre-twentieth-century female entrepreneurs of Nigeria.

Conclusion

This chapter has reflected on some of the various innovations made by Nigerian women entrepreneurs before the twentieth century, with an emphasis on ceramics, salt processing, and textiles. The discussion has focused on some of the current theoretical constructs related to entrepreneurship and innovation, and their applicability to our discourse. I have concluded my discussion with comments on the colonial and postcolonial era and argued that a renaissance in female entrepreneurship must be accompanied by inward-looking strategies and the passion for innovation manifested by innovative entrepreneurial pioneers.

I hope that the incredibly Eurocentric discourse on innovation and entrepreneurship in most current discussions on entrepreneurship will benefit from the study of these innovative African women.

GLORIA EMEAGWALI is Professor of History and African Studies at Central Connecticut State University. She has taught at numerous universities, including Ahmadu Bello University and the University of Ilorin, Nigeria, and she has been a Senior Associate Member and Visiting Scholar at Oxford University. She is the author and editor of nine books and about seventy scholarly articles.

Notes

1. Toyin Falola and Matthew Heaton, *A History of Nigeria* (New York: Cambridge University Press, 2014); Akinwumi Ogundiran, *Precolonial Nigeria: Essays in Honor of Toyin Falola* (Trenton, NJ: Africa World, 2005).

2. Toyin Falola, *Igbo History and Society: The Essays of Adiele Afigbo* (Trenton, NJ: Africa World, 2005).

3. Toyin Falola and Adam Paddock, *The Women's War of 1929* (Durham, NC: Carolina Academic, 2011).

4. Kevin Ashton, *How to Fly a Horse: The Secret History of Creation, Invention and Discovery* (New York: Doubleday, 2015).

5. Clapperton C. Mavhunga, *Transient Workspaces: Technology of Everyday Innovation in Zimbabwe* (Cambridge, MA: MIT Press, 2014), 8.

6. Peter Drucker, *Innovation and Entrepreneurship* (New York: Harper, 1993).

7. Mavhunga, *Transient Workspaces*, 12.

8. Jeff Dyer, Hal Gregersen, and Clayton Christensen, *The Innovator's DNA: Masking the Five Skills of Disruptive Innovators* (Cambridge, MA: Harvard Business Review Press, 2011).

9. Michael Tushman and Philip Anderson, *Managing Strategic Innovation and Change* (Oxford: Oxford University Press, 2004).

10. Ibid.

11. Clayton M. Christensen, *The Innovator's Dilemma* (New York: HarperCollins, 2006).

12. Drucker, *Innovation and Entrepreneurship*, 30.

13. Peter Thiel, *Zero to One: Notes on Startups, or How to Build the Future*, with Blake Masters (New York: Crown Business, 2014).

14. Niklas Zennstrom, "The Nordic Model: A Conversation with Niklas Zennstrom," *Foreign Affairs* 94, no. 1 (January/February 2015): 42.

15. Gloria Emeagwali, "Intersections between Indigenous Knowledge and Economic Development in Africa," in *Indigenous Discourses on Knowledge and Development in Africa*, ed. Edward Shizha and Ali Abdi, 31–45 (New York: Routledge, 2014).

16. Dyer, Gregersen, and Christensen, *Innovator's DNA*.

17. Thurstan Shaw, *Unearthing Igbo-Ukwu* (London: Oxford University Press, 1977).

18. Gloria Chuku, *Igbo Women and Economic Transformation in Southeast Nigeria, 1900–1960* (New York: Routledge, 2013).

19. Gloria Thomas-Emeagwali, ed., *The Historical Development of Science and Technology in Nigeria* (Lewiston, NY: Edwin Mellen, 1992).

20. Gloria Thomas-Emeagwali, "Textile Technology in Nigeria in the 19th and 20th Century," in *African Systems of Science, Technology and Art*, ed. Gloria Thomas-Emeagwali, 21–30 (London: Karnak House, 1993).

21. Chuku, *Igbo Women*, 58–66.
22. Ibid.
23. Thomas-Emeagwali, *Historical Development*, 163. See also Gloria Emeagwali, "Notes on the History of Abuja, Central Nigeria," *African Study Monographs* 5, no. 4 (1989), 191–196.
24. Thomas-Emeagwali, "Textile Technology."
25. Ibid., 26.
26. Chuku, *Igbo Women*, 69.
27. Ibid., 73.
28. Carolyn Ezeokeke, "Gender and Nupe Economy in the 19th century," in *Aspects of Niger History*, ed. T. Wuam and S. Mohammed, 145–85 (Lapai, Niger State: Ibrahim Badamasi Babangida University Press, 2014).
29. Ibid., 160.
30. Catherine Coquery-Vidrovitch, *African Women: A Modern History* (Boulder, CO: Westview, 1997).
31. Anongo Lyam et al., *Benue State in Perspective* (Makurdi, Nigeria: Aboki Monographs, 2005).
32. Ezeokeke, "Gender and Nupe Economy," 161.
33. Ibid., 163.
34. Elizabeth Edersheim, *The Definitive Drucker* (New York: McGraw Hill, 2007).
35. Toyin Falola, "Gender Business and Space Control: Yoruba Market Women and Power," in *African Market Women and Economic Power*, ed. Bessie House-Midamba and Felix K. Ekechi, 23–40 (Westport, CT: Greenwood, 1995).
36. Ibid.
37. S. Alexander Haslam, Immaculada Adarves-Yorno, and Tom Postmes, "Creativity Is Collective," *Scientific American* 25, no. 4 (July/August 2014): 30–35.
38. Keith Sawyer, *Group Genius: The Creative Power of Collaboration* (New York: Basic Books, 2007).
39. Falola, "Gender Business and Space Control."
40. Falola and Paddock, *Women's War of 1929*; Obioma Nnaemeka and Chima Korieh, *Shaping Our Struggles: Nigerian Women in Culture and Social Change* (Trenton, NJ: Africa World, 2010).
41. Felix Ekechi, "Gender and Economic Power: The Case of Igbo Market Women of Eastern Nigeria," in House-Midamba and Ekechi, *African Market Women and Economic Power*, 41–58 (Westport, CT: Greenwood, 1995).
42. Nnaemeka and Korieh, *Shaping Our Struggles*.
43. Gloria Emeagwali, "The Neo-Liberal Agenda and the IMF/World Bank Structural Adjustment Programs with Reference to Africa," in *Critical Perspectives on Neoliberal Globalization, Development and Education in Africa and Asia*, ed. Dip Kapoor, 3–14 (Rotterdam, Netherlands: Sense, 2011).
44. Gloria Emeagwali, "The Interconnections between U.S. Foreign Policy, Corporate America and Africa's Structural Adjustment Programmes," in *Africa and the Academy: Challenging Hegemonic Discourses on Africa*, ed. G. Emeagwali, 191–228 (Trenton, NJ: Africa World, 2006).
45. Gloria Emeagwali, ed., *Women Pay the Price: Structural Adjustment in Africa and the Caribbean* (Trenton, NJ: Africa World, 1995).
46. Ifi Amadiume, *Daughters of the Goddess, Daughters of Imperialism* (London: Zed Books, 2000).
47. Emeagwali, "Intersections."
48. See Howard French, *China's Second Continent* (New York: Vintage, 2015).

49. Gloria Emeagwali, "Globalisation, Sovereign Debt and Adjustment Programmes in Africa: Implications for Creditors, Debtors and Policy Makers in Europe," in *Africa in the Age of Globalisation*, ed. Edward Shizha and Lamine Diallo, 65–82 (Surrey, Canada: Ashgate, 2015).
50. Nouriel Roubini and Stephen Mihm, *Crisis Economics* (New York: Penguin, 2011).
51. Joseph Stiglitz, *Freefall: America, Free Markets and the Sinking of the World Economy* (New York: W. W. Norton, 2010); Chrystia Freeland, *Plutocrats* (New York: Penguin, 2012).

Bibliography

Amadiume, I. 2000. *Daughters of the Goddess, Daughters of Imperialism*. London: Zed Books.
Ashton, K. 2015. *How to Fly a Horse: The Secret History of Creation, Invention and Discovery*. New York: Doubleday.
Christensen, C. M. 2006. *The Innovator's Dilemma*. New York: HarperCollins.
Chuku G. 2005. *Igbo Women and Economic Transformation in Southeastern Nigeria, 1900–1960*. New York: Routledge.
———. 2013. *Igbo Women and Economic Transformation in Southeast Nigeria, 1900–1960*. Second Edition. New York: Routledge.
Coquery-Vidrovitch, C. 1997. *African Women: A Modern History*. Boulder, CO: Westview.
Drucker, P. 1993. *Innovation and Entrepreneurship*. New York: Harper.
———. 2002. *Managing in the Next Society*. New York: Truman Talley Books, St. Martin's.
Dyer, J., H. Gregersen, and C. Christensen. 2011. *The Innovator's DNA: Masking the Five Skills of Disruptive Innovators*. Cambridge, MA: Harvard Business Review Press.
Edersheim, E. 2007. *The Definitive Drucker*. New York: McGraw Hill.
Eggers, J., and R. Smilor. 1990. "Leadership Skills and Entrepreneurs." In *Leadership and Entrepreneurship*, edited by Raymond Smilor and Donald Sexton, 15–38. Westport, CT: Quorum Books.
Ekechi, F. 1995. "Gender and Economic Power: The Case of Igbo Market Women of Eastern Nigeria." In *African Market Women and Economic Power*, edited by Bessie House-Midamba and Felix Ekechi, 41–58. Westport, CT: Greenwood.
Emeagwali, G. 1989. "Notes on the History of Abuja, Central Nigeria." *African Study Monographs* 5, no. 4: 191–196.
———, ed. 1995. *Women Pay the Price: Structural Adjustment in Africa and the Caribbean*. Trenton, NJ: Africa World.
———. 2006. "The Interconnections between U.S. Foreign Policy, Corporate America and Africa's Structural Adjustment Programmes." In *Africa and the Academy: Challenging Hegemonic Discourses on Africa*, edited by G. Emeagwali, 191–228. Trenton, NJ: Africa World.
———. 2011. "The Neo-Liberal Agenda and the IMF/World Bank Structural Adjustment Programs with Reference to Africa." In *Critical Perspectives on Neoliberal Globalization, Development and Education in Africa and Asia*, edited by Dip Kapoor, 3–14. Rotterdam, Netherlands: Sense.
———. 2014. "Intersections between Indigenous Knowledge and Economic Development in Africa." In *Indigenous Discourses on Knowledge and Development in Africa*, edited by Edward Shizha and Ali Abdi, 31–45. New York: Routledge.

———. 2015. "Globalisation, Sovereign Debt and Adjustment Programmes in Africa: Implications for Creditors, Debtors and Policy Makers in Europe." In *Africa in the Age of Globalisation*, edited by Edward Shizha and Lamine Diallo, 65–82. Surrey, Canada: Ashgate.

Emeagwali, G., and G. Sefa Dei, eds. 2014. *African Indigenous Knowledge and the Disciplines.* Rotterdam, Netherlands: Sense.

Ezeokeke, C. 2014. "Gender and Nupe Economy in the 19th century." In *Aspects of Niger History*, edited by T. Wuam and S. Mohammed, 145–85. Lapai, Niger State: Ibrahim Badamasi Babangida University Press.

Falola, T. 1995. "Gender Business and Space Control: Yoruba Market Women and Power." In *African Market Women and Economic Power*, edited by Bessie House-Midamba and Felix K. Ekechi, 23–40. Westport, CT: Greenwood.

———. 2005. *Igbo History and Society: The Essays of Adiele Afigbo.* Trenton, NJ: Africa World.

Falola, T., and M. Heaton. 2014. *A History of Nigeria.* New York: Cambridge University Press.

Falola, T., and A. Paddock. 2011. *The Women's War of 1929.* Durham, NC: Carolina Academic.

Ferguson, N. 2009. *The Ascent of Money: A Financial History of the World.* New York: Penguin.

Freeland, C. 2012. *Plutocrats.* New York: Penguin.

French, H. 2015. *China's Second Continent.* New York: Vintage.

Haslam, S. A., I. Adarves-Yorno, and T. Postmes. 2014. "Creativity Is Collective." *Scientific American* 25, no. 4 (July/August): 30–35.

House-Midamba, B., and F. Ekechi, eds. 1995. *African Market Women and Economic Power.* Westport, CT: Greenwood.

Kurtzman, J. 2004. *MBA in a Box.* New York: Crown.

Lyam, A., et al. 2005. *Benue State in Perspective.* Makurdi, Nigeria: Aboki Monographs.

Mavhunga, C. C. 2014. *Transient Workspaces: Technology of Everyday Innovation in Zimbabwe.* Cambridge, MA: MIT Press.

Michalko, M. 2001. *Cracking Creativity: The Secrets of Creative Genius.* Berkeley, CA: Ten Speed.

Nnaemeka, O., and C. Korieh. 2010. *Shaping Our Struggles: Nigerian Women in Culture and Social Change.* Trenton, NJ: Africa World.

Ogundiran, A. 2005. *Precolonial Nigeria: Essays in Honor of Toyin Falola.* Trenton, NJ: Africa World.

Rose, G. 2014. "The Man Who Sells Everything: A Conversation with Jeff Bezos." *Foreign Affairs* 94, no. 1 (January/February): 000–00.

Roubini, N., and S. Mihm. 2011. *Crisis Economics.* New York: Penguin.

Sawyer, K. 2007. *Group Genius: The Creative Power of Collaboration.* New York: Basic Books.

Shaw, T. 1977. *Unearthing Igbo-Ukwu.* London: Oxford University Press.

Smilar, R., and D. Sexton. 1996. *Leadership and Entrepreneurship.* Westport, CT: Greenwood.

Stiglitz, J. 2010. *Freefall: America, Free Markets and the Sinking of the World Economy.* New York: W. W. Norton.

Thiel, P. 2014. *Zero to One: Notes on Startups, or How to Build the Future.* With B. Masters. New York: Crown Business.

Thomas-Emeagwali G., ed. 1992. *The Historical Development of Science and Technology in Nigeria.* Lewiston, NY: Edwin Mellen.

———. 1993. "Textile Technology in Nigeria in the 19th and 20th Century." In *African Systems of Science, Technology and Art*, edited by G. Thomas-Emeagwali, 21–30. London: Karnak House.

Tushman, M., and P. Anderson. 2004. *Managing Strategic Innovation and Change.* Oxford: Oxford University Press.

VerEecke, C. 1995. "Muslim Women Traders of Northern Nigeria: Perspectives from the City of Yola." In *African Market Women and Economic Power,* edited by B. House-Midamba and F. Ekechi, 59–80. Westport, CT: Greenwood.

Wuam, T., and M. L. Salahu. 2014. *Aspects of Niger History.* Lapai, Nigeria: Ibrahim Badamasi Babangida University Press.

Zennstrom, N. 2015. "The Nordic Model: A Conversation with Niklas Zennstrom." *Foreign Affairs* 94, no. 1 (January/February): 40–45.

PART III

ENTREPRENEURSHIP AS POLITICAL INITIATIVE

6 Benin Imperialism and Entrepreneurship in Northeast Yorubaland from the Eighteenth to the Early Twentieth Century

Uyilawa Usuanlele

BENIN, AN EMPIRE in southern Nigeria, was built on an enterprise in which its citizens took risks for rewards, an essential character of entrepreneurship. Various elements in the Benin worldview and experience even encouraged entrepreneurship. Some of these still exist in their proverbs, such as *A ma din, ai yan agbọn*, meaning, "If one is not daring, one cannot dominate or own the world." As emphasized by this proverb, boldness means risk taking. Apart from basic survival needs that forced people into production activities, the political and economic organization of Benin also influenced entrepreneurship through its participation and reward system. The ultimate reward sought by participants in the system was membership in the Palace Society and acquisition of a title from the Oba, which granted privileges, enhanced and protected one's status, and offered access to other economic opportunities facilitated by the Benin state and its imperialism.

This chapter seeks to account for Benin resident traders' and settlers' entrepreneurship in northeast Yorubaland (NEY) from the eighteenth to the early twentieth century, when this entrepreneurial system was pulverized by European colonialism. It argues that this pattern of entrepreneurial settlement was a response to the imposition of a royal monopoly on European trade that excluded many Benins from this lucrative trade and forced them to migrate to Yorubaland to organize supplies for the Benin monarchy's trade with Europeans. This migration and residency of Benin traders in NEY also necessitated imperialism in the area to ensure security for the Benins and the cooperation of the conquered people.

The Benin Kingdom's Economic Organization and Development before the Nineteenth Century

The Benin kingdom was one of the early states that existed in the rainforest region of West Africa before the thirteenth century. It owed its emergence to the ability of the area's inhabitants to tame and master the rainforest environment and reap surplus produce, which went into satisfying needs, tribute payments, and investment in long-distance trade. As the early settlements grew into towns, the town of Igodomigodo, later known as Benin, emerged as the dominant polity in the area and was able to subdue and incorporate neighboring settlements and towns into a kingdom. Trading and the exchange of services with settlements far and near brought Benin into contact with other groups. Diviners from Yorubaland are known to have visited Benin, and Benin craftspeople are similarly reported to have plied their trade in the Yoruba areas, even before the thirteenth century.[1] Songs have survived that eulogize Benin traders who ventured to Idoima, which could refer to present-day Idoma land, since Osaren S. B. Omoregie dates it to before the thirteenth century.[2]

As a result of these developments, Benin trading colonies began forming among these neighboring groups. Each migration included skilled artisans or craftspeople and service providers who plied their trade, as well as traders who bought and sold commodities. These movements established the trails that evolved into the four long-distance trade associations, or Ekhẹn, that existed in the nineteenth century. The fourth and least known among scholars of these long-distance links is Ekhẹn Egbamẹ,[3] which means "traders of the waterside." The Ekhẹn Egbamẹ trading association operated through the Ikpe, Igbaghon, and Orhionmwon Rivers, as well as from Ughọtọn to the western Niger delta coastal areas, to trade with Europeans. The three popularly known associations were also named after their routes: Ekhẹn Ẹgbo, to northeast Yoruba; Ekhẹn Ọria, through Esan land to the Niger River ports of Ozigono and Idah; and Ekhẹn Ikhuẹn or Irhue, through Etsako land to the Niger-Benue confluence area. The different trade routes specialized in different products as well. Ekhẹn Ọria and Ekhẹn Irhue specialized in palm oil and livestock, primarily goats and chickens; Ekhẹn Egbamẹ supplied guns, gunpowder, metals, European cloth, coral beads, gin, and salt; and Ekhẹn Ẹgbo brought slaves, various beads, antimony, potash, locust beans, leather, and cloth. The networks distributed and collected commodities from the major market towns of Eyaẹn (Ekhẹn Ọria and Ekhẹn Irhue), Usẹn (Ekhẹn Ẹgbo), and Ughọtọn (Ekhẹn Egbame). Some of these traders soon started to settle among the neighboring groups to organize the collection, buying, and selling of various goods, as well as the provision of the services that went into this trading system.

Ẹgbo Gha Wo, Ovbi Okhuo ọ Lai (If a Forest Is Tough, the Child of a Woman Will Pass through It): Organizing Trade across the Dense Rainforest of Benin and NEY

It is not known when the Benin trading settlements or colonies were first established in Yorubaland, but with the imperial expansion of Benin beginning in the fifteenth century, the forest regions of NEY and some coastal areas, including Lagos and Mahin, were incorporated into the Benin Empire. This fifteenth-century imperial expansion under Oba Ẹwuare (1440–1473) sent more Benin-Edo people to Yorubaland. With the continuing expansion and the subjection of those conquered to vassalage under the successor Obas, more Benin-Edo people poured into Yorubaland as soldiers, enforcers, or friends or supporters of Yoruba princes who had sojourned in Benin. Examples of such princes are known in Akure, Ilesa, and Owo. In Ilesa the Benin escorts of Atakumosa, or Atakukhara, were known to have settled permanently in Ilesa. One of them is recorded to have held the chieftaincy title of Osodi; others held the titles of Eijigbo and Bakinna, which put them in charge of small lineages in the Itisin quarters of Ilesa. Even the first holder of the Ogboni title, who was in charge of Benin immigrants, is claimed to have come from Igbo-Bini or Benin forest.[4] It is not clear if similar developments took place in the Akoko, Akure, Ekiti, Igbomina, Ikale, and Owo areas where Benins traded and are known to have settled.

Ewuare's conquest of NEY coincided with the coming of the Portuguese and other Europeans, which opened a new axis of trade with the coastal areas of the west Niger delta. The new European trade particularly changed the nature of relations between the Benin traders and settlers and the local Yoruba authorities. NEY had been one of Benin's main access routes to the trans-Saharan trade, and the coming of European trade in the fifteenth century transformed the NEY area into a source of commodities and a market. It also made the Benin middlemen between the coast-based European traders and the people of the interior, including northeast Yoruba. In addition to the conquest's turning these areas into tributaries of Benin, it also helped to ensure the protection of Benin traders. With the growing might of the Benin, security threats from neighbors, and the need to monopolize the new middleman position, Benin increasingly began to exclude members of neighboring groups from its territory, keeping the Benin market solely for Benin traders.

In the course of their migrations, some of the Benin soldiers and migrant traders and professional-service providers, such as hunters, medicine men, and metalworkers, founded quarters or cofounded communities. For instance, Itagbaolu is said to have been founded by an Oyo hunter and a Benin medicine man.[5] The Benin settlers in Akure town claimed that they were contemporaneous with the Alakure and that they brought Ajakpada who became the Alakure.[6] In some cases, the Benin migrant assumed political control of the community through guile or strength. Such a development is recorded for Ikere Ekiti, where a Benin prince and elephant hunter sidelined the Olukere and assumed the political leadership with the title of Ogoga of Ikere.[7]

The organization of the settler colonies differed in various NEY communities. In a conquered polity like Akure, the Oba of Benin sent a representative

Abalikale, who was more of a consul in the polity, and also appointed an Ọnọtuẹyẹvbo resident in Benin (spokesperson or mediator for the interests of the polity in the court of the Oba of Benin) for Akure.[8] The Ọnọtuẹyẹvbo approved the leader or head of the Edo settler colony in Akure, known as Ọdiọnwere. The Abalikale title was hereditary, whereas the Ọdiọnwere was not. As the head of the Benin community, the Ọdiọnwere was assisted by titled Igharefa (Iwarefa) or Igeru (numbering sixteen) and the Ediọnleyi. The Olotu Ediọnleyi (leader) became an Igeru when one of the Igeru died. Other sets of titled people known as Ikpaye, Ijagbedion, and Ikode served alongside this leader. There were also female titleholders, such as Olori Obirin Ado, Ikere, and Bamgbomo. Boys were organized into age grades, of which the highest was the Ighele; it was from this grade that they moved up to Ediọnleyi and finally to Igeru. Unlike in Benin communities where the title of Ọdiọnwere was conferred on the oldest male, among the Ẹdo nẹ Ẹkuẹ (Benin-Edo language), the Ọdiọnwere titleholder was chosen after consultation of the oracle. The Ọdiọnwere was an intermediary between Ẹdo settlers and the Deji of Akure, but the Ẹdo settlers dealt directly with the Oba of Benin without intermediaries and sent their tributes through boys who had not yet attained the Ighele grade, known as Ikọdẹ, to Benin.

The new European trade induced an influx of Benin-Edo migrants into NEY and transformed them into settler colonists who came to be known as Ẹdo nẹ Ẹkuẹ or Ado Akue (Akure/Ekiti-Yoruba language). European trade also changed the nature and character of trading relations between Benin and NEY. This development elicited demands for increased production of new goods in both Benin and Yoruba areas as the Benin assumed a new middleman position in this trade and reorganization. More importantly, since trade with Europeans was initially organized under royal monopoly,[9] the Benin traders who were excluded from direct trade with Europeans exploited Benin's inability to meet the supply needs by venturing farther afield in search of more goods to meet the demand. Many Benin-Edo traders moved into NEY territories to organize the production and supplies of the articles required for trade with Europeans and the fulfillment of local needs. According to S. A. Akintoye, "For a Benin man in Ekiti and Akoko, the opportunities were limitless for self-improvement through trade or pursuit of some industry like metalwork. These pursuits were more attractive and more reward[ing]."[10]

The presence of a large Benin settler population and the economic significance of NEY to Benin necessitated the establishment of Benin's firm control of some of the areas to ensure security for Edo traders and cooperation from the conquered people in producing the goods, which facilitated Benin's trade with the Europeans. The push for firm control also came from the wealthy titleholders residing in Benin, who were absentee NEY traders. It became the norm for a Benin trader to strike it rich in NEY, then return to Benin City to build a house and take a title while his dependents and slaves were left to handle the NEY end of the enterprise. It is not clear whether Iyasẹ Ọhẹnmwẹn ever resided in NEY, but, as Ọnọtuẹyẹvbo of Akure, he owned houses in Akure, and his sons (among them Jacob Egharevba's grandfather) and grandsons (including Igbinọba Ọtọkiti) were resident traders in Akure. Another prominent trader who retired to Benin and was also a member of the Ekhẹn Ẹgbo trading association was Ogbẹide Ọyọọ, holder of the Inẹ title, father of Agho Ọbasẹki who was Iyase from 1914 to 1920, and grandfather of Ẹghọbamiẹn, the Osuma titleholder (d. 1959). As a result of this norm, titleholders in Benin had a vested interest in the trade of NEY and were very influential in deciding the policies toward NEY. For instance, when news reached Benin of the killing of some Benin traders in Akure and the Balikale Osague, Iyasẹ Ọhẹnmwẹn demanded the invasion of Akure and volunteered to lead the army, contrary to custom; he had to be persuaded to allow his subordinate commanders to conduct the invasion.[11] His apparent motive was to protect his vested interests in Akure, which required access to profits from trade in NEY.

The resident Benin traders employed various means to grow their enterprise, including the widespread practice of marrying local NEY women. The local women's citizenship, family networks, and knowledge of the local community assisted the growth of business by ensuring security and access to the goods and services needed in these communities. For example, Obakpolor Ogagun married the warlord Ogedegbe's (Obanla of Ijesha) daughter, who was the mother of Arokun (Ayosore), wife of Oba Ovonramwen.[12] Balogun Asa's wife Atigbenro was a princess of Efon-Alaye and mother of the wife of Obaraye Igiebor Eke, who became the Obazelu of Benin. Okoro Otun, the Iyasẹ of Benin from 1920 to 1948, was the son of an Ijero-Ekiti princess and a Benin father.[13]

Trade was organized in a kind of relay system of Benin-Edo traders who established colonies in various Yoruba towns as far as the Ife-Ilesa-Ilorin area. The traders took goods from the royal factors in Benin and traders from Ẹkhẹn Egbeamẹn to Usẹn and Okeluse in the Benin-Edo-speaking area. The road from Usẹn was in a dense forest that was dangerous because of wild beasts, slave raiders (Odomuomu), thieving members of village communities, and other marauders (Izigha), who either robbed the traders or kidnapped them to sell as slaves. As a result, after paying the toll and security fees known as Dọlọdẹ (repair or secure the road), the traders assembled at Usẹn until there was a sizeable number, then were escorted along the forest road by the Ukọdẹ (road guides). The journey across the dense forest took three days of walking and two nights of sleeping.[14] Gifts or tolls were paid to the inhabitants of the communities along this forest road. In spite of this security measure, the traders were also fortified with various protective medicines against other unforeseen dangers.[15] After the traders traveled along the dense forest road, the goods were taken to the Owo area and Akure, from where the Edo settlers further redistributed these goods to Igbara-Oke, Ekiti, and finally to the Ilesa-Ife axis.[16] Another route used by the traders went from Akure through Itaogbolu-Ado-Ifaki-Otun and then to the final destination of Ilorin. The route from Otun to Ilorin was equally dangerous, and it was reported that hunters armed with guns moved along positioned in the front and back of the trading caravans on this route for security.[17]

The informants of Robert E. Bradbury, the anthropologist who worked extensively on Benin in the 1950s and 1960s, claimed that even the Akure people did not venture beyond Otun, where they met and traded with Ilorin traders. It was now left to the Benin traders to venture to Ilorin because of the high profit that the beads fetched in Benin and the west Niger delta area. In addition, they bought horses and assorted leather of different colors that were highly prized by royalty and titleholders in Benin City. As a result, some young Benins learned leather tanning and produced them in NEY for export to Benin.[18] It was probably this adventurousness and enterprise that led the Benin traders to be hailed as "the first long distance traders in Ekiti,"[19] since they even traveled beyond Ilorin.

The goods bought in Yoruba-speaking areas were taken through the same relay system and routes to Benin and the west Niger delta. The Ẹkhẹn Ẹgbo trading association brought European goods, especially gunpowder, metal appliances, gin, salt, tobacco, various textiles that were exchanged for locally woven cloth, shea butter, locust beans, beads, antimony, potash, leather, horses, and slaves. Successful travel along this forest route without robbery or attack "would get a big profit,"[20] according to Chief Osuma, a member of the Ekhẹn Ẹgbo trading association. More profit was made through various cheating techniques, which were characteristic of most trading ventures. Chief Osuma claimed that traders removed a quantity of salt from each bag before arriving in Usẹn, then sold it as a full bag, while those who took it to the Akure area removed yet more and filled the space with leaves so as to sell it as a full bag. The quantity removed was then sold separately and "that would be [the trader's] profit."[21]

The discovery and knowledge of this kind of cheating naturally caused animosity and conflicts between members of the host Yoruba and migrant Benin traders. Economic exploitation, combined with the political subordination of the host community and the superiority complex of the resident Benins, created a feeling of resentment toward the resident Benins in the host community. Akintoye reports that the "sacrosanctity attached to the person of a Benin Citizen" in NEY had changed to animosity by the late eighteenth and early nineteenth centuries, leading to violent attacks against them in some communities.[22] The identification and assault of Benin citizens were easy to perpetrate because of the peculiar bodily scarification marks that distinguished them from citizens of other polities. According to Egharevba, an argument over a small quantity of tobacco be-

:ween the Deji of Akure's wife and the Benin Balikale's wife led to a scuffle in which the Balikale was killed, which provoked Benin reprisals in the form of the reconquest of Akure in 1818.[23] These animosities and conflicts were also indicative of resentment toward the Benin for their economic exploitation through shortchanging in trade.

The Benins were able to dominate this trade not only because of their imperialism in NEY but also because of the NEY people felt insecure in Benin territory. This insecurity discouraged the NEY people from entering into long-distance trade to Benin. According to Osuma, "The Ẹkuẹ [NEY] people are afraid to enter the forest."[24] This insecurity worsened with the growth of the transatlantic slave trade in the seventeenth and eighteenth centuries, as the rising demand for slaves caused an increase in the number of kidnappings. Growing insecurity along the trade route would contribute to the formation of Ekhẹn Ẹgbo later in the eighteenth century, partly as an attempt to check this practice.

Changes and Developments in Benin Entrepreneurship in NEY in the Late Eighteenth and Nineteenth Centuries

In the eighteenth and nineteenth centuries, three developments occurred in Benin and NEY that affected Benin entrepreneurship in NEY. First, the internal political problems in Benin, particularly succession conflicts and contestation for power between the Obas and the powerful titleholders that infrequently led to civil wars in the seventeenth century, were resolved by the first half of the eighteenth century. These problems had weakened the Oba's control over trade, which came under the effective control of some powerful titleholders. In addition, there was a shift from commodities formerly controlled by the Oba to cloth, whose production was widespread and could not be easily controlled.[25] This development further weakened the royal monopoly of trade with Europeans, since more people could engage in cloth production and trade. Similarly, with the resolution of political problems, the Obas who ruled for most of the eighteenth century—Akenzua I (1713–1735), Eresoyen (1735–1750), and Akengbuda (1750–1804)—were able to concentrate their energies on fostering trade rather than on wars of expansion. The period was known as one of peace in Benin. Oba Akenzua I was known to have encouraged trade to such an extent that he became rich enough to build Owagho, a house floored with cowrie currency. His successor, Oba Eresoyen, pursued similar policies, and his principal chief, Uwangue, who was in charge of trade with Europeans, became exceedingly wealthy.[26]

Even though the preexisting embargo on trade in male slaves with Europeans was lifted, ivory, cloth, and redwood still remained the principal commodities demanded by Europeans. This new trade in cloth and slaves drove many into neighboring polities, including NEY, to organize production and supply. With a near absence of wars, which had enabled young men to earn booty and fame, a new drive developed toward self-enrichment through trade. As a result, more people ventured into trading in neighboring areas, especially Yorubaland. This influx of Benins into NEY likely reduced profit margins and necessitated the creation of the means to control the multitude of traders.

The second development that affected Benin entrepreneurship in NEY was the response to this influx of traders, low profit margins, and the security problem on the Benin-NEY trade route. One response was the formation of the Ẹkhẹn Ẹgbo trading association among Benin migrant traders in NEY in the eighteenth century. Egharevba traces its formation to Akenbo, a Benin man credited with pioneering trading expeditions into the Ekiti interior, where he amassed wealth and earned the highest nonhereditary title of Iyasẹ from Oba Eresoyen (about 1735–1750).[27] The Oba of Benin was made an honorary member, while the longest-serving member in Benin was the overall head of the association, and the Akure branch chose its leader subject to the approval of the Benin City head.

Children or descendants of pioneer members of the association were initiated into the association as infants; they paid half the membership fee, while new members paid a full fee for initiation and participation in this trade.[28] The NEY people are reported to have also joined the association very late, but it is not known when or how many joined. Nonmembers of the association were prohibited from using the forest route; according to Oba Akenzua II, violators "might be captured and sold."[29] This development was obviously a way of restricting participation in this long-distance trade and maintaining a high profit margin for wealthy traders.

The third major development that affected Benin entrepreneurship was the collapse of the Oyo kingdom, the consequent internecine wars in Yorubaland in the early nineteenth century, and the rise of the military state of Ibadan. Ibadan quickly launched a war of expansion that extended to NEY. The Ibadan invasion of NEY changed the political configuration and introduced the phenomenon of warlords, which was quickly copied. Warlordism soon became an enterprise that facilitated the slave trade and, invariably, the acquisition of wealth and power in NEY.

It was against the background of the Benin state's pro-trade policy and the established long-distance trading families' control of trade with NEY that a new succession war broke out in Benin following the death of Oba Obanosa in 1816. The war lasted almost a year, and it seems to have sent the wrong message to NEY: that Benin had been weakened by the war. Akintoye opines that the availability of guns sold by Benin traders in NEY also emboldened them to revolt against Benin imperialism,[30] since there was a seeming parity of armaments. As mentioned above, an altercation between the Deji of Akure and the Balikale resulted in the

Balikale's death. What followed was a Benin invasion of Akure from three different directions.[31]

The great effort to reconquer Akure, which was led by three of the four su-
preme commanders of the Benin army, indicates the critical importance of
Akure to Benin's trade and economy. Akure had become the only gateway left to
the great riches that came through the trans-Saharan trade, following slave-
raiding depredations disguised as jihads that were undertaken by Muslim Nupes
farther northeast among the northern Edo. Nupe marauders made that trade route
insecure, since Benin was not equipped to defend it against the Nupe cavalry. This
was also a period of increased slave trading in the transatlantic, and the ongoing wars in areas of Yorubaland farther west were yielding a large number of
slaves, which were in turn exchanged for European goods, especially firearms, to
continue prosecuting these wars.

The reconquest of Akure attracted many people from Benin as citizen-
soldiers and adventurers,[32] some of whom doubled as traders for the first time,
since their nonmembership in Ẹkhẹn Ẹgbo had previously made it difficult for
them to partake in the trade. They were supported and joined by forces raised by
the resident Benin traders to prosecute the war. Apart from the patriotic instinct
of the resident Benin traders and their desire to maintain a business climate that
was favorable to their enterprise, they were also motivated by the increased supply of slaves produced by the war. Egharevba, a grandson of resident traders and
a great-grandson of Iyasẹ Ọhẹnmwẹn, the Benin chief who was the spokesman
for Akure at the Benin palace, noted that these Benin traders in the eighteenth
and nineteenth centuries were largely into slave trading.[33] Olatunji Ojo's study
also confirms the increase of slave trading by Benin traders in the area.[34]
Egharevba recounts that Iyasẹ Ọhẹnmwẹn, the richest Iyasẹ since the eighteenth
century, was a prominent slave trader whose slaves were so numerous that "he
used to be cheated by paying twice the prices for his old slaves when they were
offered to him as new ones."[35] In 1961 Bradbury's informants in Akure confirmed
that Ọhẹnmwẹn dealt in slaves, and when he died in the 1830s, Igbinoba, his el-
dest grandson resident in Akure, inherited 202 slaves as his share of the estate.[36]
Egharevba also claimed to have inherited many slaves in Akure from his father,[37]
but they refused to follow him to Benin and he lost all of them after Oba Eweka II
formally granted freedom to all slaves in areas under his jurisdiction in 1915.[38] It
was after this formal abolition and loss of slaves that Egharevba's family finally
left Akure for Benin in 1916. It is not clear whether this was the reason many resident Benin traders relocated to Benin after the formal abolition in 1915.

Apart from slaves, Benins also traded in cannons, guns, and gunpowder,
which facilitated the acquisition of slaves. Not surprisingly, the wars in Yorubal-
and also added to the demand for guns and powder, but the wars between Ibadan

and the Egba and Ijebu limited NEY's access to supplies, and they thus had to rely on Benin, which was another route for funneling arms supplies from Lagos. Akintoye shows that in the Ekiti Parapo wars with Ibadan, "from Benin the Ekitiparapo imported a long and large muzzled variety [Dane gun] which had a longer range and could carry heavier fire than the varieties hitherto in use."[39] In addition to imported European firearms, Benin smiths also produced guns and other metal weapons for trade.[40] The traders not only bought and collected goods from the local Yoruba people but also engaged in the production of some of the goods themselves. They sought wives and slaves from specialized skilled communities, and they greatly utilized their skills in production, particularly of cloth, shea butter ointment, and locust bean paste.

NEY did not leave the trade entirely to Benin traders but rather tried to participate as much as the Benin state allowed them. Much later, they joined the Ękhęn Ęgbo, but it did not guarantee access to Benin markets since NEY traders were only allowed to trade as far as Usęn. This probably encouraged the NEY traders, led by Deji Gbogi and Olukoju, an influential woman trader, to establish Alade village and market in the Idanre territorial boundary with Benin to facilitate trade between the Ekiti, Idanre, Ondo, Owo, and Ijesa traders on one hand, and Benin traders on the other.[41]

The Benin traders in NEY were so successful and wealthy that of the nine Iyasę titleholders in the Benin kingdom between the eighteenth century and 1948, four—Akenbo, Ǫhęnmwęn, Okizi, and Okoro Otun—were intimately connected with this NEY trade route. Of these, Akenbo and Ǫhęnmwęn were traders, while Okizi and Okoro Otun had tried their hand at trading before venturing into other enterprises.

Religious and Spiritual Entrepreneurship among Benin Migrants in NEY

Apart from trade in goods, some Benins in NEY also engaged in services such as divination. One such divination skill was Ifa Ǫrunmila, which was patronized in Benin. Although Benin had its main divination systems, such as Iha Ominigbǫn or Oguęga, Olokun, and so on, some patrons usually sought a second opinion from other systems. Iha Ominigbǫn was prohibited for some time in the Benin royal court,[42] which made Ifa Ǫrunmila popular with the court and some titleholders. Egharevba reported that for a time his great-grandfather Iyasę Ǫhęnmwęn patronized Ifa Ǫrunmila, then abandoned it and banned the patronage by his descendants as a taboo.[43] Ifa Ǫrunmila divination practitioners who visited Benin from Yorubaland were quartered in the Ihogbe area under the leadership of Ehendiwo. According to Oba Akenzua II, their language was usually the Akure /Ekiti Ife dialect, which meant that they mostly came from NEY.[44]

It appears that practitioners of Benin divination systems such as Oguęga practiced in NEY, and that their absence would have made resident Benins patronize Ifa Ǫrunmila. Since conflicts and animosity sometimes developed between the migrant Benins and the host Yorubas, lack of trust would have forced resident Benins to consult and patronize diviners who were also resident Benins on personal matters. The patronage of Ifa Ǫrunmila by some resident Benins created a niche for Benin practitioners of divination, and Ifa Ǫrunmila was learned by some Benin immigrants as a profitable enterprise.

One Benin migrant who achieved wealth, fame, and power from Ifa Ǫrunmila was Okoro Otun. He was born in Benin City of an Ijero-Ekiti mother, migrated to Akure at a young age, and tried his hand at trade and divination. He later joined and fought under the warlords, where his knowledge of Ifa Ǫrunmila and medicine turned out to be beneficial for their war activities. He settled down to ply his divination trade at Itaogbolu among the warlords and mercenary soldiers. He later moved to Ijero Ekiti, his mother's hometown, where he was ennobled with the title of Eruku. He was a grand master who was patronized by Benin-Edo and Yoruba warlords, whom he fortified for war. The Benin warlord Balogun Asa Omemu ("war shield" in Benin-Edo language or "hawk" in the Yoruba language) and his army patronized him as well.[45] His fame reached Benin, and Crown Prince Aiguobasimwin (later Oba Eweka II of Benin, 1914–1933) began to patronize him.[46] He was given two chieftaincy titles, first the Esama, and subsequently the highest title of Iyasę in 1920. He was so Yorubanized that he could not speak the Edo language without mixing it with Yoruba. However, other successful Ifa Ǫrunmila diviners remained in NEY, while some who returned to Benin after the British conquest contributed to the popularity of Ifa Ǫrunmila in Benin. They did not come empty-handed; they brought along other Yoruba deities, such as Sango and Sopono, which became popular.

Another religion these Benin entrepreneurs adopted to facilitate their enterprise in NEY was Islam. The religion was not widespread in NEY, but the trading business of Benin merchants took them to the emergent jihadist city of Ilorin. Ilorin was a major market for the beads that were a highly prized and lucrative trade item in Benin and the west Niger delta area, where they were part of the paraphernalia of royalty and titled offices, as well as symbols of wealth. Those who traded in Ilorin found themselves insecure in the city because of the dominance of Muslims, with whom Benin had no relations and from whom the traders lacked protection. A descendant of one of the traders who pioneered interactions with the Muslims explained that his father claimed he felt most unsafe when the Muslims went for prayers and were left alone, particularly at night. To combat this fear and win the trust and friendship of the Muslim traders, some of these Benin traders began accompanying the Muslim traders to the mosque, which led some to convert to Islam.

One of the leading traders and pioneer converts was Elaiho Guobadia, who was renamed Ibrahim Elaiho. Initially based in Akure, he was very adventurous and traded as far as Ilorin and the Ejinrin port in Ijebuland near Lagos. He later converted to Islam in Ilorin. After the British conquest and deposition of the Oba of Benin in 1897, the power and authority of the Benin waned in NEY and the Yoruba fear of Benin migrants and settlers disappeared. Since there was no longer an Oba of Benin to protect Benin settlers, Elaiho Guobadia, who was not friendly with the Deji of Akure, moved to Ejirin and in 1899 settled in Benin City, where he proselytized Islam.[47] Some of these Muslim converts were the leading entrepreneurs and wealthy elites of early colonial Benin society.

The Muslim identity and fluency in the Yoruba language enabled some to work easily with the Lagos Yoruba traders who dominated trade immediately after the colonial conquest. They adapted quickly to the colonial demands and are believed to have pioneered cash-crop farming and plantation agriculture in Benin, as well as becoming agents of the European firms that were established in Benin territories. Of the ten leading rubber plantation owners in Benin in 1925, three—Bello-Osagie, Lawani Borokini, and Braimah—were former resident Benin Muslim traders who had returned from NEY.[48] In spite of the entreaties of Oba Eweka II, Ibrahim Elaiho declined the Benin chieftaincy title and its associated indigenous rituals and adhered to Islam. Oba Eweka II later helped him become the first native chief imam of Benin City.[49] Okungbowa and Eke, other converts from NEY, renounced Islam for the Oba's chieftaincy titles in 1918 and 1921, respectively.[50] Under the indirect rule system, holding a title office was a prerequisite for gaining access to the Native Authority Office.

Warlordism as Enterprise

The booming slave trade and the internecine wars among the Yoruba polities in the nineteenth century quickly bred warlordism among the Yoruba as a means of acquiring wealth and fame. This development had a contradictory effect on Benin migrant trading communities since it both endangered their enterprises and provided opportunities for self-enrichment and fame. The resident Benin communities and the smaller Yoruba polities of NEY needed security and protection against Ibadan, Ilorin, and Nupe Fulani warriors; roving Yoruba warlords; and slave raiders. Imperialism and the security of resident Benins necessitated the presence of some Benin soldiers along the Benin-Yoruba border areas and in some NEY communities. Some of these Benin soldiers infrequently stayed behind in NEY to seek their fortune.[51] Also, some resident Benin traders kept private armies made up of their followers and slaves who were mobilized and armed to fight and protect Benin interests.[52] With the ongoing wars in Yorubaland in the nineteenth century, many young Benin men who lacked the capital to start trading ventures migrated to NEY to seek adventure and fortune. One such adventurer was Obakpolor Ogbebor (from Ugboko n'Iyekeorhoinmwon) and renowned as Ogagun, who combined soldiering with the art of divination. He immigrated to Ekiti during the reign of Oba Osemwende and tried his hand at soldiering, which earned him the title of Ogagun, or "war captain." He later settled in Igbara-Oke and engaged in trading and divination. After amassing wealth, he returned to Benin and was given the title of Osasemwonyemwen under Oba Adolo (1848–1888).[53] He was the guardian and later father-in-law of Crown Prince Idugbowa, who reigned as Oba Ovonramwen from 1888 to 1897.

The most famous of the Benin warlords was Balogun Asa Omemu. He was the son of Omemu, head of the drummers' guilds of the kingdom. Omemu was also a Benin war commander who led Benin troops to wars in Ekiti to secure their vassalage, and he was stationed in NEY for a time. Omemu's soldiery probably inspired his son Asa to migrate to Ekiti to seek his fortune around the second half of the nineteenth century. Asa quickly learned the art of war and created his mercenary army at Itaogbolu in Ekiti. During the Ekiti Parapo wars, he joined forces with Ogedegbe of Ijesa and they served as mercenaries for weak communities and pillaged recalcitrant ones. Asa was not only a warlord but also an enforcer and protector of Benin migrants in NEY. For this he was given the Yoruba title of Balogun of Itaogbolu. He also recruited young men from Benin and Yorubaland, whom he trained as soldiers. They were divided into groups and sent out on raids and enforcement operations; in return, they gave him a share of the slaves, reported to be about two of every five enslaved people. He usually sent some to the Oba of Benin and traded others for guns and powder to be used in further depredations and trade with Ilorin.[54] To facilitate his trade with Ilorin, Asa encouraged some of his war captains, such as Obaraye Igiebor Eke, to convert to Islam to ensure their security in Ilorin.[55]

Apart from providing his soldiers with guns and powder, Asa retained some of the best diviners and medicine men to fortify his soldiers against their enemies. For his valor and protection of the resident Benins in NEY, the Oba granted him the privileges of administering the sasswood ordeal, wearing the Ukpọn Ododo (scarlet robe of Benin war commanders), and using a large umbrella, which were all privileges enjoyed by the Oba.[56] He is believed to have lived as a warlord for about forty years in NEY. When he died in 1896, his body was taken to Benin for burial.

One of the most famous of Balogun Asa's captains was Iyasẹ Okizi. According to Egharevba, "From his youth his strong aim and determination was to become a warrior either through desire for power or for wealth. But to engage in such enterprise [he] needed money and men. With this object in view, he left Benin City in the reign of Oba Adolo on a trading expedition to Idoani, where through the aid of Heaven, he acquired a great wealth in money, goods and slaves by dealing in guns and gunpowder, especially during the [seizure] and conquest of towns by Generals Ogedegbe and Asa. Here he eventually became a warrior and followed war for many years."[57]

After serving as a recruit and captain under both Ogedegbe and Asa, Okizi branched out as an independent warlord, with his army based in Ekiti. He fought in support of the Benin armies during the pacification of the rebellious Akoko and Ekiti communities and amassed wealth. He returned to Benin in 1889 under Oba Ovonramwen, and in 1890 he was conferred with the title of Iyase. He continued to lead military expeditions until the British conquest. He died in 1900.

Another notable war captain in NEY was Obaraye Igiebor Eke, a protégé of Balogun Asa. He returned to Benin as a Muslim in the 1910s and was conferred with the title of the Obazelu of Benin under Oba Eweka II.

The British invasion and conquest of Benin in 1897 ended Benin imperialism and slave trading in NEY and imposed British rule in both territories. British intervention changed the nature and character of trade by imposing British law and order and opening NEY and the formerly closed Benin territories to all in the name of free trade. Due to the psychologically devastating effect of the defeat of the Benin kingdom and the lack of imperial protection, the Benin migrant trading influence was weakened, and the big traders began to return home to Benin. Although they maintained their Ekhẹn Ẹgbo trade association long into the colonial period, they lost their monopoly over the routes as motorized vehicles and police replaced their slave porters and Ikodẹ security. The European trading firms, through their agents' penetration of the market and direct trading with the local people, gradually displaced the African independent traders. This displacement and accompanying abolition of slavery, which deprived resident Benin traders of labor and a major source of profit. The dependents of big absentee traders, smaller traders, service providers, and slaves who stayed behind in NEY started to embrace peasant farming and wage employment and struggled with absorption into the Yoruba community, which rose in influence with the ascendancy of Yoruba political hegemony in the Western Region.

Conclusion

Benin migrant entrepreneurship in NEY predated Benin imperialism in the area. With the coincidence of Benin imperialism and the introduction of European coastal trade, many Benins who were excluded by royal monopoly control of European trade flocked to NEY and other areas to organize the supply and distribution of goods needed by Europeans. In addition to trading, Benin migrants also engaged in craft production and other services from which some made their fortune.

The migrants organized themselves into a self-contained community with an administration independent of the host Yoruba rulers, and they had the protection of the Benin state and private armies to maintain Benin imperialism and protect their interests. The insecurity created by the transatlantic slave trade and continued influx of Benin fortune seekers into NEY decreased profit margins and led to the development of controls through the establishment of Ekhen Ẹgbo in both Benin City and Akure. The security facilitated by Ekhen Ẹgbo enabled Benin migrant traders to extend their enterprises farther afield, beyond northern Ekiti to Ilorin in the north and farther southwest in Ejirin.

To ensure access to goods and profit, the traders adopted new cultural practices such as Ifa Orunmila and Islam, as well as warlordism. These practices enriched them, earned them some of the highest titles in the land, and garnered political influence with which they protected and increased their wealth. Entrepreneurship in precolonial Benin was mainly geared toward acquiring wealth that facilitated the acquisition of titled offices, which were needed to protect and increase wealth and political influence. These opportunities waned with the British imperialist conquest of Benin and the imposition of colonial rule, which ended Benin imperialism and changed the nature and character of trade by inviting new competitors.

UYILAWA USUANLELE teaches African history and peace and conflict studies at State University of New York at Oswego.

Notes

1. Jacob U. Egharevba, *A Short History of Benin* (Ibadan, Nigeria: Ibadan University Press, 1968), 7; Christopher O. Ugowe, *Benin in World History* (Lagos, Nigeria: Hugo Books, 1997), 6.

2. Osaren S. B. Omoregie, *Great Benin: The Age of Odionwere, 600BC–900AD* (Benin City, Nigeria: Neraso, 1997), 29.

3. Robert E. Bradbury, "Trade and Ughoton," Osuma (informant), March 1957, BS 68, Research Notes, University of Birmingham Library, UK.

4. J. D. Y. Peel, *Ijeshas and Nigerians: The Incorporation of a Yoruba Kingdom, 1890s–1970s* (Cambridge: Cambridge University Press, 1983), 21.

5. Robert E. Bradbury, "Ita-Ogbolu," Bale and Abel Okoro (informants), February 13, 1961, BS 562, Research Notes, University of Birmingham Library, 1.

6. Robert E. Bradbury, "Akure," Odionwere and assembled edion (elders) etc. (informants), February 12, 1961, BS 563, Research Notes, University of Birmingham Library, 1.

7. Femi Adegbulu, "Edo N'ekue Phenomenon: A Study in Pre-colonial Benin Imperialism and Its Impact on Akure, Ikere and Other Communities," *Lwati: A Journal of Contemporary Research* 7, no. 2 (2010): 88–90.

8. Bradbury, "Akure," BS 563, 4.

9. Alan F. C. Ryder, *Benin and the Europeans, 1485–1897* (London: Longman, 1977).

10. S. A. Akintoye, *Revolution and Power Politics in Yorubaland, 1840–1893* (New York: Humanities Press, 1971), 28.

11. Jacob U. Egharevba, *Concise Lives of the Famous Iyases of Benin* (Nendeln, Liechtenstein: Kraus Reprint, [1946] 1973), 31–32.

12. Ekhaguosa Aisien, *The Benin City Pilgrimage Stations* (Benin City, Nigeria: Aisien, 2001), 203.

13. Paul Eke, "Chief Obaraye Eke, the Edo n'Akure Community and the Restoration of the Benin Monarchy under Oba Eweka II" (paper presented at the International Conference on Aspects of the Foreign Relations of Benin Kingdom, Benin City, Nigeria, June 24–26, 2009), mimeograph, 3–4.

14. Robert E. Bradbury, "Benin Trade and Akure," Osuma (informant), April 26, 1957, BS 58, Research Notes, University of Birmingham Library.

15. Robert E. Bradbury, "Exengbo," Osuma (informant), March 27, 1957, BS 17.1, Research Notes, University of Birmingham Library.

16. Thompson Imasogie, in discussion with author, June 3, 1986.

17. Robert E. Bradbury, "Akure," Jimba Agimajasaon (informant), February 12, 1961, BS 560/1, Research Notes, University of Birmingham Library.

18. Jacob U. Egharevba, *Some Prominent Bini People* (Benin City, Nigeria: Ribway, 1969), 56.

19. Olatunji Ojo, "Ethnic Identity and Nineteenth-Century Yoruba Warfare," accessed December 8, 2015, http://tubman.info.yorku.ca/files/2013/01/Ojo_Paper.pdf, page 16.

20. Bradbury, "Benin Trade and Akure," BS 58.

21. Ibid.

22. S. A. Akintoye, "The North-Eastern Yoruba Districts and the Benin Kingdom," *Journal of the Historical Society of Nigeria* 4, no. 4 (June 1969): 552.

23. Egharevba, *Short History of Benin*, 44.

24. Bradbury, "Benin Trade and Akure," BS 58.

25. Paula Girshick Ben-Amos, *Art, Innovation and Politics in Eighteenth-Century Benin* (Bloomington: Indiana University Press, 1999), 39.

26. Egharevba, *Short History of Benin*, 39–40.

27. Egharevba, *Concise Lives*, 23–24.

28. Robert E. Bradbury, "Benin Trade and Akure," Osuma and H. O. Emokpae (informants), April 26, 1957, BS 17, Research Notes, University of Birmingham Library; Robert E. Bradbury, "Exẹngbo etc.," Oba Akenzua II (informant), April 29, 1957, BS 59, Research Notes, University of Birmingham Library.

29. Bradbury, "Exẹngbo etc.," BS 59.

30. Akintoye, "North-Eastern Yoruba Districts," 552.

31. Three titleholders and military commanders, Ezomo, Ologbose, and Imaran (second, third, and fourth in command of the Benin Army), were involved in the invasion of Akure from different directions—Okearo/Idanre (Ezomo), Okelisa (Ologbose), and Isikan (Imaran). In addition, the Enogie (duke) of Uromi in Esan sent troops to assist in the reconquest of Akure. See Egharevba, *Short History of Benin*, 44; and Ekhaguosa Aisien, "The Role of Songs in the Recollection of the History of a People," *Benin Studies Newsletter* 1, no. 2 (May–August 1996): 2, 4.

32. Jacob U. Egharevba, *Itan Edagbon Mwen* (Ibadan, Nigeria: Ibadan University Press; Benin City, Nigeria: Ethiope, 1972), 1.

33. Ibid.

34. Ojo, "Ethnic Identity."

35. Egharevba, *Concise Lives*, 31.

36. Robert E. Bradbury, "Akure," Olowu Aghedo (informant), February 13, 1961, BS 561/4, Research Notes, University of Birmingham Library.

37. Egharevba, *Itan Edagbon Mwen*, 2–3.

38. Although the British had gradually abolished slavery in the Benin territories beginning in 1897, many slaves remained with their owners. It was only after the monarchy was restored

and Oba Eweka II installed that Oba Eweka II formally granted freedom to slaves. Large numbers of slaves came from many parts of the empire to Benin City to formally obtain their freedom. They were made to perform a ritual ceremony in which they rubbed the earth of the palace grounds with their foreheads before they were released. Thompson Imasogie and Madam Osemwowa Erebe, in discussion with author, June 3, 1986; Omoigui Oviawe, in discussion with author, June 15, 1986; Egharevba, *Itan Edagbon Mwen*, 3.

39. Akintoye, *Revolution and Power Politics*, 118.
40. Thompson Imasogie, in discussion with author, June 3, 1986.
41. Ojo, " Ethnic Identity."
42. Jacob U. Egharevba, *Iha Ominigbon* (Benin City, Nigeria: Kopin-Dogba, 1965). 4.
43. Egharevba, *Some Prominent Bini People*, 22.
44. Robert E. Bradbury, "Oromila in Benin," Oba Akenzua II (informant), July 19, 1957, BS 86, Research Notes, University of Birmingham Library.
45. Eke, "Chief Obaraye Eke," 6–7.
46. Ibid., 2.
47. Jacob Egharevba, *The Okhuaihe of Ikhuen* (Benin City, Nigeria: Author, 1974), 20.
48. Agricultural Department, Organization of M. Nevis, District Officer, Benin Division, to Resident, Benin Province, June 22, 1925, 136, National Archives, Ibadan, Nigeria (NAI).
49. Egharevba, *Some Prominent Bini People*, 77.
50. Ibid., 94; Uyilawa Usuanlele, "British Colonial Administration, Development of Islam and Islamic Education in a Non-Muslim Society, 1897–1960: The Benin Division (Nigeria) Experience," *Contemporary Journal of African Studies* 2, no. 2 (2014): 76; Eke, "Chief Obaraye Eke," 10.
51. Akintoye, *Revolution and Power Politics*, 28.
52. Egharevba, *Itan Edagbon Mwen*, 2.
53. Egharevba, *Some Prominent Bini People*, 27.
54. Eke, "Chief Obaraye Eke," 6–7.
55. Ibid., 5.
56. Egharevba, *Some Prominent Bini People*, 31.
57. Egharevba, *Concise Lives*, 37.

Bibliography

Adegbulu, F. 2010. "Edo N'ekue Phenomenon: A Study in Pre-colonial Benin Imperialism and Its Impact on Akure, Ikere and Other Communities." *Lwati: A Journal of Contemporary Research* 7, no. 2: 84–100.
Aisien, E. 1996. "The Role of Songs in the Recollection of the History of a People." *Benin Studies Newsletter* 1, no. 2 (May–August): 1, 4.
———. 2001. *The Benin City Pilgrimage Stations*. Benin City, Nigeria: Aisien.
Akintoye, S. A. 1969. "The North-Eastern Yoruba Districts and the Benin Kingdom." *Journal of the Historical Society of Nigeria* 4, no. 4 (June): 539–53.
———. 1971. *Revolution and Power Politics in Yorubaland, 1840–1893*. New York: Humanities Press.
Bradbury, R. E. Research Notes. University of Birmingham Library, UK.
Egharevba, J. U. (1946) 1973. *Concise Lives of the Famous Iyases of Benin*. Nendeln, Liechtenstein: Kraus Reprint.
———. 1965. *Iha Ominigbon*. Benin City, Nigeria: Kopin-Dogba.

———. 1968. *A Short History of Benin*. Ibadan, Nigeria: Ibadan University Press.

———. 1969. *Some Prominent Bini People*. Benin City, Nigeria: Ribway.

———. 1972. *Itan Edagbon Mwen*. Ibadan, Nigeria: Ibadan University Press; Benin City, Nigeria: Ethiope Publishing Corporation

———. 1974. *The Okhuaihe of Ikhuen*. Benin City, Nigeria: Author.

Eke, P. 2009. "Chief Obaraye Eke, the Edo n'Akure Community and the Restoration of the Benin Monarchy under Oba Eweka II." Paper presented at the International Conference on Aspects of the Foreign Relations of Benin Kingdom, Benin City, Nigeria, June 24–26.

Girshick Ben-Amos, P. 1999. *Art, Innovation and Politics in Eighteenth-Century Benin*. Bloomington: Indiana University Press.

Ojo, O. 2015. "Ethnic Identity and Nineteenth-Century Yoruba Warfare." Accessed December 8. http://tubman.info.yorku.ca/files/2013/01/Ojo_Paper.pdf.

Omoregie, O. S. B. 1997. *Great Benin: The Age of Odionwere, 600BC–900AD*. Benin City, Nigeria: Neraso.

Peel, J. D. Y. 1983. *Ijeshas and Nigerians: The Incorporation of a Yoruba Kingdom, 1890s–1970s*. Cambridge: Cambridge University Press.

Ryder, A. F. C. 1977. *Benin and the Europeans, 1485–1897*. London: Longman.

Ugowe, C. O. 1997. *Benin in World History*. Lagos, Nigeria: Hugo Books.

Usuanlele, U. 2014. "British Colonial Administration, Development of Islam and Islamic Education in a Non-Muslim Society, 1897–1960: The Benin Division (Nigeria) Experience." *Contemporary Journal of African Studies* 2, no. 2: 65–98.

7 Taking Control

Sonatrach and the Algerian Decolonization Process

Marta Musso

ALGERIA IS ONE of the ten largest producers of hydrocarbons in the world, thanks chiefly to natural gas. It is the eighth-largest supplier of oil to Europe, and the third most important methane supplier,[1] as high as 32 percent in the case of Italy.[2] In 2014 the Algerian hydrocarbons industry accounted for 34.6 percent of the total GDP of the country,[3] 60 percent of budget revenues,[4] and 95 percent of export revenues.[5] Algerian energy needs are entirely covered by domestic production, mostly from natural gas, and the country enjoys the second-cheapest energy in Africa after Libya.[6] More than 80 percent of this fundamental industry is in the hands of Sonatrach, the Algerian national oil company. Sonatrach controls all sectors of Algerian production, from exploration to extraction, transportation, refinement, and distribution. The company also operates in several countries around the world, including Libya, Spain, the United States, and Peru.[7] With a production of 2.7 million TOE (tons of oil equivalent) barrels per day of oil and gas, in 2013 Sonatrach was the twelfth most important oil company in the world for production levels, ahead of its French counterpart Total.[8]

Sonatrach is a state company, entirely owned by the Algerian state and firmly linked to the government and the army. It is the most important company in the country, and it is closely connected to the history of Algeria as an independent state. It was the first enterprise to be established in Algeria at the end of the war, and one of the main actors to promote the country's economic independence from France. Algeria's direct control over oil resources did indeed trigger one of the fiercest battles between Algeria and France, both during the war and in the first decade of the country's independence. Through Sonatrach, Algeria was able to develop a nationally controlled oil industry, managed without contributions from France.

The research presented in this chapter reconstructs the history of the company and of the Algerian oil industry from its establishment in 1963 up to the nationalization of the oil industry in 1971. In particular, the chapter focuses on the development of external networks and on the acquisition of technical competencies on the part of the Algerians, the two main factors that eventually allowed the country to acquire direct control over its resources. In only nine years, from the 1962 peace treaty that granted Algeria formal independence as a sovereign state to the 1971 nationalizations, the country was able to take direct control of the means of production, the markets, and the overall management of this complex industry. This is even more impressive when considering that the illiteracy level of the country was around 80 percent at the time of independence.[9] This struggle to obtain legal and operational control was at the very center of the Algerian politics of state building, and at the heart of its foreign relations with France, Europe, and the rest of the world.

The first section of the chapter briefly reconstructs the premises of the peace agreements between Algeria and France, and the general context in which the Saharan hydrocarbon industry developed. The second section analyzes the situation of the oil industry in the country at the time of independence, the implementation of the peace accords, and Algerians' struggle to promote the acquisition of technical and managerial competencies. The third section reconstructs the development of the Algerian oil industry and the international context that allowed for nationalizations and the final expulsion of the French companies. Overall, this chapter shows that Algeria obtained control over its hydrocarbon resources thanks to patient work in diversifying its market outlets, pressing on international law and allies, and, most importantly, investing in the professional training of a ruling class that grew around Sonatrach as the most important executive branch of the Algerian state.

The War over the Sahara

Algeria achieved formal independence from France in March 1962, after one of the longest and most violent conflicts resulting from the decolonization processes. The war lasted more than seven years and produced a toll of between 350,000 and 400,000 victims, 3 percent of the Algerian population.[10] The formal negotiations, which dragged on for almost two years between June 1960 and March 1962, were stalled several times over a fundamental issue: legal sovereignty over the Territoires du Sud, the southern territories. France claimed that the southern territories should not be considered a part of Algeria because they had a different legal status. France had annexed Algeria in 1848 with the creation of the three northern departments of Oran, Algiers, and Constantine. The two provinces that composed the southern part of the country, Oasis and Saoura, had been established in 1902 under a different administrative system. Following the 1956 oil discoveries, the French government had reorganized the *territoires* under the Organisation Commune des Régions Sahariennes (OCRS), an "international" territory composed of the desert areas belonging to several countries in the French community[11]—Niger, Chad, and French Soudan (today's Mali). The OCRS was supposedly based on international collective management, but it was effectively under the firm control of the metropole. It was a juridical and organizational tool designed by France to preserve control over the area even if the northern provinces achieved independence.

On the other side, the Algerian nationalists considered full sovereignty over the 1902 borders as a *conditio sine qua non* to engage in any peace talks. The cultural, ethnic, and historical unity claimed by the Algerian provisional government was not under discussion. During the negotiations at Melun, Lugrin, and finally Évian, both parties engaged in heated reconstructions of the history of precolonial Algeria, claiming the rightfulness of their position over the southern territories, an integral part of Algeria, or a "mer intérieure"[12] whose resources belonged to all countries touched by the sea sand. As Redha Malek, one of the negotiators for the Algerian side, wrote, "The discussions often reached absurd levels of academic and pedantic abstraction."[13]

In reality, everyone knew that the reason behind such theoretical debates was as utilitarian as it could possibly be: the prize was control over Saharan oil, the new region of hydrocarbon production that could potentially transform northern Africa into the next Middle East. The discoveries were made by several French companies in 1956 after a ten-year prospection campaign in the desert financed in large part by the French government. France considered the resources to be a fundamental aspect of its energy security and economic stability, as well as its foreign politics. With the Sahara, France was hoping to not only become a producer country but also develop its own national oil industry with the acquisition of the technology and the development of a trade area in francs. The French government had initially adopted an almost autarchic approach, limiting the possibility of investments on the part of foreign companies. However, the French projects were hampered by the lack of technology and funds; the development of a new oil region could not be implemented without the participation of US companies. Thanks to its historical firstcomer advantage in the industry, the United States was the only country to own the technology for the development of the oil industry. France tried to safeguard its interests in the Sahara while opening doors to foreign companies through a new petroleum code for the Sahara approved in 1958, which imposed on companies willing to invest the setup of joint ventures incorporated under French law in which a French company held at least half of the shares. The foreign companies also had to invest in training a French workforce and submit to Paris all the data gathered during the prospection phase. In exchange, France offered important fiscal advantages compared to the standard concession contracts of the time.

In spite of the war, the Saharan oil industry flourished between 1958 and 1962, reaching almost twenty-one million tons of annual production. Although the reserves did not prove to be as vast as those in the Middle East, it was enough to cover more than half of the French energy deficit. Two twenty-four-inch pipelines operated at full capacity, and a proposal for a third pipeline was under discussion. Work for a refinery in Algiers had started, and the construction of the first liquefied natural gas regasification plant in the world was about to begin. Even during the negotiations, investments and new production fields were open and the development of the area continued. Both foreign and French companies were confident that even in the case of a failure on the part of French negotiators, the Algerians would not have the capability, whether in terms of technology or funding, to impose any change in the contracts or outlook of the oil industry in the Sahara. France had not been able to develop the resources independently, nor had the Algerians.

On the other side of the negotiations, however, the Algerians were as determined as the French to gain control over the Saharan oil resources. Just like France, the Algerian nationalists were putting great hopes in the oil resources as the basis for their postcolonial economic independence and prosperity. Oil would bring not only economic prosperity to Algeria through revenues but also cheap energy for further industrial development, the opportunity to acquire knowledge and technical skills in a vital and booming industry, and control over a vital asset for the world economy. The negotiators were aware of the impossibility of gaining anything more than nominal control over the oil resources, and they understood that expelling the companies already operating in the area under French terms would be impossible. What they wanted, however, was to be considered the legitimate interlocutors for the companies operating in the Sahara. The Front de Libération Nationale (FLN) had been creating a parallel oil diplomacy since 1956 by secretly contacting several foreign oil companies in the United States, Italy, and elsewhere to negotiate the future of the Saharan reserves outside France.[14] Recent studies on the Évian negotiations show that the FLN was able to acquire important geotechnical information regarding the Saharan reserves, thanks to secret negotiations conducted with non-French companies.[15] The dossiers on which the Algerians worked during the negotiations were the result of diplomatic missions on the part of important members of the FLN to Italy, at the national oil company ENI, in Saudi Arabia at the American Aramco, and at Shell in London.[16] The few Algerian engineers available at the time participated in some way in these dossiers. The level of the Algerian delegation's preparation with regard to the state, size, and outlook of the oil industry in the Sahara surprised the French, who did not expect their counterparts to have obtained such a clear view of the hydrocarbon resources, especially given the secrecy of these data.[17]

Thanks to Algerian steadiness and foresight, France eventually gave up on territorial sovereignty over the Sahara and drew the negotiations to a close. The Évian accords, signed in March 1962, sanctioned the Algerians' claims to full territorial sovereignty under a cooperation scheme with France. An apposite section of the peace treaty was dedicated to the oil industry in the Sahara. The agreement recognized the Algerians' rights as the sole proprietors of the resources. The state would control new concessions and decide on the future development of the oil resources. However, everything that had already been decided under French rule would remain in place: the concessions, which lasted fifty years; the tax system; and the 1958 petroleum code that granted considerable privileges to the joint ventures. In exchange for the preservation of the status quo, France would invest in the professional training of Algerians and would promote "Algerianization" of the workforce. The treaty also included the establishment of the Organisme Technique Mixte de Mise en Valeur du Sous-sol Saharien, a French-Algerian consultative body in charge of the technical management of the mining rights. Composed of six Algerians and six French members, the *Organisme Mixte* had the responsibility of carrying out studies and the execution of public works useful in developing the Saharan resources. A long set of rules regulated its functioning so that it would be equally managed by France and Algeria. The Organisme Mixte was intended to be the body through which Algerians could directly manage the oil industry; for the French, it was intended to guarantee continuity in the management of and an adequate institutional interface for the companies in the Sahara.

All in all, the Évian agreements are usually considered a success for France, at least concerning the oil industry. Although the government was unable to preserve formal control over the Sahara, French companies were still able to preserve their stand in the area, amounting to almost 70 percent of the industry, and to leave intact all the privileges enjoyed under French rule. By virtue of the Saharan code, the companies retained the possibility of autonomously establishing prices and production levels, while the competencies of the Algerian state were limited to formally granting new concessions and collecting revenues. Because the Organisme Mixte had an equally shared board and all decisions had to be made with a majority of 50 percent plus one, the French had the power to block any decision. As Abdelatif Rebah, an Algerian economist and expert on energy problems, wrote, "The Algerian authority over the Sahara was almost entirely devolved to the Organisme Saharien."[18]

However, even though in a much weaker position, Algeria had obtained legal sovereignty over the territory and hence the right to control and nationalize the area, at least in theory. Even though no one believed the Algerians would be able to do so in the near or medium term, during the negotiations, the FLN had demonstrated that it already had important contacts with the oil industry outside France. Upon signing the accords, Bélaïd Abdessalam, one of the delegates for the Algerian side, commented with much realism, "We will be accused of being ultracolonialists, but it doesn't matter; this is the beginning of the industrialization of our country."[19]

A Forced Collaboration: From the Organisme Mixte to the Ascoop

The Évian agreements put an end to the war against France, but they did not bring peace to Algeria. The country was precipitated into chaos by terrible violence on the part of the irredentists of French Algeria, as well as that of Muslims against European Algerians and pro-French Muslims. Algerian institutions developed before and during the war included the Gouvernement Provisoire de la République Algérienne (GPRA); the Conseil Nationale de la Révolution Algérienne, equivalent to the parliament; the État Major General, the army at the frontiers headed by General Houari Boumédiène; the Union General Travailleurs Algériens (UGTA), a trade union; and the Union General des Étudiantes Musulmans Algériens. In the dramatic days of the declaration of the peace agreement, the struggle for control between the provisional government that had followed the negotiation and the army that wanted to continue the war exploded.

In June 1962 the Conseil Nationale de la Révolution Algérienne met in Tripoli to lay out the basis of the future Algerian state. Capitalism was rejected as a manifestation of colonialism that would not allow the lower classes to rise. The assembly voted in favor of a socialist program that involved the democratic socialization of the means of production, an agrarian reform to redistribute the land, and the development of state industry.[20] On July 5, five days after the referendum on the acceptance of Algerian independence on the conditions of the Évian treaty, the GPRA officially declared the establishment of the People's Democratic Republic of Algeria and tried to dismiss the État Major General. In response, the army unilaterally declared the establishment of the Bureau Politique, a parallel government opposing the GPRA. Meanwhile, the country was descending into civil war. Finally, at the beginning of August, the GPRA stepped down to recognize the authority of the État Major General and its political allies, headed by Ahmed Ben Bella, a former political leader who had been imprisoned in France since 1956. The first Algerian elections took place in September with a unique list; the single-party system, which was not part of the Congress of Tripoli's plans, eventually prevailed. On September 26 the first government of independent Algeria, headed by Ben Bella, took office. After seven years of war, it was the army that benefited from the traumatic independence process.

On many occasions Ben Bella had criticized the GPRA for signing the Évian treaty, denouncing its "neocolonial"[21] character and the selling off of Algerian oil resources. Before the ratification of the agreements in August 1962, he had asked Abdessalam, the minister of energy in the provisional government, to sign everything but to try to postpone ratification of the oil agreements. However, Louis Joxe, head of the French negotiators at Évian, insisted that either everything be ratified as one block or the entire agreement be put on hold, an option that

Algeria could not afford. In June alone, five hundred thousand European Algerians had fled the country, abandoning hundreds of small businesses. French investments in the public sectors had also stopped, leaving thousands of people suddenly unemployed. Eighty thousand public officials had left for France, leaving Algeria on the edge of administrative collapse: banks, insurance companies, post offices, communication systems, schools, hospitals, and general maintenance stopped operating.[22] According to the Algerian Teachers Union, 70 percent of primary school teachers were missing, 90 percent of secondary school teachers, and 99 percent of high school teachers.[23] These numbers show the state of Algerian society in 1962. The Muslim population was composed of a microelite of professionals; below them came an enormous mass of illiterate farmers and shepherds, a few factory workers, and many urban unemployed. The majority of the population, especially in the countryside, did not even speak French.[24]

In regard to the oil industry, Sid Ahmed Ghozali, one of the Algerian members of the Organisme Mixte, declared, "We did not even know what it was, this oil so important. . . . I did not know what an oilfield looked like, what it actually was."[25] As a matter of fact, working in the oil industry was a privilege for certain elites in France, and even more so for Algerians.[26] The complete lack of Algerian personnel capable of managing the industry was accompanied by the fact that the Saharan market was shaped around France's needs. Not only did France control almost 70 percent of the industry through joint ventures, it also managed most of the 20.7 million tons extracted from the fields. Furthermore, France was buying the oil at a higher market price than the international price because, as a producer state, it could count on the royalties in exchange. Overall, from 1962 to 1963 France ensured 63 percent of the Algerian budget, and the rest came entirely from oil revenues. Algeria was in no position to contract anything more than what was obtained in Évian. In the end, Ben Bella apparently gave the order to sign everything without even reading the documents.[27]

While the companies in the Sahara breathed a sigh of relief over the normalization of the accords, with the formal passage from French to Algerian sovereignty, the fear of possible nationalization of the oil industry began to spread. At the time, in the global oil industry only Mexico and Iran had carried out massive nationalization of oil activities, both with negative results. The international oil industry and consumer countries had enforced an embargo against the two countries, causing severe economic crises and eventually forcing the countries to partially retreat. However, nationalization of oil resources was one of the flagships of the Arab anticolonial rhetoric represented by Gamal Abdel Nasser and other Arab nationalist leaders, a group to which Ben Bella fully belonged. In October 1962 Jean Loyrette, a prominent French jurist and one of the engineers of the Saharan petroleum code, prophetically wrote in a report for the Compagnie

Française de Pétrole that it was probable that in the future Algeria would follow the model of complete nationalization rather than the French model of mixed capital; for this reason he advised the companies to be very careful in their investments.[28] Several companies operating in the Sahara commissioned similar reports on defending themselves from the risk of nationalization.

Ben Bella and his government were very ambiguous on the subject. While the possibility of nationalization in the midterm or even in the near long term looked absolutely out of reach, Ben Bella remarked more than once that the Évian agreements were a forced compromise that went against the socialist principles of Algeria. The subject was even touched on during the official presentation of Algeria as an independent state to the United Nations in October 1963.[29] The government also openly declared that it considered the Organisme Mixte as a foreign body in opposition to Algerian sovereignty. The name itself, so long and complicated, was an indication of its ineffectiveness.[30]

Minister of Energy Abdessalam, a signer of the agreements, was replaced by Laroussi Khalifa, one of the fiercest critics of the Évian agreement. Under his direction the government immediately began to be very active in the issues concerning oil, capitalizing on the networks with the international oil market created during the war. The minister's strategy was based on four main points: the establishment of a series of Algerian-only institutions for the management of hydrocarbons that worked parallel to the Organisme Mixte; the establishment of training exchanges with other countries; a real Algerianization of the workforce thanks to the UGTA; and, most importantly, the establishment of a national Algerian oil company.

During the first meeting with delegates from the companies in the Sahara in October 1962, Khalifa outlined the principles of cooperation with the Algerian government.[31] First, the companies should consider the Organisme Mixte a mere consultative body at the service of the Algerian state, not an institutional Algerian body. All the communication between the state and the companies had to pass through the Direction de l'Énergie et Carburantes (DEC) and the Bureau Algérien des Pétroles (BAP), the two formal Algerian oil institutions. The DEC and BAP were the first two bodies to be set up in Algeria in August 1962, before the Organisme Mixte was operative. They were the Algerian homologues of the French Direction des carburants français and the Bureau Recherche Pétrole, the two pillars of the state oil industry in France.

As one of his first actions as minister, Khalifa issued an appeal to all Algerian engineers and economics graduates working abroad or within Algeria to contact the ministry and come to serve in the public administration. He also commissioned a report from the Institut Français du Pétrole on how to train a specialized workforce in the oil industry. The first director of the BAP was Claude Sixou, a Jewish Algerian of French descent culture who had studied engineering in Paris. At the DEC Khalifa called on Belkacem Nabi, an engineer working at a Shell refinery in Morocco.[32] The first generation of executives in the Algerian oil industry had all studied abroad, many of them thanks to a series of scholarships for Algerian students that the GPRA had set up in several Western, Arab, and Soviet countries as part of oil diplomacy during the war. In July 1961, for example, 1,882 grants from around twenty countries were issued—947 for secondary education, 847 for the equivalent of high school and college, and 197 for engineers.[33] Most of the recipients were chosen through the Union General des Étudiantes Musulmans Algériens. The other managers usually studied in France and were members of the university section of the FLN-France. Ghozali, an Algerian member of the Organisme Mixte, was a student at the prestigious École des Ponts in Paris; he had organized a group of internships at the OCRS in preparation for its integration with the Organisme Mixte.[34] Most of the future Algerian ruling class involved with the Ministry of Energy shared this type of experience.

Another important element of immediate help that Algeria received from abroad was the choice of consultants on the hydrocarbon industry outside France. In a note to the government, Claude Cheysson, the French head of the Organisme Mixte, stated that the Algerian government was in contact with two members of the Organisation of the Petroleum Exporting Countries (OPEC): the Iraqi Nadhim Pachachi, who was relatively moderate, and the Saudi Abdullah Tariki, an ex-minister of oil who was an early advocate of nationalization on the part of producer countries. Cheysson described Tariki as a "hothead," hoping that the Algerians would choose Pachachi, who might agree to work in collaboration with France.[35] In the end, Ben Bella opted for Tariki, despite the fact that he did not speak French. The first piece of advice from the new consultant of the Ministry of Energy was to learn English.

The second point that Khalifa clarified in October 1962 was that he wanted to see immediate and effective action concerning the Algerianization of the workforce. This was a matter not just of hiring more Algerians but also of bridging the salary gaps and, most importantly, investing in the training not only of technicians but also of future executives. The UGTA was immediately effective in taking such action. On March 26, 1962, ten days after the signing of the Évian agreements, a general strike of the transport sector had paralyzed the sites of the French Société Nationale de Recherche et d'Exploitation de Pétrole en Algérie and of Compagnie Française des Pétroles, forcing the companies to close the wells. A second wave of strikes lasted throughout May. The UGTA had three main requests that corresponded to those of the government: the Algerianization of managerial and executive positions, not just the lower posts; the creation of comités d'entreprise, work councils based on the French model; and the relocation of the headquarters of the joint ventures operating in the Sahara from Paris to Algiers.

In 1962 the living conditions in the oilfields followed in full the structure and division of colonial societies. Only a handful of managers in lower posts were Algerians: SN REPAL had two Algerian engineers and Compagnie Française des Pétroles - Algérie had five. Even when highly specialized, the workers were kept in subordinate positions so that an Algerian Muslim would not give orders to a Frenchman.[36] The drillers, who occupied a dangerous and physically exhausting position, were all Algerians, but the team leaders were all European. Outside the work structures, lives in the oilfields were also divided racially. The desert presented harsh conditions, with temperatures that could reach fifty degrees Celsius during the day and drop to zero at night. The bases, small towns floating in the desert, followed the same hierarchy as the northern towns. The European elite had access to bungalows, cinemas, swimming pools, bars, and restaurants, while the low-skilled workers, in large majority Algerians from the poorer southern areas, lived in barracks and tents. When amenities were built for the low-skilled workers, the cinemas and bars were still separate for Algerians and Europeans, and only the Europeans were provided with air conditioning.[37] Algerian colors and flags were forbidden; after the independence, when the government ruled that French flags were to be replaced with Algerian flags onsite, the companies resisted the order. Although symbolic, the problem of the flag touched the core of the issue of the legitimate proprietor of a territory.

After two years of work in the field, the UGTA was able to achieve a series of objectives: comités d'entreprise in every establishment, paid strikes, mandatory training courses organized by the companies, and the end of the use of an auxiliary workforce, a practice in which personnel was hired on a daily basis according to necessity and denied any form of protection. In particular, the presence of the comités was very important to the Algerian government, since they had the aim of gaining voting rights on the board in compliance with the principle of the socialization of the means of production. Since the UGTA was firmly placed under government control, it was the first way for the Algerian establishment to have a say over the establishments. However, the comités had the clear merit of overseeing the steps toward closing the salary gaps and implementing the Algerianization process.

The third point that Khalifa clarified with the companies was that the Algerian state wanted to eventually participate in all aspects of the oil industry—the upstream sector (research and production) and the downstream sector (transportation, refining, and distribution). In the immediate future, the companies had to pass on to the BAP and DEC all geophysical data and information on drilling activities, production quotas, and distribution.[38] The first operative role of the state came with the acquisition of 40 percent of the shares of the Franco-Algerian company SN REPAL that had belonged to the Algerian governorate. SN REPAL was involved in prospection projects, the construction of the liquefied natural gas regasification plant, and the Algerian distribution network; thanks to the shares, the government had acquired about 10 percent in each of these ventures. In particular, SN REPAL was involved in the construction of a third pipeline from Hassi Messaoud to Arzew, an important and urgent task because the other two pipelines had now reached full capacity and production in the Sahara risked decline due to the lack of means for transportation. Early in 1963 the Trapal consortium was established among sixteen operators in the Sahara to present the project to the Algerian government. According to the Saharan petroleum code, the government had an obligation to facilitate the transportation of the product; however, it did not openly state that companies had the right to ownership of the infrastructures.

Thanks to the urgent character of the project, the government began to pressure the companies by stating that it would endorse the project only if it could directly acquire 51 percent of the shares. The companies refused to allow the government to hold more than 13 percent of the shares. Aside from the insertion of Algerian authorities, control over the pipelines was one of the fundamental aspects of transportation. Ownership entailed the right to decide transportation fees, an important entry in the costs of production. Negotiations went on for most of 1963 but the government did not cede, blocking the project and therefore extraction. Meanwhile, Khalifa had set up a team of experts from BAP and DEC to study the feasibility of a project that did not include the consortium at all; Algeria would construct the third pipeline by itself. Through the intermediation of the Arab Bank in Switzerland, the Ministry of Energy began to look for investors and technical contractors. No one from the Organisme Mixte was involved in the operation for fear that the French would discover the parallel project.[39] The Algerians initially turned to the United States; however, high-ranked officers in the US administration apparently tried to dissuade the government.[40] The construction companies also refused, unwilling to alienate the companies in the Sahara, some of the most important of the time: Shell, Standard Oil of New Jersey, and several American companies with important influence in the United States. Thyssen, a German company, also expressed its reluctance to go against France.[41] In the end, it was the United Kingdom that agreed to help Algeria. Several British banks offered a loan totaling £18.5 million, and the deal was signed with the Scottish construction company John Brown.[42]

In order to supervise the project, in December 1963 Ben Bella announced the establishment of the Société Nationale pour le Transport des Hydrocarbures, the Algerian national oil company. The chosen acronym for the company was initially "SNATCH," but the English explained that this would sound quite vulgar in the Anglo-Saxon world, so the company was established as Sonatrach.[43] Sonatrach was a public company modeled on the French law of 1868, with a capital of 50 million francs and shares entirely owned by the state and other public bodies. Abdessalam became its first president. The headquarters were set up in an office confiscated from the Organisme Mixte. When the government announced that the contract for the third pipeline would go to Sonatrach in venture with John Brown, it also announced that the pipeline would have a diameter of twenty-eight inches instead of twenty-four, as in the Trapal project. It would thus accommodate not only the oil extracted by the companies currently in the Sahara but also the oil that Sonatrach would directly produce in the future.

Unsurprisingly, the other companies and the French government protested vehemently against the Sonatrach project, stating that the lack of control over the pipeline was a very serious breach of the Évian accords. The consortium turned to international arbitration in The Hague, as suggested in the accords in case of dispute. However, the Algerian government ignored the arbitration, refused to appoint a third party, and stated that it would not give validity to any verdict. While the trial went on as a pantomime in Algeria's absence, the work continued in the desert under the supervision of Aït Sid Mohamed, an Algerian engineer who had graduated from the Yugoslav University of Ljubljana. Sonatrach also signed a deal with the Italian company ENI for a refinery in Arzew, a future competitor for the one built by Saharan companies in Algiers. By the end of 1964 the Algerian company was a well-established new actor in the Saharan oil industry. In only two years the government had not only established a political institution capable of negotiating with other countries but also set up a national company able to take charge of hydrocarbon transportation. In addition, the Algerians were again able to sit at the negotiating table with France, this time from a position of power.

From the Ascoop Agreement to Nationalization

After the Trapal consortium went to arbitration, the Algerian government put on hold all negotiations with the company, blocking new research projects and the release of new concessions. Ben Bella stated that they would only negotiate directly with the French state regarding the revision and settlement of the Évian accords. The Algerian government asked for three major changes: the alignment of the Saharan tax system with standard international contracts and the end of fiscal privileges for the companies; the relocation of the joint ventures headquarters from Paris to Algiers, in line with what France had required when it controlled the Sahara; and the participation of Sonatrach in all future research permits. The negotiations lasted around one year, constantly monitored by Charles de Gaulle and Ben Bella directly. None of the companies operating in the Sahara were allowed to participate in the negotiations; the Algerians knew that the French government was more interested in preserving its portion of control over the Sahara than in the profits, and that it would be willing to grant more concessions to Algeria as long as it remained in partnership with the French. According to Rebah's memoir on Sonatrach, de Gaulle instructed Cheysson, the French head of the negotiation, to "go and tell Ben Bella that the Évian accords are the Évian accords, but for me they are not the Koran."[44]

The new French-Algerian agreement was finally signed in July 1965, unlocking applications for new concessions and setting up a new type of collaboration between Algeria and France called the "Ascoop" (Association Coopérative) agreement. Although the validity of the 1958 Saharan code was once again reaffirmed, Algeria obtained a review of the tax system.[45] Furthermore, future concessions would be a monopoly of new French-Algerian joint ventures in which the two countries would share equal control while also collaborating with other partners. The Ascoop would hold the monopoly over an area of 180,000 square meters, the most promising parts of the Algerian Sahara. Sonatrach was also able to acquire from DEC and BAP the shares of SN REPAL inherited from the Algerian governorate, an operation that both the French and the other companies had tried to block for fear it would be a Trojan horse for nationalization. With the acquisition of 40 percent of SN REPAL, Sonatrach officially entered into the upstream operations of the oil industry and changed its full name to the Société Nationale pour la Recherche, la Production, le Transport, la Transformation, et la Commercialisation des Hydrocarbures.

The Ascoop agreement represented a novelty in the panorama of oil contracts at the time because it was based on government negotiations in which the companies acted as simple contractors in the area without having a say in the general strategies of oil production and distribution. In fact, the companies vehemently opposed the Ascoop agreement, including the French public bodies that controlled the majority of shares in the Sahara. However, for the French government it provided a way to retain political control over the Sahara against the foreign companies while appeasing Algeria's nationalistic objectives. Both countries presented the Ascoop agreements as a revolution in the oil industry, led by a new wave of state oilmen that represented the strengthening of state power against corporations. In reality, however, neither France nor Algeria pushed forward a real collaboration. In France, mainly due to internal political reasons, Pierre Guillaumat became the head of the French side of the Ascoop. Guillaumat was the most powerful of French state oilmen, but he was also a former dyed-in-the-wool French Algerian who had opposed the Ascoop agreement in the first place.

In Algeria, right before the signing of the contract, a coup d'état deposed Ben Bella in favor of his former ally General Boumédiène, who supported the idea of a *tout court* nationalization of the oil industry much more fervently. Despite the successes in the oil industry, the deterioration of general economic conditions and the situation of unrest in the country had eroded Ben Bella's leadership. General Boumédiène, already a fundamental figure of power in the country, eventually decided to cut out his political counterpart and take sole power. The new government displayed the authoritarian turn in Algerian politics. Khalifa, considered too close to Ben Bella, was set aside and replaced with Abdessalam. Ghozali, from the Organisme Mixte, became president of both the DEC and Sonatrach. With its members absorbed in the Ascoop project, the Organisme Mixte ceased to exist. Boumédiène's leadership was much more aggressive than Ben Bella's; the new principles of Algerian energy politics aimed to combine American capital and technology with Soviet-style governance.[46] The complete nationalization of the Algerian industry was regarded as the best solution to all Algerian economic and social problems, and oil and gas revenues were seen as the only capital that Algeria needed to accelerate its development and decrease the gap with the West.

While the Ascoop agreement remained idle, the government devoted all of its attention and investments to Sonatrach. As part of the 1965 agreement, in November the Institut Algérien du Pétrole opened as the first Algerian hydrocarbon school. The school was managed by the comités d'entreprise and the courses were organized by companies in the Sahara, which also provided the funding. The institute not only provided technical training but also instructed experts in general management and HR. At the same time, Sonatrach sealed an agreement with the University of Sheffield in the United Kingdom and with the School for Hydrocarbons owned by ENI in Italy to train Algerian undergraduates in finance, mechanical and chemical engineering, and accounting.[47] Thanks to this new influx of a specialized Algerian workforce, the company adopted a more complex structure inspired by European state companies. A series of new supply contracts were signed with Brazil, Italy, the Soviet Union, and the United States.

In 1966 the company's first project, the pipeline from Hassi Messaoud to Arzew, was inaugurated in a solemn ceremony attended by the heads of state and ministers from Spain, Soudan, Yemen, Egypt, the USSR, Italy, and Libya. Boumédiène declared that the establishment of the "first 100 percent Algerian pipeline" should be considered "a new 1st November," the day celebrated as the start of the 1954 rebellion.[48] In the same period, Sonatrach announced the establishment of an Algerian-American joint venture for drilling, Alfor, with the Texan South-Eastern Drilling Company. The contract was strongly opposed by France. Up to that point the majority of contractors operating in the Sahara had been French; this represented an important blow to the Ascoop agreement.

The following year a series of events doubled the size of Sonatrach in only a few months. In January Sonatrach acquired the distribution network from BP—350 petrol stations in the Algerian territory, corresponding to 15 percent of the entire distribution network.[49] In June 1967, when the Six-Day War broke out, Boumédiène urged all Arab countries to place an embargo against Israel's supporters, namely the United States and the United Kingdom. In order to enforce the embargo, the Ministry of Energy declared that all Anglo-Saxon companies present in Algeria would be nationalized. The directors of Shell-Algérie, Unilever-Algérie, Sinclair Mediterranean, and others were summoned to the ministry while the police sealed their offices and confiscated the establishments.[50] Overnight, the 4,500 workers in these companies became Algerian state employees under Sonatrach, increasing the number of company personnel from 955 to 5,929.[51] Engineers from Russia and Romania replaced the Western executives who left.[52] However, the nationalization did not concern Anglo-American joint ventures in which Algeria already held more than 50 percent of shares; as Boumédiène admitted, "the nationalizations were only a way to get the oil."[53]

Even though the French companies were not directly touched by the nationalizations, the repercussions of the embargo were strongly negative because many of the French joint ventures had important sales contracts with the United Kingdom. Furthermore, a new wave of strikes hit the French companies in September 1967. During the strikes, protesters closed the wells for forty-eight hours and then opened them again without incident, demonstrating that the Algerians had acquired control of the technology.[54] Interestingly, the following year a new wave of strikes saw low-skilled Algerian workers protesting against the Algerian managers and executives—the problem of class had replaced the traditional colonial divisions. These strikes were not authorized by the UGTA, and many workers were arrested.

After June 1967 it became clear that it was no longer a matter of if but rather of when nationalization would occur. Boumédiène now talked openly of the imminent nationalization of the entire hydrocarbon sector. However, everyone knew that he could not proceed in nationalizing the industry without coordination on the part of the other producer countries. The examples of Mexico and Iran and the power of retaliation by the international oil industry were such that Algeria could not have carried out such a major operation alone. Furthermore, France's strength in the negotiations was that Algerian oil was more difficult and expensive to buy than oil from the Middle East or Libya because of the geological position of the deposits. The obstacle to the nationalizations was no longer the problem of competencies or alternative markets to France but rather that of coordination with other producer countries in order to adopt a common strategy.

In 1969 Algeria officially joined OPEC, immediately becoming one of the hawks within the organization. In a series of conferences promoted by Boumédiène with OPEC and with the Arab League, he urged Third World countries to gain full control over their oil resources and end exploitation by Western companies. Boumédiène's rhetoric was already the most popular in OPEC; the majority of its members were in favor of collectively contracting a new tax system against the companies.

Beginning in 1969 when the negotiations for a planned revision of the Ascoop system began, the general climate could not have been more unfavorable to France. At the same time, negotiations between companies operating in the

Middle East and the Gulf countries were taking place and continued throughout 1970. In June Minister Abdessalam unilaterally raised the reference price for Saharan oil to a level that France would never accept. This decision clearly went against the 1965 agreement and instigated a political crisis, as the Algerians had planned. Finally, on February 4, 1971, France interrupted the negotiations unilaterally, stating that they would not let the Algerians do whatever they pleased with the Saharan oil industry. On February 14 the Gulf countries announced a new deal with the oil companies that significantly raised the tax rates in the entire area. Boumédiène ordered France to accept the same conditions, and when the delegation refused, he declared the nationalization of all Algerian hydrocarbon resources. The 1971 Algerian nationalization law put under state control, and hence under Sonatrach's control, 51 percent of oil activities and 100 percent of gas activities, becoming the third producer state in the world to nationalize. The French companies, the only remaining companies controlling more than 50 percent of shares in the joint ventures, decided to leave after negotiating the indemnities. By May 1971 most of the French personnel had left the fields controlled by Compagnie Française des Pétroles - Algérie and the other companies, replaced mainly by an Algerian workforce.

With the nationalizations, Boumédiène declared the process of independence complete, the conclusion of a second revolution that was as important as the first in guaranteeing Algeria's independence. In only nine years the country was able to take control of an industry that required high capital and high technical expertise, neither of which was available at independence. Sonatrach, a seven-year-old company, was now the most important company in northern Africa, the center of the Algerian economy, as well as its political heart. France, on the other hand, had to accept that the Évian era had concluded, that Algeria was entirely a foreign country, and that the Saharan resources would not be under French control again.

Conclusion

The fifteen years between 1971 and 1986, the golden era of OPEC, were also a period of important economic acceleration for the Algerian economy, driven mostly by Sonatrach. The annual production of oil and gas went from forty million TOE in 1971 to seventy-five million in 1978; the revenues grew from less than 2 million dinars in 1971 to almost 83 million in 1980. The number of Sonatrach employees reached eighty thousand, ten times the total in 1971, and were primarily Algerians. After thriving during the high oil prices of the 1970s and surviving the countershocks of the 1980s relatively well, thanks to more stable gas prices, Sonatrach is still one of the most important African companies and a large company among oil and gas producers.[55] As of 2013 it employed a total of 120,000 workers, 48,000 directly employed by Sonatrach and in large part Algerians—10,800 engineers, 5,129 university graduates, and 22,881 specialized workers.[56] Although the nationalization law was reviewed several times, and since 2012 the joint ventures in the Sahara have allowed up to 75 percent foreign participation,[57] Sonatrach is still fully in charge of the Algerian energy policy and the most important branch of the government.

Overall, the performance of the Algerian economy is far from bright, and the country was never able to live up to the optimism of the post-decolonization period. The same ruling class that fought the independence war and then imposed the one-party system is still in power, and it continues to control the economic and political life of the country. In general, the country suffers from all the symptoms of the so-called Dutch disease and the oil curse: underdeveloped primary and secondary sectors, few relevant economic activities outside the hydrocarbon industry, dependence on the fluctuation of oil prices, and a dual economy. Especially during the 1990s, the industrial output of public enterprises in the nonhydrocarbon sector declined by around 25 percent. Many bankrupt businesses are artificially supported by the public banking system that channels oil revenues through a system based on cronyism.[58]

However, while the problems of the Algerian economic and social system are undeniable, there is no evidence that the presence of foreign companies in the area would have improved the political and economic situation of the country. The Ascoop agreement was intended to use oil contracts as the basis for further cooperation agreements between Algeria and France. However, no other business but the oil sector was taken into consideration during the negotiations.

On the other hand, the capability of the new Algerian ruling class to seize control of the oil industry and expand it for the national benefit in terms of revenues and control over production was truly remarkable. After Algeria's success in the nationalizations, all other producer countries proceeded to nationalize their industry, imposing a decade of high prices that represented the largest transfer of wealth ever to occur without a war.[59] The creation of a company like Sonatrach represented an important empowering moment for Algeria and its economic relations with the outside world. The exacerbated nationalism of the Algerian economic structures should also be considered in light of the complete lack of an Algerian entrepreneurial class with capital to invest; all private capital in the hands of European Algerians fled the country at independence. Algerian entrepreneurs formed around the state and around the hydrocarbon industry. Thanks to the state, and in particular to the strong promotion of the workforce acquiring technical competencies, Algeria was able to overturn the colonial structures of the Sahara. One must remember that this overturn mainly benefited a small circle of technical experts who were able to take control of the industry. However, despite the many problems associated with the Algerian oil industry, Sonatrach and its technocrats represent a positive example of an entrepreneurial state that was able to make a nine-year-old country with no capital and no competencies prevail over a world power and several of the most powerful international corporations, imposing control over its territory in a process of economic decolonization that still continues.

MARTA MUSSO is Max Weber Fellow at the European University Institute. She works on the relations between state and enterprise, energy networks and foreign politics, oil revenues, and development.

Notes

1. "International Energy Statistics: Total Petroleum and Other Liquids Production 2014," US Energy Information Administration, 2014, http://www.eia.gov/beta/international/rankings/index.cfm#?iso=DZA&cy=2014.
2. "Energy Supply Security 2014," US Energy Information Administration, 2014, https://www.eia.org/media/freepublications/security/EnergySupplySecurity2014_France.pdf.
3. See *"African Economic Outlook* 2015", OECD, 2015, http://www.africaneconomicoutlook.org/sites/default/files/content-pdf/AEO2015_EN.pdf.
4. "Algeria," US Energy Information Administration, 2014, https://www.eia.gov/beta/international/analysis.cfm?iso=DZA.
5. "Algeria Exports," Trading Economics, 2016, http://www.tradingeconomics.com/algeria/exports.
6. "Algeria," US Energy Information Administration.
7. Ibid.
8. "The World's 25 Biggest Oil Companies," *Forbes*, 2013, http://www.forbes.com/pictures/eglg45emehm/12-sonatrach-2-7-million-barrels-per-day.
9. Benjamin Stora, *Histoire de l'Algérie depuis l'indépendance* (Paris: La Découverte, 1994).
10. Benjamin Stora, *Histoire de la guerre d'Algérie* (Paris: La Découverte, 1993).
11. The expression "Communauté Française" replaced the term "French Union" in 1958.
12. Declaration of George Pompidou during negotiations in Lucerne, February 19, 1961, quoted in Redha Malek, *L'Algérie à Évian: Histoire des négociations secrètes, 1956–1962* (Paris: Editions du Seuil, 1995), 94.
13. Malek, *L'Algérie à Évian*, 135.
14. See Mario Pirani, *Poteva andare peggio: Mezzo secolo di ragionevoli illusioni* (Milan: Mondadori, 2012); Irwin M. Wall, *France, the United States, and the Algerian War* (Berkeley: University of California Press, 2001); and Roberto Cantoni, "Oily Deals: Exploration, Diplomacy and Security in Early Cold War France and Italy" (PhD diss., University of Manchester, 2014).
15. See Pirani, *Poteva andare peggio*; Wall, *France*; and Cantoni, "Oily Deals."
16. Djaâfer Eskenazen, interview by Abdelatif Rebah, in Abdelatif Rebah, *Sonatrach: Une entreprise pas comme les autres* (Paris: Casbah, 2006), 35. See also Pirani, *Poteva andare peggio*; and Cantoni, "Oily Deals."
17. See Rebah, *Sonatrach*; Pirani, *Poteva andare peggio*; and Cantoni, "Oily Deals."
18. Rebah, *Sonatrach*, 28.
19. Ibid., 25.
20. Stora, *Histoire de l'Algérie*.

21. Ibid.
22. Ibid.
23. Rebah, *Sonatrach*.
24. Stora, *Histoire de la guerre*.
25. Rebah, *Sonatrach*, 64. Translation by the author.
26. Belkacem Nabi, quoted in Rebah, *Sonatrach*, 64.
27. Ibid.
28. Jean Loyrette, "Remarques sur l'organisation pétrolière en Algérie et au Sahara," October 12, 1962, Direction Géneral, Total Historical Archives, Paris.
29. Bruna Bagnato, *L'Italia e la guerra d'Algeria (1954–1962)* (Soveria Mannelli, Italy: Rubbettino, 2012).
30. Rebah, *Sonatrach*.
31. Loyette, "Remarques."
32. Rebah, *Sonatrach*.
33. Ibid.
34. Ibid.
35. de La Villerabel, "Note pour Vincent Labouret," January 13, 1964, Direction Géneral, Total Historical Archives. Translation by the author.
36. Rebah, *Sonatrach*, 108.
37. See Rebah, *Sonatrach*; "CFP 28-29-30/9/1964," Archives de Vincent Labouret, Secretaire General, Total Historical Archives, "D'Alger à In Amenas avec les travailleurs du pétrole," *Le Peuple*, September 28-29-30, 1964; and "Report on the Difficulties of the Companies in Algeria," Archives de Vincent Labouret, Secretariat General, Total Historical Archives, 1964.
38. "Algérie—Negotiations," Archives de Vincent Labouret, Secretariat General, Total Historical Archives.
39. Rebah, *Sonatrach*.
40. La Villerabel, "Note pour Vincent Labouret."
41. Djaâfer Eskenazen, interview by Rebah, in *Sonatrach*, 72.
42. La Villerabel, "Note pour Vincent Labouret."
43. "Sonatrah" or "Sonah" could not be used because in the Algerian dialect this means "low expectancy." See Rebah, *Sonatrach*. Translation by the author.
44. Rebah, *Sonatrach*, 56.
45. Petroleum Press Service (French edition), "Le bon affaire de l'Algérie," September 1965.
46. Djaâfer Eskenazen, interview by Rebah, in *Sonatrach*.
47. Rebah, *Sonatrach*.
48. Ibid., 74
49. Rebah, *Sonatrach*.
50. Environnement Petrolier et Economique: Centre de Documentation et de synthèse, "Etudes, économie et politique dans le monde," *Report année* 1967, Total Historical Archives.
51. Rebah, *Sonatrach*.
52. Environnement Petrolier et Economique, "Etudes, économie et politique dans le monde."
53. Ibid.
54. Mohamed Attlia, quoted in Rebah, *Sonatrach*, 113.
55. John P. Entelis, "Sonatrach: The Political Economy of an Algerian State Institution," in *Oil and Governance*, ed. David Victor et al., 557–98 (Cambridge: Cambridge University Press, 2012).

56. Sonatrach, *Abstract 2014*, http://www.sonatrach.com/Abstract_2014_Anglais.pdf.
57. Oxford Business Group, *Algeria 2012* (Oxford: Oxford Business Group, 2012).
58. Entelis, "Sonatrach."
59. Terry Karl, *The Paradox of Plenty: Oil Booms and Petro-states* (Berkeley: University of California Press, 1997).

Bibliography

Bagnato, B. 2012. *L'Italia e la guerra d'Algeria (1954–1962)*. Soveria Mannelli, Italy: Rubbettino.

Cantoni, R. 2014. "Oily Deals: Exploration, Diplomacy and Security in Early Cold War France and Italy." PhD diss., University of Manchester.

Entelis, J. P. 2012. "Sonatrach: The Political Economy of an Algerian State Institution." In *Oil and Governance*, edited by David Victor et al., 557–98. Cambridge: Cambridge University Press.

Forbes. 2013. "The World's 25 Biggest Oil Companies." http://www.forbes.com/pictures /eglg45emehm/12-sonatrach-2-7-million-barrels-per-day.

Karl, T. 1997. *The Paradox of Plenty: Oil Booms and Petro-states*. Berkeley: University of California Press.

Le Peuple. 1964. "D'Alger à In Amenas avec les travailleurs du pétrole." September 28/29/30.

Malek, R. 1995. *L'Algérie à Évian: Histoire des négociations secrètes, 1956–1962*. Paris: Editions du Seuil.

Oxford Business Group. 2012. *Algeria 2012*. Oxford: Oxford Business Group.

Petroleum Press Service (VF). 1965. "Le bon affaire de l'Algérie." September.

Pirani, M. 2012. *Poteva andare peggio: Mezzo secolo di ragionevoli illusioni*. Milan: Mondadori.

Présidence de la République Algérienne Démocratique et Populaire. 2003. *Projet de Programme pour la réalisation de la révolution démocratique populaire, adoptée à l'unanimité par le C. N. R.A. à Tripoli en Juin 1962*. http://www.el-mouradia.dz/francais/symbole/textes/tripoli .htm.

Rebah, A. 2006. *Sonatrach: Une entreprise pas comme les autres*. Paris: Casbah.

Sonatrach. 2014. *Abstract 2014*. http://www.sonatrach.com/Abstract_2014_Anglais.pdf.

Stora, B. 1993. *Histoire de la guerre d'Algérie*. Paris: La Découverte.

———. 1994. *Histoire de l'Algérie depuis l'indépendance*. Paris: La Découverte.

Trading Economics. 2016. "Algeria Exports." http://www.tradingeconomics.com/algeria/exports.

US Energy Information Administration. 2014. "Algeria." https://www.eia.gov/beta/international /analysis.cfm?iso=DZA.

———. 2014. "Energy Supply Security 2014." https://www.eia.org/media/freepublications/security /EnergySupplySecurity2014_France.pdf.

———. 2014. "International Energy Statistics: Total Petroleum and Other Liquids Production 2014." http://www.eia.gov/beta/international/rankings/index.cfm#?iso=DZA&cy=2014.

Wall, I. M. 2001. *France, the United States, and the Algerian War*. Berkeley: University of California Press.

PART IV

Unconventional Entrepreneurs

8   Business after Hours

The Entrepreneurial Ventures of Nigerian Working-Class Seamen

Lynn Schler

ENTREPRENEURSHIP IS RECOGNIZED as the foundation of economic growth and expansion in capitalist systems, and it is therefore promoted as a vital component for fostering growth and development in emerging economies. Much research has thus been aimed at identifying the circumstances in which it is possible to encourage and support the emergence of entrepreneurship. There is an extremely wide range of strategies proposed to achieve this goal, spanning economic, cultural, social, and political perspectives. While there is great diversity in the approaches that articulate the prerequisites for the emergence of the entrepreneurial class, there is significant consensus that the entrepreneur represents a specific kind of subjectivity in the economic landscape. The entrepreneurial class is largely posited as distinct and differentiated from the working class, and the entrepreneur is conceptualized and theorized as a certain type of economic actor.[1] Substantial research has been dedicated to identifying the defining features of an entrepreneur, with some studies emphasizing personality traits and others focusing on functionality.[2] There are both universalist models of entrepreneurship and those that see different models emerging in particular cultural contexts.[3] There is also debate regarding the optimal circumstances within which an entrepreneurial class can emerge, and here too there are both universalist and particularist paradigms. However, across much of this literature the entrepreneur emerges as a distinct subject-agent within capitalist economies. Individuals are either entrepreneurs or they are not. One can of course become an entrepreneur, but here too is an underlying assumption that entrepreneurship is a particular kind of subjectivity.

This approach to the entrepreneur as a fixed social and economic category misses out on more-complicated realities in which individuals can be part-time, partial, or strategic entrepreneurs. The complexities and fluidity of economic landscapes often enable the emergence of entrepreneurial actions and ventures among individuals who are also members of the working class. Rather than positing the entrepreneur as a distinct subject-agent in a given economic land-scape, it is important to recognize that individuals, specifically those of the working class, can initiate and maintain entrepreneurial ventures at the same time that they are employed in wage labor. Particularly in situations of economic scarcity, members of the working class often seek to supplement their incomes with businesses on the side. While these ventures are predicated on entrepre-neurial proclivity, they do not constitute an exclusive subjectivity; rather, there is an ongoing negotiation between multiple forms of subjectivity. It is therefore necessary to consider all types of economic activity in which individuals are en-gaged, and the ways in which each engagement shapes and determines individual agency and consciousness. In short, individuals can imagine themselves and their place in the world as both working class and entrepreneurial at the same time.

The notion of context is essential for enabling a more complex and fluid con-ceptualization of entrepreneurship. As we look beyond fixed categorizations, the emphasis on context helps us imagine entrepreneurship as a convergence of ac-tivity that is contingent and changing. Within specific contexts, the opportuni-ties for entrepreneurial initiatives can emerge and be exploited. To understand the meaning and potential of entrepreneurship, we must understand both the aspi-rations behind entrepreneurial ventures and the structures that enable or limit their realization. Thus, as Murray B. Low and Eric Abrahamson argue, entrepre-neurship is "a context-dependent social process."[4] Among wage earners of the working class, entrepreneurship can be a targeted strategy used to contest the in-stitutional order.[5] As Friederike Welter and Mirela Xheneti argue, resourceful individuals engage in entrepreneurial activities in order to overcome turbulent and hostile conditions.[6] However, while social, economic, and political contexts can create new opportunities, they also create restraints, and it is thus impossible to disentangle context from our understanding of the potential and significance of entrepreneurship.[7] While entrepreneurship is born as a set of aspirations, the success or failure of entrepreneurial ventures is inseparable from the cir-cumstances in which they emerge. Thus, the process of entrepreneurship must be examined within specific contexts in order to understand the extent to which it enables individuals to successfully mobilize resources to confront their economic disempowerment.

This chapter considers the entrepreneurial initiatives of working-class Nige-rian seamen and their after-hours business ventures while employed on British vessels in the late colonial era. Based on interviews with former seamen and ar-chival research, the investigation of these side businesses provides a close-up view of how members of the working class mobilized an entrepreneurial spirit and ex-ploited opportunities that arose in order to combat their disempowerment as cheap labor on colonial ships. These after-hours enterprises yielded significant profits for the seamen and their families. Beyond the economic benefits of these ventures, seamen's entrepreneurial activities became an important expression of self-fashioning. It will be seen that through these businesses, seamen circumvented economic, political, and cultural hierarchies and challenged colonial categorizations of them as a cheap and docile source of labor. The case study provides insights into entrepreneurship as both a set of aspirations that emerged in a particular context and a strategy used to negotiate and reenact social and economic boundaries.

Cheap Labor: Nigerian Seamen in the British Colonial Shipping Industry

From the very beginning of international shipping between Africa, Europe, and the New World, Africans were employed on merchant vessels as crewmen. Particularly from the eighteenth century onward, increased transatlantic traffic led to the large-scale recruitment of Africans on European ships, and these workers served as a cheaper and more efficient alternative to white sailors who suffered from the tropical climate and diseases.[8] Historians of the Age of Sail have argued that maritime employment was empowering for black seamen, offering both well-paying jobs and access to many privileges and experiences that were not available to black men ashore. W. Jeffrey Bolster argues that due to their unique positioning, the black sailors of the Age of Sail developed a "potent" masculine identity.[9] However, the technological innovations that led to the development of steamships ultimately led to the deskilling of the African crews and a steep deterioration of their status on colonial vessels. As Jonathan Hyslop notes, "It was no longer necessary to have a workforce with long experience of the sea. It took several years for a deckhand to become fully conversant with all the complexities of working on a sailing ship. By contrast, the skills of shovelling and raking coal in the holds of steamers could be picked up quite quickly. And deckhands now spent much of their time on the grinding but fairly unskilled work of scraping and painting the ships."[10] On steamships African seamen were divided into three distinct crews: sailors on deck, firemen below who stoked the steam boilers that powered the ship, and stewards in the catering and housekeeping crew. Many seamen deprecated these new shipboard tasks as less than proper seafaring.[11]

The new industrial division of labor on steamships was based on labor hierarchies entrenched in colonial racial ideologies.[12] Colonial seamen engaged in ports throughout the British Empire were paid considerably lower rates than white seamen, receiving one-third to one-fifth of a white British seaman's wage.[13] Shipping companies traveling between European and Africa became dependent on this cheap source of labor, and nearly all vessels stopped to recruit supplementary crews in the port cities of West Africa. Until World War II the vast majority of these recruits came from among the Kru in Liberia and Sierra Leone. European shipping companies would routinely stop in Freetown to pick up Kru deckhands and firemen before continuing down the coast. For their part, Kru headmen exploited this dependence and negotiated favorable terms of employment for their crews.[14]

The outbreak of World War II changed these hiring practices. The war increased demands for supplemental labor on colonial ships, since the headquarters in the port cities of West Africa oversaw ship repairs, in addition to handling the increase in cargo activity associated with the war. Janet J. Ewald argues that in times of hardship, European shipping companies historically sought out fresh sources of colonial seamen and tapped them to offset the rising costs of labor.[15] The acute need for seamen pushed shipping giants such as Elder Dempster to refocus their hiring on Nigeria. In Lagos, European shipping companies could hire seamen for much lower rates than those demanded by the Kru in Freetown. The Nigerian recruits came from a wide range of ethnic groups, including Yoruba, Igbo, Ijaw, and Urhobo, and they lacked the social cohesion and organizing skills that had facilitated the recruitment of the Kru. The lack of experience enabled shipping companies to cut the Nigerians' wages, and a new four-tiered pay scale was established during the war. At the bottom were Nigerians recruited in Nigeria, then Africans recruited in Freetown, then Africans employed from Liverpool, and finally European seamen, who were paid the National Maritime Board rates.[16] Many of the Nigerian seamen found this status demoralizing; as one recalled, "In the shipping world, we were the most poorly paid seamen."[17]

Nigerian seamen did not passively accept their low standing, and in 1942 they formed the Nigerian Seamen's Union to agitate for their rights. The union's declared objectives were "to protect the interests of its members, regulate work hours and wages, ensure adequate accommodation for all seamen on vessels and ashore, to promote the general welfare of seamen and to regulate relations between employers and employees."[18] Despite these objectives, the union did not effectively represent the seamen's needs. Archival records reveal that the union leadership was preoccupied with political struggles and infighting, leaving little time for representing seamen's grievances to colonial shipping companies. As one government review from the period stated, "The record of the Union's activities over the years makes a most pathetic reading. Almost from its inception, there have always been instances of endless strife, distrust, intrigues, tribal discrimination, police arrests, litigation, rifts of members into factions, one faction trying at one time or the other, and often quite successfully, to overthrow the other from office, and to install itself into power. No set of officials of the union would appear to have held office happily together for any reasonable length of time."[19] Thus, despite the sporadic rhetoric of demands, throughout the 1950s the union did not pose a serious threat to the shipping companies' designs to maintain the low status of Nigerian seamen on colonial vessels.

Since Nigerian seamen could not rely on their union to serve as an effective instrument through which they could improve their poor working conditions, they had to devise alternative means and strategies to protect and improve their material lives. Seamen astutely identified opportunities that could be developed and exploited to earn additional money beyond that earned through their official work in seafaring. Seamen initiated a profitable and unofficial trade that reaped considerable benefits for themselves and their families back home in Nigeria. As will be seen, seamen's independent trading ventures were evidence of their ingenuity and self-reliance. These entrepreneurial efforts provide important insights into the actions taken by working classes to resist their disempowerment in colonial labor regimes. Both the trade itself and the narratives crafted around these ventures are evidence of the entrepreneurial strategies that working classes mobilized to defy or circumvent their proletarianization and improve the material standing of themselves and their families.

A Penchant for Adventure

Q: Why did you become a seaman?

R: It was because I like to travel all over the world to see what is happening.[20]

Seamen's explanations, provided in interviews, about why they became seamen are revealing for what they can teach us about their entrepreneurial spirit. They gave a variety of responses, but nearly all of the answers they provided reflected a strong inclination toward risk taking, resourcefulness, adventure, and a belief in their own self-fashioning. Over and over, men revealed a clear sense of agency and initiative in describing what led them to sign up. They aspired to a certain lifestyle, and seafaring was a means for achieving it. As one man explained, "I saw the type of job and I liked it, and later I joined them."[21] Another simply explained, "For the purpose of adventure, nothing more."[22] Many claimed that they were drawn to the job after seeing other seamen around Lagos. As one seaman replied, "I used to see seamen coming from abroad to Lagos then. When I saw how they dressed and their actions, I was attracted to these things."[23] Another man gave a similar response: "When I was in school, I used to see the seamen from Freetown. Their manner of dress attracted me to become a seaman. Really, their clothes and shoes made me join seamen."[24] Some exploited connections to Europeans in order to get the job. One man explained that he had fought as a soldier in World War II, and when he returned to Lagos and unsuccessfully looked for a job, he turned to his British military colonel, who sent him to the Elder Dempster offices to sign on as a seaman.[25] Another man explained that he was working in a shoe store in Lagos when a British manager from Elder Dempster came in to have his shoes repaired. The two men began talking, and, according to the seaman, "he said he was teaching people on how to travel all over the world. From there, I developed an interest in what to know about the whole world. So I asked how he could help me. He said I am too small. I was fifteen years old at the time."[26] Despite his young age, he soon began working as a greaser on Elder Dempster ships. Some men exploited personal connections to local friends or family to help them get the job. Even with these connections, the men's responses implied that going to work as a seaman was a decision rooted in their own desire for travel and adventure. As one man explained, he secured the job through a connection with an Urhobo friend from back home in the Delta State, but his personal interest in becoming a seaman was piqued when he moved to Lagos and heard talk of travel abroad: "It was because it's only in Lagos that people talked about England; they say 'I want to go to England,' and from this urge to travel I went to England."[27] These narratives portray the men as proactive, risk taking, and adventurousness—traits that would eventually come into play in their entrepreneurial ventures.

Discrimination and Exploitation on Colonial Ships

While Nigerians were drawn to seafaring as a way of gaining access to new opportunities and adventures, once employed on colonial ships, they confronted many hardships. Colonial seamen often faced miserable working conditions, replete with racial discrimination and dehumanizing treatment. The archives abound with incidents of discrimination against black seamen on the part of both European crews and officers. Many black seamen suffered physical abuse, name calling, and random punishment by their officers and group beatings or other violent attacks by white seamen. The majority suffered these abuses without any recourse since they lacked any verifiable proof against those who perpetrated these crimes. Those who did complain found the European captain to be uninterested. When it was a case of a black seaman's word against that of a white seaman, there was little hope that any justice would be served. These grievances can be seen in this letter of protest from the Nigeria seamen to the shipping company:

> The habit of several white seamen, as we said, is to collectively beat up on African crew. We protest against this, because it can lead to a situation where African Seamen can join forces to retaliate [against] white seamen, leading to developments of unpleasant proportions. Captains do not call into evidence African crews to refute or say what leads to reports against them by white crews. . . . The mode of addressing them employed by white seamen borders on provocation. It is sometimes so appalling that they are confused or annoyed to [the] point of disobedience and as soon as this happens, the report reaches the Captain divorced of the circumstances under which the disobedience occurred.[28]

In the colonial era, crews were generally segregated in separate quarters. They often ate in separate areas, and African seamen complained that they were served poor-quality food compared to that of the Europeans. This segregation was the result of a ship hierarchy that reflected colonial biases linked to race and class. Ship hierarchies created clear distinctions between officers and the rank and file, and in most vessels these distinctions also coincided with racial difference. Only Europeans could advance within these hierarchies, as representatives of seamen complained in 1959: "No African seamen . . . irrespective of their number of years are in responsible posts. We always serve in a subordinate role. The African seamen who do the same type of work as white crews cannot share equal advantages with them in the sphere of working conditions, after many years of contribution to the progress of the companies."[29] White officers ate better food, lived in superior accommodations, and enjoyed unlimited rations of cigarettes and beer. The officers socialized in their own bar, which was better furnished than that of the regular seamen. While hierarchies such as these were not explicitly racist, African seamen were keenly aware of the connections between race, class, and status on colonial ships. Seamen's perceptions of discrimination touch on these intersections. As one explained, "If you talk about maltreatment from the European officers it was general. They prevented us from [entering] their quarters."[30]

Nigerian seamen complained that ship officers would not help them in times of conflict with the white crews since the officers themselves were also accused of racism. As seamen's representatives complained in 1958, "We know of instances where officers have told African crews quite openly that they hate not only them but Africans on the whole."[31] Some European officers abused their power and required Africans to work overtime for them personally. For these types of jobs, the payment was usually in kind, but sometimes Africans were not paid at all. This could be left to the officer's discretion; as one captain explained, "The chief steward may wish to have a storeroom cleared out, or have the inside of the storeroom alleyway painted. He would be paid in goods—in rice and biscuits. Likewise, the chief or second steward would have their laundry done for free or rather would pay the head washman in rice or biscuits."[32] The practice of asking African crews to do personal work for white officers was a source of great contention. As one seaman recalled, "It was a long story. That is why I said there was maltreatment by the white officers. The chief steward used to bring his car to the dock and he asked one of the black stewards to wash his car. We all resisted and refused to obey because the car in question was not the company's car, but a personal one. If you want to wash your car, take it to the car wash and pay them. The steward wanted to wash his during working hours and free of charge too. We said we weren't doing that again."[33]

Entrepreneurism and Empowerment of Nigerian Seamen

Faced with poor wages, discrimination on board, and the lack of an effective representative body, seamen had to devise autonomous strategies to protect their interests and improve their financial prospects. They therefore sought out opportunities that could be developed and exploited to earn additional money outside their official work in seafaring. Within these pockets of autonomy that were linked to the context of seafaring, seamen initiated a profitable and unofficial trade that maximized benefits for themselves and their families back home in Nigeria. Seamen's trade reflected their agency, ingenuity, and self-reliance. As they orchestrated the flow of goods across transnational networks to circumvent their disempowerment as colonial labor, they also crafted narratives about these after-hours business ventures that reflected their opportunism and resourcefulness.

Nigerian seamen used whatever meager resources they had to initiate their trading ventures. Some cash was available from their salaries. For those employed by Elder Dempster, for example, 40 percent of wages was paid in England in pounds sterling, while the remaining 60 percent was paid in Nigeria. Seamen explained that their wives claimed their allotment in Nigeria, while they used the money they received in England to buy goods for resale.[34] The interviewed seamen maintained that everyone exploited the opportunity to engage in trade since this was the only way to offset the poor salaries. As one seaman explained, "I was involved—and I am very happy to tell you that I really did a lot of buying and selling when I was working and I did that because of our poor wages."[35] Profits earned from trade fostered a sense of self-reliance among seamen, and this helps explain why the ineffectiveness of the union was not more of a cause for concern. As one man explained, "A lot of us traded on board the ship so as to have more money. And because we were involved in trading activities, we were slow to agitate for an increment in the salary. Even when the union agitated for such it had no power to push harder, but the proceeds from our trade kept us going."[36] These after-hours business ventures provided a vital supplement to wages on which the seamen and their families were deeply dependent. The seamen and their Nigerian wives stated that this extra income was used to pay their children's school fees and other household expenses that official wages would not cover.[37] One woman explained that her husband's side business was essential for their survival since his seaman's salary would barely cover the cost of food.[38] These ventures often became family businesses. Wives played a vital role back in Lagos, managing all the trading while their husbands were gone. Some opened up stores where they sold the secondhand goods their husbands brought from abroad.[39] As one of the seamen's wives explained, "On his absence I still continued to sell and he would bring more items. . . . Part of the money was sent to both our parents and the remaining I used to buy goods for my shop. I controlled the money from the shop. I paid for the children's school fees from it and he never ask me to given an account because he trusted me."[40]

Seamen's entrepreneurial ventures involved the importation of secondhand goods, such as carpets, electronics, small appliances, refrigerators, freezers, furniture, mattresses, ceramic goods, clothing, tires, and used cars,[41] from Europe to Africa, as well as the exportation of some Nigerian products to other ports in Africa and to communities in the African diaspora. Some of the items were pur-chased new in England and resold in Nigeria, where the demand for them was strong. As one of the seamen's wives recalled, "I started trading in the items he brought, such as shoes, cloth, and wigs from the UK. The wigs were brand new. I did not have a store, but before he even arrived people would be demanding them. I was able to make money from this. I needed him to go and come back so as to have more goods to sell. There was a time he stayed about one year in India."[42] Seamen would also export Nigerian staples such as *garri* (cassava flakes), yams, *egusi* (melon seeds), and *elubo* (yam flour), as well as palm wine and local beer.[43] Some also traded in wooden carvings on special order from customers in Europe or Brazil.[44]

As one seaman explained, "Yes, there is no seaman who was not involved in the trading activities. If you have a house as a seaman, you want to put chairs, table, television, stereo, and so on, no matter how little it might be."[45] Many still proudly display these items in their homes today, where they serve as material re-minders of their work and travels; some pointed these items out during inter-views. One retired seaman said, "Any old or fairly used items that were in good condition, we bought and sold them in Nigeria. You can see some of them in my living room[,] like the big mirror, the old pendulum wall clock, that flower vase, and the old stereo—[they] were bought from Europe."[46] Once seamen filled their homes with these goods, they sold any duplicates they obtained on later jour-neys.[47] Seamen and their families were often the first in their neighborhoods to have luxury items such as televisions and refrigerators, and this was often the cause of envy among neighbors. As one woman explained, "They felt we had everything in the world, so whether we eat or not, they do not know. So in most cases, they feel we are very rich."[48]

While the after-hours business was described as a vital source of supplemen-tary income, the seamen's ability to engage in these ventures was dependent on their ability to exploit social, economic, and political relations. They suffered from considerable volatility and often confronted changes in political or economic cir-cumstances on board ships, at specific ports of call, or in each country's customs policies that limited or halted their enterprises. To offset this instability, seamen nurtured positive relations with captains, immigration officers, customs officials, dockers, European retailers, African customers, and fellow crewmates. Although these relationships helped ensure the seamen's ability to buy, transport, stow, and sell goods from one continent to another, the men also had to continually adapt their activities and quickly respond to new circumstances.

During the colonial period, seamen employed by colonial shipping companies were officially allowed to transport one to four items for personal use, depending on the specific vessel they were on. However, the seamen's testimonies reveal that there was considerable disparity in the way this policy was enforced on each ship. Some captains were willing to turn a blind eye to seamen's activities, allowing them to transport items in their personal spaces or even the cargo hold. One retired seaman described the latitude that captains enjoyed in determining how much trade was permitted:

> We bought, but we were not allowed to buy goods. Whenever you wanted to do that you will have to negotiate with the captain. If he were liberal and he will allow us to buy four items, but some captains never bothered, you could buy anything, hide it and keep it in your store. But some British captains will not allow you to do that, they would tell you that you have not come to the ship to trade, you have come to work in the ship. . . . The captain called the shots. . . . No captain will tell you to trade. . . . He would overlook whatever the seamen did as regards trade. But some captains will never allow you to do that. Even before the crew get on board, the captain would have pasted a notice on the board that "No one is allow to trade." . . . The notice on the board was boldly pasted by some captains while other captains never bothered.[49]

The unpredictability of a captain's response made the seamen's ventures very risky. For example, one seaman claimed that he had invested tremendous resources after being contracted by a local dealer to carve and sell wooden objects in Canada, but his captain later threatened to sack him for conducting this side business.[50] Goods could not be brought on board without the knowledge and consent of the captain, and routine inspections were conducted. Even captains who allowed trade would often require seamen to pay freight charges and customs duties. The introduction of containers resulted in increased surveillance of goods transported by seamen since captains had to grant permission to use the containers and would charge the seamen standard freight fees. Following containerization, seamen had to organize in groups in order to fill an entire container with goods to make the trade economically viable for each individual.[51]

While captains served as the ultimate authority in determining how many items seamen could carry on board, seamen also relied on broad networks of business partners and customers at each point of their operations. Seamen purchased goods from retailers across Europe and beyond, including England, Holland, Germany, Spain, Brazil, and the Caribbean. The immense distances between various locations and the particularities of each place made trade unpredictable and risky. Customs officials could be whimsical, and seamen could face unexpected fees from officers practicing strict enforcement. This made the level of profit irregular and resulted in major losses for some.[52] Others complained that they themselves extended credit to customers that was never repaid.[53]

To offset risks and increase profits, seamen relied on relationships of trust with a vast array of retailers. While most of the transactions were based on the practice of "cash and carry," some of those interviewed claimed that it was also possible to purchase items on credit.[54] Full payment could only be rendered on return journeys that were sometimes months away, and therefore the extension of credit was only possible once seamen developed relations of trust with retailers abroad. This can be seen in the following description of relations between one seaman and his German supplier:

> He used to sell electronic appliances; it was there that I met him, and sometimes whenever I was in Germany I stayed with him and his family. I also worked with him in his shop. Here he put my honesty to the test and he found me truly honest. I got to know him when the ship I was to bring to Nigeria from Germany was not ready and I went to Bremen to buy something to sell here; that was how I met him because the ship was not ready for almost six months. When I was leaving he asked if I want to sell anything and I told him I was interested; he gave some goods to sell and I returned his money. He even told other crew members who were in the same business of buying and selling to give me their own proceeds for onward transmission to him. One day someone among our crew that I cannot identify went and duped him when I was on leave. The fraudster ordered goods in my name worth five hundred thousand *naira* at that time, and he never returned. When I went to Bremen the man asked me about the goods he sent to me; it was a long list. I said no, and when I saw the long list I wept. I told him I never sent anyone.[55]

Personal relations were central to seamen's success as entrepreneurs, and they prided themselves on their credibility as businessmen. Since there were no middlemen involved, seamen's success in independent trade was dependent solely on their personal initiative and efforts. Those interviewed were quick to link their achievements to their reputations for being upright.

There were some seamen who, for various reasons, did not take part in this after-hours business. For a few of the interviewed seamen, these side ventures were a distraction to seafaring and signaled a lack of professionalism. As one seaman charged, "Some people went there with the sole intention of making money. Some people even sold some portion of their food ration just to make additional money. All these I did not do, and you can confirm this from other seamen and they will tell you the same about me."[56] Another seaman simply claimed that it was not worthwhile financially, and instead he opened side businesses in Lagos in order to supplement his income:

> Look, you were paid for instance five kobo and you used that to buy something that you could sell for ten kobo, which adds very little value. I don't call it trade because after a trip back from Europe, before you could engage in this kind of trade again, it would take you about four to six months by which time you could have spent all you had in the previous trade. I was not very keen about this; I already started a photocopy business in Lagos Island. In fact, I was the

first person to have started that. . . . I bought the photocopy machine here in Nigeria, not abroad, and I did this business alongside as a seaman. And as I have said earlier, the seaman job was not a permanent one, so I needed something to augment my salary. More importantly, I already had children before I became a seaman.[57]

Since seamen prided themselves on their honesty and credibility, they were very quick to distance themselves from any illicit activity that was frequently associated with them. Some seamen engaged in theft and worked in cooperation with dockers to break into cargo for sale on the black markets.[58] Drug trafficking was also an extremely lucrative activity, and seamen claimed that many were lured by the high profits of this business.[59] Some crew trafficked in cannabis and cocaine between Nigeria, South America, the Caribbean, and Europe.[60] Unlike the sale of secondhand goods, drug trafficking was conducted without the consent of captains and required crew to hide the contraband somewhere on board. Small amounts of cannabis could be hidden among a seaman's personal belongings with the hope that it would not be revealed in routine searches. The carpenters, known as shippies, were well known for constructing hiding spots in the woodwork of the common areas of the ship.[61] Those engaged in drug trafficking often worked in conjunction with dockers, and even with police or customs officials who at times acted as accomplices. Thus, the crew involved in the drug trade also operated within the transnational economic networks that they established.

The narratives that seamen constructed around their side businesses reveal an act of creating a space within which they reiterated a former sense of innovation, empowerment, and influence. Time and again, seamen described their entrepreneurial activities with tremendous pride and claimed that they were innovators and pioneers in the importing and exporting business between Africa and Europe. One seaman claimed that he was the first to sell apples in Nigeria: "It depended on the items you had interest in. I, in particular, had an interest in apples. I bought apples. In fact, we seamen pioneered the importation of apples into Nigeria. We imported from France, England, and so on."[62] He also credited seamen with the start of the scrap-metal import industry in Nigeria: "The job was so attractive. We made casual friends in Europe who gave some of us these articles, including cars[,] free without asking for a dime. Therefore we didn't look into how much we earned. Our friends in Europe gave us these articles. We could bring in cars but because we couldn't afford the freight, . . . we scrapped [them]. Note that we, seamen, started scrapping cars to sell in Nigeria before the different traders started it now. We scrapped the car into parts so that it wouldn't attract any freight."[63]

Seamen's after-hours businesses also enabled an imagined redrawing of cultural boundaries between Nigeria and the Nigerian diaspora. The flow of goods from "back home" to places abroad played a role in extending a sense of familiarity and belonging outside Nigeria. Seamen thus identified the availability of Nigerian foodstuffs and alcohol in the social and cultural landscapes of Liverpool and London as a factor contributing to their sense of belonging in those places. As one seaman claimed, "[We sold] cartons of local beer (Star and Guilder) because our local beers are stronger than those ones brewed abroad. We sold all these items in Liverpool. People came to the ship and bought these items. . . . Sometimes, in those days in London, if you attended a party Nigerian local beers were served."[64]

Despite the fact that seamen fashioned themselves as cosmopolitan and empowered businessmen, a more critical investigation into their business networks reveals the resilience of some racial, cultural, and national border regimes that seamen's enterprises did not succeed in dismantling. Seamen did not enjoy full autonomy in their trading enterprises, and the circuits of their side businesses were largely limited to what Paul Gilroy has described as the Black Atlantic.[65] Thus, racial alliances and racial hierarchies played a pivotal role in directing the flows of goods and wealth within the context of seamen's trade. One seaman hinted at the limited markets available to them for trading: "Honestly, we never sold to any European but we sold in different African countries like Dakar, Monrovia, Freetown, Lagos, Gambia (Bathurst), Accra and so on. The people came to the dock and asked is there anything to sell? And we said yes; the transaction took place immediately, so no European bought the fairly used items and appliances from us—their country is good."[66] This seaman's testimony reveals a keen awareness of the racial and national boundaries that divided African seamen, clients, and port cities on the one hand, and European citizens and countries on the other. In the final reckoning, race, class, and national identities all played a significant role in shaping seamen's transnational encounters. Thus, while seamen's independent enterprises evoked moments of resourcefulness and initiative, they never fully overcame the hierarchies and inequalities enforced by the colonial context.

Conclusion

This examination of seamen's after-hours business ventures enables us to formulate a nuanced view of entrepreneurship as both a process and a strategy. Viewed from the decks of colonial vessels, the business ventures of these working-class seamen remind us that entrepreneurship is a set of actions that can only be evaluated within a particular context. Working-class seamen were shaped by experiences of discrimination and disempowerment, but they also exploited the opportunities that became available to them. Their entrepreneurship was thus an intervention that the working class mobilized against racial and class hierarchies on colonial ships. While seamen's testimonies reflect the kinds of aspirations that gave birth to their entrepreneurial ventures, their experiences also reveal the limited power of entrepreneurship to reshape economic and social hierarchies. Thus, seamen embraced entrepreneurship as a means for improving their lot, but their experiences as independent traders ultimately reminded them of the limits to their power.

LYNN SCHLER is Professor in African History in the Department of Politics and Government and Director of the Tamar Golan Africa Centre at Ben-Gurion University of the Negev, Israel. She has published books, edited volumes, and articles relating to urbanization, labor history, decolonization, and nationalism in Africa. Her most recent book is *Nation on Board: Becoming Nigerian at Sea* (Ohio University Press, 2016).

Notes

Parts of this chapter are based on the article Lynn Schler, "The Negotiations of Nigerian Seamen in the Transition from Colonialism to Independence: Smuggling to Make Ends Meet," *African Studies Review* 54, no. 1 (2011): 167–85. Reprinted with permission from Cambridge University Press. Some of the issues were also examined in Lynn Schler, *Nation on Board: Becoming Nigerian at Sea* (Athens: Ohio University Press, 2016). Reprinted with permission from Ohio University Press.

1. See Mark Casson, *The Entrepreneur: An Economic Theory* (Lanham, MD: Rowman and Littlefield, 1982); and James W. Carland, Frank Hoy, and Jo Ann Carland, " 'Who Is an Entrepreneur?' Is a Question Worth Asking," *Entrepreneurship: Critical Perspectives on Business and Management* 2 (2002): 178. A well-known critique of the "traits" approach is William B. Gartner, " 'Who Is an Entrepreneur?' Is the Wrong Question," *American Journal of Small Business* 12 (1989): 11–32. Gartner's emphasis on entrepreneurial behavior rather than personality traits does not reject the notion of the distinctiveness of the entrepreneur as an economic agent.

2. For an overview of the historical debate, see Robert Hébert and Albert N. Link, "In Search of the Meaning of Entrepreneurship," *Small Business Economics* 1, no. 1 (1989): 39–49.

3. Some examples of culturally sensitive examinations of entrepreneurship are Geert Hofstede, "Organising for Cultural Diversity," *European Management Journal* 7, no. 4 (1989): 390–97; Ana Maria Peredo et al., "Towards a Theory of Indigenous Entrepreneurship," *International Journal of Entrepreneurship and Small Business* 1, nos. 1–2 (2004): 1–20; Noel Lindsay, "Toward a Cultural Model of Indigenous Entrepreneurial Attitude" (PhD diss., Academy of Marketing Science, 2005); and Kevin Hindle and Michele Lansdowne, "Brave Spirits on New Paths: Toward a Globally Relevant Paradigm of Indigenous Entrepreneurship Research," *Journal of Small Business and Entrepreneurship* 18, no. 2 (2005): 131–41.

4. Murray B. Low and Eric Abrahamson, "Movements, Bandwagons, and Clones: Industry Evolution and the Entrepreneurial Process," *Journal of Business Venturing* 12, no. 6 (1997): 441.

5. Friederike Welter and Mirela Xheneti, "Reenacting Contextual Boundaries—Entrepreneurial Resourcefulness in Challenging Environments," *Entrepreneurial Resourcefulness: Competing with Constraints* 15 (2013): 168.

6. Ibid.

7. Ibid., 152.

8. Diana Frost, ed., *Ethnic Labour and British Imperial Trade: A History of Ethnic Seafarers in the UK* (London: Frank Cass, 1995); Diane Frost, *Work and Community among West African Migrant Workers since the Nineteenth Century* (Liverpool: Liverpool University Press, 1999).

9. W. Jeffrey Bolster, " 'Every Inch a Man': Gender in the Lives of African American Seamen, 1800–1860," in *Iron Men, Wooden Women: Gender and Seafaring in the Atlantic World, 700–1920*, ed. M. Creighton and L. Nordling, 138–68 (Baltimore: Johns Hopkins University Press, 1996).

10. Jonathan Hyslop, " 'Ghostlike' Seafarers and Sailing Ship Nostalgia: The Figure of the Steamship Lascar in the British Imagination, c. 1880–1960," *Journal for Maritime Research* 16, no. 2 (2014): 221.

11. Laura Tabili, " 'A Maritime Race': Masculinity and the Racial Division of Labor in British Merchant Ships, 1900–1939," in Creighton and Nordling, *Iron Men, Wooden Women*, 169–88.

12. Laura Tabili, "The Construction of Racial Difference in Twentieth-Century Britain: The Special Restriction (Coloured Alien Seamen) Order, 1925," *Journal of British Studies* 33, no. 1 (January 1994): 63.

13. Tabili, " 'Maritime Race,' " 180.

14. Frost, *Work and Community*, 25–27.

15. Janet J. Ewald, "Crossers of the Sea: Slaves, Freedmen, and Other Migrants in the Northwestern Indian Ocean, c. 1750–1914," *American Historical Review* 105, no. 1 (2000): 69–91.

16. Marika Sherwood, "Strikes! African Seamen, Elder Dempster and the Government 1940–42," in Frost, *Ethnic Labour and British Imperial Trade*, 130–45. See also CO 859/40/2 National Union of Seamen, February 13, 1941, Public Records Office, British National Archives.

17. Festus Adekunle Akintade, in discussion with the author, Lagos, Nigeria, December 24, 2007.

18. Board of Enquiry into the Trade Dispute between the Elder Dempster Lines Limited and the Nigerian Union of Seamen, *Report* (Lagos: Federal Government Printer, 1959), 4

19. Ibid.

20. Adeola Lawal, in discussion with the author, Lagos, Nigeria, December 21, 2007.

21. Reuben Lazarus, in discussion with the author, Lagos, Nigeria, December 16, 2007.

22. Captain Niyi Adeyemo, in discussion with the author, Lagos, Nigeria, January 25, 2011.

23. Festus Adekunle Akintade, in discussion with the author, Lagos, Nigeria, December 24, 2007.

24. Anthony Davies Eros, in discussion with the author, Lagos, Nigeria, December 15, 2007.

25. Lawrence Miekumo, in discussion with the author, Lagos, Nigeria, December 27, 2007.

26. Joseph Kehinde Adigun, in discussion with the author, Lagos, Nigeria, January 21, 2011.

27. Daniel Ofudje, in discussion with the author, Lagos, Nigeria, January 14, 2008.

28. Memorandum presented by the Nigerian Union of Seamen to Elder Dempster Shipping Lines, January 10, 1959, 4C 1908, Nigerian Union 1959–1962, Merseyside Maritime Museum.

29. Ibid.

30. Chief Charles Oloma Kose Kroseide, in discussion with the author, Lagos, Nigeria, January 17, 2008.

31. General Secretary Monday to Elder Dempster Shipping Lines, October 15, 1958, 4C 1908, Nigerian Union 1959–1962, Merseyside Maritime Museum.

32. Frost, *Work and Community*, 65.

33. Adebowale Adeleye, in discussion with the author, Lagos, Nigeria, December 16, 2007.
34. Joseph Kehinde Adigun, in discussion with the author, Lagos, Nigeria, December 17, 2007.
35. Festus Adekunle Akintade, in discussion with the author, Lagos, Nigeria, December 24, 2007.
36. Ari Festus, in discussion with the author, Lagos, Nigeria, December 24, 2007.
37. Bolaji Akintade, in discussion with the author, Lagos, Nigeria, December 24, 2007; Evelyn Miekumo, in discussion with the author, Lagos, Nigeria, December 27, 2007.
38. Bolaji Akintade, in discussion with the author, Lagos, Nigeria, December 24, 2007.
39. Evelyn Miekumo, in discussion with the author, Lagos, Nigeria, December 27, 2007; Theresa Obezi, in discussion with the author, Lagos, Nigeria, July 28, 2011.
40. Theresa Obezi, in discussion with the author, Lagos, Nigeria, July 28, 2011.
41. Ganui Agoro, in discussion with the author, Lagos, Nigeria, December 15, 2007; Adebowale Adeleye, in discussion with the author, Lagos, Nigeria, December 16, 2007; Pa Agbaosi, in discussion with the author, Lagos, Nigeria, December 15, 2007.
42. Margaret Bessan, in discussion with the author, Lagos, Nigeria, July 3, 2011.
43. Ari Festus, in discussion with the author, Lagos, Nigeria, December 24, 2007; Anthony Davies Eros, in discussion with the author, December 15, 2007.
44. Ibid.
45. Kojo George, in discussion with the author, Lagos, Nigeria, December 27, 2007.
46. Festus Adekunle Akintade, in discussion with the author, Lagos, Nigeria, December 24, 2007.
47. As one informant explained, "You cannot use two fridges if you already have one." Ganui Agoro, in discussion with the author, Lagos, Nigeria, December 15, 2007.
48. Margaret Bessan, in discussion with the author, Lagos, Nigeria, July 3, 2011.
49. Anthony Davies Eros, in discussion with the author, Lagos, Nigeria, December 15, 2007.
50. Daniel Ofudje, in discussion with the author, Lagos, Nigeria, January 14, 2008.
51. Pa Agbaosi, in discussion with the author, Lagos, Nigeria, December 15, 2007.
52. Kojo George, in discussion with the author, Lagos, Nigeria, December 27, 2007.
53. Festus Adekunle Akintade, in discussion with the author, Lagos, Nigeria, December 24, 2007.
54. Daniel Ofudje, in discussion with the author, Lagos, Nigeria, January 14, 2008.
55. Festus Adekunle Akintade, in discussion with the author, Lagos, Nigeria, December 24, 2007.
56. Muritala Olayinka alli-Balogun, in discussion with the author, Lagos, Nigeria, January 17, 2011.
57. Alex Dediara, in discussion with the author, Lagos, Nigeria, January 20, 2011.
58. Festus Adekunle Akintade, in discussion with the author, Lagos, Nigeria, December 24, 2007.
59. Chief Charles Oloma Kose Kroseide, in discussion with the author, Lagos, Nigeria, January 14, 2008; John Larry, in discussion with the author, Lagos, Nigeria, January 17, 2008; T. T. Mensah, in discussion with the author, Lagos, Nigeria, January 25, 2007.
60. Pa Agbaosi, in discussion with the author, Lagos, Nigeria, December 15, 2007; John Larry, in discussion with the author, Lagos, Nigeria, January 17, 2008.
61. Pa Agbaosi, in discussion with the author, Lagos, Nigeria, December 15, 2007.
62. Adeola Lawal, in discussion with the author, Lagos, Nigeria, December 21, 2007.
63. Ibid.
64. Anthony Davies Eros, in discussion with the author, Lagos, Nigeria, December 15, 2007.

65. Paul Gilroy, *The Black Atlantic: Modernity and Double Consciousness* (Cambridge, MA: Harvard University Press, 1993).
66. Ari Festus, in discussion with the author, Lagos, Nigeria, December 24, 2007.

Bibliography

Board of Enquiry into the Trade Dispute between the Elder Dempster Lines Limited and the Nigerian Union of Seamen. 1959. *Report.* Lagos: Federal Government Printer.

Bolster, W. J. 1996. "'Every Inch a Man': Gender in the Lives of African American Seamen, 1800–1860." In *Iron Men, Wooden Women: Gender and Seafaring in the Atlantic World, 1700–1920*, edited by M. Creighton and L. Nordling, 138–68. Baltimore: Johns Hopkins University Press.

Carland, J. W., F. Hoy, and J. Carland. 2002. "'Who Is an Entrepreneur?' Is a Question Worth Asking." *Entrepreneurship: Critical Perspectives on Business and Management* 2:178–97.

Casson, M. 1982. *The Entrepreneur: An Economic Theory.* Lanham, MD: Rowman and Littlefield.

Davies, P. N. 2000. *The Trade Makers: Elder Dempster in West Africa, 1852–1972, 1973–1989.* Saint John's, Newfoundland: International Maritime Economic History Association.

Ewald, J. J. 2000. "Crossers of the Sea: Slaves, Freedmen, and Other Migrants in the Northwestern Indian Ocean, c. 1750–1914." *American Historical Review* 105, no. 1: 69–91.

Frost, D., ed. 1995. *Ethnic Labour and British Imperial Trade: A History of Ethnic Seafarers in the UK.* London: Frank Cass.

———. 1999. *Work and Community among West African Migrant Workers since the Nineteenth Century.* Liverpool: Liverpool University Press.

Gartner, W. B. 1989. "'Who Is an Entrepreneur?' Is the Wrong Question." *American Journal of Small Business* 12 (1989): 11–32.

Gilroy, P. 1993. *The Black Atlantic: Modernity and Double Consciousness.* Cambridge, MA: Harvard University Press.

Hébert, R., and A. N. Link. 1989. "In Search of the Meaning of Entrepreneurship." *Small Business Economics* 1, no. 1: 39–49.

Hindle, K., and M. Lansdowne. 2005. "Brave Spirits on New Paths: Toward a Globally Relevant Paradigm of Indigenous Entrepreneurship Research." *Journal of Small Business and Entrepreneurship* 18, no. 2: 131–41.

Hofstede, G. 1989. "Organising for Cultural Diversity." *European Management Journal* 7, no. 4: 390–97.

Hyslop, J. 2014. "'Ghostlike' Seafarers and Sailing Ship Nostalgia: The Figure of the Steamship Lascar in the British Imagination, c. 1880–1960." *Journal for Maritime Research* 16, no. 2: 212–28.

Lindsay, N. 2005. "Toward a Cultural Model of Indigenous Entrepreneurial Attitude." PhD diss., Academy of Marketing Science.

Low, M. B., and E. Abrahamson. 1997. "Movements, Bandwagons, and Clones: Industry Evolution and the Entrepreneurial Process." *Journal of Business Venturing* 12, no. 6: 435–57.

Peredo, A. M., et al. 2004. "Towards a Theory of Indigenous Entrepreneurship." *International Journal of Entrepreneurship and Small Business* 1, nos. 1–2: 1–20.

Sherwood, M. 1995. "Strikes! African Seamen, Elder Dempster and the Government 1940–42." In *Ethnic Labour and British Imperial Trade: A History of Ethnic Seafarers in the UK*, edited by D. Frost, 130–45. London: Frank Cass.

Tabili, L. 1994. "The Construction of Racial Difference in Twentieth-Century Britain: The Special Restriction (Coloured Alien Seamen) Order, 1925." *Journal of British Studies* 33, no. 1 (January): 54–98.

——. 1996. "'A Maritime Race': Masculinity and the Racial Division of Labor in British Merchant Ships, 1900–1939." In *Iron Men, Wooden Women: Gender and Seafaring in the Atlantic World, 1700–1920*, edited by M. Creighton and L. Nordling, 169–88. Baltimore: Johns Hopkins University Press.

Welter, F., and M. Xheneti. 2013. "Reenacting Contextual Boundaries—Entrepreneurial Resourcefulness in Challenging Environments." *Entrepreneurial Resourcefulness: Competing with Constraints* 15:149–83.

9 Ace Boxing Promoter

"Super Human Power," Boxing, and Sports Entrepreneurship in Colonial Nigeria, 1945–1960

Michael J. Gennaro

From the end of World War II until independence in 1960, boxing was one of the most popular sports and forms of entertainment in Nigeria, consistently crossing race and class boundaries. It also became a major tool in the formation of a national identity during the 1950s, following Hogan "Kid" Bassey's 1957 victory in the World Featherweight Championship.[1] While many European expatriates played a fundamental role in the development of boxing and other sports in the various British colonies, in Nigeria the number of expats was relatively small. This opened a unique avenue for Nigerian entrepreneurship. Native Nigerians took a leading position in the promotion, training, coaching, and managing of boxers and boxing, and the principal figures often wore multiple hats. Super Human Power (SHP), a popular post–World War II boxer, later became a manager, trainer, and promoter.[2] Through an examination of SHP's career and influence in Nigerian boxing, this chapter investigates the entrepreneurship of sport and entertainment as a calculated business investment, one that involved risk but also financial and social rewards. The chapter focuses on the methods of self-promotion used by boxers, especially press coverage, clever nicknames, and competition in championships. All of these tactics contributed to creating and propagating a "ring persona" that would resonate with fans and society, and in turn bring the boxers and their promoters, managers, and trainers money and fame. The creation of these various personae did more than simply sell tickets to boxing matches, however; it also shaped the ideals of boxers, bodies, and manhood to sell to the public. In other words, being a boxing entrepreneur in part meant selling a form of masculinity and "modernity" to African audiences.

Nigeria: Too Few Expats and Heavy Nigerian Interest

The population of Lagos, Nigeria's colonial capital and economic hub, exploded after World War I, from 40,000 to over 126,000 by 1931.[3] However, the growth of the local European population was not proportionate to this overall increase; the number of Europeans in Lagos only grew from 300 in 1901 to roughly 1,200 in 1931.[4] By 1950 there were only 2,222 Europeans. During this period Nigerians outnumbered Europeans by a ratio of roughly ten to one.[5] The number of Europeans was therefore just large enough to run a colony, but not to sustain traditionally European pastimes, including boxing, as all-white competitions. Without African promoters, managers, trainers, and coaches, not to mention the boxers and fans themselves, boxing would have died as a sports industry in Nigeria. Nigerians' dedication ensured the existence and longevity of boxing culture in the colony. It was the commitment of individual Nigerians and not that of British Europeans that guaranteed the wild success and popularity of the sport in the colony.

The Postwar Sporting Boom

As in Europe and the United States, the desire to return to normalcy in the post–World War II period in Africa brought with it an era of revival and growth in popular leisure activities in urban areas stifled by the war.[6] The postwar period saw an increase in imports, exports, and road transportation, and consequently also in the median income of Nigerians.[7] Simultaneously, the amount of currency in circulation rose from £16,657,000 in 1946 to £51,753,000 in 1954, and more than five times as much by 1966.[8] Following World War II, more Nigerians than ever before had disposable income to spend, since wage labor for adult men had become more the norm and a reliance on women and children for income declined.[9] Some of this extra money went to leisure activities and entertainment, as seen in the rapid growth of the cinema industry and sporting leagues.[10] Sports events were relatively cheap to attend; moreover, many young men, especially the elites who had been educated in British-style schools in Nigeria, had previously been athletes or spectators and viewed sports as crucial to a new postwar urban lifestyle.[11] Sporting events were held almost daily in Nigeria, and a gate or ticket fee was charged upon entrance.

After World War II, boxing's place in Nigeria changed when it began to take a more prominent role in the sporting and social lives of Nigerians.[12] This was due to several factors: the inclusion of boxing in soldiers' military training during World War II; the creation of the Nigerian Boxing Board of Control (NBBC) in 1949; the expansion of British-style schooling, with its emphasis on sport, physical education, health, and boxing; the use of boxing training programs to combat the growing problem of juvenile delinquency; the spread of the Boys' Club movement, with boxing as a focus; and the work of several elite Nigerians and British expats, along with the growing educated middle class in Lagos, to spur a sports revolution in the colony.[13] This was aided by the increased newspaper coverage of sports, along with the expansion of travel networks and infrastructure—road, railroads, sea vessels, and airplanes—that allowed larger audiences to gather in Lagos. By mid-1957 Nigeria had transformed from a boxing backwater to one of Africa's foremost boxing colonies; in that year, Bassey won the World Featherweight Championship and in 1958 Dick Tiger won the British Empire Middleweight Championship.[14]

Entertainers as Entrepreneurs

After World War II, as the transfer of political power from British to Nigerian leaders progressed gradually but steadily, the economic transfer of private enterprises and the growth of indigenous entrepreneurship rose more organically in response to international and local pressures on the British.[15] A key area of Nigerian entrepreneurial activity was boxing events. Individual businessmen promoted the fight, secured the fighters, hired referees and judges, paid for the venue, sold the tickets, and paid the boxers' purses. They also kept the profits or paid the losses associated with each individual tournament. Like those of other entrepreneurs, their investments were calculated: they chose the best fighters they could to attract large crowds, and negotiated contracts to maximize their possible profit. They ran the risk of losing money and had to mitigate their losses. They rolled their profits into the next show and competed with other promoters to stage the best shows and secure the best fighters. Motivated not only by the lack of British personnel and the Nigerian thirst for sports entertainment, Nigerians also saw an opportunity to invest money and time into a business venture that many had themselves worked in. They knew the sport's business from their own experiences as working-class boxers, then as middle-management managers, and finally as upper-level promoters.

S. U. Fwatshak argues that Nigerian entrepreneurship should be defined as "any business activity with a market/profit orientation and aim. . . . Entrepreneurship in this context could also be a medium or small-scale producer, a distributor/petty trader and/or [one who] offers services in a market economy but lacks capitalist relations of production."[16] This definition of the entrepreneur encompasses a central part of Nigerian life often overlooked in previous studies of African entrepreneurs: the service industry and the vital entertainment services, which represented a viable avenue for Nigerians to achieve financial and social mobility. Other scholars argue that the Nigerian entrepreneur was absent in many major industries, specifically because these industries were run by expatriate firms or expatriate government firms that did not allow indigenous competition. This situation forced Nigerians to enter other professions or avenues of entrepreneurial activity.[17] In particular, Nigerian entrepreneurs used leisure spaces, especially in urban areas, to create businesses and accumulate profits. Unlike other businesses, the entertainment sector did not sell commodities but rather intangibles such as community and, in the case of boxing, ideals of masculinity and sportsmanship, as well as a new urban ideal to be "modern."

Promoters needed to sell tickets, which paid the fighters and workers, and lined their own pockets. Picking the boxers was not easy, however, and choosing the wrong matchups could prove disastrous for Nigerian promoters. There were two types of fans that promoters appealed to in order to fill seats. One type, grounded heavily in the early 1950s British style of boxing, viewed a good match as one that showed off the standup, straight left jab, crisp punches, and scientific boxing—in other words, respect for the "boxer."[18] That style of match would last to the end, with a knockout coming, if it came at all, when fighters were liable to be tired. The other type of fans believed in the carnage of the fight, in which fighting, fast hitting, knockouts, and blood were paramount—praise for the "fighter."[19] Interestingly enough, fans also wanted these fights to last a long time: they viewed a short fight with a quick knockout and poor boxing as undesirable, since they felt they were not getting their money's worth.[20] Promoters therefore had to blend these two categories. They chose and advertised fights based on how long the athletes could last in the ring and the style each pugilist employed. Choosing the right boxers gave promoters credibility and trust with the fans; fans knew that coming to certain promoters' tournaments meant an action-packed night. One such boxer who brought the fans enjoyment and later became a credible promoter was the aptly named Super Human Power.

Super Human Power

One of the first celebrities of boxing to come from the north of the colony was a cruiserweight or light heavyweight from Kano nicknamed Super Human Power. SHP traveled to fight in Lagos several times in the late 1940s and 1950s, and he was the Northern Heavyweight Champion of Nigeria.[21] He was well known in Lagos sporting circles, both for his boxing prowess and for his size.[22] The Lagosian newspapers regularly updated readers on his travels and his fights in the provinces, a rare distinction for a nonlocal. For example, in January 1951 coverage of SHP's victory over Atomic Destroyer after three rounds on Christmas Day in Kano was published in the Lagos *Nigerian Daily Times* (*NDT*).[23] He was also respected enough to be featured in the first annual Collister Belt Tournament, founded to determine the Nigerian boxer of the year.[24] SHP also worked to bring boxing to various other northern cities. For example, to help support boxing in Zaria, he routinely staged matches there, often featuring himself as the main attraction. In 1951 he defeated Smiling Terror of Zaria to retain his title of Light-Heavyweight Champion of

Nigeria. Newspapers lauded the tournament as an event in which "boxing followers in Zaria saw a demonstration of good boxing for the first time."[25]

Even during SHP's active boxing career, he simultaneously began channeling his boxing into entrepreneurial avenues as a manager of a boxing club, as well as a promoter. He founded the Northern Nigeria Boxing Club in Kano in 1952 after several years of running boxing training there, and he was responsible for encouraging many other clubs to form in the area.[26] Once formed, he promoted matches between these clubs and also sent members of his club to various places in Nigeria to promote boxing. As noted in the *NDT*, "The Northern Nigeria Boxing Club under Power is making arrangements to have inter-province boxing in Kano. He has recently completed a tour of Northern Nigeria and created several clubs and branches of his club. He started branches in Zaria, Kaduna, Minna, Sokoto, Gusau and Jos."[27] The *NDT* also reported that only a short time after the founding of his clubs, SHP wanted to bring together the best boxers of the north to get ready for interprovincial matches with Lagos.[28] Furthermore, in 1951 the *Daily Service* reported on a tournament organized by SHP on Empire Day in which twenty-eight boxers participated, many of whom were registered boxers from SHP's clubs.[29] The tournament included aptly named boxers such as Paul Royal Navy, John Torpedo, Tiger Maxwell, Young Smart, Bruce Charles, Jack Johnson, Tete Atomic, Felix Negro Flash, Godwin Terror, and Bomber James. These names, as discussed later, were key to the boxers and promoters' strategy of crafting personae and selling them to the Nigerian public in order to attract crowds. SHP understood the proper tactics of advertising and promotion from his experience as a boxer, and this included inviting boxers with catchy names.

SHP began to see success in Lagos rings, as well as in the north. One reporter in 1952 noted that the north could one day soon become a boxing center to challenge Lagos and supply a steady stream of ready talent, thanks to SHP's work.[30] The coverage of SHP's efforts in Lagosian newspapers helped to legitimize him and his activities as a boxing promoter. At the time there were two boxing clubs in Kano, and the best one, the *NDT* reported, was SHP's Northern Nigerian Boxing Club. One article reported the existence of promising boxers in Kano, Zaria, and Jos, but because they were practically unknown in Lagos, they suffered in the championship rankings for the colony.[31] SHP worked hard to secure support from Lagos to improve the sport as a whole and encourage bouts between athletes from the two regions. One thing was certain: boxing was happening in the provinces, and northern boxers were fighting professionally alongside Lagos boxers for purses and recognition.

SHP saw his role as promoting boxing throughout Nigeria. In 1952 he began the first of many trips to the east of Nigeria to garner support for boxing. SHP planned to conduct a series of exhibition matches in the east, accompanied by Bob Emmanuel, then Kano's featherweight champion. SHP hoped to create interest for interprovincial matches between east and north, increase competition, and give his boxers extra work.[32] Six weeks after SHP arrived in Aba, word of the boxing demo he staged there with Dick Tiger reached Lagos. Spectators from Aba to Port Harcourt, Calabar, Umuahia, Enugu, and Onitsha traveled up to sixty miles to attend and see the northern champ. As the paper in Lagos reported, "Wherever he went, Power told his eager admirers that boxing should not only be taken up for the glory of the sport or for money-making, but also for physical fitness and for self-defence."[33]

SHP was one of the first Nigerian promoters, but he was certainly not the only one. The 1950s saw the expansion of boxing more generally, and Nigerians filled the gaps created by this expansion in the positions of trainers, managers, and promoters. Many had formerly been boxers themselves; in the early 1950s boxing was a way to earn extra income after regular working hours. For example, Steve Tunero, a famous Lagosian boxer in the late 1940s and early 1950s, had become a manager and promoter by 1953. He decided to move to Ibadan to help facilitate the training and transfer of boxers from that region to tournaments in Lagos in order to boost the talent pool. In September 1953 Tunero staged a tournament at the Alpha Carnival African Tennis Club in Ebute Metta with boxers he had trained from Ibadan to fight against Lagosian boxers. As the *NDT* asked, "Is that not enterprising? If there is any promoter on the path of big fight promoter Nap Peregrino, I think he is this soft-spoken, unassuming but ambitious young man Steve." Tunero traveled frequently to Ibadan, which seemed to be "a fertile soil for croppers."[34] A famous former-boxer-turned-promoter from the 1940s and 1950s named Kid Richards described the difficulties of this entrepreneurial career in 1953, disclaiming the idea that promoting boxing was in any way a get-rich-quick scheme: "Believe me, it is the most risky and disappointing trade I have ever experienced. . . . Others are attempting to become boxing moguls, I don't envy them."[35] Because it was not an easy business venture, most promoters did it as a second job; for instance, Richards ran a boxing club, as did Napoleon Peregrino.[36]

Ring Personae

Boxers themselves had a hand in drumming up support and attendance at fights. A boxer who could command a large following and attract large "gates" or audiences was apt to see more fights and more money for himself. The name a boxer chose was an important aspect of his pull. Akin to branding in today's advertising, Nigerian boxers chose extravagant names and titles to promote their styles, strength, and personae.[37] These types of names remained limited to professional boxing, since the amateur boxing rules stipulated that a boxer must use his real name or a native name to conceal his identity if he did not want to use his real name. A local paper printed an article for professional boxers on how to choose a name, emphasizing that "it is among professional boxers that we come across astonishing pseudonyms as Sleeping Morris, Tony Baby Day, Hollywood Terror, Super Human Power, Tiger Jack Buffalo. Some even adopt Hollywood film star cowboy names like William Boyd, Billy the Kid, Roy Rogers, Texas Kid."[38] The importance of these names was twofold: it was a way to celebrate one's talent while also eliciting excitement in fans to see the boxers fight.

Although young men enjoyed these names, Nigerian elites felt they were tacky and embarrassing. Commenting on the choice of professional boxers' names, Horatio Agedah of the *NDT* recalled a boxing tournament where he sat beside a "foreign lady." After hearing the names from the emcee, she laughed and asked Agedah where he came up with such a name, and Agedah had to shrug: "I was embarrassed. . . . This clearly shows what laughing stocks we can make of ourselves in the ring when we choose to be called by funny and meaningless names. A young man whose real name is Mac Crimson Oghoghome could proudly adapt his name to Max Gogome for brevity or he might drop the Max and choose Crimson Ogome."[39] Agedah also describes how Nigerians in Britain have dropped or adapted their Nigeria fighting names.[40]

While upper-class Nigerians may have viewed these names as an embarrassment, there were several reasons why boxers chose them. First, the choice of a name was incredibly important to Yorubas, especially those born in the middle to lower classes, who typically did not enjoy the same ability to command naming ceremonies. Similar practices existed in other sports. For example, wrestlers of prestige in Nigeria received titles and nicknames to showcase their manliness and skill. One only has to look at the first page of Chinua Achebe's *Things Fall Apart*, where he introduces the protagonist Okonkwo's wrestling opponent Amalinze "the Cat."[41] That nickname, "the Cat," symbolized the man's wrestling ability, and with it he commanded respect in several villages, as well as drawing local fans to watch him wrestle.

Second, the circumstances of colonialism help explain the prevalence of these nicknames because the system of colonialism effectively infantilized colonized men. As an illustration, the positions held by Nigerians in the mines often had derogatory names such as "pick boys" or "tub boys."[42] The use of the term "boy" to refer to Nigerians was in fact not limited to the mines but was also found in many other positions in society, echoing perceptions of Nigerian inferiority and thus underpinning colonialism. A 1949 article in the *NDT* lamented the use of the term "boy" by Europeans in Lagos. The term, the article argued, was derogatory and too closely linked to slavery: "Would it not, therefore, in fairness and justice to our African servants, be advisable to cease bawling 'boy' at them and to treat them as human beings by addressing them by their names?"[43] Nigerian boxers did not want to be treated as boys, preferring to be seen as men who were manly and masculine in a colonial environment that infantilized them. These Nigerian

220 | Michael J. Gennaro

boxers therefore used their names as a way to direct the focus not to their imposed perceived inferiority but to their skills, abilities, and strengths.

The Art of Promoting

In order to set up a promotion, a promoter like SHP needed to secure a location for the fight. More often than not, these tended to be outdoors. Inclement weather was a constant worry for promoters since rain washed out shows completely, ruining the chance to make a profit. Rain caused the ring to become slippery and potentially dangerous for the fighters. Also, and quite understandably, fans did not like to sit in the rain. Since many venues asked for payment in advance and the NBBC required the purse to be paid in full in the event of rain, a rained-out promotion had the potential to cost a promoter a significant portion of his investment.

In addition to the venue, promoters needed to secure boxing talent with promises of payment immediately after the show. One article in 1954 lamented that boxers continually bankrupted the local promoter because they asked for too much money. In the late 1940s boxers could expect to earn five shillings per round, but by 1954 they demanded no less than one pound per round.[44] Bassey recalled that as a professional fighter in the late 1940s and early 1950s, he routinely fought for a lump sum of two pounds per fight.[45] Nevertheless, at one pound per round and with the average fight lasting eight rounds, in 1954 fighters could make eight pounds or roughly US$265 today.[46] For perspective, the Nigerian median annual income in 1950–1951 was thirty-four pounds, a sum that, if the boxer was good enough, could be earned after four fights.[47] Furthermore, even through 1954 unskilled manual laborers made roughly four shillings a day (approximately one pound per week), meaning one eight-round fight at one pound per round was the equivalent of two months' labor.[48] Since many boxers in the boom years boxed on average every two to three weeks and sometimes more frequently than that, a boxer was able to make a significant amount of money.[49]

Before the creation of the NBBC, promoters directly paid their boxers after a night's work. As mentioned previously, boxing only emerged as a popular sport in the early 1950s, and boxing promotions routinely did not draw a capacity crowd, sometimes drawing fewer than one hundred people. At a promotion in 1949 the papers noted that the fight was not sold out but the fans had a good time.[50] Stories abounded of promoters who, in an effort to recoup their losses, underpaid and sometimes did not pay their boxers at all after a fight. An interdependency existed between boxers, promoters, and managers in terms of promotion, payment, and entrepreneurship that was fragile at first because of the lack of organization and oversight in boxing. After the formation of the NBBC in 1949, however, promoters working under the NBBC's approval had to deposit the purse money with the NBBC one week in advance. This provided a protection measure for the boxers since it was the NBBC that doled out the purses, not the promoters. This ensured that promoters did not stiff the boxers with lack of payment in addition to their in-ring punishment.

African boxing entrepreneurs had to sell tickets to boxing tournaments in order to recoup their initial investment. Although boxing had become more popular in Nigeria, in the early 1950s the lack of fans at the matches remained a constant cause for concern. Unlike the Gold Coast, which boasted shows with over 3,000 paying fans, in the early 1950s Lagos found it difficult to attract more than 150.[51] Douglas J. Collister, the "Father of Boxing" in Nigeria and known locally as Deejaysee, wrote columns in the local newspapers about boxing, and he complained that Nigerian fans were not behaving like good sportsmen: "One point I would like to stress to the local fans is the promoters spend time and money in arranging these tournaments, so it is up to the local fans to help. One bad thing I have noticed in recent tournaments is the fact that a number of fans endeavour to evade paying for admittance and others pay for a shilling seat and once inside sneak into a ringside seat."[52] This was not a sportsmanlike practice, nor was it confined to small children and young men. Deejaysee was quick to point out that at this time the local promoters did not receive large sums of money: "It should surely be appreciated that all promotions are not money spinners and what little a promoter might gain in one promotion can very easily be offset by bad weather or poor attendance at another. . . . These local promoters are doing their best to put Lagos on the boxing map and so merit your consideration, fans."[53] Blackie Power, a boxer-turned-manager-and-promoter, complained in 1950 that promoters should be pitied. He noted that the attendance at pro fights in Nigeria was not enough to make money and pay boxers for their effort. Most promotions, he claimed, cost around twenty pounds to promote, and the promoter usually brought in twenty-eight pounds, leaving little money for boxers, who were routinely stiffed or underpaid.[54]

Another major problem faced by Nigerian promoters lay in the lack of available boxing talent. In the early to mid-1950s, skilled Nigerian boxers tended to leave Nigeria for Liverpool or London, many through the connections of Jack Farnsworth and Collister. Boxers such as Sammy Wilde, Reggie "Thunderbolt" Williams, Israel "Battling" Boyle, Young Panther, Slugger Chocolate, Bola "Double Hook Demon" Lawal, and Dick Tiger, to name a few of the most famous, left during this postwar period to go to the United Kingdom. As the *NDT* noted in 1952, "It is regrettable to note that ever since the exodus of West African leading boxing stars to the United Kingdom, our boxing front has been noticeably dull and promoters are always at their wits' end to attract fans to their shows. As a result, the few available box-office attractions have been monotonously busy in the ring."[55]

One possible solution to this problem was to invite more provincial boxers to fight in Lagos in an effort to spice up the local scene and hopefully uncover a few gems. The *NDT* sent out "a call to provincial boxers so that new rivalries can be made and more promotions [can be brought] to Lagos."[56] However, there was apparently not a single heavyweight in the country at the time. That class of boxers seemed to have vanished with the exit of Reggie Williams, Bob Savage, and Jack Obosi. This emigration could be attributed to the boxers' own desire to be challenged. There were a number of boxers who seemed to have reached the top and been forced to stagnate. Sammy Idowu Langford was considered unlucky since he had beaten SHP as light heavyweight champ and there were no other boxers at his level of skill; Blackie Power was considered the undisputed king of the middleweights, and he frequently appeared for fights in less than peak shape. There seemed to be no new rising stars to challenge these boxers.

Did They Make Money?

Boxing matches were not heavily attended at the start of the 1950s, and even by the end of the decade any mention of an audience of more than five hundred fans was rare.[57] One reason for this was the high cost of attending a boxing tournament, something much more expensive for the average Nigerian than a typical football game. Admittance to a football match was generally only one shilling, while boxing tickets well into the 1950s cost two shillings for the bargain or "popular" side and upwards of ten shillings for a reserved ringside seat.[58] The popular side was not always ideal for fans—it was often overcrowded, and generally consisted mainly of standing room. Promoters complained that they could easily sell out the popular side of the ring but had trouble filling reserved seats. For example, the paper complained that at one show in 1953, the reserved seats were less than one-third full, with "rows upon rows" of empty seating.[59] As mentioned previously, up until 1955 most manual laborers made one pound per week (twenty shillings) or less, and the cost of a boxing show was beyond their means.[60]

The cost of promoting boxing matches remained a continuous concern for promoters since securing boxers at a reasonable price became more difficult in the mid-1950s. Two of Lagos's top promoters, Peregrino and Tunero, both stressed that the lack of tournaments staged in Lagos was not due to a lack of fighters willing to box but rather to a lack of promoters willing to pay.[61] Peregrino complained that he made little money in 1954 because "championship bouts that formerly cost promoters no more than ten pounds, the winner receiving six pounds and the loser four, now [required] an outlay of thirty to forty pounds for the two boxers to share."[62] The cost of securing a fighter was higher than ever before, yet the size of the crowd remained similar. Promoters started to balk at fighters' asked purses since "the general belief among boxers nowadays seems to be that possession of a professional boxing license is the channel for making good money. . . . Flyweights who were once content with a purse of five shillings per round would not now accept an offer [of] less than a pound a round."[63] Peregrino begged boxers to take less money, win the crowds, and then demand a larger share of the profits when they helped create them. He saw this as the way to build a future in Nigeria in which boxers could demand two pounds per round.

Boxing promotion in Nigeria was thus not a lucrative business until the end of the 1950s. Although it is hard to find evidence of just how much money a promoter did in fact make on a single promotion, we have some information as to the range of potential profits. In 1951 Battling Roberts faced Blackie Power for the Nigerian Middleweight Championship in what the newspapers described as an exciting fight.[64] Roberts fought hard, but he was ultimately knocked out in the ninth round; he never regained consciousness and passed away at the General Hospital in Lagos the next day.[65] The boxing community and Lagos responded to the tragedy by hosting a tournament in his honor, with a portion of the proceeds donated to Roberts's family. The *Daily Service* noted that the promoter, G. M. Addy Williams, did in fact give Roberts's parents a share, roughly four pounds (fifteen shillings or twenty-four pence), which was the equivalent of one month's salary for an unskilled laborer and approximately US$145 in 2015.[66] The article noted that Williams did not give all the proceeds to Roberts's parents; it is reasonable to assume that he kept at least 25 percent and as much as 90 percent of the profits himself. If that is the case, on this particular promotion Williams would have made between six and forty-one pounds, or $208–$1,422.[67] Most promoters ran one to three tournaments each month, and with three successful promotions a promoter could make over £120 in a month. To put this profit into perspective, in 1956 a salaried Nigerian civil servant averaged £187 per annum, and unskilled workers much less.[68] This is an abstract example and cannot be taken as the norm without further evidence, but it is useful in demonstrating that, despite the small crowds, there was money to be made as a promoter, and it could be a lucrative business. Even running one successful promotion a month earned as much as one-third of a civil servant's annual salary.

Yet even with the rising popularity of boxing in Nigeria through the late 1950s, a promoter was not guaranteed to make money at every promotion. For example, Okorie, a former boxer by the name of "Black Panther," lost thirty pounds on an event due to a combination of rain and poor attendance.[69] The *NDT* commiserated: "Time and time again, the thought must go through [Okorie's] mind . . . 'just what do the Lagos boxing fans really want?' "[70] As noted previously, one of the primary concerns of promoters was how to persuade fans to attend boxing matches and pay the gate fees. Into the late 1950s fans routinely complained that the fees for boxing were too high, and Okorie believed this was one of the reasons he lost money.[71]

What Were They Selling?

Although Nigerian promoters were selling a service (entertainment), they were also crafting and selling "Nigerianness," manliness, and character to the public. Many of the ideals that the boxer and promoter were selling conflicted since fans wanted both the "gentleman" and the "fighter" in one. This 1954 newspaper description of Battling Enoch details how and why Nigerian boxers were praised in public: "Enoch's boxing genius is greatly enhanced by his quiet disposition, his gentlemanly behavior, his unassuming conduct at all times and his readiness to take good advice. Nigeria continues to send abroad to the United Kingdom and elsewhere many boys who may win laurels in various fields of sport, but I am sure Battling Enoch will also be one of our greatest 'ambassadors of goodwill.'"[72] Especially after winning the Nigerian Championship in 1953 and the West African Bantamweight Championship in 1954, Enoch was heralded as a hard-hitting fighter that fans paid to see "clad in his shimmering gown, the carriage worthy of a champion."[73] Like SHP, Enoch was both a gentleman and fighter. Young boys and men collected the pictures of boxers they idolized; one informant explained that they were drawn to particular boxers for their personality (or persona) just as much as for their skill.[74] They were seen as modern men and celebrities in Lagos, so much so that one man remembered that his father had a large picture of Bassey in their living room.[75]

Conclusion

Boxing and entertainment in general opened an entrepreneurial space for native Nigerians, in part due to the fact that there were so few British colonial officials in Nigeria and especially in the burgeoning capital city of Lagos. The service industry and, in particular, the vital entertainment services emerged as an attainable avenue for Nigerians to achieve financial and social mobility after the war. In selling boxing, however, Nigerian promoters were in fact selling an ideal of masculinity, and indeed even an archetype of an independent, modern, and strong Nigerian.

MICHAEL J. GENNARO is Assistant Professor of African History at Grambling State University. His research focuses on sport, masculinity, and boxing in Nigeria, as well as the migration of sporting talent across the British Empire.

Notes

1. See Anene Ejikeme, "Hogan Bassey: Nigerian Icon," in *Emergent Themes and Methods in African Studies: Essays in Honor of Adiele E. Afigbo*, ed. Toyin Falola and Adam Paddock, 443–56 (Trenton, NJ: African World, 2009).

2. Also known as Super Human Paul.

3. *Census 1931: Lagos Colony Population and Statistics*, 2 vols., Nigerian Archives Ibadan (NAI), Commissioner of Colony Office, Lagos (COMCOL) 1: 739. Volume 1 contains the paperwork leading up to the census and volume 2 presents the actual statistics. At the turn of the twentieth century, Lagos was still a relatively small island with a population of approximately 40,000. Unlike other Yoruba towns nearby, Lagos had a polyglot population, drawing migrants since the mid-nineteenth century. However, growth in trade before World War I led to a new, massive wave of migration from the hinterland, and by 1911 there were over 72,000 residents. By 1921 the population was estimated to be roughly 99,690 persons. The government believed that Lagos's population was actually closer to 178,000 by 1935. See Akin Mabogunje, *Urbanization in Nigeria* (London: University of London Press, 1969), 257.

4. Mabogunje, *Urbanization in Nigeria*, 264. In 1931 British persons made up the majority of Europeans (1,053), including French (37), Germans (34), and Syrians/Lebanese (134).

5. Ibid.

6. In terms of boxing, there was a similar revival of matches in Britain, especially Liverpool, as ex-soldiers wanted to either continue boxing after their service or return to weekly boxing matches as spectators. For more information about Liverpool and boxing, see Gary Shaw and Jim Jenkinson, *The Mersey Fighters 2: More Lives and Times of Liverpool's Boxing Heroes* (Liverpool: Gary Shaw, 2007).

7. Peter Kilby, *African Enterprise: The Nigerian Bread Industry* (Stanford, CA: Stanford University Press, 1965), 4. Between 1946 and 1954 imports rose from £19,824,000 to £114,069,000, and exports rose from £23,738,000 to £146,242,000.

8. E. O. Akeredolu-Ale, *Underdevelopment of Indigenous Entrepreneurship in Nigeria* (Ibadan, Nigeria: Ibadan University Press, 1975), 38.

9. Toyin Falola and Akanmu Adebayo, introduction to *Culture, Politics and Money among the Yoruba*, ed. Toyin Falola and Akanmu Adebayo (Piscataway, NJ: Transaction, 1999), 20–21.

10. See Brian Larkin, *Signal and Noise: Media, Infrastructure, and Urban Culture in Nigeria* (Durham, NC: Duke University Press, 2008). For an empire-wide case, see James Burns, *Cinema and Society in the British Empire, 1895–1940* (New York: Palgrave Macmillan, 2013). As Falola and Adebayo argue, "Thanks to wage labor, the new currencies were available to more people . . . people had more to spend, and the elite could readily imitate Westerners in habits of dress, music, food, and customs." Falola and Adebayo, introduction to *Culture, Politics and Money*, 20.

11. See Michael Gennaro, "Nigeria in the Ring: Boxing, Masculinity, and Empire in Nigeria, 1930–1957" (PhD diss., University of Florida, 2016); James Mangan, "Ethics and Ethnocentricity: Imperial Education in British Tropical Africa," in *Sport in Africa: Essays in Social History*, ed. William Baker and James Mangan, 138–71 (New York: Africana, 1987); and Lisa Lindsey, "Trade Unions and Football Clubs: Gender and the 'Modern' Public Sphere in Colonial Southwestern Nigeria," in *Leisure in Urban Africa*, eds. Paul Tiyambe Zeleza and Cassandra Rachel Veney, 105–24 (Trenton, NJ: Africa World, 2003).

12. For a detailed look at the pre–World War II boxing history, see Michael Gennaro, "'The Whole Place Is in Pandemonium': Dick Tiger versus Gene Fullmer III, and the Consumption of Boxing in Nigeria," *International Journal of the History of Sport* 30, no. 16 (2013): 1903–14; and Gennaro, "Nigeria in the Ring."

13. These sports "revolutionaries" included Nnamdi Azikiwe, Dr. Adeniyi-Jones, "Kid" Richards, Donald Faulkner, Douglas J. Collister (Deejaysee), Jack Farnsworth, P. H. Cook, and Napoleon "Nap" Peregrino, to name a few. Gennaro, "Nigeria in the Ring"; Gennaro, "'Whole

Place Is in Pandemonium.'" For British education, see Mangan, "Ethics and Ethnocentricity". For juvenile delinquency, see Laurent Fourchard, "Lagos and the Invention of Juvenile Delinquency in Nigeria, 1920–60," *Journal of African History* 47, no. 1 (2006): 115–37; and Simon Heap, "Jaguda Boys: Pickpocketing in Ibadan, 1930–60," *Urban History* 24 (1997): 324–43.

14. For more on Bassey, see Ejikeme, "Hogan Bassey." Bassey won the title in 1957 in Paris when he defeated French Algerian Cherif Hamia. Dick Tiger won his title against Britisher Pat McAteer in Liverpool. Both victories were seen as boosting the forward march to independence and Nigeria's preparedness to enter the world stage beyond the sporting arena. See Gennaro, "'Whole Place Is in Pandemonium.'"

15. Tom Forrest, *The Advance of African Capital: The Growth of Nigerian Private Enterprise* (Charlottesville: University of Virginia Press, 1994), 23, 25–26; S. U. Fwatshak, *African Entrepreneurship in Jos, Central Nigeria, 1902–1985* (Durham: Carolina Academic, 2011), 11.

16. Fwatshak, *African Entrepreneurship in Jos*, 34.

17. Kilby, *African Enterprise*, 4–5. During the closing phases of colonialism, Nigerians were prominent in many areas, especially "trade, transport, construction, services, and a wide range of small-scale manufacturing activities," such as oil refining, cement production, flour milling, brewing, printing, furniture, banking, clothing, upholstery, footwear, and metal forming.

18. See Kasia Boddy, "'A Straight Left against Sloggin' Ruffians': National Boxing Styles in the Years Preceding the First World War," *Journal of Historical Sociology* 24 (2011): 428–50.

19. Ibid.

20. One example can be seen in Ringside, "Who Will Win Tomorrow's Fight: Clottey or Martins?," *Nigerian Daily Times* (Lagos, Nigeria), February 12, year unknown.

21. "Says Sleep Morris, Lome Welterweight 'It's No Title but Challenge Fight,'" *Nigerian Daily Times* (Lagos, Nigeria), July 28, 1949; Sports Editor, "Referee Saves Sleeping Morris," *Nigerian Daily Times* (Lagos, Nigeria), August 1, 1949; "Boxing Prospects for the Collister Belt (1)," *Nigerian Daily Times* (Lagos, Nigeria), January 3, 1951; "Total Condemnation of Superman Pall Is Premature," *Daily Service*, February 2, 1951; "Superhuman Power at Zaria," *Nigerian Daily Times* (Lagos, Nigeria), August 7, 1951. "Power Expected Tomorrow," *Nigerian Daily Times* (Lagos, Nigeria), January 25, 1951, mentions that Super Human Power would be leaving Kano for the Collister and arriving in Lagos the next day.

22. SHP stood over six feet tall and fought in the lightweight and later cruiserweight divisions, between 175 and 200 pounds.

23. "Power Beats Destroyer at Kano," *Nigerian Daily Times* (Lagos, Nigeria), January 15, 1951. Power was supposed to face Bomber Agulefo. Bomber was the Ex-Serviceman's Heavy Champ and boxing champ of the Nigerian police in Jos, but he did not show up for the fight. Supporting bouts for this Christmas event saw bantams Slugger Daniel and Ojabrei Elu, both from the Nigerian Boxing Club, fight to a draw. Bruce Charles, Nigerian Boxing Club Flyweight Champion, beat Oganie, Ibadan Boxing Club champ, forcing him to retire. Light Cruiser of Gusau surrendered to Tiger Maxwell, the Nigerian Railways champion.

24. "Boxing Prospects for the Collister Belt (1)." The tournament was named in honor of Douglas J. Collister, one of the "Fathers of Boxing" in Nigeria. Collister was an avid boxing fan from Liverpool who came to Lagos in the late 1930s. He was also one of the men behind the formation of the Nigerian Boxing Board of Control in 1949. For more details on Collister and boxing, see Gennaro, "Nigeria in the Ring."

25. "Superhuman Power at Zaria," *Nigerian Daily Times* (Lagos, Nigeria), August 7, 1951. The event was originally in honor of the National Council of Nigeria and the Cameroons (NCNC). Black Bomber beat Little Kid, Dead Rain Boll lost to Poisonous Arrow, Demon Fighter beat Negro Flash, and Godwin Holy Devil beat Saw Killer Oji.

26. "Superhuman Power Forms New Boxing Club at Kano," *Nigerian Daily Times* (Lagos, Nigeria), May 10, 1952. Even before he had a proper club, SHP had more than twenty-five locals in Kano under his boxing stewardship.

27. Ibid.

28. Ibid.

29. "Empire Day Boxing Competition at Kano," *Daily Service*, May 1, 1951.

30. Staff Reporter, "Amateur Boxing in Northern Nigeria," *Nigerian Daily Times* (Lagos, Nigeria), July 10, 1952.

31. Ibid.

32. "Superhuman Power Will Tour East," *Nigerian Daily Times* (Lagos, Nigeria), October 31, 1952.

33. "Kano Boxing Champion Tours Eastern Region," *Nigerian Daily Times* (Lagos, Nigeria), December 18, 1952.

34. Sports Reporter, "Tunero Plans Big Fight for Sept 14," *Nigerian Daily Times* (Lagos, Nigeria), September 10, 1953.

35. "Is Kid Richards Really Fed Up?," *Nigerian Daily Times* (Lagos, Nigeria), July 24, 1953. Kid Richards started boxing in 1930 at the age of thirteen. He later became the manager and trainer of the Nigerian Boxing Club when his mentor, Reggie "African Hercules" Williams, left for the United Kingdom during World War II. In April 1943 he staged his first tournament, and in 1945 he started the Imperial Boxing Club, of which he became the manager, trainer, and promoter. Boxer Bob Terror wrote to the *Nigerian Daily Times* to discuss Richards, stating, "The Kid' is our local 'Peter Banasko,' and that appellation unquestionably has its own attraction. For Kid Richards is the only one in the whole length and breadth of Nigeria who not only manages but also wears the gloves when training his charge." "Healthy Rivalry in Inter-Club Boxing," *Nigerian Daily Times* (Lagos, Nigeria), July 26, 1953.

36. "Is Kid Richards Really Fed Up?" See also "Portrait: African Hercules," *West Africa*, January 12, 1952.

37. Walter LaFeber, *Michael Jordan and the New Global Capitalism* (New York: W. W. Norton, 1999).

38. Horatio Agedah, "The Nigerian Boxer and His Name," *Nigerian Daily Times* (Lagos, Nigeria), December 27, 1953.

39. Ibid.

40. Ibid. For example, "Killer" Kid Bassey became Hogan Bassey, and Young Panther became Raj Folami. Little Chocolate was now Dan Collie (meaning "friend of Collister"), and Battling Boyle just Israel Boyle. Even Small Montana now goes by his real name, Ganiyu Sulaimon, when playing soccer.

41. Chinua Achebe, *Things Fall Apart* (London: Heinemann, 1983), 1.

42. Carolyn Brown, "A 'Man' in the Village Is a 'Boy' in the Workplace: Colonial Racism, Worker Militance, and Igbo Notions of Masculinity in the Nigerian Coal Industry, 1930–1945," in *Men and Masculinities in Modern Africa*, ed. Stephen Miescher and Lisa Lindsey, 156–74 (Portsmouth, NH: Heinemann, 2003).

43. "The Name and Not 'Boy,'" *Nigerian Daily Times* (Lagos, Nigeria), July 13, 1949.

44. Horatio Agedah, "Boxing for Big Money," *Nigerian Daily Times* (Lagos, Nigeria), August 15, 1954.

45. "JM Sanderson Says: Hogan Bassey Is Nigeria's World Title Hope," *Nigerian Daily Times* (Lagos, Nigeria), June 17, 1957. Two pounds converted to roughly eighty USD in 2015. Eric Nye, "Pounds Sterling to Dollars: Historical Conversion of Currency," accessed November 11, 2015, http://www.uwyo.edu/numimage/currency.htm.

46. Nye, "Pounds Sterling to Dollars."

47. Kilby, *African Enterprise*, 3. According to Kilby, thirty-four pounds was the average for the western region of Nigeria, in which Lagos is located. The eastern region's average was twenty-one pounds and the northern region's was seventeen pounds.

48. "Five-Shilling Pay Proposal Is Rejected," *Nigerian Daily Times* (Lagos, Nigeria), August 18, 1954. A proposal for a minimum wage of five shillings a day for manual labor was rejected in the House of Representatives.

49. Fighting once a month for a year meant a boxer would receive ninety-six pounds per year, nearly three times the median average in 1954.

50. Sports Editor, "Referee Saves Sleeping Morris," *Nigerian Daily Times* (Lagos, Nigeria), August 1, 1949.

51. Blackie Power, "Pity the Poor Promoter," *Nigerian Daily Times* (Lagos, Nigeria), January 10, 1950.

52. DJC [Douglas J. Collister], "Lightweight Title Fight," *Nigerian Daily Times* (Lagos, Nigeria), March 25, 1950.

53. Ibid.

54. Power, "Pity the Poor Promoter."

55. Alade Odunewu, "Boxing Review: 'Provincial Boxers Should Flood Lagos,'" *Nigerian Daily Times* (Lagos, Nigeria), September 3, 1952.

56. Ibid.

57. "Large Crowd Watch Boxing at Makurdi," *Nigerian Daily Times* (Lagos, Nigeria), May 28, 1954. More than five hundred reportedly attended. The match was between Spider Web and Mammal Destroyer; according to the paper, "their speed kept the spectators half-seated and highly excited."

58. The popular side was the standing-only side with limited seats. Stories abounded in the newspapers of fans paying for popular-side seats, then sneaking into reserved seating.

59. K.O., "Monthly Amateur Boxing Show Begins This Week," *Nigerian Daily Times* (Lagos, Nigeria), March 16, 1953; KO, "A Plea for Better and Cleaner Boxing in Nigeria," *Nigerian Daily Times* (Lagos, Nigeria), February 9, 1953.

60. "Five-Shilling Pay Proposal Is Rejected."

61. Agedah, "Boxing for Big Money."

62. Ibid.

63. Ibid.

64. Sports Editor, "Noted Boxers Fight To-Night in Honour of Late Battling Roberts," *Daily Service*, November 30, 1951.

65. Ibid.

66. Sports Editor, "Another Blackie-KO Victim Goes to Hospital," *Daily Service*, December 3, 1951; Sports Editor, "Noted Boxers Fight"; conversion made by Nye, "Pounds Sterling to Dollars."

67. Conversion made by Nye, "Pounds Sterling to Dollars."

68. Mabogunje, *Urbanization in Nigeria*, 254. In 1956 an unskilled worker made five shillings a day, or roughly seventy-eight pounds per annum.

69. "Bassey Offered Fights for March and April," *Nigerian Daily Times* (Lagos, Nigeria), March 11, 1953.

70. Ibid.

71. Ibid.

72. Horatio Agedah, "Enoch Leaves for UK Today," *Nigerian Daily Times* (Lagos, Nigeria), July 1, 1954. Battling Enoch's real name was Enoch Adeniran Olawoyin; he hailed from Ikirun

in Oshin Division, western Nigeria. He was a tailor by trade and started boxing as an amateur at sixteen years old in 1949. He turned pro in 1950 after showing much promise.

73. "Champion Made in Two Years," *Nigerian Daily Times* (Lagos, Nigeria), January 3, 1954.

74. Abraham Adeyemi Jones, in discussion with the author, Lagos, Nigeria, May 2012.

75. "The Photographer," in discussion with the author, Ibadan, Nigeria, July 2013. "The Photographer" preferred that his identity not be revealed.

Bibliography

Achebe, C. 1983. *Things Fall Apart*. London: Heinemann.

Agedah, H. 1953. "The Nigerian Boxer and His Name." *Nigerian Daily Times* (Lagos, Nigeria), December 27.

———. 1954. "Boxing for Big Money." *Nigerian Daily Times* (Lagos, Nigeria), August 15.

———. 1954. "Enoch Leaves for UK Today." *Nigerian Daily Times* (Lagos, Nigeria), July 1.

Akeredolu-Ale, E. O. 1975. *Underdevelopment of Indigenous Entrepreneurship in Nigeria*. Ibadan, Nigeria: Ibadan University Press.

Boddy, K. 2011. "'A Straight Left against Sloggin' Ruffians': National Boxing Styles in the Years Preceding the First World War." *Journal of Historical Sociology* 24:428–50.

Brown, C. 2003. "A 'Man' in the Village Is a 'Boy' in the Workplace: Colonial Racism, Worker Militance, and Igbo Notions of Masculinity in the Nigerian Coal Industry, 1930–1945." In *Men and Masculinities in Modern Africa*, edited by Stephen Miescher and Lisa Lindsey, 156–74. Portsmouth, NH: Heinemann.

Burns, J. 2013. *Cinema and Society in the British Empire, 1895–1940*. New York: Palgrave Macmillan.

Daily Service (Lagos, Nigeria). 1951. "Empire Day Boxing Competition at Kano." May 1.

———. 1951. "Total Condemnation of Superman Pall Is Premature." February 2.

DJC [Douglas J. Collister]. 1950. "Lightweight Title Fight." *Nigerian Daily Times* (Lagos, Nigeria), March 25.

Ejikeme, A. 2009. "Hogan Bassey: Nigerian Icon." In *Emergent Themes and Methods in African Studies: Essays in Honor of Adiele E. Afigbo*, edited by T. Falola and A. Paddock, 443–56. Trenton, NJ: African World.

Falola, T., and A. Adebayo. 1999. Introduction to *Culture, Politics and Money among the Yoruba*, edited by T. Falola and A. Adebayo, 1–24. Piscataway, NJ: Transaction.

Forrest, T. 1994. *The Advance of African Capital: The Growth of Nigerian Private Enterprise*. Charlottesville: University of Virginia Press.

Fourchard, L. 2006. "Lagos and the Invention of Juvenile Delinquency in Nigeria, 1920–60." *Journal of African History* 47, no. 1: 115–37.

Fwatshak, S. U. 2011. *African Entrepreneurship in Jos, Central Nigeria, 1902–1985*. Durham: Carolina Academic.

Gennaro, M. 2013. "'The Whole Place Is in Pandemonium': Dick Tiger versus Gene Fullmer III, and the Consumption of Boxing in Nigeria." *International Journal of the History of Sport* 30, no. 16: 1903–14.

———. 2016. "Nigeria in the Ring: Boxing, Masculinity, and Empire in Nigeria, 1930–1957." PhD diss., University of Florida.

Heap, S. 1997. "Jaguda Boys: Pickpocketing in Ibadan, 1930–60." *Urban History* 24:324–43.

Kilby, P. 1965. *African Enterprise: The Nigerian Bread Industry*. Stanford, CA: Stanford University Press.

K.O. 1953. "Monthly Amateur Boxing Show Begins This week." *Nigerian Daily Times* (Lagos, Nigeria), March 16.

———. 1953. "A Plea for Better and Cleaner Boxing in Nigeria." *Nigerian Daily Times* (Lagos, Nigeria), February 9.

LaFeber, W. 1999. *Michael Jordan and the New Global Capitalism*. New York: W. W. Norton.

Larkin, B. 2008. *Signal and Noise: Media, Infrastructure, and Urban Culture in Nigeria*. Durham, NC: Duke University Press.

Lindsey, L. 2003. "Trade Unions and Football Clubs: Gender and the 'Modern' Public Sphere in Colonial Southwestern Nigeria." In *Leisure in Urban Africa*, edited by P. Tiyambe Zeleza and C. R. Veney, 105–24. Trenton, NJ: Africa World.

Mabogunje, A. 1969. *Urbanization in Nigeria*. London: University of London Press.

Mangan, J. 1987. "Ethics and Ethnocentricity: Imperial Education in British Tropical Africa." In *Sport in Africa: Essays in Social History*, edited by W. Baker and J. Mangan, 138–71. New York: Africana.

Marris, P. 1961. *Family and Social Change in an African City*. Chicago: Northwestern University Press.

Nigerian Daily Times (Lagos, Nigeria). 1949. "The Name and Not 'Boy.'" July 13.

———. 1949. "Says Sleep Morris, Lome Welterweight 'It's No Title but Challenge Fight.'" July 28.

———. 1951. "Boxing Prospects for the Collister Belt (1)." January 3.

———. 1951. "Power Beats Destroyer at Kano." January 15.

———. 1951. "Power Expected Tomorrow." January 25.

———. 1951. "Superhuman Power at Zaria." August 7.

———. 1952. "Kano Boxing Champion Tours Eastern Region." December 18.

———. 1952. "Superhuman Power Forms New Boxing Club at Kano." May 10.

———. 1952. "Superhuman Power Will Tour East." October 31.

———. 1953. "Bassey Offered Fights for March and April." March 11.

———. 1953. "Is Kid Richards Really Fed Up?" July 24.

———. 1954. "Champion Made in Two Years." January 3.

———. 1954. "Five-Shilling Pay Proposal Is Rejected." August 18.

———. 1954. "Large Crowd Watch Boxing at Makurdi." May 28.

———. 1957. "JM Sanderson Says: Hogan Bassey Is Nigeria's World Title Hope." June 17.

Nye, E. 2015. "Pounds Sterling to Dollars: Historical Conversion of Currency." Accessed November 11. http://www.uwyo.edu/numimage/currency.htm.

Odunewu, A. 1952. "Boxing Review: 'Provincial Boxers Should Flood Lagos.'" *Nigerian Daily Times* (Lagos, Nigeria), September 3.

Power, B. 1950. "Pity the Poor Promoter." *Nigerian Daily Times* (Lagos, Nigeria), January 10.

Ringside. n.d. "Who Will Win Tomorrow's Fight: Clottey or Martins?" *Nigerian Daily Times* (Lagos, Nigeria), February 12.

Shaw, G., and J. Jenkinson. 2007. *The Mersey Fighters 2: More Lives and Times of Liverpool's Boxing Heroes*. Liverpool: Gary Shaw.

Sports Editor. 1949. "Referee Saves Sleeping Morris." *Nigerian Daily Times* (Lagos, Nigeria), August 1.

———. 1951. "Another Blackie-KO Victim Goes to Hospital." *Daily Service*, December 3.

———. 1951. "Noted Boxers Fight To-Night in Honour of Late Battling Roberts." *Daily Service*, November 30.

Sports Reporter. 1953. "Tunero Plans Big Fight for Sept 14." *Nigerian Daily Times* (Lagos, Nigeria), September 10.

Staff Reporter. 1952. "Amateur Boxing in Northern Nigeria." *Nigerian Daily Times* (Lagos, Nigeria), July 10.

West Africa. 1952. "Portrait: African Hercules." January 12.

10 Healing Works

Nana Kofi Dɔnkɔ and the Business of Indigenous Therapeutics

Kwasi Konadu

THIS CHAPTER FOCUSES on indigenous forms of enterprise and leadership in the allied fields of medicine and health care in twentieth-century Africa. Although on average indigenous healers account for 60 to 70 percent of the health care delivered in African communities, especially rural ones, healers as individual practitioners or a category of analysis have rarely been studied as integral providers of value-added services to their societies. In short, healers have been written out of African economic and social histories, castaways intelligible to us only as "fetish priests," "cult officials," and ubiquitous purveyors of "witchcraft." This caricature, however, stands in stark contrast to the résumé and lifework of most African healers, embodied by prominent healers such as Nana Kofi Dɔnkɔ of Ghana.

Nana Kofi Dɔnkɔ (Sakyi) was an indigenous healer and blacksmith who lived and worked in the Takyiman (Techiman) township of the central Gold Coast/Ghana. Born to Bono (Akan) parents around 1912/1913, he was also a marginal peasant farmer whose fortune and misfortune rode the tides of the cocoa boom, and a great person who articulated a profound understanding of disease and medicine to trainees in Ghana and the African diaspora, as well as a notable group of anthropologists and historians. Although patient treatment records are extremely rare among indigenous healers, two recently discovered patient record books kept in the 1980s place his healing work in a broader perspective and form the intellectual source of this chapter.

During the 1980s Ghana's economy was in an advanced stage of economic cancer: its leading share of the world market in cocoa dropped to one-eighth, its mineral production fell by 50 percent, its inflation rose over 50 percent, production and living standards plummeted dramatically, and a military government seized power and accepted the notoriously detrimental structural adjustments of the International Monetary Fund and the World Bank. The structural adjustment scheme reinstituted the colonial economic structure by focusing on the export sector and on gold and cocoa, worsening the socioeconomic woes of most Gha-

naians and exacerbating rather than alleviating the widespread droughts and forest fires that destroyed crop production. Against this backdrop of a country ravaged by economic inertia and social anxiety, this chapter frames the work of Nana
Dɔnkɔ and provides salient perspectives on how the business of healing helped a
largely farming population deal with their social and biological ills in a time of
great uncertainty. The story places the reader in the sensory and intellectual world
of the healer; charts Nana Dɔnkɔ's therapeutic itinerary in the latter part of his
healing career, where we have the records to do so; and finally closes with an examination of a series of connected transitions in the life, community, and nation
of Nana Dɔnkɔ.

Context: A Healer's World

The Bono are an Akan people clustered principally in the Takyiman district of
Ghana's Brong Ahafo region, though they are also found in much smaller
numbers dispersed throughout Ghana and the neighboring Ivory Coast (Côte
d'Ivoire). Between late November and March, harmattan winds bringing dust and
chill permeate the early mornings and late nights, while morning mists, green
grasses, and light to heavy rains signal a rejuvenation of the land between March
and April and again from July to late August. A harvest period follows each rainy
season. The Bono of Takyiman reside in lands situated between the northern edge of
dense tropical rainforests and the southern beginnings of arid savannah terrain
punctuated by hills and rivers, the most important of which is the sacred Tano River.
Access to these ecologies allowed the Bono to create enduring systems of therapeutics and spirituality, archaeologically extending into the last two millennia.

The Tano River, which originates in Takyiman and flows north to south into
the Ivory Coast's Aby Lagoon and eventually into the Atlantic Ocean, has remained the most iconic site of therapy and spiritual culture in Akan life. However, the social use of this river and the healing technologies of Bono spiritual
culture historically existed in an interconnected web of human intuition and action, organic compounds, and inorganic or immaterial forces that constituted a
sense of the world. This world is not simply the physical world we call planet Earth
but rather the "real" world consisting of all sorts and forms of matter, energy,
force, and what might be incomprehensible to our "normal" physical senses. In
fact, our understanding of the universe and our human selves boils down to the
intimate and sometimes-volatile interactions between matter, energies, and
forces. Some we pretend to know very well in laboratory conditions; others we
know little about and proffer theories in the place of sure knowledge. In either
case, the accumulated knowledge from the deep empiricism of nature and the
cultural practices bound to it provided the Bono with their own grounded ideas
of the world and the human's place in it.

From the world of cells and life force animating our being to the world of matter and immaterial forces, humans are mobile ecosystems, connected to other kinds of ecologies. There are billions of microorganisms we cannot see that we walk past or around each day; our inability to see them makes them no less real and no less an integral part of our interconnected world. As in much of early human history, the Bono had to first figure out the human body and the constituent parts of its being, while incrementally pushing the bounds of survival in ecologies filled with threats, uncertainty, and potential. Humans have no natural predators except for other human beings. The determination of what foods to eat and in which season, which plants were medicinal or fatal, which animals were competitors, and how to battle disease-carrying insects and microorganisms that invaded the body was therefore decisive in the process of fine-tuning effective therapeutic measures for inescapable human maladies. These measures were shaped by culture, but their recourse was nature. Culture and nature were intimately bound. However, if culture was crafted out of and in response to the natural world, nature placed parameters on human culture. Arguably, when nature was viewed as a partner rather than a nemesis, it provided the conditions for human creativity and cultural nuance. Once the Bono people determined the workings of the human being and the forest-savanna landscape, hunting and farming could then provide surplus that allowed cultural development in the widest sense.

While politicians are more concerned with the dispensation of power than with the public they claim to serve, healers are preoccupied with the public good and its wholeness. A diseased society is merely a collection of traumatized bodies working against rather than with their natural, self-healing capacities—what scientists now call immunotherapy. Healers aptly recognize this disease or trauma because they see human life in the context of community and connectedness, rather than viewing people as individuals to be manipulated for the prize of power. Healers work incessantly against these forces, most often serving their communities and not their self-interest. The fundamental tension of human life is between healers and those who seek power over people. Truth be told, both manipulate, but each works with different kinds of power and toward radically different conclusions. The politician deploys the forces of deception and manipulation in order to accrue temporal power to be used against other humans, with little regard for the ruin of those individuals, while the healer understands what constitutes a human community.

The healer understands the whole human being and therefore marshals the material and immaterial resources located in his or her ecology to restore health, repair relationships, and regenerate the self-healing capacity that doggedly fights for balance within that fundamental tension. Disequilibrium is disease, and those who seek power over people thrive in diseased environments. An equally fundamental human challenge is that most humans are politicians—with or without electoral aspirations—and very few have the inborn or cultivated temperament to be a healer. It is clear why healing will never be a popular vocation, though it is necessarily an integral one. Nonetheless, the healer fights protractedly against the politician in us and in the disease settings in which afflictions thrive, working with forces that form the bookends of the human experience—physical forces and spiritual forces. These forces are no more than variations of the thematic interplay between energy and matter: if we view such forces as water, our physical world would be the solid and our spiritual world the gaseous form that water assumes. Ultimately, human beings—and the world we have inherited and shaped—are composites of these basic root forces, and the healer skillfully calibrates them to cure single individuals but also to make a people whole.

A Life of Indigenous Therapeutics

Ghana's economic and political troubles from the 1970s encroached on the 1980s, and the ubiquitous cancer of corruption—or at least the charge of pervasive corruption—infected each regime. Ghana squandered its dominant position as a global producer of cocoa as production declined precipitously and the country's support for President Hilla Limann quickly faded. The awkward tango between local politics and the forces of the global marketplace meant that each regime paid more attention to the prospects of removal by military coup than to engendering the prosperity of the country. As Jerry Rawlings's recurring calls to terminate corruption generated wide popular support, corruption within the government and the wider society cannibalized the ruling party, opening the doors for yet another Rawlings-led coup in December 1981 against Limann's inept administration. The December 31 "revolution" followed a series of military efforts to take power from Limann, but where those attempts failed, the December 31 attempt reined in the near anarchy and social distress facing the country. Through the "revolution" Rawlings established the Provisional National Defense Council (PNDC), under which the country was managed, with Rawlings as chairperson. Once the PNDC seized power, the constitution was suspended, parliament and the governing councils were dissolved, political parties were banned, and those deemed threats to national security were detained indefinitely without trial—eerily reminiscent of the Kwame Nkrumah regime.

In place of these governing structures, the PNDC installed military committees to pave the way for a promised democracy, while engendering greater public involvement in the fight against the national malady of corruption. Although Rawlings and his PNDC utilized authoritarianism, they were able to halt the country's steep economic slide and stabilize its temperamental politics through a mixture of socialist and liberal policies. The broader benefit to average citizens under PNDC rule is still being debated. Nana Kwasi Appiah, a former student of Nana Dɔnkɔ who trained during the PNDC period, noted, "I remember it was [the] PNDC era where there was a redenomination exercise, so it became very difficult for me, even traveling from my hometown (Saase) to Takyiman for my *akɔm* training for the first time. Kerosene was also in short supply and people had to queue to buy kerosene for their lamps since electricity was only in the urban centers of Ghana, leaving most of the rural areas dependent on kerosene."[1] Rawlings' push to create the conditions for anticorruption and "democracy" was no cure for the ills of the country, and healers who attended to the country's majority rural population had to engineer their own way out of the thick fog of competing forces.

While Rawlings staged his December 31 coup using the prop of corruption and the rhetoric of revolutionary change, a quiet but no less important revolution was occurring between the dominant ideologies of the enjoined fields of health and culture. The revolution of ideas and practice took place among representatives of indigenous culture and spirituality, drawn from the ranks of prominent healers and biomedical workers of African and European origin who accepted the ideology of white or European superiority in all things that mattered. Most of Ghana's and Takyiman's population lived in a world touched by politics only in abstract ways; the biomedical workers at mission hospitals, such as the Holy Family Hospital (HFH) in Takyiman, were situated in the web of individuals and local institutions that mattered in the lives of the indigenes, as well as strangers and visitors. By summer 1981 Nana Dɔnkɔ and other healers involved in the Primary Health Training for Indigenous Healers (PRHETIH) program had renamed the project Abibiduro ne Aborofoduro Nkabom Kuo (African Medicine and Western Medicine Integrated Group), marking a significant shift in their understanding of what was at stake and representing an assertion of their right to be equal partners rather than empty receptacles of biomedical knowledge.[2]

An April 1981 report prepared by Mary Ann Tregoning of the HFH, anthropologist Dennis M. Warren, Peace Corp volunteers, and PRHETIH field coordinators G. Steven Bova (1979–1980) and Mark Kliewer (1980–1981) also suggests healers were not passive receptacles. Rather, healers approached the one-way flow of Western medical knowledge with tact and from their own core self-understandings. The PRHETIH sessions that focused on medicinal herbs "were most enthusiastically received," whereas healers disregarded "those sessions that consisted primarily of advice or description" and about "family planning." The latter session received "such a low rating . . . probably because contraception was antithetical to the beliefs and practices of this highly natalistic society. In fact, one priest-healer, Nana Kofi Donkor [Dɔnkɔ], revealed that his giving advice regarding contraception was an anathema to his shrine."[3] While organizers of the

PRHETIH project envisioned a health revolution wherein healers could be used in national health delivery systems in and outside Ghana, the healers' rebellion against their prescribed role and the pejorative view held by the Ghana Ministry of Health toward healers placed project organizers and their backers in a precarious position.

With an estimated healer-to-Takyiman-township-population ratio of one to three hundred,

> most of the traditional healers interviewed [for the PRHETIH project] practice their skills upon demand. They typically return from a morning of farming to find a friend or neighbor waiting with a patient. The most prominent healer in Techiman Township, Nana Kofi Donkor, is an exception to this, however. He has set aside Friday (the principal Techiman weekly market day), and Tuesday as his special healing days. On a typical Friday, one finds seated lines of 10–20 patients waiting to consult the healer, each patient with a wooden chip with a number painted on it, modeled after a similar practice at the Techiman Holy Family Hospital. Nana Donkor does see patients upon demand on other days of the week if he is not at farm or in the forest collecting herbs.[4]

Nana Dɔnkɔ led the revolution not only in how healers practiced their evolving craft but also in the ways in which healers and biomedical practitioners worked for the health of the community in which both served, albeit with different epistemologies.

When PRHETIH field officer James Donkor helped prepare a report on the PRHETIH project that optimistically claimed, "The project continued steadily this year," this optimism was based on some promising results.[5] The final two groups of healers from Takyiman had completed the PRHETIH coursework, while healers from the localities of Krobo and Tuobodom were interviewed for two additional cohorts.[6] Guided by Nana Dɔnkɔ and his exemplary practice, healers who completed the PRHETIH program also had a decisively immediate impact on health outcomes for the Takyiman community. The HFH served some 83,000 patients in the Takyiman area in 1981, with patients coming from a forty-mile radius. The HFH received an average of 300 to 350 patients a day. The forty-four healers who received primary health training were an integral part of the 26 percent decrease in the outpatient department and in the more than 80 percent drop in that department's diagnoses of malaria, gastroenteritis, respiratory tract infection, and skin diseases in 1981.[7] According to HFH reporting, most of the maladies "could [and did] receive first line treatment in the villages and/or be prevented by decent water supply and sanitation facilities," though malaria remained the most intractable health problem for all.[8]

In 1981 a North American visitor to Nana Dɔnkɔ's compound was struck by its apparent "state of perpetual pandemonium." At sixty-eight or sixty-nine years of age, Nana Dɔnkɔ and his healing practice showed little sign of slowing down. The visitor continued,

> One can arrive any given morning to the sound of wild drumming, and the sight of a half-dozen young priests and priestesses covered in white powder, gyrating wildly across the compound. Occasionally one falls unconscious, eyes rolled back, only to be helped back up to continue dancing. Amidst this clamor, older priests demonstrate how to grind roots, bark, and leaves into medicines, and how to sacrifice and butcher goats, providing food for priests and deities alike. For Kofi Donkor is a teacher, initiating young trainees into the priesthood . . . [and] when we arrived at [Kofi Dɔnkɔ's compound, the] . . . initiates were undergoing intensive possession experience and training.[9]

As this training session for indigenous healers ended, "a more reserved crowd quietly filtered in and took orderly seats on a bench along one wall. They were outpatients, come to Kofi Donkor's weekly clinic to employ his healing knowledge. Each held a small piece of wood with a number brightly painted on it, an idea Donkor picked up at a modern hospital."[10] Nana Dɔnkɔ's ability to adopt an effective technique or procedure without undermining the cultural platform on which his healing practice stood was precisely why he was so effective and why the hospital—and the biomedical practitioner in general—was constrained in understanding and holistically treating patients. Patients were not simply diseased organisms; they had histories, aspirations, deferred dreams, ancestral linkages, and a range of material and psycho-emotional conditions that weighed, in one lived moment or another, heavily on the individual and his or her community. Viewed from this perspective, Nana Dɔnkɔ argued convincingly, "It is always better for a patient to consult a traditional healer. We are more conversant than Western doctors, and it is our rapport with patients that leads to our success."[11]

Healers like Nana Dɔnkɔ delivered some 70 percent of the health care in the Takyiman district. We can assume that the picture in Takyiman, with over forty-five thousand villages that accounted for three-fourths of Ghana's total population, more or less reflected the country as a whole. Doctors at the HFH, such as Dutch husband-and-wife physicians Willem and Magda Boere, had no doubt of the healers' capacity and what role they should play in Takyiman and in the national health care system. As Willem conceded, "The healers have the potential to help us with our overwhelming caseload. . . . I already refer patients with psychiatric diseases to Kofi Donkor's place." In a remarkable statement that should not be taken lightly, Willem continued, "It is difficult to find convincing evidence that *our* medicine [that is, biomedicine] is more effective than theirs. Take snakebite, for example. Seventy percent of the snakebites in this area are nontoxic. So if a patient with snakebite consults a traditional healer, he will always cure seventy percent. But we with our antivenom, on the other hand, can cure seventy-five percent. But that is just not convincing statistically."[12]

Overall, Willem was right. The number of patients that flowed through Nana Ɔnkɔ's compound daily supports Willem's case. One day in summer 1981,

> [a] woman carrying a small child and holding the token marked with a bright number 'one' took a seat opposite [Kofi] Donkor. Serene and grandfatherly, he immediately put the mother and child at ease. His popularity was obvious. Nearly 40 patients had come that day, some from more than 30 kilometers away. . . . After receiving medicine, each patient had his or her condition and treatment recorded in a large record book, and a small payment was elicited. This payment was purely a token gesture, to foster a bond of obligation between patient and healer. . . . It is only after a cure has been effective that proper compensation can be offered.[13]

More statistically convincing are two record books Nana Dɔnkɔ kept during the 1980s, providing an unprecedented, big-data view of a "modern" healing praxis and the communities served.

In a 1980 interview Nana Dɔnkɔ asserted, "My work is like that of a medical doctor and so anybody can come to me."[14] This English translation and the statement itself deserve further attention. Nana Dɔnkɔ was ɔbenfoɔ—one with a high degree of knowledge and skill within a system of spiritual practice and cultural acumen. Counterparts are rare and cross-cultural comparisons are imprecise, but if we had to pin the term ɔbenfoɔ down to something familiar, that something would be a doctorate degree for healers since ɔben is another term for "medicine," properly called *aduro* (pl. *nnuro*). Though the ɔbenfoɔ knows the properties and uses for all types of indigenous medicines, he or she employs aduro rather than *aduto* (*adu*: medicine; *to*: to throw), medicine of neutral value but whose outcome is fashioned by the intent of the user. Those healers or individuals supplied by healers target the aduto with their ill intent and "throw" (that is, leave or deliver through spiritual means) the aduto to cause destruction or malice on another person. The target of successful aduto develops a sickness (ɔyare) and becomes a diseased person (ɔyarefoɔ). In some cases, the perpetrators or recipients of aduto, who may retaliate with their own deployment of aduto, can transform an individual into an invalid (ɔyare-susow) or cause an epidemic (ɔyaredɔm) in a community. The diseased person or community may seek out the hospital (ayaresabea) and a medical doctor (ɔyaresafoɔ), but they soon realize neither hospital nor doctor can heal, though the latter might offer some relief. Patients need *ayare-sa*, the holistic act or art of healing. Therefore, in 70 percent of the encounters between a range of illnesses and infected patients, the patients consulted or sought therapeutic intervention from indigenous healers. In these encounters and in cases where doctors referred patients to him, Kofi Dɔnkɔ was the embodiment of ɔben (medicines of high spiritual potency) and appropriately known as ɔbenfoɔ to all who remained "amazed at his endurance when it came to seeing his patients. Nana [Dɔnkɔ] would sit in the same spot for hours, talking and diagnosing his patient."[15]

The efficacious delivery of *health* with *care* was the hallmark of Nana Dɔnkɔ's healing practice. Sadly, we have few statistics regarding the daily workings of his healing craft, but the record books that he kept during the 1980s put his practice into a broader perspective. To some extent, these record books also allow us to imagine his previous decades of practice. As noted previously, the "condition and treatment [of patients were] recorded in a large record book," but there were two such books and a collection of index cards that together disclose some remarkable and unprecedented insights into at least 70 percent of the Takyiman community and beyond. In fact, Nana Dɔnkɔ's reach was transnational as both a trainer of healers and a healing practitioner. Nonetheless, patient data were kept on loose, unorganized, and fragmented index cards and in two large notebooks with the heading "Kofi Donkor Herbalist Clinic Nyafoma—Techiman B.A." For instance, on February 20, 1987, Nana Dɔnkɔ treated Adwoa Fordjour (Fodwoɔ) and Ayuba Muhamed from Dɛɛma and recorded the information on small, two-by-two-inch index cards with "outpatient card" and "bring this card on each visit" written on each side.

These cards, or at least what remains of them, are too fragmented to derive a reliable picture of the individuals and families Nana Dɔnkɔ treated. However, the two surviving record books are much more fascinating in their details and revealing in the profile generated for individual patients and the broader communities to which they belonged. While the first record book ("book 1") recorded 2,073 patients between 1982 and 1988, the second book ("book 2") contains records of some 5,670 patients who visited Nana Dɔnkɔ between November 1982 and December 1986.[16] Taken together, from this total of 7,743 patients we can determine an average of between 1,291 and 1,936 a year; if we multiply the latter yearly average by the sixty or so years of Nana Dɔnkɔ's healing career, which seems more accurate, he would have diagnosed and treated over 116,000 patients, assuming he worked on nonshrine days as well. Although we are working with incomplete and literally tattered records and will never know what complete records would have revealed, these imprecise numbers more than justify Nana Dɔnkɔ's acclaim and legacy.

For the 2,073 patients recorded in book 1, a strong statistically significant relationship exists between patients and the variables of occupation, age, village, and region of origin. In those cases in which patients listed their occupation, a sample size of 585 reveals that 380, or 65 percent of patients, were farmers, followed by traders (16 percent) and students (3.1 percent). Of the total number of patients recorded, 1,747 or 84.3 percent originated from the Brong Ahafo region, 15.1 percent from the Ashanti (Asante) region, several individuals from northern Ghana and the Volta region, and one person, named Afia Douhs, from Togo. Although the average age among patients was eighteen years, Nana Dɔnkɔ cared principally for children aged one to three and adults aged twenty to thirty. Individuals aged thirty made the most visits to his healing center, but many infants who had not yet turned one year old also received his care. Analyzing the 108 patients who made the most frequent visits, the majority came to Nana Dɔnkɔ's compound for healing services in 1984, followed by 1987, 1986, and 1983. Readers may recall that Ghana had one of the highest birthrates in the world during 1984–1985; this may explain the age of those who paid the healer a visit, as well as the volume of visits. Although most of Nana Dɔnkɔ's patients hailed from the Brong Ahafo region, only 28 percent came from the Takyiman township. The remainder came from outside the township—some 12 percent from Akomadan, 4.8 percent from Aworowa, 4.6 from Nkenkasu, and 4.3 from Tanɔso—but within the Takyiman district and Brong Ahafo region.

If the geographic reach of Nana Dɔnkɔ's practice was noteworthy, his wide appeal among patients who self-identified their religious orientation is remarkable. Of the 682 who disclosed their religious affiliation, 31.2 percent were Roman Catholic, 16.7 percent Muslim, 14.4 Methodist, 9.5 Seventh-Day Adventist, 4.7 percent Presbyterian, 4.5 percent True Church members, and 4.1 percent Pentecostal. Six individuals identified themselves as members of Musama (an "independent African church"), three as members of an African faith church, and two as Halaluya. We can presume the more than 1,200 individuals who did not self-identify a religion affiliation were adherents of the spiritual culture that Nana Dɔnkɔ embodied, precisely because that spirituality was not a separate institutional form and practice outside of the culture in which they lived.

Nana Dɔnkɔ identified and treated some seven hundred illnesses, as evidenced in books 1 and 2. Patients most often complained about illnesses centered in the stomach or abdomen (*yafunu yadee*), fever with jaundice (*asram*), illness affecting the flesh or innards (*honam yadee*), illness associated with childbirth (*awoɔ*), malarial fever (*ahobene*), and illness preventing pregnancy (*anidane*). Forty-eight individuals came "for medicine." The treatment protocol or method for delivering the medicines for most of these illnesses involved a combination of drinking the medicinal preparation and receiving it through enema, bath, or *dudo*. Dudo is a type of medicine consisting of various herbs, bark, and roots kept in a black pot with water; the liquid is used for bathing as a preventive and cure, and the ingredients are specific for each ailment. Using the Ghanaian currency (*cedi*), most payments for treatment consisted of between twenty to forty cedis (40 percent) and one hundred cedis (23 percent), though in-kind payments of chickens (*akokɔ*), eggs (*nkosia*), or alcoholic drink (*nsa*) were included in practice. One-fourth of the patients in book 1 identified as married, with 10.4 percent indicating "under husband" (that is, a woman who is married). The married couple who individually or jointly consulted Nana Dɔnkɔ most frequently were Yaa Donkor and Kwaku Nyamekyɛ. Kwaku was a sixty-year-old farmer and Methodist from the Asante region—the village or township of Akomadan, to be precise—who visited Nana Dɔnkɔ six times "for medicine" and other times for afflictions resulting from "negatively charged" medicines (*aduto yadeɛ*). Apparently, the sickness (*yadeɛ*) derived from ill-intended medicines (aduto) were severe and protracted, causing Kwaku to make frequent visits to Nana Dɔnkɔ's compound in search of protective and nullifying medicines.

In book 2 the number of patients is more than double that recorded in book 1 but for a shorter period. Between November 1982 and December 1986 some 5,670 patients flowed into Nana Dɔnkɔ's compound. Just over one-fourth originated in the township or district of Takyiman; the rest—mirroring the profile given for book 1—came from Akomadan (10.6 percent), Aworowa (6.4 percent), and Afrancho (3.9 percent). Both Akomadan and Afrancho are in the northern parts of the Asante region. The patients from these locales consisted of infants or toddlers (several months to three years old) and adults aged twenty to thirty-five, per the entries for the 3,209 individuals for whom age was listed. The average age was nineteen years old. Consistent with book 1, the most frequently treated illnesses were awoɔ (11.2 percent), anidane (5.9 percent), ahobene (5.7 percent), yafunu and honam yadeɛ (4.7 percent each), and asram (4.2 percent). Although book 1 included treatments administered through baths, enemas, and oral application, book 2 added vapor therapy (*pu* or *pru*), steam baths, and nasal drops to Nana Dɔnkɔ's repertoire.

Also unique to book 2 is the robust data on payment (*aseda*, "giving thanks"). Of the 2,076 patients for which payment data was recorded, one-fourth or 22.2 percent gave thanks with 400 cedis, an alcoholic drink, and a chicken. Some 11 percent did the same but with 200 cedis; 7.1 percent the same but with 600 cedis; and a combined 8.4 percent made the same offerings but with either 100 or 140 cedis. We should bear in mind that aseda was only given after the patient declared that his or her illness—social, physical, psychic, or otherwise—had been effectively treated. Thus, patients were empowered and payments were contingent on pragmatic outcomes. Since women's illnesses topped the list of most frequently treated maladies, it should not be surprising that women paid most often, either for themselves or for their children. The top women in the latter category were Adwoa Manu, Grace Yeboah, Alima Kramo, Abiba Kramo, Adwoa Akoma, and Adwoa Amponsah. In this list, we see the three major types of patients ordered by religious affiliation or spiritual adherence: *kramo* is the Akan term for a Muslim, Grace was a Christian name received through baptism or upon entering school, and *manu* (second-born child) and *akoma* (heart) represent the indigenous spiritual culture. Most intriguingly, patients named Adwoa Manu, Afia Sarpong, Akua Mensah, and Grace Yeboah made the most visits to Nana Dɔnkɔ's healing facility.

In 1988, when book 1 ends, the Ghana Psychic and Traditional Healers Association issued a "Certificate of Competence and Authority" to "Oduyefo—Okomfo Kofi Donkor." The certifying document indicated Nana Dɔnkɔ was "a member of the above association and has been critically examined by the Board of Examiners of the National Executive and has been found qualified and competent in various fields of Herbal Treatment."[17] The certificate was issued on February 29, 1988, with a picture of Nana Dɔnkɔ and with signatures from the national chairperson and secretary. Nana Dɔnkɔ also had a membership card; although it was not filled out, it contained the aims and objectives of the association.[18]

As a member of the Takyiman community and its subset of healers, Nana Dɔnkɔ also played the ubiquitous role of attending funerals as family head (*abusuapanin*) and prominent healer (*ɔbosomfoɔ*). Attending to life as a healer also meant attending to matters of death and temporal transition, all filled with ritual obligations, observances, and participation in the fundamental ebb and flow of Ghanaian society. For example, on June 20, 1984, Nana Dɔnkɔ attended the funeral of *ɔbaapanin* Nana Amma Tabuaa, the fifty-four-year-old "Queenmother of [New] Kenten," who had recently passed.[19] Funerals occurred often, and they were usually held on Saturdays. Regardless of the deceased's social standing, most funerals were announced on small two-by-two-inch or three-by-three-inch cards that indicated the chief mourners, kin, and invited personalities. Nana Dɔnkɔ was frequently invited; in one way or another, many of the mourned were his patients or relatives of his patients. Like the index cards that recorded patient information, the backs of these funerary announcements were used to record important information. For example, on January 5, 1988, a note on the back of the funeral announcement for Kwadwo Krah read, "We functioned from morning to evening and had an amount of five hundred and thirty cedis (530.00). With the above amount old man [an affectionate term for Nana Dɔnkɔ] authorized me to give 300 [cedis] to his wife as feed allowance and also one hundred cedis to buy pito [a beverage with low alcoholic content brewed from fermented millet]. It has now left with 180 cedi."[20]

Nana Dɔnkɔ also accounted for life's priorities on the back of those funerary announcements. On one he noted that he and his family worked "from morning to evening," earned 530 cedis that day; gave much of his daily earnings to his wife, Afia Monofie; bought pito to share with family; and saved the rest. Though profound in his understanding of disease and medicine, Nana Dɔnkɔ was deeply pragmatic and engaged in community affairs and in much of the mundane activities of other Ghanaians. On September 2, 1990, Nana Dɔnkɔ and his elder sister *ɔkɔmfoɔ* (spiritualist-healer) Adwoa Akumsa and family participated in a send-off party for J. K. Tuffour at the community center in Takyiman. Tuffour had recently retired from the police force after twenty-eight years of service.[21] One striking example of Nana Dɔnkɔ's participation in such activities concerned the national weekly lotto that was established in 1958 as the Department of National Lotteries, one year after Ghana's political independence. In 2006 the Department of National Lotteries morphed into the National Lotto Authority after having its processes automated in 1979 with mechanized lotto coupons. Nana Dɔnkɔ probably played the national weekly lotto beginning in the 1960s, though only two lottery tickets, dated September 17, 1988, were found among his papers. Lotto players simply chose five numbers from one to ninety, and winners would cash in their prize coupons at regional offices. Nana Dɔnkɔ would have done so at the regional office in Sunyani. As one can imagine, the lotto was extremely popular during the political and economic turbulence of the 1960s, 1970s, and 1980s. This steady popularity continued into the early 1990s as economic decline in Ghana, before the Gulf oil crisis, raised petroleum prices by 2 percent, affecting transport and foodstuff prices. For a largely farming population, Ghana's common folks bore the brunt of this, and their burden grew with inflation pegged at 37 percent and a gross domestic product at 2.7 percent. Farmers and families like that of Nana Dɔnkɔ stubbornly pushed their lives through the jagged contours of Ghana's unstable political economy.

By 1990 claims of subversive activity and executions by firing squads were recurring themes, along with criticism of PNDC policies, while the second phase of the Economic Recovery Program and extradition treaties between Ghana and its eastern neighbors were implemented under Rawlings's vision for Ghana. Rawlings's National Commission for Democracy expanded Ghana's administrative districts from 65 to 110 and officially recognized the newly created Upper West Region. The commission also presided over national efforts to register voters for district assembly elections across the country, instituted a new minimum wage (set at 218 cedis in 1990), and sought to provide a road map for Ghana's political future. A 1990 clergy meeting asked for a debate on this future, and an opposition group based in London called the Democratic Alliance of Ghana echoed the clergy in protest and demanded multiparty constitutional rule. The Movement for Freedom and Justice in Accra joined the chorus. Rawlings's ruling administration did not ignore these calls for transition, but he wanted to be the architect of that transition. In this moment of flux, more than half of the cocoa and coffee plantations were sold to private individuals and businesses in Ghana and abroad, signaling yet another reordering of economy policies along lines praised by the International Monetary Fund and World Bank. In Takyiman the district had also been restructured, reducing the landmass by 25 percent and shrinking its population.[22] With only 39 percent of the majority rural populace of Ghana having access to safe water and 43 percent to health services, the HFH had little choice but to revive the PRHETIH program through the appointment of Samuel Oduro-Sarpong as program coordinator in October 1990. Sarpong prepared for the 300 identified healers and the 124 ready for training.[23]

In 1991 the seventy-nine- or eighty-year-old Nana Dɔnkɔ was visited by Margaret Yeakel-Twum, a student associated with anthropologist Michael Warren. Yeakel-Twum's observations at Nana Dɔnkɔ's compound provide an important snapshot of his healing practice and the patients he treated. Yeakel-Twum described Nana Dɔnkɔ's "shrine room" as a "dark room with two small windows, each with a light grate covering the opening." Inside "there were nine [*abosom* (spiritual forces) represented by brass pans] that were housed in this shrine room."²⁴ The compound area had been transformed into a clinic. Yeakel-Twum wrote,

I would arrive at the clinic and find patients waiting to be seen. Some patients stayed at the clinic for extended treatments or if their homes were a long distance away. Many of the patients who sought out Kofi Donkor did so on references from friends or relatives, often traveling from far away areas. Those who waited did so very patiently and quietly, never seeming to be in a hurry to leave. There were days when those who were waiting were not doing so for treatment but to bring payment of some sort for previous services rendered. At this clinic, no one was turned away if they could not pay and payment was not expected until the treatment was effective. Women would proudly bring in babies to show Kofi Donkor, proving that his treatments for their infertility had worked again. . . . Infertility was one of the major complaints of women who came to the clinic, which was presented as always a women's problem.²⁵

Yeakel-Twum observed Nana Dɔnkɔ treating boils (*mpɔmpɔ*), malnutrition (*asenam*), snakebites (*ɔwɔka*), and many other conditions, but she regarded his clinic as surprisingly unique because the HFH referred their patients to him. "There were other herbalists in the area who had clinics in their compounds," she continued, "but Kofi Donkor's seemed [to] be the oldest and most established clinic in this area."²⁶ Nana Dɔnkɔ's healing facility was well stocked with herbs, a wide range of dried bark, roots, and leaves, gathered locally as well as from distant areas, that were arranged in a cabinet. A fresh pile of medicines lay in the middle of compound, and Yeakel-Twum "was always amazed [when] Nana Kofi Donkor would stand up from his chair, put his crutch under his arm, hobble over to this pile and proceed to point out to his son or another family member the pieces of plant material he needed to work with. Nana [Dɔnkɔ] had slipped and broken his hip about a year ago and was dependent on the crutch for mobility. . . . It truly was fascinating to watch this process, as I knew very well that Nana knew exactly what plant the root, stem or bark originated from."²⁷ In addition, while "Nana [Dɔnkɔ] used his extensive knowledge of herbs in his diagnosis, he also used a stethoscope that had been given to him as a gift from a visiting African-American. He would listen, in particular, to the breathing of the youngest patients who were brought in for treatment."²⁸

Through his "herbal clinic," Nana Dɔnkɔ also taught and certified healers trained under his leadership. On December 22, 1991, he had a letter written on behalf of his kin and recent healing graduate Nana Akua Asantewaa Asubɔnten, authenticating her status as Asubɔnten ɔkɔmfoɔ. Nana Dɔnkɔ dictated, "This is to certify that Nana Akua Asante[waa] Asubonteng Bono Priestess has been an apprenticeship at the above clinic for a period of four years. During her period of stay, she studied the following: Bono traditional culture, Bono medicine and traditional religion. . . . I recommend her for traditional healing license and certificate." The letter was signed with Nana Dɔnkɔ's thumbprint or index finger print inside the stamped seal of the "Nana Kofi Donkor Herbal Clinic."[29] Nana Dɔnkɔ also trained Kwasi Appiah and Akwasi Owusu around the same time. Both hailed from the Asante region. Appiah's family migrated from Koforidua to farm cocoa in Asante. He trained for the ɔbosom (Akumsa) his great-grandparents collected to build their town, whereas Owusu trained for an ɔbosom his uncle had found in the forest and brought to their village of Boɔho, eight miles north of Kumase, in the 1970s. While Appiah returned to his hometown after graduation, Owusu remained in Takyiman, bought a plot of land and built a house, initiated his own healing practice, and in the process named his first son after Nana Dɔnkɔ—Kwame Sakyi.[30]

Alongside Nana Dɔnkɔ's training and certification of healers, the reconstituted PRHETIH under new field coordinator Oduro-Sarpong represented a different certification process centered on the imperatives of biomedicine and the Christian orthodoxy gripping the nation.[31] The reincarnation of the PRHETIH program came with some new faces in its personnel and some changes from within. Oduro-Sarpong was the first Ghanaian and non–Peace Corp field coordinator; joining him was HFH matron Elizabeth Dwamena, who was a manager of PRHETIH program. After studying the Dormaa Healers' Project and attending courses in Kumase and at the Centre for Scientific Research into Plant Medicine in Akwapem, Oduro-Sarpong recruited 180 of 300 herbalists for the PRHETIH program. He also mapped out year-end goals: register all herbalists in the Takyiman district, train and graduate healers in the program, construct an arboretum, and establish a "databank on all healers in the district" that would allow for follow-up visits and supervisions. Through Oduro-Sarpong, changes to the PRHETIH emblem on its certificates were made, from the "old one [that] portrays a doctor and a fetish priest" to one that would "portray a leaf crossed with a hypodermic Syringe." As Oduro-Sarpong reasoned, the "former emblem does not represent all the categories of the healers who are made up of Christians, Muslims, Fetish Priest(esses) and 'Ordinary' herbalists. The new symbol will signify the cooperation between all users of herbs (leaf) and all Western Medical practitioners (syringe)." The new changes to the revitalized PRHETIH program were publicized through press releases to the *People's Daily Graphic*, the state-owned daily newspaper.[32] The Ghanaian state, under Rawlings's PNDC, also reveled in this mood of change.

Transitions

In 1994 the HFH was named a district hospital for Takyiman, qualifying it for more government funding and enabling it to offer greater care to the poor. However, the hospital had to celebrate its fortieth anniversary amid the rebuilding of its maternity unit, which had been destroyed by a tornado the previous year. Unlike the HFH, the government's care for the poor through its community health insurance plan was duly criticized for its inability to improve health care among the impoverished, but more so for its inability to adequately address the politics and "ethnic" clashes that had erupted in northern Ghana. The subplots to these clashes were, on one hand, the cumulative effect of military and civilian rule, inflation, currency devaluation, failed structural adjustment schemes, and indebtedness, and, on the other hand, the country's inequalities and antagonisms running beneath a veneer of democratic progress following the 1992 presidential elections. The 1994 "ethnic" rivalries over land and political authority exploded in the bloodiest conflict of its kind in the history of the nation, amid Ghana's almost-unquestioned acceptance of things foreign and an attendant view of the United States as "God's country." In February 1994, some five hundred people were killed in the conflict that gripped the Northern Region of Ghana, with thousands of refugees fleeing to Togo.

The new Rawlings regime imposed an extended state of emergency and dispatched national armed forces to the area. After several people were killed in the regional capital of Tamale, negotiations began but were marred by claims of plots to overthrow the government and by opposition parties withdrawing from the reconciliation process. By August a peace agreement had been reached and a cease-fire went into effect, allowing a negotiating team to focus on its task of facilitating stability. Ironically, the new president and constitution returned to old tactics of arresting individuals who allegedly conspired to overthrow the government, charging them with crimes against the state. Further arrests and killings in the region did not resolve the tensions but rather increased suspicion and conflict among the participants involved and toward the new government. Nana Dɔnkɔ had often traveled to northern Ghana, learned from its healers, and had many patients who traveled from that region to Takyiman to seek out his therapeutic offerings. His approach to the people of Ghana was simple: treat all, regardless of their political or religious standing and affiliation, with an affirmation of their humanity and with care. The Rawlings regime, and consequently the people of Ghana, would have benefited greatly from such a human approach.

The conflicts that erupted in northern Ghana were not contained there and had consequences for the rest of country. With newly paved roads between Tamale and Takyiman, and between Takyiman and its regional capital of Sunyani, "people [were] mobile," as HFH officials observed.[33] However, the extended state of emergency placed travel restrictions on all moving to and from northern Ghana. Takyiman was the crossroads between northern and southern Ghana, and so the restrictions emanating from the conflicts also affected those who needed hospitalization or the indigenous therapeutics offered by Nana Dɔnkɔ and company, the flow of goods and services, and the hundreds of thousands of food producers and the commerce they transacted at the Takyiman market. The Takyiman market was the largest three-day market, and the township was the fastest-growing commercial center in the country. Approximately 90 percent of its residents were farmers who planted cassava, yams, maize, and beans and engaged in small-scale trading; 2 percent were full-time merchants; and just over 5 percent were civil servants. The conflicts affected the arrival and departure of people, produce, and manufactured goods through the commercial hub that was Takyiman, as well as the number of inpatients and outpatients at the HFH, both of which decreased during the protracted conflicts.[34] For Takyiman inhabitants, the six doctors at the HFH translated into one doctor per 20,133 individuals, while the nine mission hospitals (seven Catholic, two Protestant) in the Brong Ahafo region served about 69 percent of the regional population.[35]

HFH records clarify the features all mission hospitals shared but also which programs differentiated the HFH in its response to the exigencies of the times. The HFH developed a credit union called Abosomankotere (chameleon) in May 1971 with 165 members; 1994 reports suggest the credit union continued "to thrive with 201 members."[36] The HFH responded to the 130 HIV/AIDS cases brought to the hospital with an educational campaign targeting every single village in the district, including schools.[37] To help in the fight against malnutrition and anemia, the 169 active HFH-trained traditional birth attendants were deployed alongside the 201 PRHETIH healers located in ten communities, though further training was put on hold since officials were more concerned with the "supervision of trained traditional healers."[38] While leaders of diverse cultural groups grappled with the burial of indigent and abandoned group members, the HFH was challenged by a new life-and-death matter: abortions.[39] Of the sixty-eight cases of induced abortions, about half were done through the insertion of herbs deep into the vagina, and 22 percent were married women who explained that they did so because their last baby was born too young, while 47 percent were unmarried women who had no trade or only incomplete schooling.[40] The unborn, the living, and the deceased remained entangled because they embodied the community in both its transformations and its transitions.

For Nana Dɔnkɔ and family, life and temporal death were not statistical matters but rather the filaments of the human experience. On April 17, May 7, and June 12, 1995, Nana Dɔnkɔ was admitted to the HFH. While there, Christian fanatics tried their best to convert him, but their theological arguments failed. Nana Dɔnkɔ, we are told, could not accept that he had "sinned" and that Jesus would cure his illness if he confessed these "sins." Gravely ill, he proclaimed that he had committed no acts of negativity (*bɔne*) toward anyone. During the three months in and out of the hospital, Catholic priests also sought to convert Nana Dɔnkɔ through baptism. According to Nana Dɔnkɔ's family, the healer "understood the pastor's language, but [Nana Dɔnkɔ] gave [the clergyman] a good [proverbial] response and did not change his beliefs."[41] On August 8, 1995, Nana Dɔnkɔ made his transition to *asamando* (where the ancestors dwell) around age eighty-four at his compound in kɔmfoɔkrom (healer's village). In observance of this moment, family and community appropriately exclaimed, "ɔkɔ akuraa" (he or she has gone to the village), "ɔkɔ baabi" (he or she has gone someplace), and "*dupɔn kɛseɛ atutu*" (a great tree has been uprooted).

Relatives nearby described his transition in the following way. Nana Dɔnkɔ expected to pass seven days before he did. As a child's belonging in the Akan world requires waiting seven days before he or she is named—and therefore registered as a member of the human community—so too healers reserve this same right on their way to an ancestral community. On the seventh day, his wife, Afia Monofie, prepared pounded yams made into dough (*fufu*) and a light soup (*nkwan*) for him. While eating, Nana Dɔnkɔ fell to the ground, shaking, in front of the eating table. He then went into his bedroom, followed by some family members, who witnessed the healer fall again, but this time into a deep trance state. He requested those with him to remove the iron bracelet (*kaa*) on his hand and iron ring (*kawa*) on his finger. Water and schnapps were brought into the room almost immediately. Water was poured on the mouth of Nana Dɔnkɔ before the animating life force that fought so hard to stay on earth around 1912/1913 left his physical body. Nana Dɔnkɔ's passing occurred when preparations were being made for the annual yam or harvest festival; for this reason, funerary plans were put on hold and his body was sent to the HFH mortuary for preservation—*Nana kɔ aduro mu* (Nana went into medicine). Nana Dɔnkɔ's body remained on view for seven days before the burial, and thousands of individuals from near and far paid the first of several periodic respects to a person who embodied the best of them and what they could become.

KWASI KONADU is Professor of History at the City University of New York. He is author of *Indigenous Medicine and Knowledge in African Society*, *A View from the East: Education and Black Cultural Nationalism in New York City*, *The Akan Diaspora in the Americas*, *Transatlantic Africa, 1440s–1888*, and *The Ghana Reader: History, Culture, Politics*.

Notes

1. Nana Kwasi Appiah, in discussion with the author, Saase, Ashanti, Ghana, September 27, 2012.

2. Dennis M. Warren, G. Steven Bova Sr., Mary Ann Tregoning, and Mark Kliewer, "Ghanaian National Policy towards Indigenous Healers: The Case of the Primary Health Training for Indigenous Healers (PRHETIH) Program" (paper presented at the annual meeting of the Society for Applied Anthropology, Edinburgh, April 12–17, 1981), 12.

3. Ibid., 14.

4. Ibid., 21, 24 (quotation).

5. Ibid., 4.

6. Holy Family Hospital, *Annual Report* (Techiman, Ghana (unpublished report) 1981).

7. Ibid., 2.

8. Ibid., 1.

9. *Travel Account to Accompany the Study Guide for the Film "Bono Medicines"* (Lone Rock, IA: J. Scott Dodds Productions, 1982), 5. The sacrificial use of goat is inaccurate. Asubɔnten taboos goat, and so the visitor either misidentified the animal used or simply invented the use of goat.

10. Ibid., 5–6.

11. Ibid., 6.

12. Ibid., 13–14 (italics mine).

13. Ibid., 7.

14. Nana Kofi Donkor, in discussion with Raymond Silverman, Techiman, Ghana, April 20, 1980, p. 211.

15. Nana Kwaku Sakyi, in discussion with the author, Miami, June 14, 2012.

16. "Kofi Donkor Herbalist Clinic Nyafoma—Techiman B.A.," unpublished record books kept at Kofi Donkɔ's family compound. I have transcribed both books and created a Microsoft Excel file for each. The statistical analysis that appears in this section derives from these files. These data sets are in this author's possession.

17. Ghana Psychic and Traditional Healers Association's Certificate of Competence and Authority (registered no. 3377) to "Oduyefo—Okomfo Kofi Donkor," 1988. Copy in author's possession.

18. Copy of certificate and card in author's possession.

19. Funeral announcement for Akosua Antwiwaa, December 15, 1984. Copy in author's possession. Note that the date of the announcement card and the date of the event Kofi Dɔnkɔ or a scribe wrote on that card were not the same. I have used the latter.

20. Funeral announcement for Kwadwo Krah, November 15, 1980. Copy in author's possession. Note that the date of the announcement card and the date of the event Kofi Dɔnkɔ or a scribe wrote on that card were not the same. I have used the latter.

21. Invitation and program for Mr. J. K. Tuffour, September 2, 1990. Copy in author's possession.

22. Holy Family Hospital, *Annual Report* (Techiman, Ghana, 1990), 13.

23. Ibid., 8.

24. Margaret Yeakel-Twum, "Medicinal Plants and Traditional Healers in Ghana, West Africa" (unpublished paper, University of Minnesota, 1991), 9.

25. Ibid., 12.

26. Ibid., 13.

27. Ibid.

28. Ibid., 14.

29. Nana Kofi Donkor to unnamed individual, Techiman, Ghana, December 22, 1991.

30. Nana Kwasi Appiah, in discussion with the author, Takyiman, Ghana, December 25, 2001; Nana Akwasi Owusu, in discussion with the author, Takyiman, Ghana, December 25, 2001.

31. Samuel Oduro-Sarpong, "Primary Health Training for Indigenous Healers (PRHETIH) Project: Holy Family Hospital" (unpublished document, April 1991), 1.

32. Ibid., 2.

33. Holy Family Hospital, *Annual Report* (Techiman, Ghana, 1994), 13.

34. Ibid., 3.

35. Ibid., 3, 20.
36. Holy Family Hospital, *Annual Report* (1990), 5; Holy Family Hospital, *Annual Report*
1994), 5.
37. Ibid., 12, 18.
38. Ibid., 6, 12, 15–16 (quotation).
39. Ibid., 19.
40. Ibid., 9.
41. Kofi Sakyi and family, in discussion with the author, Techiman, Ghana, July 2009,
anuary 2011.

Bibliography

Holy Family Hospital. 1981. *Annual Report*. Techiman, Ghana (unpublished).
———. 1990. *Annual Report*. Techiman, Ghana: Unpublished Report.
———. 1994. *Annual Report*. Techiman, Ghana: Unpublished Report.
. Scott Dodds Productions. 1982. *Travel Account to Accompany the Study Guide for the Film "Bono Medicines."* Lone Rock, IA: J. Scott Dodds Productions.
Oduro-Sarpong, S. 1991. "Primary Health Training for Indigenous Healers (PRHETIH) Project: Holy Family Hospital." Unpublished document, April.
Warren, D. M., G. S. Bova Sr., M. A. Tregoning, and M. Kliewer. 1981. "Ghanaian National Policy towards Indigenous Healers: The Case of the Primary Health Training for Indigenous Healers (PRHETIH) Program." Paper presented at the annual meeting of the Society for Applied Anthropology, Edinburgh, April 12–17.
Yeakel-Twum, M. 1991. "Medicinal Plants and Traditional Healers in Ghana, West Africa." Unpublished paper, University of Minnesota.

11 Entrepreneurs or Wage Laborers?

The Elusive Homo Economicus

Ralph Callebert

In 2009 I first presented some early research findings at the history and African studies seminar of the University of KwaZulu-Natal in Durban, South Africa. I had embarked on a project researching the lives and livelihoods of Zulu migrant dockworkers in that city up to 1959. I argued that although these workers were certainly wage laborers and frequently engaged in collective working-class action, entrepreneurial and individual strategies of advancement were equally important to their lives and economic decision making. Jeff Guy (1940–2014), the late and eminent historian of the Zulu Kingdom and colonial Natal, shared an incisive insight on this occasion. I no longer recall his exact words, but I can paraphrase his comments as follows: In the 1970s and 1980s, scholars of Africa found radical proletarian wage laborers everywhere they looked; in the 1980s and 1990s, we stumbled upon strong, enterprising women and diverse forms of resistance and agency—or what James C. Scott discussed as the weapons of the weak.[1] Finally, in the early twenty-first century, scholars are more likely to celebrate an indomitable entrepreneurial spirit among Africa's poor and informal workers, who have a seeming capacity to constantly find new ways to "create something from nothing."[2]

It would seem that historians and other scholars of Southern Africa have often been on a quest to find their ideal subjects, regardless of whether these subjects were proletarian radicals or neoliberally celebrated entrepreneurs. There is, of course, a good deal of truth to each of these accounts. Many African workers did form part of a working class, something that older, conservative accounts of African labor generally did not acknowledge, and many of the African poor do eke out a living through informal entrepreneurial activities. However, both accounts fail to grasp the social realities of African workers and entrepreneurs because neither considers African economic history on its own terms. Both assume the applicability of Western-derived concepts. These accounts presuppose, on the one hand, a notion of wage labor based on European and North American experiences of work from the last two to three centuries or, on the other hand, a universal economic market rationality and entrepreneurial spirit embodied by the *homo economicus*. The latter concept is, with a notable masculine bias, also sometimes rendered as the "economic *man*." As I argue with particular reference to the history of dockworkers in Durban in the 1950s, many African workers and entrepreneurs, today as in the past, fit into neither of these Eurocentric conceptualizations.

Finding Proletarians, Finding Entrepreneurs

As African workers in South Africa's system of oscillating labor migration, Durban's dockworkers were not afforded the rights of industrial citizenship—that is, the right to unionize or strike, or to participate in collective bargaining.[3] Nevertheless, this lack of industrial citizenship did not result in a passive acceptance of the racial and government-imposed industrial order. In fact, their militancy has been central to a substantial literature on dock labor in Durban. David Hemson has written the seminal study on these workers and stresses that they had a long history of often-uncompromising working-class action. Others writing on work in the Durban harbor have also focused mainly on unionization and industrial action.[4] In their proletarian radicalism, therefore, Durban's dockers were not all that different from dock laborers all around the world.[5]

However, historians have emphasized not only the working-class nature of dockworkers. Much of the literature on African workers from the 1970s and 1980s also discusses their working-class consciousness and organization. This is especially the case for South(ern) Africa, which has often been seen as more "modern" and industrialized than the rest of the continent.[6] For many authors, their interest in class struggle reflected their political commitments. Hemson, for example, was active in the Durban Student Wages Commission that protested low African wages, and he became a union organizer. Moreover, validating African workers as a modern proletariat was particularly political in the context of white minority regimes. Here the modernist teleology of the development of an African working class and the emergence of the modern African industrial *man*, another concept with a strong masculine bias, countered conservative narratives that rendered Africans essentially different, essentially rural, and incapable of forming a modern working class.[7] The latter account justified segregation and the denial of political and industrial rights to a population that purportedly could never achieve the necessary intellectual and cultural attributes required to participate in the political and electoral process or in the institutions that govern industrial relations. The liberal anthropologists of the Rhodes-Livingstone Institute thus argued that African migrant workers could become—and were becoming—a true modern and urban working class; that they too could be part of Western progress.[8]

Eager to affirm Africans as modern workers or to find a radical proletariat, progressive scholars frequently overlooked other identities and more complicated aspects of African workers' livelihoods. Racial, ethnic, and gender identities did not always receive the attention they deserved, and the petty entrepreneurial activities many workers engaged in were scarcely discussed. However, the last decades of the twentieth century brought a focus on gender, on the resilience of rural and ethnic identities, and on more-individual and smaller-scale forms of agency and resistance than those afforded by class-based organization.[9]

If the 1970s and 1980s were characterized by a quest for African proletarians, the early twenty-first century begot a comparable infatuation with entrepreneurs. The neoliberal love affair with entrepreneurship has even taken on ontological dimensions—in other words, entrepreneurship has come to be seen as a characteristic that is central to what it means to be human.[10] In the Global South it is especially the informal entrepreneur who embodies the late-capitalist ideal of entrepreneurial creativity.[11] For popular authors such as Hernando de Soto and Dambisa Moyo, overextended governments and "dead aid" crush the inherent entrepreneurial spirit of the poor in Latin America, Africa, and elsewhere. To unleash this productive and commercial energy and to empower the poor to help themselves (that is, pull themselves up by their bootstraps), we therefore simply have to remove these obstacles.[12] In this discourse, which generally pays little attention to the structural and macroeconomic causes of poverty, the poor are easily romanticized as valiantly working to fulfill their inherent and individual creative potential. They do so in the face of destitution, oppressive overregulation, corrupt governments, and cultural obligations to kin, traditional authorities, and dependents; these are collective demands that impede individual accumulation.

This seemingly universal appeal of entrepreneurs is not limited to former Goldman Sachs and World Bank economists, as a quick glance at the copious literature on informal entrepreneurialism in Africa would illustrate. Although certainly not all of this literature uncritically celebrates the informal economy as the poor displaying their agency and helping themselves, its size does reflect a general preoccupation with African informal entrepreneurs.[13]

Wage Laborers or Entrepreneurs?

In many ways Zulu migrant dockworkers in mid-twentieth-century Durban did form the radical and militant working class that Hemson and others have described. During the 1940s Zulu Phungula emerged as a militant and uncompromising leader whom some dockworkers still remembered when interviewed in 2009.[14] Despite lacking the legal ability to unionize or strike, Phungula and a small committee of organizers led dockworkers in several strikes during World War II. Even after the authorities exiled him from Durban in 1949, workers' defiance endured through leaderless resistance.[15] Industrial actions continued to cause disruptions in port operations until 1959, when authorities and employers increased their control over the labor force through the institution of monopoly hiring, the abolishment of casual labor, and enforced residence in compounds. The 1960s thus became a decade of comparatively successful repression of workers' militancy, not only on the docks but also throughout the city. However, dockworkers revived resistance in Durban with a strike in 1969. This strike was a precursor to the 1972–1973 Durban Strikes, in which dockworkers were equally involved, and which rekindled resistance against apartheid even before the 1976 Soweto Uprising.[16]

Despite all this convincing evidence of dockworkers' frequent engagement in collective working-class actions, the dockers interviewed for this research hardly formed a typical proletarian working class. A focus on their harbor employment and their engagement in strikes tells only part of their story and reduces their experiences to their waged employment. Many of these workers and other members of their households—as well as people outside their households, as we will see—engaged in small-scale entrepreneurial activities. They did so despite persistent attempts by the apartheid state to root out informal or unlicensed African businesses, and more generally to limit independent income-generating opportunities for Africans since these offered alternatives to underpaid wage labor and enabled African family life in the city. The existence of such opportunities thus posed a challenge both to institutionalized labor migration and to urban segregation.[17] This account of households relying on entrepreneurial activities in the face of official attempts to quell African enterprise seemingly validates neoliberal avowals that overextended and intrusive governments stifle people's innate entrepreneurial spirit. Nevertheless, I argue that just as we cannot simply subsume these workers under the concept of wage laborers derived from Western experience, these worker-entrepreneurs also did not possess a universal entrepreneurial essence that was waiting to be liberated.

While these workers clearly engaged in wage labor and were not afraid to defend their interests as a working class, few dockworkers' households had dock wages as their only source of income—in some cases it was not even the household's main source of income. Even though wages on the docks were generally better than what the majority of African workers earned, the Zulu-speaking migrant dockworkers combined their waged employment with continued investment in the rural homestead economy and with mostly small-scale, informal trade. All interviewees maintained access to land in the rural reserves or on white farms. Growing rural populations, which were partially the result of apartheid-era influx controls, meant that the land available to Africans was increasingly insufficient to meet their consumption needs.[18] Nevertheless, access to land continued to play an important role in sustaining consumption levels for most dockworkers' households. Many households thus continued to invest some of their income in agricultural production. The produce from the land and the milk from the livestock, and occasionally their meat, reduced the need to use scarce cash for everyday consumption.

Furthermore, several wives and mothers earned extra cash by selling some of their produce. These women were not the only ones to engage in petty trade. More than half of the interviewed dockworkers were involved in some form of small-scale trade: they sold *dagga* (marijuana) in the city or cigarettes and sweets at their workplaces; they also pilfered loose food from the holds of ships and from the wharves. This food, which frequently spilled from broken bags and crates, was collected by the workers to sell at home in the rural areas or in the urban townships. As in many ports around the world, both workers and employers generally considered this practice acceptable. In Durban it was also crucial to dockworkers' small businesses. The harbor's predominantly casual labor regime also afforded workers some flexibility to spend time on their side businesses and thus facilitated their entrepreneurialism.[19] Their wives and mothers were involved in these strategies since they were the ones selling the pilfered goods in the rural areas. Some dockworkers also entered into commercial partnerships with urban women, with whom they may or may not have had romantic or sexual relationships. These women sold pilfered goods in the townships or informal settlements.

All interviewed workers wanted to, and did, retire in the rural areas. While their intent to return to their rural homes was significantly influenced by cultural and social expectations, it was also the result of the many restrictions Africans faced in the cities under early apartheid. Moreover, the continued practice of customary tenure in the reserves gave migrants a tangible stake in rural society. Livelihood strategies that involved commercial activities allowed the more successful dockworkers to retire to their rural homes much earlier than most African workers could at that time. They could leave behind the racially segregated city and the arduous labor that they did not enjoy. Moreover, those dockworkers who engaged in small-scale trade generally managed to retire to their rural homes earlier than those who did not: some left urban wage labor after as little as four to six years. These patterns thus seem to confirm the image of informal entrepreneurs pulling themselves up by their bootstraps. However, few dockworkers had any intent to become part of an entrepreneurial class; rather, they used these strategies to escape dependence on urban wage labor and to hasten their return to their rural homes. Most did not sustain their investments in their informal businesses after they achieved that goal since they usually preferred to invest in cattle and dependents. Colonial reformers frequently considered such supposedly unproductive investments irrational, yet there was a clear logic to them. This logic, however, was not a universal market logic, and their informal trade was not just another example of what Adam Smith describes as humans' innate "propensity to truck, barter, and exchange."[20]

Market Society as a "Stark Utopia"

Cattle were in many ways a productive investment. They were a source of milk, meat, and draft power. Moreover, money could be made from breeding and selling livestock. Several dockworkers built up their herds as a form of self-reproducing capital that carried them through their rural retirement, selling the cattle one head at a time when they needed money. Nevertheless, cattle were more than commodities to be bought and sold, or a source of meat and other animal products. They played an indispensable social role in African communities across Southern Africa. Young men needed access to cattle to be able to marry and become homestead heads; cattle provided a symbolic presence at their rural homes for absent migrant workers and thus a public claim to continued belonging in the rural society; and the practice of *ukusisa*, the loaning out of cattle to poor rural dwellers who had no cattle of their own, fostered clientelistic relations. The well-known aphorism "Money has no calves" reminds us not only that cattle is a self-reproducing form of capital but also that money cannot be seen by others. Cash establishes no visual and public presence for migrants and cannot mark the symbolic transition into manhood that is achieved through the transfer of cattle as bridewealth. Money cannot fulfill the same social function as cattle.[21]

The value of cattle and other livestock therefore cannot be reduced to its monetary exchange value or to the milk they produce. Cattle are not simply subject to a formalist and reductionist market valuation; they cannot be reduced to numbers. Consequently, decisions about cattle can seem irrational within a formal market logic, such as when people did not sell their cattle when prices were high or when their herds exceeded the grazing capacity of the reserve lands. Colonial officials and reformers, and later development practitioners, have frequently pathologized such decisions as symptoms of a "cattle complex," that is, an obsession with cattle as a source of status rather than as an economic resource.[22] Land was equally irreducible to monetary valuation.[23] Of course, reserve land could not be bought or sold, and Africans could not buy land outside the reserves. Nevertheless, land too had a social and cultural significance beyond its value as a productive asset. Land provided continued access to rural society and allowed migrant workers to build their *umuzi* or homestead. Building an umuzi and leaving the paternal homestead established a man as a homestead head and was an important marker of manhood and adulthood.

Rather than being irrational, however, decisions that value land and cattle beyond their market price or productive potential follow a different economic logic, one that cannot be reduced to a purportedly universal market logic. Inspired by Karl Polanyi, I argue that there is no "rational" universal market logic that can be dissociated from culture; the economic sphere is always embedded in social relations.[24] Even if the Western market economy that matured in the nineteenth century seems to approach a disembedded economy entirely divorced from social, cultural, or political considerations, the self-adjusting market that necessarily would be at the heart of such a market society "implied a stark utopia" that "could not exist for any length of time without annihilating the human and natural substance of society."[25] Polanyi thus argues against a tendency to assume a universal economic rationality in which values are purely derived from a market logic and devoid of social or cultural value;[26] he named this tendency "formalism." Against this formalist tradition, he posits a substantivist approach to economic anthropology that considers economic behavior to be "interwoven with the general fabric of social, political, and religious life."[27] Hence the pursuit of financial gain becomes just one of several considerations.[28]

The more-than-monetary value of cattle is perhaps most pronounced in the practice of *ukulobola*, marriage through the exchange of cattle as bridewealth. Not only are the cattle worth more than their monetary exchange value, marriage is also more than a contractual agreement between two individuals. Marriage through ukulobola is an investment in affines and thus in a social and economic support network. The relationship with affines and kin is ultimately a social rather than a biological one, and it is the circulation of cattle that shapes these relationships. Building and maintaining these social networks of support also require forms of labor that cannot be subsumed under either waged work or entrepreneurial labor, and that do not adhere to a market logic. The gift economy that is central to the production and reproduction of these social relations is irreducible to a market economy or even a strict system of reciprocity.[29] The making of claims on those who have resources and the fostering of relations with people who may be able to help you when you are down on your luck—that is, the maintenance of networks of support—are forms of distributive labor that are often crucial to the survival of the poor. These forms of labor cannot be dissociated from their social context and reduced to mere calculations.[30] Land and labor are thus what Polanyi calls "fictitious commodities,"[31] and in this context cattle are as well.

It would therefore be a mistake to assume that Durban's dockworkers were gifted with an instinctive and universal profit motive, which is a key characteristic of the *homo economicus* or of an essentialist entrepreneurial spirit.[32] The pursuit of profit, while of course important for the survival of their households, was less a goal in itself than the means to achieve an intent, determined in part culturally and socially, to return to their rural home. I do not suggest that people were not looking for gains but rather that money was not the only measure of such gains; cattle, dependents and affines, the status of homestead head or *umnumzane*, and so on were equally part of their considerations. In other words, these households did not exist in a precapitalist, nonmarket utopia. Their lifeworld was neither a purely market-based society nor its antithesis, a society entirely devoid of money and markets, neither of which can ultimately exist.[33]

Moreover, we cannot see the entrepreneurialism of these workers as separate from their wage labor since these activities were crucially dependent on their employment on the docks. If they had not worked on the docks, they might never have engaged in this small-scale trade. The opportunities to pilfer offered by dock employment and the flexibility of casual labor made these strategies possible. Consequently, informal trade was more a creative way in which dockworkers took advantage of the opportunities port employment offered in order to break their dependence on wage labor than it was the outcome of an entrepreneurial essence. Indeed, in order to escape rural poverty and dependence on unpleasant urban employment for their members, these households strategically combined different economic activities that included wage labor, cultivation, animal husbandry, pilferage, small-scale trade, the commercial labor of women who were not part of these households, and non-market-based distributive (rather than productive) labor.

Locating the Household

Much as we cannot consider cattle, land, and labor mere commodities in this context, dockworkers' households equally defy easy identification with standard models of the household. These were not traditional Zulu homesteads nor Chayanovian peasant households that carefully balanced self-exploitation against the drudgery of their labor. We also cannot apply the neoclassical model of the profit-maximizing unitary household.[34] These households were not simply rural homesteads with a missing migrant laborer since urban wages and informal businesses were crucial to their reproduction. Neither are these examples of proletarian households that were forced by apartheid laws to reside in rural reserves and engage in oscillating labor migration since the rural economy was equally vital for their survival. Even township women selling pilfered goods contributed to the reproduction of dockworkers' households to which they did not belong, while having their own households and livelihood strategies. The households studied here thus did not exist in one place but rather in two or three separate locations, and they were composed of mutually dependent yet separate spheres of consumption and production (that is, the rural homestead, their workplace on the docks, and the urban township) that together reproduced the household as a whole.

These spheres were mutually dependent since none of them could reproduce the household on its own, yet they were also separate because distance and the difficulty of communication granted a measure of autonomy to different members in different locations. Men and women in these different locations made decisions about employment, cultivation, commerce, and consumption both in consultation with each other and on their own initiative. They pooled income but also tried to keep it out of the hands of other household members as they both struggled for and negotiated over the control of the household's resources and strategies.

Women selling produce would at times refrain from telling their husbands about such income in order to keep exclusive access to these cash resources. Men investing their wages in cattle also kept this money out of the hands of women who could not access or sell cattle, even if such decisions can scarcely be reduced to this rationale.[35] While different members had a common interest in reproducing the household, they generally also had distinct priorities, such as investing in cattle, becoming a homestead head, or managing everyday consumption. Several dockworkers' wives thus took pride in the fact that their "children never went to bed hungry,"[36] while their husbands were more likely to see becoming a homestead head and owning cattle as the measure of their success since owning cattle is the "life of a man."[37]

Neoclassical models of the household tend to obscure these gendered, generational, and other conflicts within the household since they assume solidary units of decision making acting to maximize their profit. More useful for our understanding is Jane I. Guyer's account of households as "constituted by a series of implicit or explicit contracts, not by total subsumption of the members into a solidary unit whose internal relationships can be taken as given."[38] Indeed, the households of Durban's dockworkers are best characterized as complex sets of relations between individuals who combined resources and made joint decisions, but also had their own strategies and resources over which they struggled with other members. The central dynamic of the household was thus not simply cooperation, as Amartya K. Sen notes, but rather cooperative conflict.[39] This mix of conflict and cooperation mirrors Kwame Gyekye's discussion of the Akan art motif of the two-headed crocodile to illustrate how communalism and individuality are not mutually exclusive in African social thought. The two heads symbolize individuality, as the heads struggle and compete with each other for food, yet they do have the same basic interest since they have one stomach.[40] Similarly, members struggle over the household's resources and strategies, but they are also bound in their common interest in allowing the household to survive, prosper, and reproduce. Rather than unitary, these households are "amphibious."

These multicentered households bridged the rural and urban spheres, and the formal and informal economies. Their multifaceted livelihoods were yet another reason why dockworkers did not conform to Eurocentric expectations of economic and political behavior either as wage laborers or as entrepreneurs. Both their entrepreneurialism and their wage labor should be understood within the context of these intricate livelihoods. Consequently, they did not necessarily behave as either radical proletarians acting in solidarity with a broader working class or as individual entrepreneurs looking out for their own interests. These workers and their leaders engaged in an idiosyncratic mix of collective working-class action and protests in support of the interests of African petty entrepreneurs.[41] These diverse forms of militancy included strikes, go-slows, and overtime boycotts but also calls for economic nationalism and commercial segregation, as well as virulent anti-Indian sentiments. Dockworkers were on the front lines of the 1949 anti-Indian pogrom, and several dock leaders called on the authorities to restrict trade in African areas to African traders.

This seeming contradiction does not signify that dock leaders' working-class rhetoric was part of a disingenuous attempt by an African petty bourgeoisie to appeal to the working class, as it was for some African leaders.[42] Neither was nationalist violence only a surrogate for frustrated working-class action.[43] Indian traders represented competition for aspiring African entrepreneurs, who evicted these traders in the 1949 pogrom and took over their businesses. These different approaches to socioeconomic advancement, reflecting both working-class and entrepreneurial concerns, mirrored the multifaceted livelihoods of many dockworkers' households. Workers thus defended their interests as wage laborers, as small-scale traders (or as workers aspiring to escape their dependence on wage labor through commercial strategies), and as rural dwellers who insisted on their right to return to their rural home regularly without losing their employment. Moreover, dockworkers did not merely wear the two hats of wage laborer and entrepreneur and defended their interests in either one capacity or the other. There was a functional relationship between those two since their employment on the docks made their entrepreneurial strategies possible. Both of these activities were integral parts of their households' livelihood strategies, and thus their interests as wage laborers or as entrepreneurs cannot be separated.

However, these livelihoods were precarious. The opportunities that dock employment offered to aspiring entrepreneurs slowly eroded during the 1950s and were drastically curtailed with the decasualization of dock labor in 1959. Apartheid authorities continuously tried to limit Africans' opportunities to earn an income outside the strictly controlled system of labor migration and cheap African labor. Decasualization was an important strategy to achieve this goal, and it resulted in lower pay rates and reduced flexibility to combine wage labor with commercial activities. Of course, decasualization also stifled militancy in this notoriously strike-prone sector for a decade.[44] Moreover, workers could no longer choose where to present for hiring, a practice that had given pilferers the opportunity to select those ships on which they could handle interesting goods. There was also increased pressure to live in the closely policed compounds, in which it was difficult to run informal businesses or hide pilfered goods. All these developments complicated entrepreneurial strategies. Such strategies were made all but impossible by the 1950s "clearing out" of uMkhumbane, an informal settlement that was the hub of African petty trading in Durban, and by containerization in the 1970s, which took away many opportunities for pilferage.

The Elusive *Homo Economicus*

It would thus seem that Durban's dockworkers did not fit very well into either the account of radical proletarians forming a militant working class or that of innate entrepreneurs imbued with an individualistic profit motive and a universal "propensity to truck, barter, and exchange." These universal categories derived from Western experience have limited purchase in this context, and even in the West their wholesale applicability is often questionable. Moreover, this is not only the case for 1950s Durban since the *homo economicus* tends to be elusive in much of the African continent.

The concept of this "economic person" is generally attributed to John Stuart Mill, though the phrase does not appear in his work. It refers to his theoretical abstractions in "On the Definition of Political Economy; and on the Method of Investigation Proper to It" (1836).[45] In this essay Mill describes a hypothetical subject whose motives and interests have been reduced to a limited number of reductive but well-defined factors. He argues that his abstractions to such a narrow range of relatively simple motives make this theoretical man particularly useful for analysis. Mill undertakes an "ethology" of this hypothetical person but also acknowledges that these motives can never be entirely separated from other interests and that this model has geographical and historical limitations.[46] However, he sees such exceptions to his model only as the result of secondary disturbing causes, as aberrations to a general law.[47] As such, the idea of a universal human who behaves in certain predictable ways is not challenged: this human just has to be recovered from the messy real world with its irrational impulses and disturbing causes of geography, culture, and history—lived reality is a layer of uncertainty to be peeled away to reveal the abstract rational and predictable economic human.

The phrase "economic man" or *homo economicus* was coined by Mill's critics in the late nineteenth century, who considered his abstractions vulgar and were uneasy with what they considered an unabashed expression of human selfishness. For John Kells Ingram, Mill "dealt not with real but with imaginary men— 'economic men' who were conceived as simply 'money-making animals.'"[48] While such critiques may have reduced the human complexity of Mill's economic man even further from a few incentives to one, later shifts in economic theory transformed this *homo economicus* into a mere rational decision maker. In today's usage the economic man is defined by his rational method of decision making. This mirrors the shift from what was once known as political economy to neoclassical economics—a science of choice, as most starkly formulated by Lionel Robbins.[49] Such models, whether they take into consideration one or several motives, rely on a hypothetical subject who operates in a particular market society in which the subject makes choices according to a market rationality. The idea of the *homo economicus* thus assumes the universality of a specific disembedded market economy that only matured in the West in the nineteenth century. This market society, Polanyi reminds us, "alone was economic in a different and distinctive sense, for it chose to base itself on a motive only rarely acknowledged as valid in the history of human societies, and certainly never before raised to the level of a justification of action and behavior in everyday life, namely, gain. The self-regulating market system was uniquely derived from this principle."[50] Such a self-regulating market economy and its requisite market society could never exist for an extended time since it would wreak havoc on social existence and would thus inevitably beget society's protective response to reembed the economy into society.

The assumption of a universal *homo economicus* or of the applicability of the purportedly normative "free" wage labor relationship from the West relies on an ethnocentric perspective.[51] Decisions about consumption, production, and the distribution of resources—that is, economic behavior—cannot be reduced to a universal, formalist market logic. Labor, moreover, is human activity and therefore essentially social. Thus, labor, consumption, and distribution cannot be fruitfully considered outside their social, political, and cultural contexts. This is why Polanyi's substantivism focuses on livelihood, that is, on the place of economy in human society, and not just on a formalist focus on the market.[52]

Such a cultural and social reading of the economic sphere is nothing new to the literature on Africa, and neither are examples of economies that do not operate along the lines of a universal market and of workers who do not quite behave like wage laborers. In *Marginal Gains* Guyer shows how profits in Atlantic West Africa were made in the interstices between two different economic systems with different methods of valuation.[53] Sara Berry's *No Condition Is Permanent* discusses how and why African farmers and rural dwellers often behaved in a seemingly irrational way within the paradigm of neoclassical economics. The story of "African rural economic life is filled with examples of farmers who prefer not to register their land rights, even though it is legally and administratively feasible to do so; employers who don't dismiss redundant or unproductive workers; laborers who work without pay, though hiring-out is an option; lenders who do not charge interest, and borrowers who pay back more than they owe."[54] In this context economic and sociopolitical incentives are not mutually exclusive or somehow separable. Economic investment cannot be divorced from investments in the social networks that allow one access to crucial resources, such as land, labor, or necessary permits. Consequently, investing one's surpluses in the maintenance of these networks—that is, in status, political access, dependents, and so on—is not irrational; these are investments in the means of negotiation over such access.

In short, Eurocentric assumptions about the working class or the neoclassical and equally ethnocentric understanding of the *homo economicus* as an individual decision maker with a predominant (or even exclusive) interest in maximizing his or her profit do not work very well in much of sub-Saharan Africa. The decisions regarding their livelihoods that dockworkers and other members of their households made were never purely economic and market driven, and they cannot be divorced from their social, cultural, and political context. As such, these decisions are as much social as they are economic. Durban's dockworkers were both wage laborers and entrepreneurs, just as they were husbands, African, Zulu, fathers, homestead heads, and so on. However, their lives and livelihoods cannot be reduced to any one of these categories.

Postscript

Returning to Guy's insightful remarks cited at the beginning of this chapter, I wish to draw further on the work of Polanyi. In "Our Obsolete Market Mentality," he maintains that the privileging of one motive (or a few) in our understanding of decision making probably has as much to do with how economists believe we should make decisions as with how we actually do so. Under the scathing subtitle "Birth of a Delusion," Polanyi posits that liberal economic theory is not "concerned with actual, but with assumed motives, not with the psychology, but with the ideology of business. *Not on the former, but on the latter, are views of man's nature based.* For once society expects a definite behavior on the part of its members, and prevailing institutions become roughly capable of enforcing that behavior, opinions on human nature will tend to mirror the ideal whether it resembles actuality or not."[55] Our choices to focus on specific aspects of economic and social life have more to do with the ideology of the capitalist market society than with social realities in Durban and its surrounding countryside. The changing interpretations Guy notes therefore reveal more about the intellectual and ideological milieu in which these accounts were written than about African livelihoods.

RALPH CALLEBERT teaches African history and critical writing at the University of Toronto. His current research explores understandings of labor and work outside the Global North.

Notes

1. James C. Scott, *Weapons of the Weak: Everyday Forms of Peasant Resistance* (New Haven, CT: Yale University Press, 1987).

2. Carol Hymowitz in *Forbes* and quoted in Andrew Pendakis, "Sovereigns of Risk: The Birth of the Ontopreneur," *South Atlantic Quarterly* 114, no. 3 (2015): 604.

3. On South Africa's institutionalized labor migration, see Jonathan Crush, Alan Jeeves, and David Yudelman, *South Africa's Labor Empire: A History of Black Migrancy to the Gold Mines* (Boulder, CO: Westview, 1991).

4. David Hemson, "Class Consciousness and Migrant Workers: Dockworkers of Durban" (PhD diss., University of Warwick, 1979); Mike Morris, "Stevedoring and the General Workers Union," pts. 1 and 2, *South African Labour Bulletin* 11, no. 2 (1986): 90–114, and no. 4 (1986): 100–118; Jeremy Baskin, "GWU and the Durban Dockworkers," *South African Labour Bulletin* 8, no. 3 (1982): 18–33; Bernard Dubbeld, "Breaking the Buffalo: The Transformation of Stevedoring Work in Durban between 1970 and 1990," *International Review of Social History* 48, no. 1 (2003): 97–122.

5. On militancy and radicalism in dock labor, see Frank Broeze, "Militancy and Pragmatism: An International Perspective on Maritime Labour, 1870–1914," *International Review of Social History* 36, no. 2 (1991): 165–200.

6. For an excellent but inevitably dated overview of the literature on labor in Africa, see Bill Freund, *The African Worker* (Cambridge: Cambridge University Press, 1988). For an updated review of the study of labor in South Africa, see Bill Freund, "Labour Studies and Labour History in South Africa: Perspectives from the Apartheid Era and After," *International Review of Social History* 58, no. 3 (2013): 493–519.

7. However, writing about the African working class was not exclusive to Southern Africa; see Richard Sandbrook and Robin Cohen, eds., *The Development of an African Working Class: Studies in Class Formation and Action* (London: Longman, 1975).

8. James Ferguson, *Expectations of Modernity: Myths and Meanings of Urban Life on the Zambian Copperbelt* (Berkeley: University of California Press, 1999), ch. 1.

9. This account is necessarily simplified. A good overview of the critiques of liberal and Marxist historiography can be found in Christopher Saunders, *The Making of the South African Past: Major Historians on Race and Class* (Cape Town: David Philip, 1988), chs. 16–18.

10. Pendakis, "Sovereigns of Risk."

11. Ibid., 604–5.

12. Hernando de Soto, *The Mystery of Capital: Why Capitalism Triumphs in the West and Fails Everywhere Else* (New York: Basic Books, 2000); Dambisa Moyo, *Dead Aid: Why Aid Is Not Working and How There Is a Better Way for Africa* (New York: Farrar, Straus and Giroux, 2009).

13. On the changing perceptions of the informal economy in sub-Saharan Africa, see Deborah Potts, "The Urban Informal Sector in Sub-Saharan Africa: From Bad to Good (and Back Again?)," *Development Southern Africa* 25, no. 2 (2008): 151–67.

14. Seventy-seven interviews with former dockworkers and their relatives, as well as with representatives from the shipping industry, were conducted by Sibongo Dlamini, by Snegugu Lerato Mchunu and the author, and by the author in 2009 and 2014.

15. See also Ralph Callebert, "Working Class Action and Informal Trade on the Durban Docks, 1930s–1950s," *Journal of Southern African Studies* 38, no. 4 (2012): 847–61.

16. On the political nature of these strikes, see Peter Cole, "No Justice, No Ships Get Loaded: Political Boycotts on the San Francisco Bay and Durban Waterfronts," *International Review of Social History* 58, no. 2 (2013): 185–217.

17. Stein Inge Nesvåg, "Street Trading from Apartheid to Post-apartheid: More Birds in the Cornfield?," *International Journal of Sociology and Social Policy* 20, no. 3/4 (2000): 34–63.

18. Charles Simkins, "Agricultural Production in the African Reserves of South Africa, 1918–1969," *Journal of Southern African Studies* 7, no. 2 (1981): 256–83.

19. See Ralph Callebert, "Cleaning the Wharves: Pilferage, Bribery and Social Connections on the Durban Docks in the 1950s," *Canadian Journal of African Studies* 46, no. 1 (2012): 23–38. On pilferage in other ports, see Linda Cooke Johnson, "Criminality on the Docks," in *Dock*

Workers: International Explorations in Comparative Labour History, 1790–1970, ed. Sam Davies et al., 721–45 (Aldershot, UK: Ashgate, 2000).

20. Adam Smith, The Wealth of Nations (London: Penguin Classics, [1776] 1986), 117.

21. For more on cattle in the Zulu social structure, see Jeff Guy, "Colonial Transformations and the Home," in Ekhaya: The Politics of Home in KwaZulu-Natal, ed. Meghan Healy-Clancy and Jason Hickel, 23–47 (Pietermaritzburg, South Africa: University of KwaZulu-Natal Press, 2014).

22. For example, see Union of South Africa, Report of the Native Economic Commission, 1930–1932, U.G. 22-1932, 19. For a discussion of this cattle complex as an example of an 'invented' tradition in the context of colonialism, see James Ferguson, The Anti-politics Machine: "Development," Depoliticization, and Bureaucratic Power in Lesotho (Minneapolis: University of Minnesota Press, 1994), ch. 5; and Emmanuel Kreike, "De-globalisation and Deforestation in Colonial Africa: Closed Markets, the Cattle Complex, and Environmental Change in North-Central Namibia, 1890–1990," Journal of Southern African Studies 35, no. 1 (2009): 81–98.

23. This continues to be the case today. See Derick A. Fay, "'Keeping Land for Their Children': Generation, Migration and Land in South Africa's Transkei," Journal of Southern African Studies 41, no. 5 (2015): 1083–97.

24. Both Marcel Mauss and Émile Durkheim similarly highlight the noncontractual element of the private contract, that is, the social glue that makes seemingly asocial market transactions possible (state, law, custom, social order, morality, and so on). See Durkheim, The Division of Labor in Society (New York: Free Press, [1893] 1997), ch. 7; and Mauss, The Gift: The Form and Reason for Exchange in Archaic Societies (London: Routledge, [1925] 2001).

25. Karl Polanyi, The Great Transformation: The Political and Economic Origins of Our Time (Boston: Beacon, [1944] 1957), 3.

26. On the irreducibility of the social to the market, see Raji Singh Soni and Ralph Callebert, "A Political Economy of the Humanities: Turning Tables with Marx and Kant," Australian Humanities Review 59 (2016): 1–22.

27. J. R. Stanfield, "Karl Polanyi and Contemporary Economic Thought," Review of Social Economy 47, no. 3 (1989): 267.

28. On substantivist and formalist approaches, see Karl Polanyi, "The Economy as Instituted Process," in Trade and Market in Early Empires: Economies in History and Theory, ed. Karl Polanyi, Conrad M. Arensberg, and Harry W. Pearson, 243–70 (Glencoe, IL: Free Press, 1957).

29. Cf. Mauss, The Gift.

30. On the importance of a distributive political economy, see James Ferguson, Give a Man a Fish: Reflections on the New Politics of Distribution (Durham, NC: Duke University Press, 2015), esp. ch. 3.

31. Polanyi, Great Transformation, ch. 6.

32. See ibid., 30.

33. Though often read as constructing a moralist and nostalgic dualism between market and nonmarket societies, Mauss's account of The Gift does not support such a dichotomy. In fact, Mauss was very critical of what he saw as a Bolshevik antimarket ideology. See Keith Hart, "Marcel Mauss: In Pursuit of the Whole," Comparative Studies in Society and History 49, no. 2 (2007): 473–85.

34. Alexander V. Chayanov, The Theory of Peasant Economy, ed. Daniel Thorner, Basile Kerblay, and R. E. F. Smith (Homewood, IL: American Economic Association, 1966); Howard N. Barnum and Lyn Squire, "An Econometric Application of the Theory of the Farm-Household," Journal of Development Economics 6, no. 1 (1979): 79–102.

35. Cattle in this context are a special-purpose money, that is, money that can only serve specific purposes and can only be used by certain people, as opposed to general-purpose money, which can serve all money purposes and be used by anyone. See Viviana A. Zelizer, "The Social Meaning of Money: 'Special Monies,'" *American Journal of Sociology* 95, no. 2 (1989): 342–77.

36. Fikile Mlotshwa, interview with Snegugu Lerato Mchunu and the author, Bulwer, KwaZulu-Natal, South Africa, June 25, 2014.

37. Mzenkosi Duma, interview with Sibongo Dlamini, Mkhunya North, KwaZulu-Natal, South Africa, November 13, 2009.

38. Jane I. Guyer, "Household and Community in African Studies," *African Studies Review* 24, no. 2/3 (1981): 99.

39. Amartya K. Sen, "Gender and Cooperative Conflicts," in *Persistent Inequalities: Women and World Development*, ed. Irene Tinker, 123–49 (New York: Oxford University Press, 1990).

40. Kwame Gyekye, *An Essay on African Philosophical Thought: The Akan Conceptual Scheme* (Cambridge: Cambridge University Press, 1987), 143–46, 159–61.

41. I discuss this in more detail in "Working Class Action."

42. Paul La Hausse, "The Message of the Warriors: The ICU, the Labouring Poor and the Making of a Popular Political Culture in Durban, 1925–30," in *Holding Their Ground: Class, Locality and Culture in 19th and 20th Century South Africa*, ed. Philip Bonner et al., 19–57 (Johannesburg: Witwatersrand University Press, 1989); Iain Edwards, "Cato Manor, June 1959: Men, Women, Crowds, Violence, Politics and History," in *The People's City: African Life in Twentieth-Century Durban*, ed. Paul Maylam and Iain Edwards (Pietermaritzburg, South Africa: University of Natal Press, 1996), 111.

43. For a discussion of explanations of the pogrom as a "surrogate targeting of Indians for broader African grievances" (109), see Jon Soske, "'Wash Me Black Again': African Nationalism, the Indian Diaspora, and Kwa-Zulu Natal, 1944–1960" (PhD diss., University of Toronto, 2009), ch. 3.

44. Decasualization followed a global trend in port labor and a colonial African trend of stabilization of urban labor. See Klaus Weinhauer, "Power and Control on the Waterfront: Casual Labour and Decasualisation," in Davies et al., *Dock Workers*, 580–603; and Frederick Cooper, *Decolonization and African Society: The Labor Question in French and British Africa* (Cambridge: Cambridge University Press, 1996).

45. John Stuart Mill, "On the Definition and Method of Political Economy," in *The Philosophy of Economics: An Anthology*, ed. Daniel M. Hausman, 52–68 (Cambridge: Cambridge University Press, 1994).

46. Joseph Persky, "The Ethology of *Homo Economicus*," *Journal of Economic Perspectives* 9, no. 2 (1995): 223, 228.

47. Mill, "On the Definition and Method," 60.

48. Quoted in Persky, "Ethology," 222.

49. Persky, "Ethology," 222–23; Stanfield, "Karl Polanyi," 266–67.

50. Polanyi, *Great Transformation*, 30.

51. Though Polanyi's work helps us uncover the ethnocentrism in assumptions of a universal market rationality, his account of global history in *The Great Transformation* focuses almost entirely on Europe and its offshoots. See Keith Hart, "Karl Polanyi's Legacy," *Development and Change* 39, no. 6 (2008): 1135–43.

52. "To study human livelihood is to study the economy in this substantive sense of the term." Karl Polanyi, *The Livelihood of Man*, ed. Harry W. Pearson (New York: Academic, 1977), 20.

53. Jane I. Guyer, *Marginal Gains: Monetary Transactions in Atlantic Africa* (Chicago: University of Chicago Press, 2004).

54. Sara Berry, *No Condition Is Permanent: The Social Dynamics of Agrarian Change in Sub-Saharan Africa* (Madison: University of Wisconsin Press, 1993), 14.

55. Karl Polanyi, "Our Obsolete Market Mentality," *Commentary* 3, no. 2 (1947), https://www.commentarymagazine.com/articles/our-obsolete-market-mentality/. Emphasis in original.

Bibliography

Barnum, Howard N., and Lyn Squire. 1979. "An Econometric Application of the Theory of the Farm-Household." *Journal of Development Economics* 6, no. 1: 79–102.

Baskin, Jeremy. 1982. "GWU and the Durban Dockworkers." *South African Labour Bulletin* 8, no. 3: 18–33.

Berry, Sara. 1993. *No Condition Is Permanent: The Social Dynamics of Agrarian Change in Sub-Saharan Africa.* Madison: University of Wisconsin Press.

Broeze, Frank. 1991. "Militancy and Pragmatism: An International Perspective on Maritime Labour, 1870–1914." *International Review of Social History* 36, no. 2: 165–200.

Callebert, Ralph. 2012. "Cleaning the Wharves: Pilferage, Bribery and Social Connections on the Durban Docks in the 1950s." *Canadian Journal of African Studies* 46, no. 1: 23–38.

———. 2012. "Working Class Action and Informal Trade on the Durban Docks, 1930s–1950s." *Journal of Southern African Studies* 38, no. 4: 847–61.

Chayanov, Alexander V. 1966. *The Theory of Peasant Economy.* Edited by Daniel Thorner, Basile Kerblay, and R. E. F. Smith. Homewood, IL: American Economic Association.

Cole, Peter. 2013. "No Justice, No Ships Get Loaded: Political Boycotts on the San Francisco Bay and Durban Waterfronts." *International Review of Social History* 58, no. 2: 185–217.

Cooke Johnson, Linda. 2000. "Criminality on the Docks." In *Dock Workers: International Explorations in Comparative Labour History, 1790–1970,* edited by Sam Davies, Colin J. Davis, David de Vries, Lex Haarma van Vos, Lidewij Hesselink, and Klaus Weinhauer, 721–45. Aldershot, UK: Ashgate.

Cooper, Frederick. 1996. *Decolonization and African Society: The Labor Question in French and British Africa.* Cambridge: Cambridge University Press.

Crush, Jonathan, Alan Jeeves, and David Yudelman. 1991. *South Africa's Labor Empire: A History of Black Migrancy to the Gold Mines.* Boulder, CO: Westview.

De Soto, Hernando. 2000. *The Mystery of Capital: Why Capitalism Triumphs in the West and Fails Everywhere Else.* New York: Basic Books.

Dubbeld, Bernard. 2003. "Breaking the Buffalo: The Transformation of Stevedoring Work in Durban between 1970 and 1990." *International Review of Social History* 48, no. 1: 97–122.

Durkheim, Émile. (1893) 1997. *The Division of Labor in Society.* New York: Free Press.

Edwards, Iain. 1996. "Cato Manor, June 1959: Men, Women, Crowds, Violence, Politics and History." In *The People's City: African Life in Twentieth-Century Durban,* edited by Paul Maylam and Iain Edwards, 102–42. Pietermaritzburg, South Africa: University of Natal Press.

Fay, Derick A. 2015. "'Keeping Land for Their Children': Generation, Migration and Land in South Africa's Transkei." *Journal of Southern African Studies* 41, no. 5: 1083–97.

Ferguson, James. 1994. *The Anti-politics Machine: "Development," Depoliticization, and Bureaucratic Power in Lesotho*. Minneapolis: University of Minnesota Press.
———. 1999. *Expectations of Modernity: Myths and Meanings of Urban Life on the Zambian Copperbelt*. Berkeley: University of California Press.
———. 2015. *Give a Man a Fish: Reflections on the New Politics of Distribution*. Durham, NC: Duke University Press.
Freund, Bill. 1988. *The African Worker*. Cambridge: Cambridge University Press.
———. 2013. "Labour Studies and Labour History in South Africa: Perspectives from the Apartheid Era and After." *International Review of Social History* 58, no. 3: 493–519.
Guy, Jeff. 2014. "Colonial Transformations and the Home." In *Ekhaya: The Politics of Home in KwaZulu-Natal*, edited by Meghan Healy-Clancy and Jason Hickel, 23–47. Pietermaritzburg, South Africa: University of KwaZulu-Natal Press.
Guyer, Jane I. 1981. "Household and Community in African Studies." *African Studies Review* 24, no. 2/3: 87–137.
———. 2004. *Marginal Gains: Monetary Transactions in Atlantic Africa*. Chicago: University of Chicago Press.
Gyekye, Kwame. 1987. *An Essay on African Philosophical Thought: The Akan Conceptual Scheme*. Cambridge: Cambridge University Press.
Hart, Keith. 2007. "Marcel Mauss: In Pursuit of the Whole." *Comparative Studies in Society and History* 49, no. 2: 473–85.
———. 2008. "Karl Polanyi's Legacy." *Development and Change* 39, no. 6: 1135–43.
Hemson, David. 1979. "Class Consciousness and Migrant Workers: Dockworkers of Durban." PhD diss., University of Warwick.
Kreike, Emmanuel. 2009. "De-globalisation and Deforestation in Colonial Africa: Closed Markets, the Cattle Complex, and Environmental Change in North-Central Namibia, 1890–1990." *Journal of Southern African Studies* 35, no. 1: 81–98.
La Hausse, Paul. 1989. "The Message of the Warriors: The ICU, the Labouring Poor and the Making of a Popular Political Culture in Durban, 1925–30." In *Holding Their Ground: Class, Locality and Culture in 19th and 20th Century South Africa*, edited by Philip Bonner, Isabel Hofmeyr, Deborah James, and Tom Lodge, 19–57. Johannesburg: Witwatersrand University Press.
Mauss, Marcel. (1925) 2001. *The Gift: The Form and Reason for Exchange in Archaic Societies*. London: Routledge.
Mill, John Stuart. (1836) 1994. "On the Definition and Method of Political Economy." In *The Philosophy of Economics: An Anthology*, edited by Daniel M. Hausman, 52–68. Cambridge: Cambridge University Press.
Morris, Mike. 1986. "Stevedoring and the General Workers Union." Pts. 1 and 2. *South African Labour Bulletin* 11, no. 2: 90–114; no. 4: 100–118.
Moyo, Dambisa. 2009. *Dead Aid: Why Aid Is Not Working and How There Is a Better Way for Africa*. New York: Farrar, Straus and Giroux.
Nesvåg, Stein Inge. 2000. "Street Trading from Apartheid to Post-apartheid: More Birds in the Cornfield?" *International Journal of Sociology and Social Policy* 20, no. 3/4: 34–63.
Pendakis, Andrew. 2015. "Sovereigns of Risk: The Birth of the Ontopreneur." *South Atlantic Quarterly* 114, no. 3: 595–610.
Persky, Joseph. 1995. "The Ethology of *Homo Economicus*." *Journal of Economic Perspectives* 9, no. 2: 221–31.

Polanyi, Karl. (1944) 1957. *The Great Transformation: The Political and Economic Origins of Our Time*. Boston: Beacon.

———. 1947. "Our Obsolete Market Mentality." *Commentary* 3, no. 2. https://www.commentary magazine.com/articles/our-obsolete-market-mentality/.

———. 1957. "The Economy as Instituted Process." In *Trade and Market in Early Empires: Economies in History and Theory*, edited by Karl Polanyi, Conrad M. Arensberg, and Harry W. Pearson, 243–70. Glencoe, IL: Free Press.

———. 1977. *The Livelihood of Man*. Edited by Harry W. Pearson. New York: Academic.

Potts, Deborah. 2008. "The Urban Informal Sector in Sub-Saharan Africa: From Bad to Good (and Back Again?)." *Development Southern Africa* 25, no. 2: 151–67.

Sandbrook, Richard, and Robin Cohen, eds. 1975. *The Development of an African Working Class: Studies in Class Formation and Action*. London: Longman.

Saunders, Christopher. 1988. *The Making of the South African Past: Major Historians on Race and Class*. Cape Town: David Philip.

Scott, James C. 1987. *Weapons of the Weak: Everyday Forms of Peasant Resistance*. New Haven, CT: Yale University Press.

Sen, Amartya K. 1990. "Gender and Cooperative Conflicts." In *Persistent Inequalities: Women and World Development*, edited by Irene Tinker, 123–49. New York: Oxford University Press.

Simkins, Charles. 1981. "Agricultural Production in the African Reserves of South Africa, 1918–1969." *Journal of Southern African Studies* 7, no. 2: 256–83.

Smith, Adam. (1776) 1986. *The Wealth of Nations*. London: Penguin Classics.

Soni, Raji Singh, and Ralph Callebert. 2016. "A Political Economy of the Humanities: Turning Tables with Marx and Kant." *Australian Humanities Review* 59:1–22.

Soske, Jon. 2009. "'Wash Me Black Again': African Nationalism, the Indian Diaspora, and Kwa-Zulu Natal, 1944–1960." PhD diss., University of Toronto.

Stanfield, J. R. 1998. "Karl Polanyi and Contemporary Economic Thought." *Review of Social Economy* 47, no. 3: 266–79.

Union of South Africa. 1932. *Report of the Native Economic Commission, 1930–1932*. U.G. 22-1932.

Weinhauer, Klaus. 2000. "Power and Control on the Waterfront: Casual Labour and Decasualisation." In *Dock Workers: International Explorations in Comparative Labour History, 1790–1970*, edited by Sam Davies, Colin J. Davis, David de Vries, Lex Haarma van Vos, Lidewij Hesselink, and Klaus Weinhauer, 580–603. Aldershot, UK: Ashgate.

Zelizer, Viviana A. 1989. "The Social Meaning of Money: 'Special Monies.'" *American Journal of Sociology* 95, no. 2: 342–77.

PART V

African Enterprise in the Shadow of Colonization

12 The Socioeconomic Bases of the Growth of Microentrepreneurship in the Igede Area of Central Nigeria in the Nineteenth and Twentieth Centuries

Mike Odugbo Odey

THIS CHAPTER EXPLAINS the nature of the growth of small-scale entrepreneurial activities among the Igede people in central Nigeria through networks of social capital formations that eventually metamorphosed into small but genuine spirit of entrepreneurship. The origin and development of microentrepreneurial behavior among the Igede people of Benue State are largely traceable to the concept and practice of moral economy long before the advent of Western political economy in central Nigeria. In the Igede area microentrepreneurial growth found expression in a number of different activities that flourished under the rubric of social entrepreneurship, involving individuals and groups who provided sustainable solutions to the needs of social groups and the environment, and from which the traditional form of entrepreneurship—with its desire for profit maximization—later developed. The central argument here is that, despite its initial unconventional nature when juxtaposed with the praxis of entrepreneurial tradition and literature, social entrepreneurship thrived and constituted the basis on which the conventional typology of business consciousness and gain sprang up and grew in an inseparable nexus between the two. Thus, in this chapter, the concept of social entrepreneurship is used as the dominant framework of analysis, along with related themes, to explain the development of microentrepreneurship in the Igede area of Benue State in central Nigeria during the nineteenth and twentieth centuries.

The first objective of the chapter is to explain the inseparable links between social entrepreneurship and the traditional definitions of entrepreneurship as exhibited in Igede history during the period. The second objective is to demonstrate how the dynamics and uniqueness of social networks led to the development of entrepreneurship in the Igede area. Along the way, the chapter argues that the history of entrepreneurship in Africa was in place long before the advent of Western capitalism. Third, the analysis shows how the development of Igede history largely thrived as a typology of social entrepreneurship over time. The basic sources of information used in the analysis were the Nigerian National Archives, Kaduna, oral information, the internet, and secondary sources related to the issues involved. The chapter argues that the development of entrepreneurial activities in Africa assumed different forms without the influence of European capitalism, which is characterized by huge industrial technology and capital. The relevance of the argument in the chapter lies mainly in its connection to the larger space of African economic history and the development of the continent at large.

Perspectives

A genuine understanding of the subject matter in this chapter requires a clear view of the three related concepts of social entrepreneurship, moral economy, and microentrepreneurship. They are particularly relevant as a framework of analysis and are also useful for explaining the socioeconomic bases of the growth of microentrepreneurship in the Igede area during the nineteenth and twentieth centuries.

Although social entrepreneurship is an emerging concept in entrepreneurial literature, it is well known in many parts of the Western world and has been a significant concept for explaining entrepreneurial history and development. A social entrepreneur is "someone who recognizes a social problem and uses entrepreneurial principles to organize, create, and manage a venture to make social change."[1] Furthermore, social entrepreneurship provides an innovative way to solve social problems and produce social benefits or change, which is, as it were, like the return of the invisible men who were expelled from the mainstream literature of economics but are now restored due to their importance in microeconomic value and the theory of innovators and entrepreneurship.[2] Social entrepreneurship is generally concerned with the enhancement of social capital or investment in human capital for the development of other sectors in an economy, within which all other core issues of sustainable development coalesce.[3] While the traditional or orthodox meaning of entrepreneurship pertains to production and distribution to maximize profit, social entrepreneurship *ab initio* is not about profit making. However, in order for social entrepreneurs to achieve their goals, they must necessarily use the principles of entrepreneurs. *Ipso facto*, social entrepreneurs will always look for profit in one way or another to achieve their ultimate goals.

Social entrepreneurship is a modification of and is derived from the traditional concept of entrepreneurship. Other than in the Western world, the concept is relatively new and not in popular usage in other parts of the globe, especially sub-Saharan Africa. It involves social interaction and is expressed in several ways. Undoubtedly, social entrepreneurship constitutes the basis for the emergence of microentrepreneurship among the Igede people of central Nigeria, as explained in this chapter. It is simply about how people use innovations or brilliant ideas to overcome seemingly insurmountable social and economic problems to create new products and services, thereby improving people's lives. It is also an agent of social transformation. That is, the concept of social entrepreneurship cannot be used in the exclusive sense of the parent word "entrepreneurship."

Against this background it is easy to argue from a broader perspective that entrepreneurship is both a social and economic activity. Indeed, an entrepreneurial spirit is ingrained in the cultural ecology and social history of people and not limited to any part of the world or any particular type of economy, whether industrial or agrarian. However, in the past, due to racial prejudice and socialist dogma, Western intellectuals did not take seriously the development of African business culture as the expression of a genuine spirit of entrepreneurship and hard work, but rather interpret it as mere subsistence behavior.[4] Perhaps because entrepreneurial studies and history began in Europe, the assumption exists that African entrepreneurial history should follow the same development pattern. While the two may be similar in several respects, differences abound in many ways due to differences in geographical and historical contexts. It is a well-known fact that much of the African entrepreneurial spirit lies in Goran Hyden's argument that 'small is powerful: the structural anomaly of rural Africa,"[5] as a genuine reflection of the resilience of African farmers who, despite all odds, remain independent inventors, cannot be obliterated by other social classes, and are the owners of their means of production. Indeed, the capacity of the African peasantry for generating huge wealth may be small, but it is powerful enough to withstand the hazards of the agrarian, weather-driven culture; manage the conflicts of capital and labor; and coexist with the capitalist mode of production. It is also capable of generating wealth for investment. According to Yvette Monga, it is a fundamental truth that African precapitalist societies exhibited a genuine spirit of entrepreneurship through hard work, ventured onto unfamiliar paths for profit making, and provide "a number of strong examples of progressive economic behavior embedded in particular features of indigenous social organizations."[6]

It is against this backdrop that we should attempt to understand the significance of social entrepreneurship for the growth of microentrepreneurship within the context of Igede traditional institutions and social relationships. For example, age-group associations, cooperative labor organizations, women's dance and singing groups, household and lineage groups, and similar social groups served social as well as economic purposes. A more comprehensive understanding of entrepreneurship history among the Igede people of Benue State in central Nigeria is contingent on a clear perspective of their social and economic organizations.

Linked to this is the fundamental truth that entrepreneurs' traditional institutional risk-averse behavior is intended to produce social benefits, as exhibited in predominantly agrarian communities described as having a "moral economy," which is one of the basic characteristics of most precolonial economies and a necessary antecedent of postcolonial political economic development. James Scott underscores the significance of moral economy as a framework for analyzing "the centrality of risk and subsistence security among peasants in pre-capitalist societies."[7] James Scott's idea of the technical arrangements of "safety first" correspond to a "subsistence ethic" within the peasant social structure and constitute what Edward Thompson calls a "moral economy," which is focused on survival and simple reproduction systems.[8]

Scott's idea of the moral economy of the peasantry is comparable to Goran Hyden's "economy of affection"[9] and Karl Polanyi's morality of reciprocal giving eventually becomes a viable investment opportunity. Most peasant economies essentially first underscore the necessity of everyone's survival before other considerations such as economic gain. However, this does not in any way obliterate the desire for wealth, as clearly expressed in Thompson's formulation in *The Making of the English Working Class*.[10] Among other things, Thompson refers to this as "subsistence ethic" since it affects the social relations of production and behavior. For the most part, this is the main concern of most rural people in less developed economies whose focus remains on the survival and safety nets of the community with "adaptive flexibility." Here, safety nets include the availability of food, the price of subsistence commodities, the proper administration of taxation, and goodwill or the operation of charity. The canon law of moral economy is that it has a plausible correlation to the concept of social entrepreneurship; most peasant societies are structured in an adaptive manner and in such a way that the subsistence needs of the rural poor remain sacrosanct. In other words, rather than being directed at the maximization of economic gains, societal behavior is geared toward survival needs first, but it veers into business ethics as long as it is used to generate other essential elements in the overall development of society. The Igede society falls within the framework of moral economy as so far expressed, and in the present analysis it is imperative to link it to the emergence and development of microentrepreneurship in the area.

The third concept worth clarifying is microentrepreneurship, within which other related terms, such as "small and medium enterprises," are subsumed. Microentrepreneurship is an important component of entrepreneurship and includes small- or medium-size businesses or both. In the context of the present analysis, one must avoid insisting that microbusinesses must have a capacity of up to N 1 million and N 1.5 million, a staff capacity of about ten people, and annual turnovers of the business owner, as experts have always suggested. Here the term "microentrepreneurship" refers to all start-up businesses whose origins are traceable to social entrepreneurship, having begun from scratch and expanded to anything bigger. Against this background, "microentrepreneurship" refers to all family or household businesses; unskilled businesses that allow anyone to participate without hindrances, such as those that were involved in agricultural production for overseas and export trade during the colonial period; artisans; migrant laborers; and businesses dominated by women, such as the foodstuff trade. All these can be regarded as small-scale businesses or microenterprises. Due to the fluid nature of small and medium businesses in Nigeria, S. T. Kpelai argues that the term "SMEs [small and medium enterprises] has become a common nomenclature for describing the three classes of entrepreneurship businesses": small, micro, and medium businesses.[11]

There is no specific or comprehensive literature on the development of entrepreneurship in Igede history. However, one can glean the complex details within the context of generalized African economic history works in which the concept of entrepreneurship and its development are mentioned in passing. Even then, there are too many deficiencies in the historiography on indigenous African entrepreneurship during the nineteenth century and the early colonial period. One of the earliest works on entrepreneurship in Nigeria that supports the idea that microentrepreneurial development is plausible in the informal sector and is central to economic growth is Tom Forrest's *The Advance of African Capital: The Growth of Nigerian Private Enterprise.*[12] It is similar in content to *The Native Economies of Nigeria* by Daryll Forde and Richenda Scott.[13] Another important work, on the growth of Hausa entrepreneurship through groundnut production, which was given a boost by the development of railway transport in Northern Nigeria, is by Jan S. Hogendorn.[14] Anita Spring and Barbara E. Mc-Dade have edited one of the most recent and comprehensive analyses of African entrepreneurship in different regions of the continent.[15] Sara S. Berry's volume is a beautiful analysis of the development of nineteenth-century Yoruba cocoa entrepreneurs "as a process of capital formation in a land surplus economy."[16] John Tosh's appraisal of tropical agriculture, rightly regarded as a revolution through the productive activities of small cash-crop producers for export, also explains the remarkable development of African entrepreneurship during the colonial period.[17] Polly Hill's case study of Batagarawa in Katsina Province provides a good example of rural capitalism and entrepreneurial growth in its own right.[18] These and several other pioneering explanations of the development of entrepreneurship in Africa provide important reference points in the discourse on early African business enterprise. However, most of these early perspectives are rather vague, patchy, and localized to specific geographical regions of the African continent. In addition, they generally overlook a number of important details in the emergence of entrepreneurship and its changing dynamics in many other regions of the continent. These details need further interrogation for a systematic reconstruction of entrepreneurship history in Africa, a gap that this chapter attempts to fill in part. These earliest available works present a version of indigenous African entrepreneurship dominated by women. For instance, in works by Mike O. Odey,[19] I. L. Bashir,[20] B. F. Bawa,[21] and S. U. Fwatshak,[22] each author deliberates in his own way on the multifaceted development of African entrepreneurship in central Nigeria, especially women's microentrepreneurial engagements in agricultural production and foodstuff trade, small-scale tin mining, iron smelting, pottery, woodcrafts, weaving, tanning, salt mining, and trade in these products, which led to small businesses and economic growth in these areas. Apart from this, in two separate volumes, Paul T. Zeleza[23] also critically examines various aspects of entrepreneurial growth in different parts of Africa in the nineteenth and twentieth centuries.

In Igede and the rest of central Nigeria, the basic structure of every household rested on traditional agricultural production; the household was made up of the head, the wife (or wives), the children, and other relatives who could be mobilized into the labor force to boost productivity when necessary. The allocation of family members to specific workplaces was the prerogative of the family head, and women were usually responsible for marketing the produce in local and border markets. Productive activity and trade constituted the basic economic activity of each household, by which petty cash was generated for other investments. These women's activities in food production and foodstuff trade constituted the hub of microentrepreneurship in central Nigeria over time. Most of these small-scale enterprises involving women were flexible, dynamic, and always in transition toward more-complex market economies connecting diverse groups and crossing ethnic boundaries in the region. Furthermore, local women were very knowledgeable about when to take more or less of their farm produce to each market. They also knew how to adapt to changing circumstances in the operations of local markets and take advantage of new opportunities within the larger economic system in the region.

Microentrepreneurial activities in Igede in central Nigeria mainly depended on agricultural production and petty trading in foodstuffs and, to a lesser extent, on craftworks by people with limited or no formal education. According to Forrest, the process was more or less a continuum through which influential and relatively wealthier individuals eventually rose from microentrepreneurship to large-scale entrepreneurship.[24] In fact, most of the indigenous Nigerian entrepreneurs during the precolonial period were apprentices who were very resourceful, resilient, and adaptable to changing circumstances. Although Hill did not study Igede rural society in particular, her works describe striking similarities in how agricultural production and produce trade constituted the easiest means by which to earn cash in a genuine spirit of entrepreneurship. She describes rural capitalism or indigenous economies as "the basic fabric of existent economic life which involved production of export or other cash crops, subsistence farming, cattle rearing, fishing for cash or subsistence, internal trading in foodstuffs, transportation, economically motivated migration, indigenous credit-granting systems and so forth."[25]

In the very remote past, the general conception of an entrepreneur was as an individual who has the ability to manage large production projects and available resources without risk. However, in the seventeenth century the idea of risk management in production systems was added to the conception of entrepreneurship and still remains an important aspect. During the British Industrial Revolution in the eighteenth century, experts on the subject tried to distinguish between a provider of capital (as a factor of production) and the one who needed and used it. In the nineteenth and twentieth centuries, entrepreneurs were seen purely from the economic point of view as organizers and operators of big or small enterprises with the ability to generate wealth. An entrepreneur is one who "shifts economic resources out of an area of lower gain into an area of higher productivity and greater yield," which goes beyond the literal translation of the French word *entrepreneur* as "one who undertakes" to encompass the concept of value creation.[26]

Joseph A. Schumpeter later moved beyond the basic concept of value creation as an invaluable contribution to what is perhaps the most useful idea regarding entrepreneurship.[27] Schumpeter argues that every entrepreneur has a certain attitude that is inevitable and must be taken as an imperative force for economic progress without which economic growth would be impossible, static, and even subject to decay. Schumpeter's idea of entrepreneurial spirit also involves an individual who identifies a commercial opportunity, which could be a material, product, service, or business, and has the ability to organize a venture and implement it. Successful entrepreneurship sets off a chain reaction, encouraging other entrepreneurs to reenact the idea and ultimately propagate the innovation to the point of "creative destruction," in which the new venture and all its related ventures effectively render existing products, services, and business models obsolete.[28] While Schumpeter sees the entrepreneur as an agent of change within the larger economy, Peter F. Drucker views entrepreneurs as those who constantly search for change, respond to it, and see it as an opportunity to exploit.[29] Drawing from both perspectives, Israel M. Kirzner sees entrepreneurs as people whose critical ability lies in their "alertness."[30] Most experts also agree that entrepreneurs are innovators who use a variety of new and untried methods to make new products. From the African perspective, an entrepreneur is not seen as participating in mass production through the factory system or the use of industrial machines to make new products. In other words, in the African context and for the purpose of this chapter, an entrepreneur is an individual with the initiative and the ability to mobilize factors of production, including social capital and ultimately economic wealth.

Despite continuous scholarly refinement and changes in the definition of entrepreneurship, some elements have remained constant and run through most of the perspectives, regardless of time and disciplinary leanings. These include the ability to take risks and make profits, the ability to maximize factors of production more efficiently and turn them into something of greater value to society, and the ability to enhance economic growth and development by using social capital. More specifically relevant to the preceding argument, Schumpeter further explains, "Entrepreneurs have not accumulated any kind of goods, they have created no original means of production, but have employed existing means of production differently, more advantageously. Economic development in our sense is only accomplished in the form of carrying out new combinations of existing goods."[31]

From the perspectives described here, an entrepreneur is not only a capitalist or a technologist but also one who has the capacity and the innovation to engage in social networking or effective factor mixing in any productive or commercial activity—whether small or large in scale and formal or informal—whose ultimate goal is to bring about economic development and improvement in people's lives in the society at large. This broad-spectrum approach is perfectly in line with Ernst F. Schumacher's challenge concerning the complexity and devastation of technological doctrine: that "small is beautiful" and powerful indeed.[32]

Entrepreneurs are those who generate wealth and bring about new results and profits through their actions, initiative, and resourcefulness. In contemporary parlance, an entrepreneur is either an aggressive competitor or a collaborator in wealth creation and the focal point in the dynamics of economic growth and development, whether as a capitalist or creditor business manager who is always motivated by profit. Whether one sees the entrepreneur as a breakthrough innovator, an early exploiter, or upstart, most intellectuals associate entrepreneurship with people who possess exceptional abilities to seize new opportunities, commitment, and the drive to pursue their goals with an unflinching willingness to bear the inherent risks. For the purpose of this chapter, the basic description of an entrepreneur that will be used to reconstruct the history of entrepreneurship in the Igede area of central Nigeria is essentially as a middleman who shuttles between businesses in an attempt to put to work what has not been tried before, whether social capital or business consciousness, in order to ultimately generate wealth for the good of society.

Geographical and Historical Contexts

Since the nineteenth century, there has been a gradual but consistent growth of small and medium enterprises, and what may fall under the general nomenclature of "microentrepreneurship," in the Igede area of central Nigeria. Igede land comprises both the Oju and the Obi local government areas—created in 1976 and 1986, respectively—in Benue State and has common boundaries with Yalla-Ogoja in the southwest in Cross River State, the Tiv in the west, and the Idoma in the north.

After the first group's arrival from the Oyihu, their legendary place of birth, the second wave of Igede migrations involved the dispersion of the thirteen clans to their present locations, each with its group of villages from the first nucleus settlement in the Igede forest. However, some clans (Ainu) claimed they did not pass through that route to their present locations. One can still find a complex mixture of initial arrivals and later arrivals cohabiting in Igede villages as one group, commonly referred to as *Idakwu* (mixed settlement).

The Igede ethnic group is currently the third largest in Benue State. In the early colonial period the Igede population numbered a little over 150,000,[33] and by the 2006 population census it was about 500,000. The physical environment in which Igede entrepreneurial activity thrived is naturally well endowed with adequate rainfall. However, the Igede people appear to be among the poorest in Nigeria.

Socioeconomic Bases and the Development of Microentrepreneurial Activities in the Igede Area of Benue State, Nigeria

The entrepreneurial history of the Igede people is traceable to several microsocial and mircoeconomic activities. For the most part, these appear to be rather simple but unique in several ways, and they began as part of the microentrepreneurial development in central Nigeria. The best way to understand this developmental process is to critically examine the workings of social groups and associations in the Igede area when people came together, either for the purpose of improving their lives through social networks or economic life, which were the genesis of social entrepreneurship and the overall development of the Igede people. Most of these community associations and activities were characterized by a wide range of common historical and cultural elements, especially language, traditions, and inseparable kinship bonds among the Igede people. Community associations can sometimes be overtaken by ethnic sentiments with negative tendencies; however, for the most part, community associations in the Igede area were geared toward problem solving and played important roles in the developmental process of the area. As elsewhere, Igede community associations were formed to address a broad range of issues outside of state interests, such as religion, community, business, professional concerns, and ethnic group consciousness. Their purpose was to develop the area, such as through the expansion of small farmers' agricultural production, the provision of sociophysical infrastructure, and the development of the nonfarm rural industrial sector. The basic and most important associations that formed the base of microentrepreneurial development in the area over time are discussed here.

Age-Group Alliances and the Growth of Social Entrepreneurs and Community Development

Age groups (*ikpa*) in Igede were basically precolonial organizations comprising individuals who were all born within a certain period of time ranging from one to twenty-four months. Age groups were the hub of most social activities and were very important for personal identity, social recognition, and entrepreneurial engagements. An Igede person who did not know his or her age-mates and failed to be actively involved in age-group engagements was regarded as a social pariah. In fact, even today it is a taboo for any Igede person not to know his or her age-mates. According to retired sergeant major Isaac Ikpa, "Age grade formations among Igede people of Benue State in Nigeria began in 1910."[34] Since that time, about sixteen such groups have been recognized, from the most senior down to the youngest.

Each age group was identified with a specific name derived from a historical event in the Igede area: Alewu-Ogonye (1910), Alewu-Abirikpa (1912), Alewu-Inyumegi (1914), Alewu-Owaya (1916), Alewu-Umoko (1918), Alewu-Oboche (1921), Alewu-Ochinyi (1923), Alewu-Ogoo (1925), Alewu-Ohiri (1927), Alewu-Umoji (1929), Alewu-Ikoti (1931), Alewu-Ideri (1933), Alewu-Igbagiri (1935), Alewu-Inaba (1937), Ibokini (1939), and Alewu-Ikorota (1941). For example, "Alewu-Owaya" refers to those born in Igede when the telegraph wire was introduced in 1916, while "Alewu-Ohiri" refers to the age group of people who were born when the British pound sterling (*ohiri*) was introduced in Igede in 1927. Alewu-Ikoti were those born in Igede when the area courts were introduced in 1931; Alewu-Ideri, when the farthing was introduced in 1933; Alewu-Inaba, when the Igede numbering system was established in 1937; and Alewu-Ikorota, when tarmac roads were heard of or introduced in 1941. It was impossible for individuals to progress from one age group to another; a person was expected to remain a member of his or her age group as long as he or she lived, in order to consolidate the achievements of the group in perpetual competition with other groups. The only exception occurred if an individual quarreled with other members or if he or she was excommunicated. As time went on, the military role of age groups in Igede became less important, while the social importance and, much later, the economic importance continued to increase.

The primary objectives of most age groups were social recreation and other mutually beneficial activities. Throughout Igede history, men's age groups were more like social clubs called *Okum*, and they were devoted to certain social functions such as singing and dancing in bands. Usually a number of age groups came together to form one Okum as a higher level of social organization. Membership was voluntary and progressive from one Okum to another on an annual basis.

The relevance of age groups and their activities to the development of social entrepreneurship in Igede lies in the growth of individual initiative, talent, and social capital, which could be harnessed to achieve other group and individual goals. Without the age-group system, some persons would never have worked hard enough to be known in their immediate communities, and competitive community development programs between different age groups would not have been practiced. Furthermore, age groups helped make people conscious of their social and economic needs, out of which surplus resources were generated for different individuals and over time the genuine spirit of entrepreneurship developed. For instance, to be recognized by fellow age-group members, one was expected to demonstrate good behavior and be able to provide a good meal and calabash of palm wine for members, which required hard work. It was in this way that different individuals generated the initial capital and wealth for personal investments in other ventures.

These groups worked, played, and traveled together as one social group. For instance, to boost their productive capacities and earn money for investment purposes, age groups engaged in rotational group farming, moving from one farm of fellow group members to another until each member's farm was cultivated. Reciprocal, communal age-group work was one of the most strategic forms of labor organization to boost productivity and generate personal wealth. Paul Bohannan sees this production strategy as creating "an atmosphere of revelry and happiness."[35] Women split into work groups at different stages ranging from weeding to harvesting, and they later stored farm produce before it was taken to the markets. In the Igede area, as in the rest of central Nigeria, the reciprocal labor system was the most viable strategy for maximizing productivity to meet export demands for produce during the colonial period. It varied from place to place and existed under different names throughout central Nigerian history. In some places communal work groups were organized within the same age groups, and in others the work was divided between males and females during peak periods of commodity production to meet higher demands for local consumption and export trade. Indeed, collective age-group labor proved more efficient than individuals working alone and resulted in higher productivity and the emergence of female entrepreneurship and economic growth in the Igede area long before the twentieth century.[36]

Similarly, when a member of an age group wanted to marry, his or her group colleagues would facilitate the process in the same manner by coming together to work on a farm to earn money for the dowry. Over time, such monies were not only used for social purposes such as marriages but were also invested in other ventures for wealth creation and profit maximization. This partly spurred the growth of social entrepreneurship among the Igede people of central Nigeria in the nineteenth and twentieth centuries.

Village and Community Alliances for Higher Production and the Growth of Social Entrepreneurship

Besides age-group formations, other social networking that led to wealth generation involved different communities participating in social activities not for monetary gain but rather for the sustainability of society. These included women's dance and singing groups (*imary* and *alihi*) and efforts to clear village playgrounds where sporting activities took place, footpaths to the village and greater community, and streams that supplied drinking water. Over time, this also constituted another important basis for the gradual development of social entrepreneurship among the Igede people.

Another dimension of this was the formation of larger community groups in different Igede villages that worked together in cycles to harvest different agricultural produce, such as palm tree oil and kernel extracts, yams, and rice. Different communities invested their proceeds to train apprentices, pay school fees, or build houses and a number of other things on a rotational basis from one family or another. Without such innovations among families as a strategy for community development, several Igede elites and intellectuals would not have had the opportunity to become what they are today because no single household had the wherewithal or capability to generate enough resources to educate a child in school without the combined efforts of friends, relatives, or the larger community. All these were part of the genesis of social entrepreneurship among the Igede people that later became the entry point for the growth of traditional entrepreneurship in the area. The offspring of these social network members in turn became entrepreneurs in diverse fields, and today they form the majority of the Igede educated elite.

Iron Smelting, Blacksmithing, and the Development of Microentrepreneurs in Igede

Iron smelting and blacksmithing were very important and popular economic activities in Igede precolonial history. With iron technology, agricultural tools and other implements, such as hoes, javelins, and cutlasses, as well as iron currencies, were produced and circulated. Those who had the skills to make iron tools were socially revered and had the advantage of generating money in the form of iron rods (*okpoko*) much earlier than others. Iron smelters produced two types of currencies, both of which were introduced in the nineteenth century: *okobo*, with trifurcated, stubby arms, about 5.08 centimeters long; and *ubeje*, with thinner arms, about 12.70 centimeters long.[37] The earliest form of currency in Igede was known as *ikona*.[38] These currencies significantly facilitated the exchange of goods and growth of small-scale enterprises. For example, apart from the exchange of goods in early local and border trade, the currencies were also useful for marriage purposes and the storage of wealth. At that time, the rich in Igede were those who had thirty or more iron rods and multiple wives and children who could be mobilized for labor for productive activities. The highest producers of yams and owners of livestock were regarded as heroes or very rich. It was from such humble beginnings that enterprising people began to emerge and invest in other small-scale businesses to develop the Igede area.

It is not clear how the Igede people acquired the skill of iron production, but because the technique existed in two centers of iron production in Nigeria, especially in Awka and Nok, which were close to the Igede area, it is reasonable to suggest that the Igede people acquired ironworking techniques from either of these two centers, as suggested by Antony G. Hopkins in his explanation of diffusionist theory.[39] According to Hopkins, the knowledge of ironworking reached West Africa during the first millennium BC, and by 500 BC the technology had reached Nok village in northern Nigeria. It has been widely argued that, through the process of diffusion, the knowledge of iron came to Africa from Asia, and, by extension, the knowledge of ironwork came to the Igede area through trade with eastern and other parts of central Nigeria. However, available evidence regarding the knowledge of iron in some parts of Africa seems to cast doubt on the diffusionist assumption.[40] According to Bassey Andah, iron technology in Africa was an indigenous technological innovation, and diffusionist theory should be dismissed as mere speculation.[41]

Ironworking involved two methods of production. The most popular was to place crude lumps of iron ore in a shallow pit or clay furnace under hot charcoal until they melted and became soft. The iron was then taken out of the fire and hit with a heavy iron hammer into the shape of the desired tool. The embers of the charcoal were fanned to a constant level through a bellows system. Skillful Igede metallurgy workers began to emerge as microentrepreneurs since "the very act of making tools [was] a stimulus to increasing rationality rather than the consequence of a fully matured intellect. In historical terms, man the worker was every bit man the thinker."[42]

The Development of Handicrafts and Microentrepreneurship in Igede

In addition to iron and blacksmithing, it is important to isolate and further examine other traditional Igede handicrafts during the precolonial period due to their revolutionary importance. Such handicrafts included basket and mat making, pottery, food processing, beer brewing, and hand looming. Among other economic activities, these constituted the basis on which microentrepreneurial activities developed among the Igede people of central Nigeria. Men specifically handled ironworking, blacksmithing, basketry, rope making for roofing, mat making, and game hunting for elephants and lions, which led to title holding. On their part, women specialized in pottery, brewing, and clay work. However, there was no rigid classification along gender lines in craftsmanship. As iron production in the Igede area gradually declined due to an inadequate supply of pig iron and negligence, cottage industries and handicrafts began to assume new levels of importance and see wider participation. Thus, both men and women demonstrated great skills in the production of material goods or handicrafts in addition to their efforts in the initiative of boosting food production. The range of goods produced was simple and without any form of specialization in the materials produced. Distribution was also minimal.

Among the Igede of central Nigeria, only women dug clay for pottery from large deposits of clay ponds or quarries. The clay was then powdered and mixed with powdered gravel; molded into the desired shape, such as that of a pot or plate; sun dried for several days; burned by fire; and sometimes perfected in a hearth, at which point it was ready for use or sale. Clay and pottery products were used as household goods, ornaments, and items for decoration and rituals. Pottery technology was widespread throughout central Nigeria, and its development as a craft constitutes a good example of the emergence of small-scale business enterprise in the nineteenth and twentieth centuries. The most significant aspect of this handicraft in Igede is that it provided an avenue for skilled Igede women who risked digging in the underground clay tunnels in order to make money.

Cotton Cloth Weaving

Skilled Igede women were also well known for weaving Igede traditional clothes (*ogodogodo*) by hand. The process of weaving was long and labor intensive, from the harvesting of cotton seed and hanging of the pure cotton wool on wooden handles to the weaving of the cotton material. At this stage expert weavers would turn the prepared cotton cloth into a variety of materials, including long chair clothes, towels, and the long strips used by elders, called *igbagiri*. The same weavers engaged in dyeing (*enyi-ido*) the cloth to a desired color, from which the current Igede national dress, characterized by blue and white, derived its inspiration. The innovations were borrowed from Igede neighbors, domesticated, and dominated by women who gradually emerged as small-scale enterprising individuals. These women, who had no previous training or cash, gradually became better off than their counterparts who joined dance groups as "women of honor" (*alihi*), and they began to empower and improve the social and economic conditions of others.

Brewing

The brewing of beer using traditional methods, called *oburukutu*, requires more than a passing comment because it was one of the earliest ways to invest cash in Igede-area microbusinesses in the nineteenth and twentieth centuries. It is not

clear whether the practice was indigenous to Igede women or borrowed from elsewhere. Like the handicrafts of cloth weaving and clay pottery, the process of
brewing beer was exclusively dominated by women. It depended on the availability of millet and guinea corn, which were seasonally harvested between December and March. The brewing process was complex and long, taking about five days
of Igede's market week. The grain was usually measured out in the desired quantity
and soaked overnight. It was then washed, rinsed, covered with green leaves, and
left for a few days to facilitate germination before being powdered into flour. It
was later soaked and boiled in hot water. The malt was stored overnight in large
basins and pots and sieved the next day. At this stage the malt could be consumed
as a nonalcoholic beverage called *ere ojuegbeju ka* or *apio*. To complete the brewing process to create beer or another alcoholic drink, a smaller quantity of dried
flour and some alcohol that had been preserved for a longer period of time were
added to the apio. Igede women still claim that other ethnic groups in the region
can only process the sweetened type, not the alcoholic beverage, and that they are
the best-known brewers of traditionally made beer in central Nigeria.[43]

Emerging Patterns of Small-Scale Trade as an Example of Microentrepreneurship

In the conventional wisdom of Western economists, trade appears to be understood as the basis of all productive activities. However, the primary goal of farmers during the precolonial period of Igede history was initially survival and not
trade. In fact, prioritizing sales of farm produce before consumption was considered a frivolous or prodigal act during the precolonial era, though I maintain that
it was the basis of Igede moral economy. This is why the advent of colonial rule,
with its introduction of free-market enterprise, was seen as an evil influence on
the Igede moral economy.

Even the man who distinguished himself as a successful farmer was morally
bound not to sell the produce but to give it to less privileged relatives, in-laws, or
whomever was in need of food. However, that was in the very remote past when
the "economy of affection" was wholeheartedly embraced.[44] All that gradually
changed even before the advent of colonial rule, which provided a catalyst that
brought large improvements in different socioeconomic activities and the development of indigenous entrepreneurship in Nigeria. Thus, most of what was
produced by farmers, local craftsmen, and women was exchanged in local markets.
This was when "the Igede had a little contact with the outside world with considerable movement of pots, palm-wine, and firewood along the dry-season Oju-
Otukpo road to the Otukpo market."[45]

The emergence of markets in the Igede area began as a natural process in
response to population growth, increasing community and individual interaction,

and the expansion of subsistence needs and ways to meet them. For instance, when subsistence production fell short of individual village or community demands, the natural response was to make up the difference from other sources, as clearly predetermined by the different ecologies and needs present in the Igede area and that of their immediate neighbors long before the advent of the British colonial rule. This was a common practice throughout the West African. There were instances in which people deliberately met and exchanged goods and services at specific places and times as a matter of necessity and according to the dictates of human ecology. The nature of such trade and the existing markets were not necessarily patterned on the Western style. They had weaknesses and imperfections; however, trade existed and gradually transformed from a site of microentrepreneurial engagements to a site of macrolevel ones. This process was present in three emerging trade patterns in the West African subregion: areas with marketplaces but no market principles, those with marketplaces but peripheral market principles, and those where marketplaces dwindled but market principles were becoming stronger.[46] The needs of different groups in different places encouraged different forms of exchange systems in the Igede area, which naturally led to evening markets (*ihi-obi*) and other methods for the exchange of farm and nonfarm products, carried out at the village playground. In the evening markets, different individuals, especially women and children, brought their goods, mainly farm produce and soup condiments, to be sold to those in need. So significant were the evening markets in Igede economic life that the advent of colonial rule did not disrupt or displace it.

The Igede, Idoma, Tiv, and Iyala areas in central Nigeria all have the five-day market week. The Igede markets were, and still are, Ihiobila, Ihiejwo, Ihiokwu, Ihigile, and Ihio. Their origins are not known; however, they are generally traced to the founders from whom they derived their names. These markets were previously located in places within walking distance. Today, however, each has produced smaller markets throughout Igede land. Markets with the same nomenclature can be held in two or more places on the same day. Igede markets are characterized by periodicity and the rural nature of the open country, which serves as a center for the collection, bulking, and distribution of local food products from local food processing and local craft and industrial products. The rotating operation allows buyers and sellers of farm produce, mainly women, to prepare for the next market on a continuous basis. Long-distance traders from different places such as Otukpo and Ogoja flood these market centers each week. Other trade links between Igede land and outsiders were the Wanakom-Ukele axis through Adum-Owo, and to Ogoja/Iyala through the Oboru-Oho and Itakpa/Igabu routes. Another route went through Uwokwu and Idele to Izzi (Njelele in Igboland) and Utonkon in the southwest. The items sold were generally soap (*ucha buru*), groundnuts, benniseed, iron implements, yams, tobacco, palm oil, and palm kernels. The Igede people bought salt from Iyala in Cross River State (Imanyala) and pig iron from the south. From the existing oral evidence, one can corroborate the gradual development of microentrepreneurship and the growth of markets and border trade, which moved in tandem in Igede land during the nineteenth and twentieth centuries.

Economically Motivated Igede Migrant Laborers in Yoruba Cocoa Farms in Western Nigeria

One outstanding aspect of the life of the Igede people was the massive and economically motivated long-distance immigration to Yoruba cocoa farms in southwestern Nigeria after the World War II period. The contributing social factors were relatively important; however, most economic historians agree that economic reasons are central to human migration for purposes of personal improvement and well-being. These long-distance migrations for economic reasons were very important in the overall development of the Igede people's entrepreneurial history. The Igede area was relatively poor, and long-term migration to Yoruba cocoa farms was one definite way by which to alleviate widespread poverty and generate cash for small-scale businesses. The long-distance movements and permanent relocations to the Yoruba cocoa farms involved almost every family and village over a long period of time.

Informants generally agree that the Agatu people from Idoma land in central Nigeria were the first to introduce Igede migrant laborers to the economic opportunity of working on Yoruba cocoa farms. The 1950s marked the peak of cocoa exports, which acted as a pull from the savannah region in the north to the western region, especially along the Ibadan, Akure, and Agege axis. The Yoruba called most emigrants from Igede who worked as either masters or servants on the cocoa plantations Agatu or Alejo, which were general names for strangers. The Igede masters (*oga*) usually drafted young Igede boys of school age from different Igede villages as servants (*anche*) and engaged them on cocoa farms from morning till evening, seven days a week, for a period of about one year before they were paid in cash. In some cases masters and servants would stay for one or two more years, either to earn enough money for their prospective business when they returned to Igede or to work and have their own tomato, cassava, or pepper farms in order to establish their personal businesses, build houses, or buy lorries before returning to Igede land. The ability of Igede masters to mobilize and organize the labor of young boys as servants on the cocoa farms was unique, enterprising, and perhaps the most successful story in the overall process of microentrepreneurial development in Igede history. The enterprise also required the ability to generate the initial capital for hiring the boys as servants by paying their parents in advance before they traveled to the cocoa farms, with the prospect of generating more cash for future investments by the masters and servants alike.

Berry has articulated in great detail the broader picture of the labor constraints on the cocoa plantations during the colonial period in Nigeria, and how the demands for labor were met from other parts of Nigeria.[47] The most significant point about the responses of Igede migrant laborers to cocoa plantations and export trade is how the activities facilitated the emergence of small-scale enterprises by those who participated in them. Some of the earliest small-scale entrepreneurs in this category who were well known throughout the Igede area include Christopher Ogah from Ohirigwe village; Ode Egbere from Ito and Aboyi Ogbu Oho-Oboru village; Alex Ikpe from Ainu village; and Micah Onmah, Joseph Ageh, and Ogbaniko from Ito. Others were Oddah Ogilegwu from Ohuhu-Owo, one of the first owners of a grinding machine in Onyike-Igede, and Edwin Ola, owner of a sawmill. One of the most successful labor masters from the Ito area was Ode Ochong, who built a petrol filling station at Ito Barracks. Another was Ondah Imeje, whose son acquired a university education in Ogun State in western Nigeria before returning to Igede. Ode Egbere from Ito, who was one of the earliest bread bakery owners, retired and returned from western Nigeria to Igede after several years to begin his microbusiness. Several other successful Igede labor masters later returned to Igede land to establish rice mill businesses, beer parlors, timber and lumber businesses, and motorbike hiring businesses at Onyike Market, the largest business hub in Igede land. An exceptional example was Aboyi Ogbu from Oho-Oboru, who settled permanently in Yoruba land on his own cocoa farm in Ibadan and Ore, as well as owning a fleet of lorries and houses that he rented to Igede tenants who stayed in Yoruba land for longer periods. Many were unable to set up businesses of this magnitude but were able to send their children to school, from which a group of Igede educated elites emerged over time. Even today, most educated elites of Igede extraction trace their rise to these labor migrations to Yoruba cocoa farms.

The most significant point here, which generally applies to the praxis of entrepreneurial tradition that is broadly related to the growth of microentrepreneurship among Igede people, is how these migrations to Yoruba cocoa farms were organized and mobilized using available economic resources. Indeed, most of them relied on the existing social and traditional relationships that enabled them to borrow money as the basic means of generating the initial financial resources to hire the servants needed to work for cash. Such monies attracted interest. Some of the parents of the young laborers were partly paid up front for their children's expected earnings. Another significant practice of the labor masters was to retain their farmland back in Igede while in Yoruba to avoid being alienated from their land during their extended absence. This was considered part of the risk they had to take, just as they did not know whether the loans from social groups and advance payments to parents for young migrant laborers would yield the desired results. This willingness to accept risk is a characteristic of all entrepreneurs.

Conclusion

The central focus in this chapter is on the nature, origin, and development of small-scale businesses in the Igede area of Benue State, central Nigeria, through simple but viable social and economic activities that served as the bases of microentrepreneurial growth during the nineteenth and twentieth centuries. Most of the small-business activities analyzed in the chapter represent the best examples of what may be referred to as the earliest start-up businesses among the Igede people in central Nigeria. One of the contributions of the chapter is its argument that social entrepreneurship is a significant model for the reconstruction of entrepreneurship history in Africa. The most important conclusion here is that the development of entrepreneurship among the Igede did not follow the overbeaten path described by Western intellectuals. Rather, the development of microentrepreneurship among the Igede people generally began on the platform of men's and women's social clubs, age groups, community associations and work groups, very humble craftsmanship, and economically motivated migrant laborers moving from Igede to western Nigerian cocoa farms during the post–World War II period. All these socioeconomic activities under the rubric of Igede moral economy were transformed into what can be regarded as microentrepreneurial activities in foodstuff trade and a wide variety of craftsmanship that metamorphosed into traditional entreprencurship in the Igede area.

Among other things, the chapter is an important reflection on Igede business initiatives that were conducted through a variety of social and economic activities. These included an investment of social capital and networking in indigenous knowledge, arts, and crafts as a deliberate effort to bring about a better society. This chapter argues that the entrepreneurial history of the Igede people is naturally embedded in their "economies of affection," out of which business consciousness, conscious capitalism, an entrepreneurial spirit emerged and developed over time. It would be impossible for anyone studying the history of Igede business enterprises to overlook these humble beginnings. This is why it is fundamental to understand the socioeconomic activities in the Igede area as the basis for the emergence and growth of the microentrepreneurial efforts of its people. The overall development of the Igede area in central Nigeria depended primarily on these social and economic activities over time. Finally, the chapter provides a new platform for future directions of study, from which a more robust intellectual engagement in African entrepreneurial history will emerge, using the Igede example as a springboard.

MIKE ODUGBO ODEY is Professor of Economic History at Benue State University, Nigeria. He is author of *The Development of Cash Crop Economy in Nigeria's Lower Benue Province, 1910–1960* and *Food Crop Production, Hunger, and Rural Poverty in Nigeria's Benue Area, 1920–1995*. He specializes in development issues and entrepreneurial, agricultural, and environmental history.

Notes

1. Roger L. Martin and Sally Osberg, "Social Entrepreneurship: The Case of Definition," *Stanford Social Innovation Review* 5, no. 2 (Spring 2007), https://ssir.org/articles/entry/social_entrepreneurship_the_case_for_definition.
2. William J. Baumol, "Entrepreneurship, Innovation and Growth: The David-Goliath Symbiosis," *Journal of Entrepreneurial Finance and Business Ventures* 7, no. 2 (Fall 2002): 1–10.
3. United Nations Development Programme, "Measuring Development: GNP per Capita versus Human Development" (1997), cited in Charles Keyley Jr. and Eugene R.Wittkopf, *World Politics: Trend and Transformation* (New York: Macmillan, 1999), 129.
4. John Iliffe, *The African Poor: A History* (Cambridge: Cambridge University Press, 1987).
5. Goran Hyden, *Beyond Ujaama in Tanzania: Underdevelopment and the Uncaptured Peasantry* (Los Angeles: University of California Press, 1980), 9.
6. Yvette Monga, "A Historical Perspective on African Entrepreneurship: Lessons from the Duala Experience in Cameroon" (1983), in *African Entrepreneurship: Theory and Practice*, ed. Anita Spring and Barbara E. McDade (Gainesville: University Press of Florida, 1998), 169.
7. James Scott, *The Moral Economy of the Peasant* (New Haven, CT: Yale University Press, 1976), in Michael J. Watts, *Silent Violence: Food, Famine and Peasantry in Northern Nigeria* (Berkeley: University of California Press, 1983), 105.
8. E. P. Thompson, *The Making of the English Working Class* (Harmondsworth, UK: Penguin, 1961), in Michael J. Watts, *Silent Violence: Food, Famine & Peasantry in Northern Nigeria* (Berkeley, University of California Press, 1983), 106.
9. Guran Hyden, *Beyond Ujaama in Tanzania*, 14.
10. Thompson, *English Working Class*.
11. S. T. Kpelai, *Entrepreneurship Development in Nigeria* (Makurdi, Nigeria: Aboki, 2009), 32.
12. Tom Forrest, *The Advance of African Capital: The Growth of Nigerian Private Enterprise* (Charlottesville: University of Virginia Press, 1994).
13. Daryll Forde and Richenda Scott, *The Native Economies of Nigeria* (London: Faber and Faber, 1945).
14. Jan S. Hogendorn, *Nigerian Groundnut Exports: Origins and Early Development* (Zaria, Nigeria: Ahmadu Bello University Press, 1978).
15. Spring and McDade, ed., *African Entrepreneurship*.
16. Sara S. Berry, *Cocoa, Custom and Socio-economic Change in Rural Western Nigeria* (Oxford: Clarendon, 1975), 8.
17. John Tosh, "The Cash Crop Revolution in Tropical Africa: An Agricultural Appraisal," *African Affairs: The Journal of the Royal African Society* 79, no. 314, Jan. 1980, 79–94.

18. Polly Hill, *Studies in Rural Capitalism in West Africa* (Cambridge: Cambridge University Press, 1977).
19. Mike O. Odey, *The Development of Cash Crop Economy in Nigeria's Lower Benue Province, 910–1960* (London: Aboki, 2009).
20. I. L. Bashir, "Some Conceptual Issues in African Entrepreneurship: Myths and Realities," in *Policy Issues in Small-Scale Industrialization in Nigeria*, ed. I. L. Bashir and Ode Ojowu, 11–21 (Jos, Nigeria: University of Jos Press, 1990).
21. B. F. Bawa, "Agricultural Development in the Lowlands" (PhD diss., University of Jos, 995).
22. S. U. Fwatshak, *African Entrepreneurship in Jos, Central Nigeria, 1902–1985* (Durham, NC: Carolina Academic, 2011).
23. Paul T. Zeleza, *A Modern Economic History of Africa*, vol. 1, *The Nineteenth Century* Dakar, Senegal: Codesria, 1993).
24. Forrest, *Advance of African Capital.*
25. Hill, *Studies in Rural Capitalism*, 3.
26. Jean Baptiste Say, *Cathéchisme d'économie politique* (London: Sherwood, 1816).
27. Joseph A. Schumpeter, *Theory of Economic Development* (Cambridge, MA: Harvard University Press, 1934).
28. Joseph A. Schumpeter, *Capitalism, Socialism, and Democracy* (New York: Harper, 975), 82–85.
29. Peter F. Drucker, *Innovation and Entrepreneurship* (New York: Harper Business, 1995).
30. Israel M. Kirzner, *Perception, Opportunity and Profit* (Chicago: University of Chicago Press, 1979).
31. Schumpeter, *Theory of Economic Development*, 118.
32. Ernst F. Schumacher, *Small Is Beautiful* (London: Blond and Briggs, 1973).
33. NAK/SNP/206/1933–1935 (1935), National Archives, Kaduna, Nigeria. Secretary, Northern Province. A. Frampton, "Notes on Igede District of Idoma Division," in Daryll Forde, ed., *Peoples of the Niger-Benue Confluence* (London: Lowe and Brydone, 1970).
34. Isaac Ikpa, quoted in Ogwuna Oboh et al., *Igede Gedegede: Selected Essays on Igede Culture and Language* (Makurdi, Nigeria: Onaivi, 1987), 1/4.
35. Paul Bohannan, *Tiv Economy* (London: Longman, 1968), 72.
36. Mike O. Odey, "Perspectives on the Growth of Small Scale Commodity Trade in Central Nigeria up to the 1970s," in *Proceedings of the Third International Conference on Innovation and Entrepreneurship*, Durban, South Africa, March 19–20, 2015, ed. Deresh Ramjugernath, 126–34 Reading, UK: Academic Conferences and Publishing International, 2015).
37. NAK/SNP/206/1933–1935 (1935), National Archives, Kaduna, Nigeria. Secretary, Northern Province. A. Frampton, "Notes on Igede District of Idoma Division," in Forde, *Peoples of the Niger-Benue Confluence.*
38. Mike O. Odey, "The Political History of Igede People from the Pre-colonial Period to 923" (BA history project, University of Jos, 1980).
39. Antony G. Hopkins, *An Economic History of West Africa* (London: Longman, 1973).
40. Zeleza, *Modern Economic History of Africa*, vol. 1.
41. Bassey Andah, "Iron Age Beginnings in West Africa: Reflections and Suggestions," *West African Journal of Archaeology* 9 (1983): 135–50, quoted in Zeleza, *Modern Economic History of Africa*, 1: 174.
42. Walter Rodney, *How Europe Underdeveloped Africa* (London: Bogle-L. Ouverture, 1976), 10.
43. Grace Ohie Ogah (popular traditional brewer of "*ogbette* beer"), in discussion with the author, Ohirigwe Igede, Nigeria, December 20, 2001.

44. Goran Hyden, *Beyond Ujaama in Tanzania*, 14.
45. Forde, *Peoples of the Niger-Benue Confluence*, 140.
46. Bohannan, *Tiv Economy*, 73.
47. Sara S. Berry, *Cocoa, Custom and Socio-economic Change in Rural Western Nigeria* (Oxford: Clarendon, 1975), 8.

Bibliography

Andah, B. 1983. "Iron Age Beginnings in West Africa: Reflections and Suggestions." *West African Journal of Archaeology* 9:135–50.
Bashir, I. L. 1990. "Some Conceptual Issues in African Entrepreneurship: Myths and Realities." In *Policy Issues in Small-Scale Industrialization in Nigeria*, edited by I. L. Bashir and O. Ojowu, 11–21. Jos, Nigeria: University of Jos Press.
Bashir, I. L., and O. Ojowu, eds. 1990. *Policy Issues in Small-Scale Industrialization in Nigeria*. Jos, Nigeria: University of Jos Press.
Baumol, W. J. 2002. "Entrepreneurship, Innovation and Growth: The David-Goliath Symbiosis." *Journal of Entrepreneurial Finance and Business Ventures* 7, no. 2 (Fall): 1–10.
Bawa, B. F. 1995. "Agricultural Development in the Lowlands." PhD diss., University of Jos.
Berry, S. S. 1975. *Cocoa, Custom and Socio-economic Change in Rural Western Nigeria*. Oxford: Clarendon.
Bohannan, P. 1968. *Tiv Economy*. London: Longman.
Drucker, P. F. 1995. *Innovation and Entrepreneurship*. New York: Harper Business.
Forde, D., ed. 1970. *Peoples of the Niger-Benue Confluence*. London: Lowe and Brydone.
Forde, D., and R. Scott. 1945. *The Native Economies of Nigeria*. London: Faber and Faber.
Forrest, T. 1994. *The Advance of African Capital: The Growth of Nigerian Private Enterprise*. Charlottesville: University of Virginia Press.
Fwatshak, S. U. 2011. *African Entrepreneurship in Jos, Central Nigeria, 1902–1985*. Durham, NC: Carolina Academic.
Hill, P. 1977. *Studies in Rural Capitalism in West Africa*. Cambridge: Cambridge University Press.
Hogendorn, J. S. 1978. *Nigerian Groundnut Exports: Origins and Early Development*. Zaria, Nigeria: Ahmadu Bello University Press.
Hopkins, A. G. 1973. *An Economic History of West Africa*. London: Longman.
Hyden, G. 1980. *Beyond Ujaama in Tanzania: Underdevelopment and the Uncaptured Peasantry*. Los Angeles: University of California Press.
Iliffe, J. 1987. *The African Poor: A History*. Cambridge: Cambridge University Press.
Tosh, J. "The Cash Crop Revolution in Tropical Africa: An Agricultural Appraisal," *African Affairs: The Journal of the Royal African Society* 79, n. 314, Jan. 1980, 79–94.
Kirzner, I. M. 1979. *Perception, Opportunity and Profit*. Chicago: University of Chicago Press.
Kpelai, S. T. 2009. *Entrepreneurship Development in Nigeria*. Makurdi, Nigeria: Aboki.
Martin, R. L., and S. Osberg. 2007. "Social Entrepreneurship: The Case of Definition." *Stanford Social Innovation Review* 5, no. 2 (Spring). https://ssir.org/articles/entry/social_entrepreneurship_the_case_for_definition.
Meillassoux, C., ed. 1971. *The Development of Indigenous Trade and Markets in West Africa*. Oxford: Oxford University Press.

Monga, Y. 1998. "A Historical Perspective on African Entrepreneurship: Lessons from the Duala Experience in Cameroon" (1983). In *African Entrepreneurship: Theory and Practice*, edited by Anita Spring and Barbara E. McDade, 169–80. Gainesville: University Press of Florida.

Polanyi, K. 1957. *The Great Transformation*. Boston: Beacon.

Oboh, O., O. Agocha, I. Ode, J. Adima, and J. Aja. 1987. *Igede Gedegede: Selected Essays on Igede Culture and Language*. Makurdi, Nigeria: Onaivi.

Odey, M. O. 1980. "The Political History of Igede People from the Pre-colonial Period to 1923." BA history project, University of Jos.

———. 2009. *The Development of Cash Crop Economy in Nigeria's Lower Benue Province, 1910–1960*. London: Aboki.

———. 2015. "Perspectives on the Growth of Small Scale Commodity Trade in Central Nigeria up to the 1970s." In *Proceedings of the Third International Conference on Innovation and Entrepreneurship*, Durban, South Africa, March 19–20, edited by Deresh Ramjugernath, 126–34. Reading, UK: Academic Conferences and Publishing International.

Rodney, W. 1976. *How Europe Underdeveloped Africa*. London: Bogle-L. Ouverture.

Say, J. B. 1816. *Cathéchisme d'économie politique*. London: Sherwood.

Schumacher, E. F. 1973. *Small Is Beautiful*. London: Blond and Briggs.

Schumpeter, J. A. 1934. *The Theory of Economic Development*. Cambridge, MA: Harvard University Press.———. 1975. *Capitalism, Socialism, and Democracy*. New York: Harper.

Scott, J. 1976. *The Moral Economy of the Peasant*. (New Haven, CT: Yale University Press).

Spring, A., and B. E. McDade, eds. 1998. *African Entrepreneurship: Theory and Practice*. Gainesville: University Press of Florida.

Thompson, E. P. 1961. *The Making of the English Working Class*. Harmondsworth, UK: Penguin.

Tosh, J. 1980. "The Cash Crop Revolution in Tropical Africa: An Agricultural Appraisal." *African Affairs: The Journal of the Royal African Society* 79, no. 314 (January): 79–94.

Watts, M. J. 1983. *Silent Violence: Food, Famine and Peasantry in Northern Nigeria*. Berkeley: University of California Press.

Zeleza, P. T. 1993. *A Modern Economic History of Africa*. Vol. 1, *The Nineteenth Century*. Dakar, Senegal: Codesria.

13 Ethnicity, Colonial Expediency, and the Development of Retail Business in Colonial Turkana, Northwestern Kenya, 1920–1950

Martin S. Shanguhyia

A COLONIAL ECONOMIC history of Turkana,[1] a semiarid, expansive area in Kenya's northwestern borderlands with Uganda, South Sudan, and Ethiopia, has to take into account the global capitalism that late nineteenth and early twentieth-century British colonialism helped import into eastern Africa. A closer analysis of that history reveals the extent to which colonial capitalism shaped and was in turn shaped by the pastoralist economy—including the precolonial trade to which it was linked—that has been the mainstay of the Turkana livelihood from the time of this community's settlement in the Lake Turkana Basin. The extent to which pastoralist societies and their livestock economies have interacted with capitalism—in its Western connotation—has provided a rich context for examining the actions, reactions, and consequences of their intersection with local states and particularly with the pastoralist communities.[2] This chapter contributes to our understanding of these processes by focusing on Turkana's economic experience under British colonial rule between 1920 and 1950, a period in which colonial expansion into the region placed value on notions about the role of pastoralist resources and related economic externalities—trade in particular—in the colonial project of development in a region characterized by hardship.

Thus, the expansion of British colonial rule in northwestern Kenya during the early decades of the twentieth century encountered a Turkana community whose fortunes and misfortunes were based on a pastoralist economy. The emergence of international colonial borders in this region; the area's geographical remoteness; frequent drought in its semidesert environment; and internecine, interethnic conflict between the Turkana and other African communities across the border with Uganda, Sudan, and Ethiopia rendered the pastoral economy indispensable but shaky, and helped convince colonial authorities of the need to diversify the economic base of the Turkana outside pastoralism. As colonial rule in the area progressed, the economic value of livestock, tobacco, and food grains in local and regional markets persisted, and even appreciated, amid an increase in local demand for new imported merchandise. Such economic potential was deemed a good thing for a community that for many years had appreciated pastoralism only as a means of survival and one that was only coming into contact with "progress" and "modernization" via colonization.

However, the refrain within colonial vision and policy for the area was that the best way for the Turkana pastoralist to reap the full benefits of the expanding economic opportunities occasioned by colonial trade was for him to become, among other things, a business retailer. Among other factors examined in this chapter, an inflow into Turkana of Asian (Indian) and especially Somali businessmen seeking to benefit from the budding colonial markets at the expense of the Turkana was a major reason behind such thinking within the colonial ranks in Turkana and in Nairobi, the headquarters of the Colony and Protectorate of Kenya. The colonial administration's response proved paternalistic as it positioned the colonial state as the "protector" of local pastoralists from what many colonial officials perceived as the commercial exploitative tendencies of itinerant Somali businessmen. Government intervention involved strict administrative measures to close out these "alien" traders as a precondition for cultivating successful indigenous Turkana retail businessmen, and to regulate market prices for stock and other essential commodities.

The history of business enterprise among the Turkana and their colonial relations moves beyond the military and livestock management themes that dominate studies done on the community,[3] yet the history of the development of colonial trade in Turkana cannot be understood outside those themes. As is demonstrated in the chapter, British colonial officials' rationale for intervening in local and regional trade in Turkana was indirectly linked to a protracted military confrontation with the Turkana that was concluded shortly before 1920. Colonial suppression of Turkana armed resistance resulted in considerable loss of livestock in the community, which produced economic uncertainty in the area to the extent that the colonial administration's push for economic "modernization" after about 1920 involved the promotion of trade in foreign merchandise and the diversion of local livestock as a principal commodity in that trade.

Colonial officials also rationalized that the modernization of trade would in turn help popularize a modern cash economy in a community given to the barter system of commodity exchange. In essence, this was a deliberate strategy aimed at strengthening the colonial tax regime based on cash and not livestock payment. Trade, cash, and colonial taxation were in turn connected to colonial biases against pastoralism and a nomadic lifestyle. As Vigdis Broch-Due and Todd Sanders have lucidly put it, colonial policy makers in Kenya held stubbornly to the view that pastoralists were content with livestock wealth, which led them to develop a revulsion toward work and in turn rendered them idle and "unproductive." Colonial officials therefore coerced them into commodifying their labor by using taxation as an instrument to turn them into industrious individuals, a "civilizing" mission that failed to bear fruit.[4] Such views notwithstanding, the push for a cash economy failed to supplant barter trade between the Turkana and some of their neighbors, but both coexisted as modes of economic exchange. This therefore forced the local administration to sanction barter trade as a means to ensure economic and social control of the communities involved in colonial trade.

Overall, an analysis of the development of trade in colonial Turkana reveals the extent to which expansion in imperial territorial possessions was intertwined with a corresponding flow of goods in and out of frontier areas of the British Empire. Turkana was a vast district, one in which the semidesert environment presented transportation and communication challenges. This made it difficult for both the colonizers and the colonized to access food supplies and essential commodities in the far-flung, remote parts of the Kenya Colony. In Turkana District a few carefully sited administrative centers, particularly Lodwar and Lokitaung, were staffed by colonial officers and their African support staff, isolated from the rest of the colony by vast distances, and these required a constant supply of manufactured wares and food supplies.[5] This made it imperative for the colonial state to step in and regulate the flow and value of livestock and merchandise. In doing so it enunciated and implemented policies that unearthed a range of attitudes and notions about fairness, exploitation, ethnicity and race, honesty, material accumulation, and development. The extend to which these aspects shaped the emergence of entrepreneurial activities in this part of Kenya, and Turkana responses to those activities, is a major theme in this chapter.

The British colonial authorities thus used the emerging colonial economics in northwestern Kenya to frame social virtues in interethnic commercial relations, and to draw conclusions about what officials thought determined social, economic, and moral differences between the Turkana and other ethnic groups. According to colonial administrators, the Turkana possessed wealth in livestock—colonial disregard for the importance of pastoralism notwithstanding—but were ignorant of its market value by colonial standards and thereby susceptible to exploitation by Somali businessmen. The latter were portrayed as dishonest "parasites" in their business dealings, a race bent on striking "gold" at the expense of innocent and ignorant Turkana pastoralists. These factors reinforced colonial notions about the Turkana as conservative, traditional, less progressive, averse to modernization, and lacking the economic sophistication required to secure their livestock wealth from foreign (Somali) exploiters. Yet, in reality, the Turkana were not passive as these processes unfolded. Many of them continued to regard livestock as central to their livelihoods and channeled cattle, sheep, and especially goats into the highly-regulated colonial trade regime as a way of coping with the

ncreased mobility of commodities and people. A negligible number emerged as
he leading modern retail traders that the colonial government aimed for. In all
hese changes, the Somali, operating away from their traditional home bases in
northern and northeastern Kenya, became victims of the economic and cultural
imperialism of the Colony and Protectorate of Kenya. This victimization only
ended following the administration's failure, at least by 1950, to create a monopoly of indigenous Turkana retailers to supplant Somali traders.

Early Regional and Local Trade in Turkana, circa 1880s–1930

During the last two decades of the nineteenth century, the Turkana were among
those African pastoralists who played a central role in what Richard Waller and
Neal W. Sobania refer to as "regional networks of exchange."[6] The Turkana were
an important part of the trade networks that linked the Karamoja Plateau, the
Lake Turkana Basin, and Ethiopia. Before the onset of colonial rule in what later
developed into the British East Africa Protectorate (later Colony and Protectorate of Kenya), the Turkana exchanged commodities with traders from the Horn
of Africa, the east coast of Africa, and their neighbors within the Greater Karamoja Region. In the 1880s and 1890s early European adventurers into the common geographical frontiers of Kenya and Ethiopia reported that the Turkana
community and Abyssinians engaged in brisk trade with Asian traders. These
traders acquired slaves, ivory, and livestock from Turkana country and its environs and left behind tobacco, grain, and firearms.[7] Some of these European visitors
established friendly relations with the Turkana in order to acquire basic services
such as food and water in return for the exotic merchandise that they brought
into the area. This contrasts sharply with the frequent episodes of violence perpetrated by Ethiopian and Arab-Swahili ivory hunters and slave dealers who
ventured into the Lake Turkana Basin.[8]

The Turkana exchanged livestock for grain, spears, and ostrich feathers with
the several Nilotic communities living to the west on the Karamoja Plateau that
became part of the Uganda Protectorate. Alliances and intermittent warfare in
the Karamoja communities during the nineteenth century led to a high demand
in iron-bladed spears among the Turkana, creating a lucrative trade in this item.
Some of the communities, the Jie in particular, cashed in on the Turkana demand
for agricultural products to export sorghum, given that the arid environment
made it difficult for many members of the latter community to cultivate their
land.[9] Thus, aside from demands created by regional warfare, ecological changes
caused by dramatic shifts in seasonal climatic patterns also dictated the degree
to which commodities were exchanged between the highland and plateau dwellers (Karamoja communities) and the lowland dwellers of the Lake Turkana Basin, mainly the Turkana pastoralists. This exchange became pronounced in times

of natural disasters such as drought, when Turkana pastoralists preferred to trade livestock for food items, particularly grain, from their agro-pastoralist neighbors on the Karamoja Plateau.[10] Similarly, to the northeast and north of Lake Turkana, trade with agricultural communities from the Sudan and Ethiopia was important beyond the intermittent interethnic conflicts and social interaction. Particularly important was trade with the Dassanech (Merille) of Ethiopia, which ensured the exchange of calabashes and iron for millet.[11] They also exchanged livestock, fish, and tobacco among themselves and with communities such as the Pokot (Suk), Samburu, and Marakwet, who, like the Turkana, were constituted into the Kenya Colony.[12]

Before the advance of colonialism into Turkanaland, firearms and tobacco were the most sought-after commodities in Turkana. Tobacco was consumed to help overcome feelings of hunger, likely the result of prolonged food scarcity, especially during drought seasons. Compared to spears, guns were essential not only for defense against Abyssinian slave raiders and other enemies but also for raiding fellow Karamoja pastoralists to replenish family herds. Consequently, some scholars have perceived guns and tobacco as critical to the sustenance of Turkana livelihoods.[13] The colonial administration later initiated serious disarmament measures to end violent cattle-raiding activities. However, tobacco remained an essential commodity sold in Turkana for most of the colonial period, followed by millet.

The intrusion of colonialism in this region altered the terms and flow of pre-existing trade but did not completely undermine its value to the communities involved in it, including the Turkana. British colonial incursion into Turkana started about 1903 and was forceful and gradual. Colonial troops pushed in from the already-pacified areas of Kenya to the south of Turkana, from the adjoining Pokot and Baringo Districts in the north-central part of the Great Rift Valley. The fact that access to resources determined the initial British push into Turkana cannot be underestimated. Given that much of Kenya, Uganda, and Sudan were under some British colonial control at least by 1910, lawlessness resulting from persistent ivory poachers in the Turkana-Ethiopia frontier areas threatened the emerging colonial administrations in the region. Furthermore, a rinderpest epidemic shortly before 1910 set the Turkana's traditional livestock-raiding missions to replenish their herds in a southerly direction into the British-controlled Pokot and Baringo areas (southern Turkana borderlands). This elicited a punitive colonial response against the raiders that led to the eventual British decision to conquer the Turkana. Equally important to this decision was the threat that Ethiopia's expansion into the area posed to Britain's imperial mission in eastern Africa for control of the Lake Turkana region.[14] Early British colonial administrators in Kenya and Uganda considered the Ethiopian southern frontiers bordering Turkana to be volatile and therefore a security threat to the pacified areas of the two colonies. The conquest of Turkana, they hoped, would end Ethiopia's southern expansion while improving law and order on the frontiers. Colonial pacification of Turkana led to considerable loss of the local pastoralists' livestock. Between 1905 and 1918, when the community was subdued, almost 150,000 livestock were confiscated as punishment for Turkana belligerence.[15] The resource base that sustained Turkana subsistence and trade was thus severely compromised. At the same time, the new district colonial administration soon realized the area's vulnerability regarding access to food supplies by local European administrators and their African support staff. The need for Turkana pastoralists to supply meat to government employees in the district became imperative, while some of the livestock acquired by the local administration was exported to European-settled areas and towns in Kenya. For instance, in 1927 and 1928 a total of about 4,025 livestock was bought by the government and exported to other parts of the Kenya Colony.[16] This marked the beginning of the integration of Turkana into the larger colonial economy regulated by a modern, alien state.

This regulation was gradually extended to the general trade involving other commodities that entered Turkana. Consequently, in the early years of colonial rule, the government began devising ways to make the demand and supply of livestock sustainable for the colonial economy. Commercial activities, especially the buying and selling of livestock, proceeded under the oversight of the colonial administration. Local officials considered this mission as a necessary benevolent service for a pastoralist community that they considered extremely conservative, as R. Greene, the assistant district commissioner of Turkana, made clear in 1926: "They [Turkana] are very conservative people and do not want to change their customs. It is therefore difficult for them to see how any good can come of our administration which they naturally resent."[17] This comment referred to the challenges the administration faced in its efforts to channel Turkana livestock into a rigidly controlled colonial economy.

As far as economic business was concerned, preexisting local and regional trade was encouraged, but plans had been put in place to encourage the use of cash in buying and selling and to regulate the market value of livestock and other trade commodities. The rationale for this was the official feeling that traders coming into Turkana exploited the existing traditional barter system to defraud the Turkana of the true market value of their livestock, such value being determined in terms of cash. Indeed, in 1926, while reflecting on the state of trade in the district, the district commissioner (DC) observed, "Chief articles of trade are tobacco, beads, axes, and cowries which are exchanged for sheep and goats. The prices paid are very poor."[18] Internal trade flowing into the district, particularly from the south through Baringo and Pokot, proved lucrative to a considerable number of Turkana who exchanged goats for tobacco, maize meal, knives, and copper wire. American khaki was also imported and purchased by those who could afford it.

Although the Turkana seemed to "thrive fairly well" in this trade, they also became suspicious of the monetary value assigned to their livestock. Local government officials blamed them for purchasing tobacco from itinerant traders at "ridiculous" prices—usually in the form of livestock—rather than buying the product directly from the growers at reasonably cheaper rates.[19] Government attention shifted toward controlling the entry into Turkana of these itinerant or "alien" traders, many of them Somali. At the same time, the Turkana were encouraged to take the position of these outside traders, buy merchandise in bulk, and sell it to the members of their own community, thus ending their reliance on Somali traders. The idea was that a Turkana trader was unlikely to exploit his fellow "tribesman." This proved wishful thinking as the few Turkana retailers who emerged in the 1940s sometimes hiked the price of some commodities with a view to making a profit from the booming trade.

The Colonial Crackdown on Itinerant Somali Traders

By the time of the British arrival in mainland East Africa, the Somali dominantly inhabited—as they still do—northeastern Kenya and some of its northern parts. Like the Turkana, they inhabited a semiarid environment that marked their Northern Frontier District, and pastoralism was their mainstay economic activity. However, unlike the Turkana, the Somali were ardent long-distance traders who, as Peter T. Dalleo reveals, were actively involved in every aspect of regional trade as producers, consumers, merchants, financiers, and caravan leaders.[20] They dealt mainly in game trophies, particularly ivory, rhino horn, and ostrich feathers, as well as slaves, livestock, and livestock products. They supplied these to many parts of northern and northeastern Kenya, Somalia, and the East African Indian Ocean coastal locations. They were also important agents in the distribution of imported manufactures into the interior of Kenya, especially cotton cloth, copper wire, spices, tea, and firearms.[21]

Following the establishment of effective colonial control over the Somali of Kenya shortly after World War I, the British administration institutionalized new measures that curtailed Somali trade activities. The most important of these measures involved strict game laws and livestock activities to prevent ivory and rhino poaching, and the requirement that all trade in the colony be conducted in permanent *dukas* (shops) in certain town centers. These policies undercut Somali long-distance trading activities and traditional modes of sustenance, and prompted their opposition to the colonial administration.[22] As is revealed later in this chapter, most of these measures, especially the policies on shops, were also implemented in Turkana to control Somali and other alien traders in the district.

It is likely that Somali traders were already present in Turkanaland during the last two decades of the nineteenth century—which preceded colonial rule in the region—when many long-distance traders and adventurers entered the area in the 1880s and 1890s. This is further confirmed by the fact that those traders were already involved in regional trade networks and dealt in principal trade items such as ivory and firearms, the two commodities that were part of the commercial enterprise in precolonial Turkana. The expansion of British colonial rule into Turkana aided the movement of Somali into the district. Some came as members of the King's African Rifles, which suppressed Turkana resistance in the years between 1910 and 1918. Many others entered the district as colonial aides in transport work, given that early colonial officers considered the Somali very skilled as camel cyces and donkey "boys."[23] Many of these Somali colonial employees opted to stay in Turkana after their demobilization or retirement from government employment and put their hand to retail businesses. Other Somali were attracted to Turkana by the economic opportunities the district offered when the area was opened up by the colonial administration. It was the commercial activities of these individuals that the administration sought to curtail on the rationale that they exploited the local Turkana people in the emerging colonial trade.

Somali keen on trade initially entered Turkana from the south, where much of the internal trade flowed into the district from the more productive regions of western Kenya. By the mid-1920s shops owned by these traders began to appear at centers such as Kolosia and Lokichar. In 1926 Somali traders owned ten of twenty shops operated by alien traders in Kolosia, while by 1928 six shops in Lokichar were under Somali management. Arab, Asian (Indian), and Sudanese traders owned a few of the shops at these centers.[24] The main imports sold at these outlets were maize meal, tobacco, *amerikani* cloth, knives, beads, and wire, and these were sold in exchange for Turkana livestock.

Government intervention in trade commenced during 1928 and was occasioned by an influx of itinerant stock traders in the wake of a decline in Turkana livestock due to famine. The administration was determined "to secure for the natives a fair deal when selling their stock."[25] Somali traders were suspected of exporting from the district livestock acquired cheaply or illegally from the Turkana. In the administration's view, this practice concealed the actual volume of trade in livestock, particularly the highly prized smaller stock—sheep, goats, and donkeys. By the government's estimation, the export figures for these small livestock gave a completely inaccurate idea of the actual amount of trade.[26] As long as the volume of trade increased, more Somali became involved, thereby raising fears within the district administration that these traders were taking over business in Turkana. In 1929 the DC for North Turkana raised an alarm on the dangers of increased Somali entry into Turkana: "The Somali traders have increased by well over 100% and this number answers present requirements, although there is a constant demand for further entrance into the district. . . . It is most undesirable that a Somali immigration should turn Northern Turkana into a Somali Reserve . . . this trend of affairs should carefully be watched."[27] These incoming traders devised ways of purchasing female stock with the aim of breeding herds in their designated residential areas within Turkana. District officials perceived this development as posing a "very real danger" to the Turkana's position in local trade, and it led to the official conviction that, unless the Somali traders' practice of breeding stock was prevented, this group was likely to establish a commercial "Somali Colony" for the purpose of exploiting local pastoralists.[28]

Prospective Somali traders were now required to obtain licenses before entry into Turkana. Many did not receive the license due to the strict requirements imposed by the administration before it granted the permit to trade. Second, beginning in 1930 those who obtained licenses after a grueling vetting process were banned from buying female stock to prevent them from becoming stock farmers in Turkana. Despite this second measure, the purchase of female stock continued surreptitiously. Government inspections of Somali shops in trading centers in the southern, central, and northern parts of the district revealed an accumulation of "vast herds of stock of both sexes." Further inspection showed little or no merchandise of value in the shops, a confirmation of fraudulence in the livestock trade. This led to an administrative decision to further restrict many Somali traders attempting to enter Turkana by denying them licenses. The few who were able to obtain licenses were expected to carry out their trade activities at shops strategically located at government administrative centers for the purpose of closer surveillance.[29] Somali traders were also required to use cash when purchasing goats and sheep from the Turkana.[30] The push for a cash transaction fit the government's desire to consolidate its tax base in Turkana by requiring that colonial taxes be paid in shillings. The Somali livestock "fraudsters" offered such competition to government livestock rations that the introduction of sales for cash ensured that the losses suffered by the government could be recouped through a secure tax base.

Inspection of Somali shops in the major trading centers in Lodwar, Kaptir, Lokitaung, Lorgum, and Kakuma was carried out during 1933 to ensure that no stock was kept there or sold illegally. Many such shops were closed as traders resisted the policy requiring them to stop selling stock around the shops. Only two shops belonging to Somali traders remained in operation in southern Turkana during 1933. On the northern frontiers of Ethiopia, a few Somali were allowed to run shops. As a result, seven Somali *dukas* were active in Lokitaung, and one in Todenyang at the Omo delta on the Ethiopian border. Todenyang was a busy border town that was characterized by frequent tensions and conflicts between the Turkana and the Dassanech over fish, land, and trade in grain. However, n times of peace the center also teemed with business in millet and livestock. A Somali shop was allowed there "as an experiment" to serve the mainly Abyssinian soldiers that policed the opposite side of the international border.[31] This commercial arrangement at the border center served the political and security needs of the British colonial administration, given the volatile interethnic relations in his border region.

In the meantime, a crackdown on Somali stock trade ensured that the government became the major buyer of goats in fairly large numbers, mainly to provision civil and military staff in the far-flung administrative centers of Turkana. For instance, in 1935 the government purchased a record 19,959 goats from the Turkana to be used for food rations for government employees. In the same year 10,088 sheep and goats were exported from Turkana, three times the number exported in the previous year. There is less evidence that the Somali traders contributed significantly to this export, given the restrictions imposed on them. The Turkana may have sold this stock directly to the government. Many Somali traders were relegated to importing camels into Turkana from the Northern Frontier District, a venture that did not fare well since the Turkana resisted buying these camels because the "alien beasts would bring disaster to the land."[32]

Thus, the government crackdown left few and often unviable economic opportunities for Somali traders operating in Turkana. Only very few were allowed to do business, under stringent conditions and with permission from Nairobi through the provincial commissioner's office. In fact, at the height of the government crackdown on these traders shortly before the war, sixteen of them were running shops across Turkana in 1935.[33] The colonial strategy was to limit their numbers in the district as much as possible so as to ensure "accountability" and "fairness" in trade in ways that would benefit the Turkana. As trade appreciated after the Depression and the famine years between 1930 and 1933, those who had exited the district due to financial instability demanded to return, hoping to "share the profits of prosperity with their rivals who weathered the storm."[34] Such demands only served to stiffen regulations regarding entry into Turkana by potential alien traders. Most were now required to pay credit (collateral) to the government in the form of either cash or a specific number of goats before obtaining a permit to enter the district to conduct trade. This measure was implemented after the government realized that a Somali trader always went "ahead of Government Safaris" and purchased large quantities of livestock, thereby making it difficult for the administration to acquire sufficient stock for government use and export.[35]

As the government's demand for livestock increased, the administration was forced to turn to licensed Somali middlemen to meet this demand. This came at a time of government demand for a high quality standard of goats sold at all markets. In a rational response, these middlemen raised the prices of their goats so as to make a profit. They realized that selling at official government rates would lead to a loss. For this they were deprecated as exploiters and forced to either sell at government-controlled prices or lose their licenses. The middlemen made up for the losses by directing some of their stock to the more established regional markets outside Turkana, particularly to Kenya's top beef markets in Kitale, Nakuru, and Nairobi, where they earned huge profits.[36]

A further measure taken by the district administration involved the keeping of a profile of all Somali already living, working, or trading in Turkana. A register was kept of these Somali that showed "all necessary particulars." They were also prohibited from acquiring helpers from among the Turkana since such helpers were thought to facilitate the devious Somali business activities that the state was seeking to eradicate. A measure was put in place to ensure that any helpers for Somali traders were Somali, not Turkana, in origin and from outside the district. These helpers were also required to acquire entry permits from the government. Even after entering the district, restrictions were imposed to prevent them from branching off into local trade. In his district handing-over report at the end of 1937, R. D. F. Rayland elaborated on these measures: "Each Somali trader is allowed a helper of his own race and care should be taken to see that such helpers do not branch out on their own before they have earned the right to do so by several years' service. Any attempting to do so may profitably be expelled for breach of conditions of their permit. . . . I have always dealt in all Somali matters myself as they require strict personal scrutiny."[37] Furthermore, Somali traders already living in the district were allowed to stock no more than ten goats for their milk requirements. Kept away from the lucrative trade in cattle, goats, and sheep, many of them turned to trade in alternative livestock, especially mules and ponies that they acquired from Ethiopian refugees fleeing the Italian occupation of their country. Even then, the government preferred that they dispose of these livestock outside Turkana to prevent them from selling the stock to the local community at exorbitant prices.[38]

The outbreak of World War II provided the administration with a convenient pretext to expel Somali traders from the district. Tensions and insecurity in the northern borderlands caused by the Italian conquest of Ethiopia provided the government with a justification to close down Somali shops and order their owners to leave the district. "It was thought necessary," the DC explained, "for their own safety as for the safety of others, that these people should leave the district."[39] Many of the departing traders lost an estimated three thousand livestock to the Turkana through looting. The few Asian traders based in Lodwar also left due to insecurity from the Italian bombardment of the town in 1940. These enforced departures failed to stop trade in Turkana; however, they led to a glut in goods at market centers, particularly livestock, that the Somali middlemen had previously dispensed to buyers. District officials therefore decided to seek individuals to facilitate trade, and they turned to the Turkana to play that role. It was only after the war that the government hesitantly considered readmitting prospective Somali traders into Turkana, and only after a concerted effort to create an enterprising group of Turkana retailers in an attempt to permanently replace the Somali had met with minimal success.

Creating Turkana Business Retailers

From the late 1920s through the 1940s the colonial government pursued a variety of ways to have the Turkana play an active role in colonial trade, all which were aimed at undermining the Somali position in business within Turkana. Approaches that were pursued included but were not limited to encouraging the Turkana to establish shops in leading market centers, enabling them to participate in trade as middlemen, transitioning them to a cash economy, and cultivating a culture of mass consumption of imported manufactures. In 1928 the administration began to urge the Turkana to set up their own shops alongside those owned by Somali and Asian traders. This strategy was aimed at breaking the Somali monopoly in buying and selling, as well as helping spread the prices and profits for many of the principal commodities to make them affordable.[40]

The Turkana were also urged to adopt the use of cash in buying and selling to ensure the economic value of their livestock, instead of relying on the barter system that the Somali traders used to undervalue goats. The government's belief that cash would reflect the near-market value of Turkana stock was clear: "Shillings are regarded with distrust and the average Muturkaneit [Turkana] appears to prefer to barter a goat for a piece of cloth worth shs. 1/50, rather than sell the goat for shs. 5/-, and pocket the balance."[41] Consequently, policies were launched to popularize the use of cash by the Turkana. For instance, following the rule that forced Somali traders to purchase livestock from the Turkana for cash, beginning in 1930 the latter were now required to pay their hut taxes in shillings.[42] The new cash policy seemed to help in the circulation of money and goods, particularly livestock, as confirmed by the fact that by 1935 75 percent of Turkana taxpayers in the southern portions of the district were reported to be paying their taxes in cash following a lucrative market for their goats.[43] However, it must be emphasized that the adoption of a cash economy proceeded slowly in the following years. Barter trade remained popular because it tended to guarantee the value of traditionally premier commodities, especially livestock and tobacco. Thus, although the use of cash in economic transactions was encouraged and even sometimes enforced, it failed to supplant barter trade for years to come. The same applied to the idea of paying taxes in cash, as was revealed in a 1951 official report: "The privilege of taxpaying is still enough of a novelty for the Turkana to be delighted to show off his ability to meet his dues."[44]

As effective administration spread to the northern areas of the district bordering Ethiopia and Sudan in the 1930s, trade in those areas increased as well. The Turkana living in those borderlands bartered goats and cattle for millet with the Dassanech of Ethiopia.[45] The western parts of the district also benefited from external trade with communities in the eastern parts of the Uganda Protectorate, particularly the Bagisu, who exchanged grain for Turkana livestock. During these years the variety of items flowing into Turkana increased as well. Aside from traditional items, Western manufactures started to appear in large volume, particularly cotton products such as blankets and cloth. However, their low demand among the Turkana raised concerns from the administration; the DC lamented, "Their wants are few and one seldom sees them wearing clothing of European manufacture. The trade blanket which plays such a part in petty trade elsewhere is seldom to be met with. Cotton goods are more suited to the climate, but meet with little sale."[46]

Only those Turkana living near government stations—and they were few—had a tendency to buy *amerikani*. Most preferred traditional trade items, such as spears from the Jie, gourds from the Teuso, and tobacco from the Dodoth in Uganda, because of their affordability and suitability to local subsistence needs. This slow response of local consumers to Western products reinforced colonial notions that the Turkana were so steeped in their pastoral lives that they were averse to progress, the latter being measured by the ability to cultivate a taste for Western goods introduced through modern trade. The fact that they were less sophisticated in their consumption patterns was made clear by the DC's 1933 remark that "the needs of the Turkana are at present few and simple—spears, gourds, beads, and tobacco constitute their main requirements."[47] Campaigns were therefore launched to have the Turkana buy and use the new manufactures and also sell them as a way of dislodging the Somali in merchandise trade.

The four years leading up to the outbreak of World War II witnessed an unprecedented increase in trade in Turkana District. This was especially true regarding business in millet, tobacco, and spears, which were items that flowed in from neighboring colonial territories and from Turkana's neighboring districts within Kenya. Large numbers of government and privately contracted lorries (trucks) loaded with manufactured goods also entered the district from Kitale, a town in the north-central Rift Valley that owed its origins to European settler agriculture based on maize cultivation. By 1939 maize meal rivaled millet as the major food item, with a high demand in Turkana. This demand was aided by drought and food shortages that forced the Turkana to barter their hides and skins—usually used for clothing and shelter—for maize meal.

The outbreak of the war brought a large number of British imperial troops into Kenya's northern borderlands to help fend off Italian threats in neighboring Ethiopia. Many of the troops were stationed in Turkana at Lodwar and Lokitaung, and they created a high demand for food supplies that was met by the provision of Turkana livestock for meat. Following the forced departure from the district of many Somali traders with the coming of the war, there was surplus livestock that the government stepped in to purchase at prices "better than what the Somalis gave."[48] Unfortunately, as far as the administration was concerned, the Turkana failed to take advantage of the war's economic opportunities to stake their claim to local and regional trade, and they were perceived as deferring the commercial proceedings to the few Somali traders who were allowed to remain in the district.

A few Turkana took the initiative of obtaining tobacco directly from Marakwet, an area that was the chief source of that commodity. However, Somali traders still found ways to dominate the acquisition of tobacco, which they in turn used as currency to pay for Turkana livestock in extremely small quantities, thereby making enormous profits. The reigning official perception was that the Turkana as sellers (of livestock) and buyers (of subsistence commodities such as millet and tobacco) were exploited at both ends of commercial relations. This status quo convinced district officials that the remedy for the existing imbalance in trade was in the hands of the Turkana people. It was up to them, not the Somali traders, to ensure that they reaped a fair profit from the tobacco-livestock trade. "The only way to achieve this," the DC concluded, "is by the Turkana trading their stock themselves without the assistance of [Somali] middlemen."[49] The number of Turkana middlemen involved in trade was decried as lamentably low. The ultimate government solution to this problem was thus to get the Turkana to play a direct role in buying and selling.

The war conditions that led to the departure of many Somali traders and the closing of their shops provided the government with an opportunity to support a group of potential Turkana retailers to complement the services of the few alien traders in the district. As noted earlier, the idea of encouraging the Turkana to establish individual shops had emerged before the war. It had failed to take off partly due to the aggressive competition posed by Somali traders. As economic fortunes in Turkana added value to livestock and other commodities during the war, and as trade led to an increase in the volume and range of goods flowing into Turkana, the ordinary Turkana pastoralist ceased to be just an observer, contrary to the picture painted by official perceptions. Evidence of his involvement is revealed by the large amount of cash in circulation, resulting from the increased buying and selling during the war. The Turkana provided a market for merchandise, which they purchased using cash earned from their labor and livestock as part of the war-effort program for the colonial state. During the war the Turkana made a fortune by offering their labor and livestock as part of the war effort, but the cash they earned was deemed to be of little value due to the small number of shops in which the money could be spent. In order to get them to spend money, the government raised taxes, with the hope that this increase would cause a spike in the selling and buying of livestock and manufactures in order to generate further cash flows.[50]

Aside from these measures, the more official government strategy of incorporating the Turkana into colonial trade focused on encouraging them to establish retail businesses in certain market centers from which many Somali businessmen had been forced to leave. Many within the administration were still convinced that this approach would be effective at undermining Somali dominance in trade and allow the local community to gain control of the economic proceedings. Active involvement by a few Turkana in some form of retail business appears to have picked up during the war, particularly in 1942. The war may have receded from Turkana's frontiers by that year, but the economic boom it had generated became the basis on which local participation in retail trade was pushed by the administration. Of the thirteen shops registered in the district for that year, ten were operated by Turkana traders, and these were stocked with soap, matchboxes, and tobacco that were acquired in exchange for livestock, although a considerable amount of cash was also used in purchasing these commodities.[51] The two notable Turkana traders who emerged during this time were Barowa Akhono and Kaka, with the latter registering fair success in retail trade during the 1940s.

Akhono's initial rise resulted from being the son of a colonial chief, but he emerged as a trader in the prewar years. He may have been one of the few indigenous business entrepreneurs in colonial trade who did not have to cope with intense Somali competition. He began to experience a measure of success in the early years of his trading career following the government crackdown and expulsion of Somali traders from the district. Due to this success, his fellow Turkana were constantly urged "to follow his example."[52] By the mid-1940s Akono had become one of the most established retailers in Lodwar and Lokitaung, although he began to encounter competition from a few Somali and Asian traders who were allowed to open shops at these centers. He appears to have weathered this competition at a time when other Turkana traders could not and were reported to be retiring to their *manyattas* (villages).[53]

Officials attributed the failure of these traders to the Turkana's natural disposition as "ignorant" and "honest," which unscrupulous alien traders took advantage of to exploit them, as was plainly stated by the local DC: "The comparative honesty of the Turkana coupled with their complete ignorance of the mysteries of buying and selling makes them easy meat in the commercial world."[54] Although the government considered Akhono to be experienced in matters of trade and needing much support from the administration, he was still viewed as a typical Turkana whose honesty rendered him vulnerable to Somali businessmen. Indeed, he was criticized for being a stooge of Somali traders who "buy him turbans and pat him on the back" in an effort to defraud him.[55] Although in 1948 ıe still owned shops in Lodwar and Lokitaung, Akhono fizzled out of business ɔefore the end of that decade. However, given his commercial experience, after ı950 he was sought out by the district administration to maintain a supplies shop ın Todenyang to serve hundreds of poor Turkana who lived on the nearby banks ɔf Lake Turkana.

In 1942 Kaka appeared as a distinct trader in Turkana during the Allied cam-ɔaign against the Italians in Ethiopia. The government hired him as a transporter ınd supplier of commodities for British troops, after which he established shops ın Lodwar and market centers in Namaroputh (at the Omo delta) and Lokitaung, ɔn the Kenya-Ethiopia border. These two centers thrived on cross-border barter :rade in livestock and millet, to the extent that Lokitaung was given the nickname "Mecca of Barterers" by local colonial observers.[56] Kaka started his retail busi-ness in Lodwar, where the district administration helped him secure a shop that ıad been abandoned by an Asian trader at the outbreak of the war. However, he concentrated his commercial efforts farther north on the Ethiopian borderlands, where he monopolized the lucrative trade in millet that was brought across the ɔorder from the Dassanech community in Ethiopia. He was responsible for dis-tributing this grain to other parts of Turkana, including Lodwar. He also emerged as the leading retail dealer for imported manufactures that he redistributed across Turkana.[57] Those Turkana with livestock to dispense of and with cash to be spent flocked to Kaka's shop to purchase manufactured goods. Kaka's role in the sup-ply of goods was a principal reason why public consumption of merchandise was ɔn an upward trend in the late 1940s.[58]

By 1947 Kaka had become one of the "big three" traders in Lodwar, from which he sent most of his millet for resale to the central and western areas of Turkana. Since supply of this grain was essential for the food needs of the Tur-kana in both famine and good years, the government sought ways to have Kaka monopolize the trade in this item in its source areas, especially in Namoruputh. This led to a further crackdown on Somali and Asian traders who hoped to open shops in the borderlands with Ethiopia, where most of the millet came from. Kaka's main competitor in the grain trade was U. G. Patel, the Asian trader who ıad lost his shop to Kaka in Lodwar but was eventually permitted to open an-other shop in Lokitaung. However, as part of the government strategy to have Kaka monopolize the millet trade in this region, Patel was denied a license to ɔpen another *duka* next to Kaka's in Namoruputh, the main center of trade in millet from Ethiopia.[59]

Thus, the idea of commercial monopoly was directly imposed to help Kaka fend off serious competition from alien traders. This case reinforces further how the government deliberately set Somali traders against Asian shop owners. These traders were accused of hoarding essential commodities and thereby depriving Kaka's shop of essential merchandise, and of deliberately raising the price of essential commodities. The consensus within the administration was that in order to drive prices down in Lokitaung, there was a need to promote competition in business there along the lines of "nationality and religion." A price control enforcement unit was also sent into Lokitaung to monitor the prices these traders charged for commodities.[60] Price control in both the barter and cash trade had been instituted a few years earlier as a deterrent for Somali exploitative tendencies, but it increasingly became a convenient tool in the colonial government's efforts to regulate alien traders and cultivate the existence of Turkana traders.

The success registered in the retail trade in Turkana by Kaka, and partly by Akhono, was not replicated by many Turkana, at least by 1950. While many of them joined colonial trade due to state tax demands and by the dynamics of demand and supply, they played an active role in provisioning livestock, clearly the largest item in colonial trade in the district. In this way Turkana pastoralism was a vital component in the exchange and flow of commodities in a modern, highly regulated colonial economy served by local and regional trade. This was the case in spite of British colonial officials' degrading perception of Turkana pastoralism and the lifestyle this mode of production supported.

Commercial business as fostered through the shop system that developed in concert with colonial trade was not tailored to the economic needs of the Turkana. The shop system was encouraged by the colonial government mainly as a means to ensure economic and social control of "undesirables" entering or living in the district, primarily the Somali. Therefore, colonial efforts to establish the Turkana in retail businesses failed to produce the degree of participation from the Turkana that the government desired. This failure was partly due to the fact that retail businesses focused on manufactured merchandise, which required the help of modern transportation services that were rare in Turkana. Unlike the Turkana, the Somali had mastered the use of camels and donkeys in long-distance trade and tapped into this experience to operate retail trade in Turkana before the colonial crackdown on their business entrepreneurship in the district. As emphasized earlier, pioneer colonial officials in Turkana recognized this skill among the Somali and relied on them as camel and donkey cyces to meet the colonial administration's transportation needs in the expansive Turkana semi-desert environment. Itinerant and established Somali traders used this draft service and experience to their advantage as they sought to profit from the lucrative trade that developed in Turkana.

Limited by transportation challenges resulting from Turkana's unforgiving physical landscape, aspiring Turkana retailers found it difficult to buy, move, and stock merchandise in their shops. Only a few, such as Kaka, had access to truck services, which explains these individuals' comparative success in retail business. Even then it took days, even months, for merchandise to reach shops in the far-flung market centers of Lokitaung and Namoruputh. In their criticism of the Turkana as a community that showed no interest in the benefits of modern trade, colonial officials overlooked these technical and physical challenges and instead decried the absence of essential commodities in these shops. In 1945, following his inspection of shops in the aforementioned two market centers, the district officer at Lokitaung observed, "Kaka's Lokitaung *duka wallah* [shop assistant] is quite useless and due to his slackness the *duka* at Namoruputh has been continually out of sugar, soap, and tobacco."[61] The problem was more about the movement of goods between the two market centers than the laxity of the *duka wallah*. More often than not, the selling and buying of livestock and grain proceeded outside shops in large quantities. Shops were only frequented by a few, mainly those with a taste for foreign manufactures and by those who lived near government administration centers.

Undeterred by the slow growth in Turkana's retail trade through the *duka* system by the close of the 1940s, the government still hoped that it was only a matter of time before this would be realized. This perspective was clear in L. E. Whitehouse's handing-over report to his successor as DC: "Trade should be allowed to develop gradually and . . . for the next few years . . . emphasis should be placed on getting the Turkana themselves to take a growing and more efficient part in this aspect of development of their country. Apart from those who are already established in trade in the district, no non-Turkana of any race should be made welcome until Turkana had proved their worth as traders."[62]

Whitehouse's observations raise two important conclusions. First, they reinforced the long-held colonial conceptualization of the Turkana society and its pastoralist economy as static, conservative, and resistant to changes introduced by the infiltration of Western influence. Such a view presented the community as adhering to wealth in cattle that they "conserved avariciously," slow at consuming foreign manufactures, and lacking a "superfluity of possessions."[63] In spite of the flow of manufactured commodities in the district, in the early 1950s the Turkana individual was still considered averse to buying and using these manufactures. "A few calabashes, and his stool . . . a pillow by night comprise his furniture. Under the impact of modern times, drinking cups of used tins, saucepans, and metal pots have made their appearance. But usually, the [Turkana] hut is innocent of these signs of progress."[64]

Second, Whitehouse's observations reveal the official insistence in the late 1940s on "creating" a modern Turkana trader by means of excluding Somali and other alien traders from the district. However, with the volume of goods on the increase and the failure to turn large numbers of Turkana into modern retailers, the administration relaxed its policy of restricting Somali involvement in trade in Turkana during the second half of the 1940s. In a gradual way, official policy began to advocate the need for the government to work with Somali traders already established in the district rather than lift the ban on the entry of new traders or former businessmen who were trying to return to the district. As part of this approach, Farah Issa, a Somali sergeant major who had recently retired from the colonial police service in Turkana, was allowed to live and trade in the district. This decision was based on the fact that Issa was "reasonable" and should be rewarded for his long and good service in Turkana. The district administration built him a modern brick shop in Lodwar "as a model for further *dukas*."[65] Issa was also charged with the responsibility of ensuring order and cleanliness in all Lodwar shops. However, like all other Somalis operating in the district, he was under surveillance and subjected to restrictions. There were not many Somali traders as lucky as Issa. Between 1943 and 1950 the administration rejected many pleas and applications by Somalis seeking entry into Turkana for purposes of trade. These applicants were derided as "poor sick creatures" whose sole intention was to make profit at the expense of the Turkana pastoralist.[66]

The ban on Somali entry was finally lifted in 1949, but restrictions on trade were maintained. The lift came about when Asian traders had also started to establish themselves as retailers in the southern and central areas of Turkana. Tensions emerged, particularly in Lokichar, between the newcomers and aspiring local Turkana businessmen who began to grasp the economic potential that expansion in regional and local trade presented.[67] Such tensions were generally uncommon since many Turkana preferred to purchase valuables from these alien retailers while selling them livestock. By the close of the 1940s the British colonial efforts to create a sizeable group of retailers from Turkana pastoralists by undermining Somali commercial entrepreneurship in northwestern Kenya had come to naught.

Conclusion

The sedentary nature of agricultural communities and the value that colonial officers gave to their crops is well understood. The same cannot be said about pastoralist communities such as the Turkana. Although their integration into the colonial economy brought some commercial opportunities, those benefits did not immediately accrue to the local community. Before that integration, the importance of their livestock in regional commercial relations in the years preceding colonialism was critical to their survival. Even after the establishment of colonial rule, livestock remained essential to the survival of the Turkana community and the area they inhabited. The colonial encounter with this community initially led to degrading notions of the pastoralist economy, which was viewed as offering little to satisfy the needs of a modern, Western economy. However, as the need to integrate this region and its inhabitants into that economy became inevitable, livestock and related precolonial items proved invaluable to the economic and, by extension, political aspirations of the British colonial state in Kenya. That state continually intervened and altered the terms of trade in Turkana to meet its aspirations in ways that promoted imperial trusteeship over local communities. Thus, the colonial government offered to serve as the protector of Turkana economic welfare by seeking to use trade to place a premium on pastoralist resources—livestock in particular—that were seen as threatened by the exploitative activities of non-Turkana traders who were drawn into Turkana country following the increase in regional and local trade. The policies used to regulate the trade relations that emerged there reveal the moral workings of colonial capitalism on the frontiers of twentieth-century European empires and help us understand how complex the colonial aspirations to "create" modern African traders were. These aspirations were not only linked to Western notions of trade monopolies and economic competition that defined classical economics but also used to define cultural values that drove economic relations, as well as values such as fairness, honesty, and exploitation, among others. Furthermore, as the British discovered in colonial Turkana, any efforts to promote such relations were not without the temptation to use ethnicity and race to achieve the desired economic state. Economic regulation, aimed at promoting indigenous—Turkana—entrepreneurs, was seen as a means to achieving social control of communities in an environment in which a lack of such control was perceived as undermining access to resources by the colonial state, and the social control of those communities considered vulnerable to the intense economic competition that colonial trade brought to rural Africa.

MARTIN S. SHANGUHYIA is Associate Professor of African History at Syracuse University in New York. He is author of *Population, Tradition, and Environmental Control in Colonial Kenya.*

Notes

1. The term "Turkana" denotes both the area and the community that lives there, hence "Turkana District" and "the Turkana community or people."
2. Such a classic study that analyzes both the historical and the recent impact of capitalism on pastoralists in different parts of the world, including Africa, is Claudia Chang and Harold A. Koster, eds., *Pastoralists at the Periphery: Herders in a Capitalist World* (Tucson: University of Arizona Press, 1994). More contemporary aspects of these developments are examined in Andy Catley, Jeremy Lind, and Ian Scoones, eds., *Pastoralism and Development in Africa: Dynamic Change at the Margins* (New York: Routledge, 2012).
3. Turkana's military engagement with British colonialism is well accounted for by John Lamphear, "Aspects of Turkana Leadership during the Era of Primary Resistance," *Journal of African History* 17, no. 2 (1979): 225–43; and John Lamphear, *The Scattering Time: Turkana Responses to Colonial Rule* (Oxford: Clarendon, 1992). With regard to Turkana pastoral relations, especially in the precolonial period (carried out in the late colonial period), see P. H. Gulliver, *The Family Herds: A Study of Two Pastoral Tribes in East Africa, the Jie and Turkana* (London: Routledge and Keagan Paul, 1955); and, more recently, J. Terence McCabe, *Cattle*

Bring Us to Our Enemies: Turkana Ecology, Politics, and Raiding in a Disequilibrium System (Ann Arbor: University of Michigan Press, 2004).

4. Vigdis Broch-Due and Todd Sanders, "Rich, Poor Man, Administrator, Beast: The Politics of Impoverishment in Turkana, Kenya, 1890–1990," *Nomadic Peoples*, n.s., 3, no. 2 (1999): 36.

5. The geographical extent of colonial Turkana District was estimated at 24,677 square miles, about half the size of England. It was second only to the Northern Frontier District, the largest administrative unit in the colony, located in the north and part of northeastern Kenya. See John S. S. Rowlands, "Report on the Grazing Areas of Turkana District of Kenya" in John S. S. Rowlands and D. O. Lokitaung, *An Outline of North Turkana History, 1951*, DC/TURK/3/3, Kenya National Archives (hereafter KNA).

6. Richard Waller and Neal W. Sobania, "Pastoralism in Historical Perspective," in *African Pastoralist Systems: An Integrated Approach*, ed. Eliot Fratkin, Kathleen A. Galvin, and Eric Abella Roth (London: Lynne Rienner, 1994), 45.

7. Extracts from "A. Donaldson Smith (Arnold 1897), through Unknown African Countries" and "Memorandum: Turkana Frontier Affairs: Historical Prior to 1928," all available in "Political History of Turkana," 1943, DC/TURK/3/1, KNA; M. Abir, "Southern Ethiopia," in *Pre-colonial African Trade: Essays on Trade in Central and Eastern Africa before 1900*, ed. Richard Gray and David Birmingham, 119–37 (London: Oxford University Press, 1970).

8. Lamphear, "Aspects of Turkana Leadership."

9. For details on trade in iron and iron implements in the region, see Ralph S. Herring, "Iron and Trade in Labwor, Northeastern Uganda," *Trans African Journal of History* 8, no. 1/2 (1979): 75–93, esp. 80 and 87 as relates to the Turkana. Regarding Jie export of grain to Turkana, see John Lamphear, "The People of the Grey Bull: The Origin and Expansion of the Turkana," *Journal of African History* 29, no. 1 (1988): 27–39.

10. The occurrence of disasters and the inertia this generated on the exchange of food for survival in Karamoja in the precolonial and colonial period are well accounted for. See, for instance, Beverley Gartrell, "Prelude to Disaster: The Case of Karamoja," in *The Ecology of Survival: Case Studies from Northeast African History*, ed. Douglas H. Johnson and David M. Anderson, 193–217 (Boulder, CO: Westview, 1988).

11. "Political History of Turkana."

12. As regards precolonial trade between communities in the Lake Turkana Basin, though its emphasis is not on the Turkana, see Neal Sobania, "Fishermen, Herders: Subsistence, Survival, and Cultural Exchange in Northern Kenya," in special issue, *Journal of African History* 29 (March 1988): 41–56.

13. Especially see J. Terence McCabe, "The Failure to Encapsulate: Resistance to Penetration of Capitalism by the Turkana of Kenya," in Chang and Korster, *Pastoralists at the Periphery*, 201.

14. On the details for each of these factors, see Gulliver, *Family Herds*, 7–8; Lamphear, "Aspects of Turkana Leadership," 230–32.

15. McCabe, "Failure to Encapsulate," 201.

16. Southern Turkana District Annual Report, 1927, 1928, DC/TURK/1/2, KNA.

17. "Southern Turkana District Annual Report," 1927, 1928.

18. Turkana Annual Report, 1926, DC/TURK/1/2, KNA.

19. Turkana Annual Report, 1927, DC/TURK/1/2, KNA.

20. Peter T. Dalleo, "The Somali Role in Organized Poaching in Northeastern Kenya, c. 1909–1939," *International Journal of African Historical Studies* 16, no. 4 (1975): 473.

21. Ibid., 472–74.

22. Ibid., 473.

23. Turkana Annual Report, 1926; "Political History of Turkana." Cyces were camel or don-key caretakers who were usually employed by the colonial administration to shepherd cara-vans transporting officials or goods in parts of Kenya such as Turkana, which lacked efficient roads due to the arid and semiarid nature of the landscapes. Most of them were Somali, but a few Indians were also hired for this purpose.

24. Southern Turkana District Annual Report, 1927, 1928.
25. Southern Turkana District Annual Report, 1928.
26. Southern Turkana District Annual Report, 1929, DC/TURK/1/2, KNA.
27. North Turkana Annual Report, 1929, DC/TURK/1/3, KNA.
28. Southern Turkana District Annual Report, 1930, DC/TURK/1/2, KNA.
29. Turkana Province Annual Report, 1930, DC/TURK/1/4, KNA.
30. Ibid.
31. Turkana District Political Records, 1933, DC/TURK/1/2, KNA.
32. Turkana District Annual Report, 1935, DC/TURK/1/2, KNA.
33. Ibid.
34. Turkana District Annual Report, 1936, DC/TURK/1/7, KNA.
35. Ibid.
36. Ibid.
37. R. D. F. Ryland, Turkana District Handing Over Report, 1937, DC/TURK/2/1, KNA.
38. Ibid.
39. Turkana District Annual Report, 1940, DC/TURK/1/7, KNA.
40. Southern Turkana District Annual Report, 1928.
41. Southern Turkana District Annual Report, 1929.
42. Turkana Province Annual Report, 1930.
43. Turkana District Annual Report, 1936.
44. An Outline of North Turkana History, 1951, DC/TURK/3/3, KNA.
45. Turkana District Political Records, 1933.
46. Turkana Province Annual Report, 1930.
47. Turkana District Political Records, 1933.
48. The conditions that led to an increase in trade during this period are widely mentioned in Turkana District Annual Report, 1936, 1937, 1939, 1940, DC/TURK/1/7, KNA.
49. Turkana District Annual Report, 1937.
50. Turkana District Annual Report, 1940; Turkana District Annual Report, 1941, DC/TURK/1/7, KNA.
51. Turkana District Annual Report, 1942, DC/TURK/1/7, KNA.
52. Turkana District Annual Report,1940.
53. Turkana District Annual Report, 1943, DC/TURK/1/7, KNA.
54. Ibid.
55. Ibid.
56. Outline of North Turkana History.
57. Kaka's trading ventures are widely mentioned in W. F. P. Kelly, Safari Diaries, March 1942, DC/LOK/4/1, KNA; Turkana District Handing Over Report,1943, DC/TURK/2/6, KNA; Turkana District Handing Over Report, 1944, DC/TURK/2/6, KNA; and Turkana District Handing Over Report, 1946, DC/TURK/2/7, KNA.
58. Turkana District Handing Over Report, 1946.
59. Turkana District Handing Over Report, July 1947, DC/TURK/2/5, KNA; J. R. Nimmo, Handing Over Notes, Turkana District (Lokitaung), 1947, DC/TURK/2/5, KNA.
60. Turkana District Handing Over Report, December 1949, DC/TURK/2/5, KNA.

Rowlands, J. S. S. 1951. "Report on the Grazing Areas of Turkana District of Kenya." In J. S. S. Rowlands and D. O. Lokitaung, *An Outline of North Turkana History, 1951.* DC/TURK/3/3. Kenya National Archives.

Ryland, R. D. F. 1937. Turkana District Handing Over Report. DC/TURK/2/1. Kenya National Archives.

Sobania, N. 1988. "Fishermen, Herders: Subsistence, Survival, and Cultural Exchange in Northern Kenya." In special issue, *Journal of African History* 29 (March): 41–56.

Southern Turkana District Annual Report. 1927. DC/TURK/1/2. Kenya National Archives.

Southern Turkana District Annual Report. 1928. DC/TURK/1/2. Kenya National Archives.

Southern Turkana District Annual Report. 1929. DC/TURK/1/2. Kenya National Archives.

Southern Turkana District Annual Report. 1930. DC/TURK/1/2. Kenya National Archives.

Turkana Annual Report. 1926. DC/TURK/1/2. Kenya National Archives.

Turkana Annual Report. 1927. DC/TURK/1/2. Kenya National Archives.

Turkana District Annual Report. 1935. DC/TURK/1/2. Kenya National Archives

Turkana District Annual Report. 1936. DC/TURK/1/7. Kenya National Archives.

Turkana District Annual Report. 1937. DC/TURK/1/7. Kenya National Archives.

Turkana District Annual Report. 1939. DC/TURK/1/7. Kenya National Archives.

Turkana District Annual Report. 1940. DC/TURK/1/7. Kenya National Archives.

Turkana District Annual Report. 1941. DC/TURK/1/7. Kenya National Archives.

Turkana District Annual Report. 1942. DC/TURK/1/7. Kenya National Archives.

Turkana District Annual Report. 1943. DC/TURK/1/7. Kenya National Archives.

Turkana District Handing Over Report. 1943. DC/TURK/2/6. Kenya National Archives.

Turkana District Handing Over Report. 1944. DC/TURK/2/6. Kenya National Archives.

Turkana District Handing Over Report. June 1944. DC/TURK/2/6. Kenya National Archives.

Turkana District Handing Over Report. 1946. DC/TURK/2/7. Kenya National Archives.

Turkana District Handing Over Report. July 1947. DC/TURK/2/5. Kenya National Archives.

Turkana District Handing Over Report. June 1948. DC/TURK/2/8. Kenya National Archives.

Turkana District Handing Over Report. February 1949. DC/TURK/2/9. Kenya National Archives.

Turkana District Handing Over Report. December 1949. DC/TURK/2/5. Kenya National Archives.

Turkana District Political Records. 1933. DC/TURK/1/2. Kenya National Archives.

Turkana District Safari Report. November 30–December 13, 1945. DC/LOK/4/1. Kenya National Archives.

Turkana Province Annual Report. 1930. DC/TURK/1/4. Kenya National Archives.

Waller, R., and N. W. Sobania. 1994. "Pastoralism in Historical Perspective." In *African Pastoralist Systems: An Integrated Approach,* edited by E. Fratkin, K. A. Galvin, and E. A. Roth, 45–68. London: Lynne Rienner.

Epilogue
African Entrepreneurship, Past and Present

Moses E. Ochonu

In precolonial Africa, entrepreneurship was not a narrow, bounded vocation. Instead, it inhered in particular ways of doing things, and in any organized activity that promised personal or communal benefit. In this capacious definitional universe, enterprising warriors were entrepreneurs. They transformed the art of warfare from a regimented, sporadic activity to one with its own routines, rhythms, and protocols. Warrior guilds, whether in precolonial Ibadan, Asante, Dahomey, Buganda, or Zulu, were centers of entrepreneurship. When systematized and conceptualized as a professional business venture, as it was in many precolonial African kingdoms, warring involved planning, management, delegation, tasks, goals, deliverables, compensation, the creation of value in the form of war spoils, the distribution of dividends, and reinvestment in the processes for improving war making.

War making entailed postoperational accounting, overheads, the calculation of profits, and periodic stocktaking. It was a business, and the guilds, warrior cults, and military training programs of precolonial African kingdoms were business schools of sorts. Warlordism, as Uyilawa Usuanlele's chapter showed in regard to precolonial migrants from Benin Kingdom, was a carefully organized business endeavor in its own right but was also connected to trade, politics, craftsmanship, and entrepreneurial spirituality. This conceptualization is a perfect segue into an important argument in this volume: entrepreneurship mapped onto many spheres of precolonial and colonial African life, notably the political and cultural spheres.

I have chosen this unlikely example of warring to illustrate a theme that runs through the chapters of this volume, an epistemological postulation at the core of this book: in Africa, entrepreneurial pursuits were not shaped by the narrow permutations of combining the forces of production—capital, labor, and knowledge—to produce a profit. Entrepreneurs occupied multiple positions and professions in society; entrepreneurship was only one of several elements that defined them. Moreover, their entrepreneurial lives often existed in symbiosis with the demands, responsibilities, and ethics of the wider culture. Given this reality of multiple entrepreneurial trajectories and entwinements, it is perhaps more productive to speak of "entrepreneurial Africans" than of "African entrepreneurs." The latter assumes a consistent, permanent occupational identity of people whose lives were consumed and defined solely by their entrepreneurial engagements. The former category is a more accurate description because, as the chapters of this volume collectively do, it advances the premise that almost all occupational groups of Africans were capable of entrepreneurial thinking and action and were entrepreneurial at different points in their lives. In other words, we understand many groups of Africans to have thought and acted like entrepreneurs, regardless of their professions. Our analysis in this volume was guided by the belief that Africans did not have to be entrepreneurs in the strict, restrictive definition of the term in order to have demonstrated entrepreneurial instincts or to have accomplished entrepreneurial breakthroughs.

Entrepreneurial Africans existed and operated at the interstices of profits and power, commerce and culture. Profit making was coextensive with social obligations. Entrepreneurs were mindful of societal expectations on them and on their innovations and crafts. Society, in turn, recognized that entrepreneurs had special gifts that had to be nurtured and liberated from the sociopolitical routines of quotidian life. Entrepreneurial pursuit was a for-profit endeavor for the most part, but profits and service to society went together, fed into each other. Political power holders cultivated entrepreneurs and were entrepreneurs in their own rights. Entrepreneurs, for their part, cultivated the protective, logistical, and spiritual resources deposited in the political realm. Ultimately, the idea that individual profit making could and should coexist with the provision of societal benefit and that entrepreneurial projects should catalyze society's economic potentials was an unwritten but well-understood rule of business in most of the contexts analyzed in the chapters of this book. As African scholars, businesspeople, and policy makers search for an African business ethos, they will do well to consider the African historical partnership between profits and people, a partnership demonstrated in several of the stories told in this book.

The overarching argument in this volume is that African entrepreneurial experiences, past and present, are complex and defy the narrow entrepreneurial notions or conceptual formulations that originated in the West. We therefore posit the need not just for a more expansive theory of entrepreneurship that addresses the typologies of African entrepreneurial lives showcased in this volume but also for a new academic subfield dedicated to the study of African business and entrepreneurship history. The proposed field will access the methods, theories, and concepts of several disciplines to analyze case studies and manifestations of entrepreneurial innovations across a vast array of African occupational and socioeconomic fields.

The study of the African entrepreneurial past can be a chronological enterprise divided into the familiar periodization of African history—precolonial, colonial, and postcolonial—with scholars paying keen attention to the dynamics and forces shaping entrepreneurial behaviors in each period. The chapters in this volume have already outlined directions for such studies. Explorations of precolonial business activities in this volume pivot on the importance of mobility and networks for entrepreneurial pursuits. This is a theme that can be further developed into a systematic study of precolonial business networks within and across Africa's several regions. Other chapters in this volume focused on how the novel economic and structural interpellations of the colonial period—a cash-crop economy, taxation, integration into the world economy, and migrant labor regimes—shaped a particular kind of African entrepreneurial behavior and birthed new commercial and productive niches replete with new markets and value chains. Several chapters directly or indirectly charted new ways of studying entrepreneurial trends in the postcolonial period, with sustained attention to how entrepreneurial Africans fared under multiple postcolonial economic regimes: developmental statism, modernization programs and plans, economic collapse, neoliberal structural adjustment, and globalization. Other chapters anticipate future globalizing trends and their potential impact on innovation, small-scale business ventures, and the vast informal trade and service-delivery sectors of African economies.

Looking ahead, it is important that the past and present of African businesspeople, business communities, and entrepreneurial successes and failures be studied on their own terms so that the insights from such studies can enrich and inform expanding global academic and policy debates on the role of entrepreneurs in forging a new, inclusive global prosperity.

MOSES E. OCHONU is the Cornelius Vanderbilt Chair in African History at Vanderbilt University. He is author of *Africa in Fragments: Essays on Nigeria, Africa, and Global Africanity*; *Colonialism by Proxy: Hausa Imperial Agents and Middle Belt Consciousness in Nigeria* (IUP), which was named finalist for the Herskovits Prize; and *Colonial Meltdown: Northern Nigeria in the Great Depression*.

Index

Mossi, 55, 72
Moyo, Dambisa, 254
Mufuruki, Ali A., 32
Muslims, 8, 64, 69, 74, 77n29, 99, 163, 165–66,
    168, 178, 179, 182, 241, 242, 246; Muslim
    women, 83, 87–88, 90, 92, 99, 104
Mwanza, 36, 37

Nairobi, 121, 297, 305, 306
Nasser, Gamal Abdel, 179
National African Company. *See* Royal Niger
    Company (RNC)
National Council of Nigeria and the
    Cameroons (NCNC), 94, 226n25
National Council of Women's Societies,
    96, 100
nationalism, 21, 31, 36, 189; economic, 261
nationalization, 42–43, 45, 173, 174, 177, 179–80,
    181, 185, 186, 187–89
natural gas, 173, 176, 182, 186, 188
natural resources, 4, 54, 116, 301
neoliberalism, 1, 2, 5, 9–10, 129, 252, 254,
    255, 322
Netherlands, the, 32–33, 41; Holland, 204
networks, 5, 101, 104, 122, 140, 141, 174, 180;
    community, 32; business, 34, 37, 40, 46,
    53–54, 62, 74, 75, 130, 204, 207, 322;
    distributive, 61, 183, 186; economic, 7, 21, 53,
    206, 258; entrepreneurial, 31, 39, 46, 68, 322;
    ethnic, 17; kinship, 37, 58, 93, 159; social, 115,
    122, 124, 143, 258, 263, 273, 280, 281, 284, 291;
    transnational, 130, 202, 206; travel, 215.
    See also trade: networks
Niger, 63, 64, 65, 67, 69, 70, 175; lower, 71;
    Middle Niger region, 60, 61; Niger Coast
    Protectorate, 84; Niger Republic, 64, 67;
    western, 156, 157, 160, 165
Nigeria, 14, 22, 55, 63, 64, 83, 84, 93, 94, 96, 99,
    100, 102, 104, 128, 140, 142, 144, 147, 198, 199,
    202, 203, 205, 206, 207, 213–14, 217, 219, 221,
    223–24, 226n24, 227n35, 277, 282, 285; central,
    22, 66, 71, 117, 139, 142, 144, 273, 275, 278,
    280–81, 283, 285, 286, 287, 288, 289, 291;
    colonial, 11, 21, 22, 87, 91, 104, 290; eastern, 8,
    94, 139, 141, 142, 143, 144; Eastern Region, 94,
    228n47; independence, 95, 101, 226n14;
    Nigerian diaspora, 206; Nigerian market, 86,
    145; Nigerian people, 85, 102, 213–15, 218, 219,
    221, 222, 224; Nigerian women, 83, 85–86, 89,
    94, 98, 102, 104, 139, 141, 144, 147; northern,
    53, 71, 72, 84, 87, 90, 91, 101, 103, 117, 139, 217,

277, 285; Protectorate of Northern Nigeria,
    84; Protectorate of Southern Nigeria, 84–85
    southeastern, 92, 93; southern, 155;
    southwestern, 289; western, 53, 100, 139, 141,
    144, 228n47, 228n72, 290, 291. *See also*
    National Council of Nigeria and the
    Cameroons (NCNC); Nigerian Boxing Board
    of Control (NBBC); *Nigerian Daily Times*;
    Northern Nigeria Boxing Club; seamen:
    Nigerian; unions: Nigerian Seamen's Union
Nigerian Boxing Board of Control (NBBC),
    214, 226n24
Nigerian Daily Times, 216, 217, 218, 219, 221–22,
    223, 227n35
Niger River, 65, 116, 156
Nikki, 64, 65, 72
Nima, 118, 122
Nkrumah, Kwame, 235
Nnoruka, Eunice Abiana, 93, 94, 95, 96
Northern Nigeria Boxing Club, 217
Nugent, Paul, 121
Nupe, 65, 66, 71, 89, 139, 142, 143, 163, 165
Nwonaku, Nywanyiemelie Mgbogo, 8, 93
Nyamwezi, 15, 24n33, 83
Nyerere, Julius, 16, 41, 42, 45
Nzimiro, Mary, 94

Odey, Mike Odugbo, 278
Oduro-Sarpong, Samuel, 244, 246
Oguntubi, Comfort, 101
Oguta, 92–93
Ọhẹnmwẹn, Iyasẹ, 159, 163, 164
Oju, 281, 287
Okizi, Iyasẹ, 164, 167, 168
Ollivant, G. B., 98, 102
Oman, 33, 35
Omemu, Balogun Asa, 165, 167
Omoregie, Osaren S. B., 156
Onitsha, 84, 92, 93, 94–96, 218
Oonk, Gijsbert, 34, 42
Organisation Commune des Régions
    Sahariennes (OCRS), 174–75, 181
Organisation of the Petroleum Exporting
    Countries (OPEC), 181, 187, 188
Organisme Technique Mixte de Mise en Valeur
    du Sous-sol Saharien, 177, 179, 180–81, 183,
    184, 186
Ossomari, 92, 93
Otun, Okoro, 159, 164, 165
Owo, 139, 157, 160, 164, 288, 290
Oyo, 65, 157, 162

Lightning Source UK Ltd.
Milton Keynes UK
UKHW020412090322
399769UK00002BA/50